perceptions of europe

a comparative sociology of european attitudes

Edited by
Daniel Gaxie, Nicolas Hubé
and Jay Rowell

ecpr PRESS

First published by the ECPR Press in 2011

Paperback first published by the ECPR Press in 2013

The ECPR Press is the publishing imprint of the European Consortium for Political Research (ECPR), a scholarly association, which supports and encourages the training, research and cross-national cooperation of political scientists in institutions throughout Europe and beyond.
ECPR Press
University of Essex
Wivenhoe Park
Colchester,
CO4 3SQ, UK

Typeset by AnVi Composers
Printed and bound by Lightning Source

British Library Cataloguing in Publication Data
A catalogue record for this book is available from the British Library

Hardback ISBN: 978-1-907301-15-5

Paperback ISBN: 978-1-907301-15-5

www.ecpr.eu/ecprpress

ECPR – Studies in European Political Science

Series Editors:
Dario Castiglione (University of Exeter) and
Vincent Hoffmann-Martinot (Sciences Po Bordeaux)

ECPR – Studies in European Political Science is a series of high-quality edited volumes on topics at the cutting edge of current political science and political thought. All volumes are research-based offering new perspectives in the study of politics with contributions from leading scholars working in the relevant fields. Most of the volumes originate from ECPR events including the Joint Sessions of Workshops, the Research Sessions, and the General Conferences.

Books in this series

The Domestic Party Politics of Europeanisation: Actors, Patterns and Systems
ISBN: 9781907301223
Edited by Erol Külahci

Interactive Policy Making, Metagovernance and Democracy
ISBN: 9781907301131
Edited by Jacob Torfing and Peter Triantafillou

Perceptions of Europe: A Comparative Sociology of European Attitudes
ISBN: 9781907301155
Edited by Daniel Gaxie, Jay Rowell and Nicolas Hubé

Personal Representation: The Neglected Dimension of Electoral Systems
ISBN: 9781907301162
Edited by Josep Colomer

Political Trust: Why Context Matters
ISBN: 9781907301230
Edited by Sonja Zmerli and Marc Hooghe

Please visit www.ecpr.eu/ecprpress for up-to-date information about new publications.

| contents

| list of figures and tables

Figures

Tables

| contributors

PHILIPPE ALDRIN is a professor of political science at the University of Nice-Sophia Antipolis, and a member of the Centre for European Political Sociology (GSPE-PRISME) and of the ERMES (UNS) research team.

GIULIANO BOBBA is a post-doctoral researcher in political science at the Faculty of Political Science of the University of Torino.

MARIE-HÉLÈNE BRUÈRE is an assistant research engineer at the University of Paris 1 Panthéon-Sorbonne, and a member of the European Sociological and Political Science Centre – Sorbonne Political Research Centre (CESSP-CRPS).

DOROTA DAKOWSKA is a senior lecturer in political science at the Strasbourg Institute of Political Studies (IEP) and a member of the Centre for European Political Sociology (GSPE-PRISME).

MARINE DE LASSALLE is a senior lecturer in political science at the University of Strasbourg, and a member of the Centre for European Political Sociology (GSPE-PRISME).

DANIEL GAXIE is a professor of political science at the University of Paris 1 Panthéon-Sorbonne, and a member of the European Sociological and Political Science Centre – Sorbonne Political Research Centre (CESSP-CRPS).

NICOLAS HUBÉ is a senior lecturer in political science at the University of Paris 1 Panthéon-Sorbonne, and a member of the European Sociological and Political Science Centre – Sorbonne Political Research Centre (CESSP-CRPS).

KATARZYNA JASZCZYK is a doctoral student in political science at the University of Warsaw's Institute of Applied Political Studies, and a member of the European Sociological and Political Science Centre – Sorbonne Political Research Centre (CESSP-CRPS).

CHRISTÈLE MARCHAND is a doctor in political science at the University of Avignon, and a member of the CURAPP research team.

PATRICK LEHINGUE is a professor of political science at the University of Picardie, and a member of the CURAPP research team.

JEAN-MATTHIEU MÉON is a senior lecturer in information and communication science at the University Paul Verlaine of Metz, and a member of the CREM research team.

SÉBASTIEN MICHON is a CNRS researcher and lecturer at the University of Strasbourg, and a member of the Centre for European Political Sociology (GSPE-PRISME).

MURIEL RAMBOUR is a doctor in political science, and an associate member of the Centre for European Political Sociology (GSPE-PRISME) and of the European Sociological and Political Science Centre – Sorbonne Political Research Centre (CESSP-CRPS).

JAY ROWELL is a CNRS researcher and lecturer at the University of Strasbourg, and the director of the Centre for European Political Sociology (GSPE-PRISME).

PIERRE-EDOUARD WEILL is a doctoral student at the University of Strasbourg, and a member of the Centre for European Political Sociology (GSPE-PRISME).

| preface

This volume presents the essential results of the Concorde research project funded by the French National Research Agency (ANR) and directed by Daniel Gaxie. The research was carried out between January 2006 and June 2009 and aimed at understanding and explaining the attitudes of various categories of citizens towards 'Europe'.[1] The Concorde programme initially included four French research institutes based in Paris (University Paris I – Sorbonne Centre for Political Research (CRPS) with Marie-Hélène Bruère, Daniel Gaxie, Nicolas Hubé and Muriel Rambour), Strasbourg (University of Strasbourg – Centre for European Political Sociology (GSPE), with Philippe Aldrin, Dorota Dakowska, Marine de Lassalle, Sébastien Michon, Jean-Matthieu Méon, Jay Rowell and Pierre-Edouard Weill), Amiens (University of Picardie – Centre for Administrative and Political Research (CURAPP) with Patrick Lehingue and Christelle Marchand) and Berlin (Centre Marc Bloch, directed by Pascale Laborier). The original idea was to compare the attitudes of German and French citizens. In late 2007, a team from the University of Turin, led by Alfio Mastropaolo and Giuliano Bobba, decided to join the programme and the comparison was extended to include Italy. In March 2008, a convention was signed with the Centre de Civilisation française et francophone in Warsaw to conduct interviews in Poland. Dorota Dakowska organised a team of interviewers, with the assistance of Katarzyna Jaszczyk. Ondrej Novotny, who was writing a doctoral thesis at the Université Libre de Bruxelles at the time of the research, followed the project. He introduced a few elements of comparison based on the research he was conducting in the Czech Republic. Thus, thanks to the dynamic of the project we were able to extend the geographical frame of the comparison, although it remains asymmetrical, due to the importance of the French institutions and researchers that initiated the project. Dozens of interviewers from various countries, including students in participating universities, were involved in several phases of this collective survey. They are too many to mention here, but we thank them for their participation; we also thank the hundreds of people who agreed to meet us to answer our questions. Last but not least, we thank Marie-Hélène Bruère, who coordinated the publication of this volume; Jean-Yves Bart, who has faced and overcome many hurdles in translating the original text into English; and Emma Gormley and Kemo Weibel Simone for their hard work on the translations of early versions of some of the chapters.

---

1   Our survey shows that many citizens perceive European integration in a confused way. Only a tiny minority thinks of the European Union when asked about European issues. Others spot a mysterious entity or consider a few neighbouring countries. The use of inverted commas is therefore used to highlight the differing views of what constitutes 'Europe' in the eyes of the interviewees.

The book is structured in four sections:

The first section presents the approach used in the research project. Many scholars have written on the attitudes of citizens towards 'Europe'. Their studies have produced a vast number of statistical results based on secondary analyses of questionnaires conducted with samples of the population in each Member State of the European Union (EU). Despite their insights, these studies raise a number of methodological issues and are hampered by several blind spots, which are analysed in Chapter 1. Eurobarometer surveys constitute the main source of these studies on Europeans' attitudes towards European construction. In Chapter 2 our examination shows that the status of these surveys as an academic and political instrument and their methodology, based on closed-ended questions, need to be debated. The Concorde project was thus conceived as a reaction to our dissatisfaction with standard methods of observing and interpreting citizens' attitudes towards 'Europe'. Our aim was to use more in-depth survey techniques in order to better account for the complexity and the diversity of 'ordinary' citizens' perceptions and reactions. We also sought to bridge the gap between research traditions such as the sociology of political attitudes and the sociology of Europe. These research questions and alternative methodologies are presented in Chapter 3. This book relies mainly on in-depth semi-directive interviews, with open-ended questions, conducted with samples of citizens from the relevant Member States. In addition to these individual interviews, we organised focus groups and collected various materials emanating from spontaneous interventions of citizens related to 'European issues' (letters to newspapers or magazines, responses to online questionnaires developed by pro-European organisations).

The second section focuses on the analysis of attitudes towards 'Europe'. In Chapter 4 a number of ideal types that can be used to characterise the dispositions of various categories of the public are presented. The results based on observations made in France are compared at the end of the chapter with those obtained in other countries. The diversity of the 'mechanisms' structuring the attitudes of ordinary citizens is emphasised in this chapter. In Chapter 5 the ambivalence of these attitudes and the difficulty in ascertaining a clear and coherent stance on Europe in most cases is analysed in more detail. The focus in Chapter 6 is on the thorny question of comparison and discusses the content and the influence of collective national experiences of European integration.

The third section analyses the resources and instruments mobilised by various categories of citizens to express points of view on 'Europe'. The various types of arguments and discourses mobilised by citizens to express their views on 'Europe' are discussed in Chapter 7. In Chapter 8 it is considered whether and, if so, to what extent, the ability to express opinions on 'Europe' depends on specialised knowledge. The focus in Chapter 9 is on the means of gathering information and levels of information of different categories of the public. It takes into account their feeling of being informed (and not informed) in order to establish what seems obscure and uncertain to them, and what appears more familiar, providing respondents with discursive elements that they can rely on to develop their viewpoints.

The fourth section seeks to compare attitudes towards 'Europe' in various segments of the public. In Chapter 10 it is shown that the knowledge and perceptions of European citizens also depend on the organisation and the visibility of the EU. It describes the links between attitudes and ways of experiencing this original polity. The focus in Chapter 11 is on interviewees from popular milieus, both because they are the most remote from European issues and, consequently, because their reactions are all too often ignored in specialised literature. In Chapter 12, on the other hand, the spontaneous interventions of ordinary citizens on 'Europe' is studied, identifying the fractions of the public that are sufficiently aware of European issues to express themselves autonomously and spontaneously beyond opinion surveys.

chapter one | what we know and do not know about citizens' attitudes towards europe

Daniel Gaxie

Scholars of European studies have been interested in the perceptions of European integration by EU citizens for a long time now, often with a note of normative apprehension around the key question of positive or negative attitudes towards European construction. The unease is caused by the idea that a widespread gap has developed between 'elites', perceived as staunch supporters of the European cause, and the increasingly sceptical 'masses'. According to proponents of this approach, this has been confirmed by the results of several referendums in Denmark, France, the Netherlands, and Ireland. Until the early 1990s, it was thought that a permissive consensus among the unconcerned European public initially allowed political elites to impose European integration (Carruba 2001: 144; Coman and Lacroix 2007). This consensus has been progressively eroded by effects of EU institutions and decisions on the everyday lives of Europeans: the introduction of the Euro, the austerity policies established to meet the demands of the monetary union, or the increase in the number of Member States (enlargement) (Della Porta and Caiani 2007). This evolution is often considered as worrying, since the attitudes of the public are supposed to support the political foundation of integration (Deflem and Pampel 1996: 120; Gabel 1998b: 333; for a slightly different analysis see Delmotte 2007: 21).

These academic and political concerns have inspired hundreds of studies on the attitudes of European citizens towards European construction. Many statistical results, explanations and interpretations, often contradictory, have been published. We will not be able to present an exhaustive overview of this literature in this chapter; rather, we will discuss a number of blind spots and methodological issues.

Most research carried out in this field relies on the secondary analysis of Eurobarometers. On this basis, three types of interpretation have been put forward: the 'utilitarian' approach, a 'values-based' interpretation, and hypotheses related to the specificities of national experiences of European integration.

The utilitarian approach

The most common explanation put forward is that the more individuals benefit from European construction, the more they are likely to have a positive outlook on the integration process. There has been some discussion on which types of benefits – 'objective' or 'subjective', 'individual' or 'collective' ones – are most strongly correlated to attachment to Europe. A few statistical elements give credit to the idea that national macroeconomic factors influence support for integration. Some authors have also explained that citizens from countries that are net beneficiaries of the EU are more likely to support integration, whereas contributing countries are more likely to be against it (Hooghe and Marks 2004). At the same time, it seems logical to think that each individual perceives national economic conditions through their own economic situation (Gabel and Whitten 1997).

One of the most solidly established results in European studies is that education, occupational skill and income have a positive impact on the degree of attachment to Europe (Bélot 2002; Binnema and Crum 2007). In order to explain these results, Gabel and Palmer (1995) have argued that the liberalisation of the European labour market has had varying effects, depending on the level of education and occupational skill. They have interpreted education and occupational skill as elements of individual human capital, which they argue is a key indicator of the ability to adapt to competition entailed by the liberalisation of the labour market. Well-off citizens are also thought to profit more from this liberalisation, since they enjoy more investment opportunities in financial markets. Moreover, the central objective of the European Central Bank is to curb inflation, which is seen as another advantage for those in possession of financial assets. On the other hand, Europeans with low incomes are mostly seen as victims of the liberalisation of the capital markets. This liberalisation is even liable to worsen their situation, as capital is more mobile than workers. Low-income citizens are also considered to be more dependent on social expenditures, which are also reduced by the free movement of capital and the European monetary policy. From this perspective, 'the utilitarian theory provides a robust explanation for variation in support for integration. Across various sets of nations and years, citizens' support for integration is positively related to the level of economic benefits they expect to derive from European integration' (Gabel 1998b: 351). The authors define these economic benefits (and costs) in more or less detail. Some scholars link attitudes towards integration with traditional class divisions (Deflem and Pampel 1996). Workers and low-income categories are thought to worry about losing their jobs, receiving lower wages, decreasing social expenditure and/or their position in collective bargaining. Simon Hix (1999) develops a more sophisticated social class theory. He contends that attitudes towards integration are not only related to human capital but also to the 'location of social interests'. Regardless of their education, occupational skill and income, individuals have opinions and demands that vary according to their economic sector (for example, non-market public sector, production for the national or international markets, financial services, European multinationals or the farming sector). Several authors have also criticised several elements of Gabel's utilitarian theory. Some have objected that individuals are not necessarily aware of the benefits or costs induced by European integration. Others have emphasised that people with high levels of education, occupational skill and income are those who support moderate parties, which are the main supporters of European construction. Therefore, they might support integration for political reasons as well as economic ones. Liesbet Hooghe and Gary Marks (2004: 416) suggest a modified utilitarian theory: 'Citizens who feel confident about the economic future – personally and for their country – are likely to regard

European integration in a positive light, while those who are fearful will lean towards Euroskepticism.' In their view, when citizens form judgements on European integration, they do not take into account the possible resulting benefits or costs for themselves; rather, they express an optimistic or pessimistic inclination deriving from their economic situation.

Value-based explanations

Value-based explanations are presented as an alternative or a complement to utilitarian theories. Some researchers argue that citizens do not evaluate the EU on the basis of perceived personal benefits, but that they rather take into account various representations, emotions and values (Bélot 2002: 29). Others admit that citizens may consider the economic consequences of integration, but go on to add that feelings of group membership also matter and are arguably decisive (Hooghe and Marks 2004: 415). Proponents of value-based explanations consider territorial identities first. They stress that support for European integration increases when the feeling of belonging to Europe is present (Dell'olio 2005: 102). Symmetrically, citizens who have a feeling of exclusive national identity often hold negative opinions towards European integration (Cautrès and Grunberg 2007: 22). But identification with Europe is also known to be positively correlated to the level of education and social class, in the same way as exclusive national identifications are negatively correlated with them. These identifications are however thought to have a specific statistical effect on European attitudes when controlled for education and social classes (Dell'olio 2005: 103).

European or national identities are also associated with other values presumed to influence attitudes towards Europe. Specialists emphasise the role of xenophobia, which is statistically associated with the exclusive feeling of national membership. The two attitudes are alleged to contribute to the fear of change, and especially of European unification, perceived as a threat to national integrity (De Master and Le Roy 2000). By contrast, those who identify themselves with Europe are assumed to be less predisposed to share hostile opinions on minorities and foreigners (Citrin and Sides 2004: 180). Other authors associate identity with a larger set of attitudes. Allegiance to the national polity is said to be associated with xenophobic, authoritarian, rigorist, anti-universalist, ethnocentric, materialist and pessimistic attitudes. 'Authoritarian' attitudes are, for instance, inferred from answers to questions on the death penalty or whether schools should emphasise discipline and effort. Symmetrically, those who feel European or assert both their national and European identities are considered more prone to express positions defined as universalist, humanist, tolerant, cosmopolitan, and post-materialist. Several interpretations of these correlations are proposed. Some argue that authoritarian, ethnocentric and pessimistic world views reinforce the attachment to an organising pattern embodied by the nation state. Symmetrically, those who share universalist world views are assumed to be more likely to defend new forms of political regulation (Cautrès and Denni 2000: 348). Another explanation is that those who share exclusive feelings of national identity oppose Europe because they fear losing their national identity as well as social benefits (Cautrès and Grunberg 2007: 24). Other authors argue that the EU has favoured contacts between people of different nationalities and origins, and that those who are the most afraid of foreigners are accordingly less likely to support integration (De Master and Le Roy 2000: 421).

Researchers focusing on 'values' have tried to articulate this factor with utilitarian hypotheses. Hooghe and Marks (2004: 416) argue that economic preoccupations are decisive in contexts where the economic consequences of European integration are clearly perceived. When such conditions are not met, identities override. They add that the more a country's elites are divided, the more national identity is mobilised and stimulates negative perceptions of Europe. In the opposite case, either national identity is not mobilised or it favours supportive attitudes. In a similar perspective, De Master and Le Roy (2000) point out that statistical links between indicators of xenophobia and critical views on European integration are weaker when interviewees live in countries which, like Belgium, Ireland, Portugal and Spain, receive high levels of EU funding. They add that these countries have a Catholic culture and that the ecumenical culture of Catholicism might encourage internationalism and a more open attitude towards foreigners.

National context-based explanations

Many authors argue that national differences relating to support of European integration are more important than individual socio-demographic or ideological variations (Deflem and Pampel 1996: 136; Dell'olio 2005: 96) They dismiss the common assumption that all Europeans have the same perception of the EU and suggest taking into account the manner in which each national community sees the integration process (Diez Medrano 2003: 5). Citizens of Member States are supposed to have a distinctive experience of integration, a sense of their position within the EU, and a shared view of their country's role in the world (Harmsen 2007: 81). These national evaluations of integration are also affected by party competitions and institutional opportunity structures. The majoritarian logic of British politics might, for instance, amplify expressions of Euroscepticism due to an overriding electoral incentive for each of the two larger parties to maintain themselves as a ' broad church', which gives relatively radical minorities a disproportionate amount of influence over determining parties' attitudes on European issues. But as Harmsen (2007: 81) emphasises, 'nothing comes from nothing, and Euroscepticism provides good copy for politicians and journalists alike, because it resonates with long established British perceptions of Europe and the Europeans'. This 'resonance' hypothesis is crucial in the interpretations of attitudes towards Europe based on national political cultures (Risse 2004: 265). National visions of Europe are interpreted as an outcome of a top-down process driven by elites, more especially politicians and columnists, who constantly formulate and reformulate their views on European construction according to different national and international evolutions, as well as their own power interests. But ideas have to resonate with existing identity constructions that define the range of acceptable opinions in a given national context. Invented by certain actors, internalised by opinion-makers in political parties, media and pressure groups, national frames of Europe become consensual and spread to the mass public. These perceptions are analysed as elements of national identities. They are embedded in institutions and the country's political culture and serve as collective interpretation routines. The members of the 'imagined communities' refer to views of the relationships between their countries and Europe that reactivate their vision of themselves and of their differences from other national populations (Marcussen *et al.* 1999). Accordingly, from the German point of view, European construction is regarded as redemption of the past, an alternative to nationalism, a protection against hegemonic and xenophobic inclinations, a way of reassuring the world about the country's peaceful intentions and a guarantee for democracy and the social market economy (Diez Medrano 2003). Spanish citizens are thought to be grateful towards Europe for its contribution to modernising the country and democratising its political system (Diez Medrano 2003). Italians welcome the benefits of structural funds and the opportunities for correcting the effects of national 'pathologies' (Della Porta and Caiani 2007). From a French point of view, Europe is a 'French Europe', supporting the national 'mission civilisatrice' and strengthening its role in Europe as well as its influence in the world (Marcussen *et al.* 1999: 621). Conversely, Europe is said to be perceived by the British as a threat to the national lifestyle, the country's role in the world, its special relationship with the United States and the Commonwealth, self-government, the constitutional monarchy, the parliamentary tradition and sense of political responsibility (Marcussen *et al.* 1999: 626).

Some scholars who stress the importance of national context also emphasise the specific effects of history on the perceptions of each country. Others suggest a more systematic model. Therefore, the 'goodness of fit' hypothesis refers to the difficulties countries face in bringing their institutions and public policies closer to European standards. A large distance between a country and the European average (characterised by low level of labour coordination and a high level of capital coordination), imposes high costs to comply with European legislation, therefore resulting in a greater likelihood of critical opinions (Hooghe and Marks 2004: 416). In this perspective, British Euroscepticism is seen as a result of a poor fit. From a Scandinavian viewpoint, the EU's institutional system is regarded as a threat to more transparent and participative decision-making models as well as to the high level of social protection (Harmsen 2007: 86).

These explanations based on national political culture presuppose the existence of a national perception shared by all citizens. Studies are based on an analysis of statements made by political parties, politicians and the quality press defining national visions of European integration as a means to identify interpretation frameworks. It is generally assumed that voters who devote little attention to European issues reflect the views of the leaders and political parties they have chosen to support (Aspinwall 2002: 103). The alternative hypothesis positing that political elites take stances according to the public's electoral preferences (Carruba 2001: 153) seems more fragile. Some examples of political responses to the mobilisations of categories that are particularly aware of European policies, such as farmers, have been observed. Likewise, there have been attempts in the decision-making circles of some countries to circumvent the majority of negative votes in the European referendums. Yet, it is probably more realistic to agree with Carruba that national elites take into consideration the electoral constraint whenever there is one, but that they also make use of whatever leeway they have to promote European integration. Considering the low levels of interest and information on European issues, it is unlikely that political elites take stances according to the public's preferences. Quite the contrary, it is known that Europe is the 'touchstone of dissent' between pro-European centre-right or centre-left government parties and more marginal Eurosceptic political organisations, factions or actors. It has also been observed that national elites and the mass public are more often pro-European when their governments are regularly drawn from centrist coalitions. Therefore, it could be argued that it is because the mass public supports centrist parties and governments that it subscribes to pro-European positions (Aspinwall 2002: 106). Then again, it has also been observed that most leaders become pro-European (as well as more moderate) when they govern.

Diverse and sometimes contradictory explanations

This overview of the academic literature shows that authors rely on well-established statistical correlations as a basis for a number of diverging interpretations, which are sometimes contradictory. For example, the observation that positive views on European integration are more likely when the level of education or income is higher is interpreted in different ways. As we have seen, support for the integration process is often explained by 'instrumental' economic motives based on a 'utilitarian' cost/benefit assessment, which is itself correlated with social status. Other specialists have explained that the higher the level of education and income, the more, on the one hand, they consider themselves to be 'European' and on the other hand, the more they share universalist, humanist, tolerant, cosmopolitan and post-materialist world views that predispose them to support European construction. Significantly different explanations are also given to the 'utilitarian' label. We have seen that some authors consider that the wealthiest are the most likely to benefit from the opportunities offered by integration. We have also seen that others make an equally convincing case for the idea that people who enjoy favourable economic conditions are also more optimistic and confident about their own future and that of their country, and are hence predisposed to have a positive outlook on European integration regardless of the benefits they can draw from it. Some studies explain national differences through different collective experiences of European construction. Others explain that perceptions of Europe depend on the costs of adjusting to European standards. These culturalist or utilitarian explanations of national differences are in turn contradicted by the hypothesis positing that citizens follow the positions of the parties and leaders they support.

The articulation of explanatory factors

The articulation of these various explanations raises a number of issues. Some researchers consider that their own interpretations contradict those that have been suggested by others. But most scholars do not claim to reject competing hypotheses. Sarah de Master and Michael K. Le Roy (2000: 419), for instance, accept the argument according to which European realities are assessed through a cost/benefit ratio. They only object to the fact that it does not take into account motivations like the desire to preserve national integrity from foreign influences, even though these motivations inform the evaluation of European integration in addition to considerations of economic self-interest. Attempts to articulate these diverse explanatory factors have seldom been made. The oft-quoted paper by Matthew Gabel (1998b) concludes, for example, that the utilitarian hypothesis is the most robust explanation of the attitudes towards integration. He, however, goes on to say that 'class partisanship' (i.e. the idea that members of a 'social class' adopt attitudes which 'reflect' the positions of the political party they support) exerts an 'independent influence'. Other explanations, such as support for government (citizens project their judgements of their own government onto the question of integration), 'political values' (for instance, post-materialist attitudes) and 'cognitive mobilisation' (a high level of political awareness and well-developed skills in political communication enable citizens to identify with a supranational political community), also appear acceptable to him, but only for the citizens of certain states and during certain periods. However, neither Gabel nor De Master and Le Roy clarify the relationships between what they consider to be causes of attitudes towards integration. For example, how can the disposition to preserve national integrity combine with the utilitarian evaluation of personal interests? Should we believe that national or European identities prevail when the personal interests of individuals are not at stake in European integration? Or when they do not give priority to their economic interests? But then, why would certain individuals have no personal interests involved in European integration, or why would they play down the importance of their interests? If we consider that both utilitarian motives and the influence of government parties contribute to shaping attitudes towards Europe, it appears necessary to specify which citizens give priority to their personal interests or follow the views of their parties, and which ones simultaneously consider both elements of appreciation.

Each individual has a certain level of education, income and occupational skill, party preferences (or lack thereof), territorial identifications and materialist or post-materialist, tolerant or authoritarian, cosmopolitan or xenophobic, optimistic or pessimistic attitudes. All these elements are thought to influence attitudes towards European integration, but it is necessary to specify which individual characteristic is 'activated' when judgements on Europe are formulated, by whom, at what moment and why. One of the rare attempts to unify explanatory factors suggests that identities are the prevailing factor and that economic utilitarianism only influences attitudes towards Europe when the economic effects of integration are significant and identifiable (Hooghe and Marks 2004: 416). However, the authors do not mention who is liable to distinctly perceive the significant economic consequences of integration, in which circumstances and why.

The limitations of probabilistic explanations

Quantitative studies provide probabilistic results. We know for instance that people who have a high level of education and income are statistically more likely to support European integration than others. We also know that, even though there are proportionally fewer of them, people who share these same features can also express negative opinions. However, in the literature, there are hardly any explanations for these cases. It is possible that levels of education, income and occupation are oversimplifying factors. It has been suggested that in addition to occupation, the economic sector, for instance public or private, as well as its position in regional, national or international competitions needs to be taken into account (Hix 1999). However, even if finer instruments were used to provide more precision on the individuals' economic situations, they would probably reveal cases that contradict statistical trends and require further explanations. Similarly, if we admit that apparently 'xenophobic' and 'authoritarian' attitudes are more frequent in the working class, and that they are statistically associated with negative perceptions of the EU, we should also study the reasons why certain members of the same classes do not share these attitudes, or why some who hold such attitudes do not always have negative perceptions of the EU. Statistical trends should, of course, be taken into account, but it seems necessary to consider the individuals whose reactions contradict predominant probabilities.

Statistical correlations and causal interpretations

The great majority of studies on attitudes towards Europe are based on correlation measurements obtained from a quantitative secondary data analysis. Because they do not have other empirical material, some authors are prone to overestimating the importance of their statistical processing. In some cases, correlations are tacitly interpreted as causal links. Hence, those who write that a given factor 'explains' the highest percentage of variance of a dependent 'variable' forget that the word 'explanation' has a different meaning in statistics and social science. When some authors claim that an 'independent variable' 'organises', 'structures', or 'accounts' for an attitude towards Europe, they are using a tacitly causal language in order to interpret simple correlations.

In most cases, however, a distinction is made between statistical observations and causal interpretations. For instance, Matthew Gabel explains that education, occupational skill and income are positively correlated with positive attitudes towards integration because educated and skilled people are more capable of adapting to economic competition induced by the liberalised European labour market. Conversely, Gabel's interpretation of negative correlations is that low-income European citizens are generally victims of market liberalisation (1998b: 337). In this oft-quoted article, the author attempts to measure the impact of various factors considered as 'explanatory' of the support for European integration. The paper relies on regression analyses of several indicators of ordinary citizens' attitudes towards European integration (constructed by quantifying the responses to several opinion questions) on various independent variables. The author adds the differences in levels of support for integration obtained when comparing high and low levels of education, the highest and lowest incomes, skilled and non-skilled occupations, and proximity or distance from a border. After interpreting these variables as indicators of 'utilitarian' attitudes, he observes that their combination produces statistical effects that are more significant than any other indicators of the other explanatory factors reviewed in his article (party preferences, support for a government party and 'materialist' and 'post-materialist' attitudes). He reaches the conclusion that the statistical data confirms that the 'utilitarian' theory is the best explanation for attitudes towards Europe.

Regardless of the objections which can be advanced on measurement methods,[1] the major problem with Matthew Gabel's argument lies in the logical jump from statistical observations to the confirmation of a causal theory. We have long known that variables such as education, occupation and income are statistically associated with opinions on European integration. In spite of, or because of the various co-linearities that link them, we can admit that adding their 'effects' on opinions on integration results in the strongest correlations. But, based on this, we cannot conclude that 'across various sets of nations and years, citizens' support for integration is positively related to the level of economic benefits they expect to derive from European integration' (Gabel 1998b: 351). This interpretation is undoubtedly an interesting one, and is partially confirmed by the results of the study presented in this volume. But the statistical data mobilised by Gabel do not constitute evidence of the validity of the interpretation he suggests. With the same statistical data, we could also argue that in all nations and in every period, citizens' support of European integration depends on their confidence in their personal future and the future of their countries (Hooghe and Marks 2004), or that it depends on ideological support for the market economy. The expected economic benefits, confidence in the future and support for market economy are three speculations (amongst many others) in the interpretation of the causal links that form the basis of correlations between positive opinions of European integration on the one hand and education, occupation and income on the other hand. None of the statistical elements produced by secondary data analyses, like those of Eurobarometers, enables us to choose between them.[2]

---

1. One could for instance question the possibility of measuring the 'independent statistical effects' of variables that are as strongly inter-correlated as education, income and occupational skill. We can object that when adding up the 'statistical effects' of education, income and occupational skill, one adds two or three times the same reality, which is partly present in all three variables. Hence, it would not be surprising that such an addition produces the most significant statistical effects.

2. This difficulty explains the fact that many authors prefer to stick to a more modest and tentative register when proposing causal interpretations of their statistical results. In an older paper, Matthew Gabel and Guy D. Whitten (1997: 81) argued: 'Given that economic growth and develop-

The statistical information drawn from databases is suggestive, but it does not contain any direct information on the causal links. In this sense, it is causally silent. To take another example, we can observe a correlation between support for government parties and positive opinions on European integration. This correlation might be spurious and support for government parties, just like positive opinions on European integration, might be dependent on a third factor without being linked together. It might, for instance, be argued that moderate fractions of the public support European integration and also support government parties, for reasons that are not (or not chiefly) related to European issues. If we assume that the correlation is not spurious, several possible interpretations can be put forward. We can, for instance, speculate that most government parties support European construction and that they manage to convince their supporters that this position is well founded. Research in sociology of public opinion also suggests that some citizens who trust government parties might reproduce their arguments without having a clear-cut personal opinion on the question. It is also possible that certain citizens with a particularly high awareness of European issues and who are in favour of integration support a given party because it adopts positions that are close to their own. Another possibility is that these various hypotheses apply to distinct fractions of the public and are hence compatible. Here again, however, merely observing a concomitant variation between positive opinions on integration and support for government parties does not provide any indication on the effective existence or the reasons of a causal link between the two phenomena.

Gaps in the knowledge of subjective representations

The academic literature on ordinary citizens' attitudes towards Europe is somewhat paradoxical. On the one hand, it strives to verify hypotheses with empirical observations. At the same time, many interpretations are solely based on intuition. Secondary data analyses from surveys attempt to infer subjective perceptions and representations of European citizens through the distribution of responses to closed-ended questions. However, they do not provide any first-hand information on what the interviewees consider when responding. Many authors have gone to great lengths to explain the reasons why citizens support or oppose the integration process, but few have tried to observe them directly. Currently, little is known about the subjective perceptions and reasons why citizens have positive or negative views on the EU. Few researchers have strived to comprehend – in the sense of a comprehensive sociology – what citizens think about Europe and how they think about it.[3]

---

ment are both central motivations for integration and among the predominant responsibilities of the European Union (EU), it *seems reasonable* that the EU public would evaluate integration based upon economic criteria.' (my emphasis)

3.   We can only mention a few rare studies focusing on direct interviews with citizens on the reasons and motives of their attitudes towards Europe; mainly Bélot 2000, Medrano 2003 and Meinhoff 2004.

We know that working-class categories are more likely than other groups with higher social positions to favour the death penalty, to approve the idea that 'schools should give priority to discipline' and to assert a national identity rather than a European one, at least when they are interviewed on these topics. In the same research conditions, they are also more likely to answer that their country's membership in the EU is not a good thing and that they are against efforts to unify Europe (Cautrès and Denni 2000; Cautrès and Grunberg 2007; Grunberg and Schweisguth 2003). However, there is no empirical 'evidence' on causal links between these responses. Correlations can be observed between 'opinions' (or responses) on the death penalty and European integration, but this does not imply that interviewees make reference to the death penalty when asked about European integration. A possible objection, obviously, is that opinions on the death penalty are simple indicators of an underlying 'authoritarian' attitude. But in that case, it is necessary to show that such an attitude is activated when formulating judgements on European construction. This requires an observation of the instruments of judgement effectively mobilised by different categories of citizens, specifying which ones are likely to be interpreted as indicators of an authoritarian attitude, and identifying the fractions of the public that use them. Many authors argue that territorial identities (for example, the claim to feel 'French only' rather than 'French and European') are the most decisive explanatory factors of attitudes towards Europe. However, at this point, very few direct empirical observations (on a large scale) establish that Eurosceptics refer to threats on their national identities when they express negative views on European construction. It is not enough to observe such political statements from a few political movements to conclude that this argument is reproduced by those who oppose European integration, or even only by supporters of these movements. Attitudes defined as 'intolerant', 'nationalist', 'authoritarian', 'anti-universalist' or 'xenophobic' can be considered as explaining reactions towards European integration only if people justify their perceptions of European integration with reasons likely to be interpreted as indicators of such attitudes. Here again, it is impossible to establish a causal link merely on the basis of an apparent correlation.

Researchers infer the presence of attitudes from opinions and reactions expressed by individuals. These opinions and reactions result from perceptions, considerations and motives that rely on cognitive and evaluative instruments. These instruments are related to the diverse socialisations experienced by individuals depending on (among other things) social mobility, position, living conditions, experiences and social ties. Few studies have attempted to explain these complex articulations of the components of attitudes towards Europe. Of course, the relationships between true opinions, occasional answers, justifications, rationalisations, declared and undeclared motives, and objective reasons, are complex. The subjective experience of Europe is not always adequately conveyed in the considerations and the elements of judgement expressed during an interview. Interviewees are not always willing to discuss the social conditions (in this sense 'objective') associated with these ideas and judgements, or often do not even think about doing so. Nonetheless, the motives and reasons put forward in interviews to support or oppose European integration can reveal certain elements of the subjective perceptions of the integration process. They can also give a number of clues on the 'objective' conditions that are associated with them, especially when interviewees are asked about their life experiences. It is impossible to explain attitudes towards Europe without comprehending what individuals perceive of it and how they perceive and evaluate it. Many speculations, intuitions, presuppositions, fictions and preconceived ideas have been mobilised to explain the subjective reasons that lead individuals to express attitudes of support or opposition to European integration. These studies should rely more heavily on sound empirical observations.

Indifference towards the sociology of opinion and citizens' information levels

It has long been established that there are 'significant pockets of ignorance' (Franklin *et al.* 1994: 458), a limited understanding, and little interest for European issues in the general public (Slater 1982: 77). A number of scholars have emphasised that European construction has been an elite-driven process, and that the public's low information and awareness level has given them a great deal of freedom. These scholars have repeatedly stated that many European issues are of a technical nature and that they have limited direct effects on citizens, even though their degree of salience has increased with the adoption of the Euro, the Schengen Agreement and the enlargements (Carruba 2001: 141–2). However, the low levels of information and interest of the mass public, as well as the differences between various fractions of the public have been strangely ignored by many authors studying European attitudes. We have known for decades now that opinion surveys may record more or less significant proportions of responses given with little conviction, some of which tend to be random (Converse 1964). We know that these behaviours are particularly pronounced when information and interest levels are the lowest.

Since the early 1980s, hundreds of articles and books have been devoted to the task of completing analyses, which, like that of Converse, have been labelled as 'minimalist'. These studies have discussed at length 'shortcut(s)', 'rules of thumb' and 'judgement heuristics' mobilised by people who are summoned to give opinions on political issues even though their information, sophistication and interest levels are low (Popkin 1991; Sniderman *et al.* 1991; Lodge and McGraw 1995; Lupia and McCubbins 2000). Specialists in public opinion and opinion polls have lamented the fact that researchers claim to explain opinions or votes by inventing models that tacitly presuppose that all citizens are adequately and equally informed on political issues (Zaller 1992). They have shed light on the fact that during interviews, many people come up with 'opinion statements' on the spot, using whatever comes to mind at the time. Certain responses to opinion polls are accordingly analysed as results of immediately accessible 'considerations': any reason that might help an individual give an answer to the question asked (Zaller 1992: 36, 40). Politically aware citizens take into account a large number of considerations, which are relatively coherent and also match these citizens' predispositions. Less politicised interviewees integrate fewer considerations, which are less coherent. It follows that the most aware interviewees are more likely to express opinions, and express opinions that are ideologically coherent with their predispositions (Zaller 1992: 52). These observations suggest dismissing the pre-supposition that all individuals have pre-existing structured attitudes that are re-vealed by questions in opinion polls. Conversely, they suggest that some individu-als have inconsistent views on certain issues (Zaller 1992: 54). Such caveats are all the more important when studying remote and abstract subjects such as certain European issues. Regardless of this, many scholars who study citizens' attitudes towards Europe seem to assume that all citizens are capable of giving opinions on all the political issues of European construction, and that they could all be lo-cated on a single axis, a political one, opposing the sceptics on the one hand and the staunchest supporters of integration on the other. Based on a correspondence analysis, two researchers have identified three dimensions of the 'opinions' relat-ing to European integration, which account for 33 per cent of the global inertia of the responses analysed. The first axis, which accounts for 15.6 per cent of the inertia, reveals an opposition between opinions in favour and against Europe. The second one, (9.10 per cent) opposes those who express assertive opinions to those who express uncertain and less structured viewpoints. The third dimension (8.2 per cent of inertia) distinguishes strong opinions from conflicting ones (Cautrès and Denni 2000). For reasons related to the inevitable sample bias and to the use of closed-ended questions, we can assume that the impact of the first dimension was overestimated, and that the second and the third dimension were underestimated. At any rate, it appears that almost all publications so far have focused on the first dimension, or have tacitly reduced the space of attitudes towards Europe to this one dimension; the other two have been almost completely ignored. The second dimension is sometimes even artificially suppressed because of the very question-able habit of excluding 'don't know', 'no opinion' or 'no answer' responses from the analysis (see Gabel 1998b: 340 or Dell'olio 2005: 96), or even assimilating them to neutral and intermediary opinions (Inglehart 1970: 49).

The overall low level of information and individual differences in awareness of European issues are not coherent with the culturalist explanations that posit the existence of a national experience of European integration, of collective routines of understanding and of a common view shared by all nationals of their country's place in the EU and the world. Likewise, such explanations do not concur with the observation that, until now, Europe has provided the basis for the emergence of a new political cleavage and has never played a major role in electoral competitions (Hix 1999; Binnema and Crum 2007). Indeed, few empirical observations on an idea of Europe shared by all the fractions of a national public have been made. Juan Díez Medrano has pointed out the existence of a correlation between the recurrence of certain themes in newspapers and responses made by interviewees of the three countries considered in his study. However, local elites are over-repre-sented in his samples, and most of the examples of judgements on Europe that he cites in his book are from leaders of local party organisations, unions, chambers of commerce and craft industries, columnists of local newspapers, political repre-sentatives, spokesmen for organisations of women, farmers or youth. Similarly, it is in each country's quality press that he seeks the frames of interpretation that are supposed to be shared by the entire national community, without considering how or whether it might reach the general public.

Limits of surveys relying on closed-ended questions

The use of Eurobarometer-based databases prevents specialists of European studies from taking into account the actual information and interest levels of the interviewees. Many scholars whose work relies on such material consider it self-evident that all those who answer a question have an opinion on this question, that all answers are expressions of equally deeply-rooted opinions, and that they are the product of similar *modus operandi*. Typically, responses to the question on whether the EU is a 'good' or 'bad' thing or something that is 'neither good nor bad' are assumed to be a 'satisfactory manner of measuring preferences incorporating all relevant political issues' (Carruba 2001: 145). The low rate of 'no answer' responses to most of the questions asked in opinion polls is interpreted as a confirmation of a shared capacity to express opinions on all European issues, including those that are quite remote from the preoccupations of many citizens (Cautrès and Denni 2000: 325). Some specialists have, however, suggested that there could be several forms of support or opposition to European integration, but this avenue of research has seldom been explored.

Opinion surveys question samples, presumed to be representative of the entire population, on a wide array of difficult and often technical issues. For instance, respondents interviewed in 2005 were asked about their confidence in European institutions, the political union of Europe, the presidency of the European Council, monetary union, common foreign policy, security and defence policy, the European constitution, enhanced cooperation, the priority action areas of the EU, the increase of the EU's budget, the role of the EU regarding world economic growth, environmental protection, world peace, democracy in the EU, the creation of a ministry of foreign affairs of the EU, the performance of European economy, the strengthening of European integration, the relevant territorial level for addressing the issues of immigration, unemployment, environmental and health issues, etc. When responses to such questions are added together for statistical processing, the same weight is granted to the reactions of all interviewees. The responses are homogenised, without taking into account the fact that respondents are unequally familiar with the themes in question.

Respondents are expected to give opinions on complex European issues. They often discover the existence of the issue when they are asked the question, but are aided by the use of closed-ended questions. They are asked about issues that they might find abstract, complex, obscure or remote, but they are only asked to choose between simple and short responses. All they have to do is say 'yes', 'no', 'I agree', 'I disagree', 'for', 'against', 'it's a good thing', or a 'bad thing', 'it's important', 'it's not important', 'attached', 'not attached'. They know that the interviewer is not going to ask them to explain and justify their views in detail. Yet, observation shows that many of the interviewees have more difficulties when they have to formulate answers to open-ended questions (Gaxie 1990) and all the more so when they are asked to explain the reasons for these answers.

Closed-ended questions tend to reduce the frequency of 'no answer' and 'no opinion' responses, not only because they make the respondents' task easier, but also because of their formulation. The possibility of not answering exists, but it is rarely explicitly suggested, and the interviewers are often instructed to discourage it. Observation shows that on unfamiliar subjects, the percentage of people who do not answer the question is noticeably higher when 'no opinion' is one of the options given to the interviewee (Gaxie 1990). Asking a question and suggesting different responses without suggesting the possibility of not having an opinion amounts to pushing the interviewee to respond. Some of the responses obtained in such circumstances can be considered as low-intensity opinions, or even survey artefacts. The reasons why more interviewees express negative views on Europe when asked about (relatively) more familiar subjects, such as the Euro or social protection, rather than on more general and abstract questions, such as, for instance, the respective powers of the EU and Member States, requires closer investigation (Cautrès and Denni 2000: 325).

It is potentially thorny to add up formally identical responses to close-ended questions without precaution. When researchers make such totalisations, they presuppose that all the interviewees who have given formally identical responses have not only understood the question, but have also understood it in the same way. Responses to questions including ambiguous terms such as 'political Union', 'integration', 'democracy in the EU', or 'trust in the institutions', should not be added up without previously studying the meanings that the interviewees give them. If interviewees understand the same question differently, they are in fact responding to different questions. Similarly, we cannot presuppose that formally identical responses to an abstract question – on European construction for example – are all based on the same abstract viewpoint.

Opinion polls on European issues can produce artificial results when they elicit responses on topics that have never been considered before. An analogous observation pushed Ulrike Hanna Meinhoff (2004) to develop a survey technique which avoids considering that interviewees are familiar with a topic just because they responded. She chose to ask interviewees to comment on photographs. These photographers showed facades of buildings adorned with the European flag, or signs mentioning the EU in the construction of infrastructure. She observed that none of the interviewees referred to Europe or the EU in their comments. Only when explicitly asked about their attachment to Europe did they begin to address the topic. Indeed, few people would discuss on their own initiative all the topics presented to them in opinion surveys, and few have had opportunities to discuss them with friends or relatives.

The point of this overview of the literature is of course not to invalidate all secondary quantitative database analyses. They are obviously useful and necessary, and have provided many important results. We are merely pleading for more rigour in the methodology and the interpretation of their findings. Rigour should not only be exercised when measuring, but also when controlling measures. Measures should not only be considered as satisfactory because they provide hard data. If the soundness and the significance of the responses are uncertain, the relevance of the statistical processing will be doubtful, regardless of the level of significance. Advocating more rigour in the observation of opinions entails diversifying methodologies. Obviously, we do not suggest doing away with statistical measures and processing, but more open-ended questions should be introduced into opinion surveys. Before starting to process responses, it would be necessary to find out what the interviewees have in mind when they respond, which entails having the means to observe the reasons and motives of their responses. The aim of this volume is to introduce methodological and theoretical pluralism in a research field which has until now been massively dominated by a specific and relatively superficial use of surveys. There should be more reliance on in-depth interviews, collective interviews, spontaneous documentary sources and first-hand observations in order to provide more precise and realistic descriptions and explanations of the diversity and the complexity of citizens' attitudes towards European integration.

chapter two | the eurobarometer and the making of european opinion

Philippe Aldrin

A debatable, yet seldom debated, monopoly on expertise

The European Commission has claimed that a 'European public opinion' exists and has therefore scrutinised its mood swings for more than thirty years. Well before the Brussels institution created the semi-annual survey programme called Eurobarometer (EB) in 1973, Jacque-René Rabier, its founding father, inferred a rise of a 'European political awareness' and the existence of a 'consensus in favour of European integration' from the results of the very first European-wide polls,[1] saw the rise of a 'European political awareness' and of a 'consensus in favour of European integration' (Rabier 1965: 53 ff.).[2] Four decades and six hundred opinion surveys later, this prophetic intuition has become an institutional truth. Indeed, the regular publication of the EB surveys, and the echo created by them, have since largely contributed to naturalising the idea of a European public opinion in European political, intellectual and media circles. Furthermore, the extensive database that they now constitute has been institutionalised to the point where it now prevails as the essential source of information on the state of public opinion in Europe, as well as the reiterated statistical evidence of support for the Community process by the majority of Europeans. Among the EB's so-called 'trend' questions,[3] the one that aims to measure support for the EU – 'Generally speaking, do you think that [your country]'s membership of the European Union is: a good thing/a bad thing/neither good nor bad' – invariably elicits a majority of 'positive' answers. Over the 1998–2008 period, more than 52 per cent of respondents on average chose the first option. While the (slight) drop of the number of positive answers and the latest electoral trials have recently led the writers of EB reports to

---

1. This programme systematised experiments with 'European polls' conducted in the 1950s and 1960s. 'Just as a barometer can be used to measure the atmospheric pressure and thus to give a short-range weather forecast, this Euro-barometer can be used to observe, and to some extent forecast, public attitudes towards the most important current events connected directly or indirectly with the development of the European Community and the unification of Europe.' (EB1, 1974). We refer to the EB reports following the nomenclature used by the Commission, which assigns them a number based on order of publication. When there is no additional precision, 'EB' refers to the so-called 'standard' EBs; when other EBs are discussed (Flash, Special surveys, etc.), this will be mentioned.

2. This consensus was soon said to be a 'permissive' one (Lindberg and Scheingold 1970).

3. These questions are named 'trend' questions because they have been asked since the early stages of the programme.

reconsider the enchanted vision of a spontaneous and generalised Europhilia,[4] the scores obtained by this answer are now held as evidence of Europeans' approval of political Europe. A few weeks after the 2005 referendums, in which both French and Dutch voters rejected the constitutional treaty, the heads of state and government gave this reminder in the conclusions of the European Council: 'We have noted the outcome of the referendums in France and the Netherlands. We consider that these results do not call into question citizens' attachment to the construction of Europe' (Declaration by the Heads of State and Government, European Council, 16–17 June 2005, Brussels, SN 117/05). In the aftermath of another less encouraging verdict expressed in the voting booths, this official certainty was partly based on the EB's longitudinal results and post-referendum surveys.[5] An instrument like the EB, which virtually holds a monopoly over the analysis of Europeans' opinions and so assiduously supports both the European integration project and the supranational path (both spearheaded by the backing institution) should attract sociological curiosity. How is the EB made? Who makes it? According to which methods? Which means (material, human, conceptual) are used and which aims (institutional, political, ideological) are sought? Does the EB have an influence – and if so, what kind – on political, media and scholarly perceptions of 'European public opinion'? Surprisingly, a review of the academic literature on the topic reveals that there has been very little research attempting to shed light on these questions,[6] even though the literature on European opinion makes systematic and liberal use of EB data (Inglehart and Reif 1991; Bréchon and Cautrès 1998).

In the context of the Concorde research programme, it has occurred to me that it would be useful to consider the various processes – manufacturing, publication, mediatisation, uses, secondary exploitations – at work in the equivalence between EB and European public opinion. The analysis presented in this chapter thus explores the instrument's several dimensions: as a Community programme for measuring opinions; as an instrument of political governance used within the EU's institutional game and at the interfaces of European decision-making; as a dominant, or even exclusive source of data on the Europeans' attitudes. In order to try to understand the EB's unprecedented dominance (as surveys backed and published by a political institution) over the general knowledge of Europeans' opinions on Europe, I will first analyse the questionnaires and raise some methodological issues. Then I will go on to study the ins and outs of the institutionalisation of EB results, to understand how a monopolistic and official production of 'European public opinion' has come to prevail.

---

4. A survey report published in February 2005 claims: 'We note growing support for the European Union membership in the majority of Member States [...]. However, beneath this increase lie differences in opinion. In 7 countries, this rise comes hand in hand with an increase in respondents regarding membership as a bad thing' (Special EB 220, wave 62.2: 7).

5. According to them, even in countries that voted 'no', a large majority of citizens support membership in the European Union: 88 per cent of French respondents (Flash EB 171), and 82 per cent of Dutch respondents (Flash EB 172).

6. For an analysis of the EB's political uses, see Smith 1998.

(Sociologically) questioning the questionnaire

To understand the place that the EB now holds, we need to go back to the origins of the instrument. This historical analysis, however, is made more difficult by the numerous accounts provided by the EB's founders (Rabier 1993; Melich 1998), who have shaped a powerful founding mythology, in the spirit of a general discourse on the 'heroic' early stages of the European Community (Dumoulin 2007). Embedded in this etiological discourse, the EB's genesis is short-circuited by an indigenous objectivation of sorts, against and with which the process of sociological objectivation has to unfold. The sociological deconstruction of the founding mythology requires dissociating the study of the EB surveys' production chain and the analysis of their social uses and effects. Hence, in this first part, the focus is on the EB reports, considered mainly on the basis of their properties as material objects containing indications on methodology (how the questionnaires are conceived, how the data are interpreted), survey set-up (how the questionnaire is administered), and the rhetoric of evidence (how the data are treated and modelled, conclusions) (see Topalov 1999), which specifically concern the political opinions collected by the instrument. This will be an internal analysis, and thanks to close attention to possible biases – immanent (inherent to the analysis of opinions through closed-ended questions), induced (generated by the conception and the administration of the questionnaires) and topical ones (linked to the specificities of the theme imposed and the public required to contribute) – of the EB method, I will endeavour to identify their effects on the orientation and dispersion of the data.

Recording political opinions on Europe in surveys

Opinion surveys relying on closed-ended questions entail a number of inherent biases, inscribed in the hypothesis on which such an approach is based, and which may be reinforced by their practical application (intellectual and material conception of the surveys, modes of administration of the questionnaire). While I do not wish to stir up the controversy between those who use and defend opinion surveys (Cayrol 2000) and those who denounce both their epistemological foundations and their effects (Bourdieu 1993; Champagne 1990; Lehingue 2007c), surveys, like any other method of empirical observation, should be subjected to scientific discussion. Such a discussion starts with the two 'sociological' assumptions that condition the very existence of opinion surveys: persons asked to respond to a survey have an opinion on the theme of the survey that can be recorded, measured and classified; their opinions display to the same extent the qualities – sincerity, consistency, stability – that justify their interpretation through various statistical operations of distribution, aggregation, comparison or cross-study with the respondents' properties (age, gender, level of education, occupation, place of residence). The sociological critique of these assumptions is as old as the introduction of surveys in democracies (Blondiaux 1994), but has never offset the promise of this 'science of opinion' that offers the illusion of a social cartography of political attitudes and of the predictivity of votes. Yet, we cannot dismiss the hypothesis positing that

persons who are requested to respond by an interviewer do not always have a previously constituted or even latent opinion on the questions asked (Converse 1964).
In such situations, the practice that consists in making the respondents choose between pre-worded answers in a closed-ended list and then considering that their
compliance with the request amounts to an opinion arguably produces opinions
that are entirely artefactual, 'by-products' of the interaction between pollster and
pollee (Lehingue 2007c: 137). Assigning the status of 'opinions' to these data and
submitting them to extensive statistical treatment can therefore be problematic.
This ultimately depends on the type of solicitation and the modalities of responses
offered by the survey. How do EB surveys fare on this issue?

The political questions of European Commission surveys include a wide range
of demands, such as classifying options, comparatively evaluating predictions,
engaging in self-assessment or introspection, or choosing a side in political controversies. Sometimes the solicitation involves the respondents themselves, about
a choice they will or would have to make as citizens; sometimes it requires that
they put themselves in the shoes of leaders facing the imperative of hierarchising
priorities and launching initiatives. This last type of solicitation implies varying
levels of realism (depending on the respondent's social status, age, and interest in
politics) and complexity (depending on the precision, technicality, or lexical specificity of the question), as these questions from the EB database show:

Excerpt 1 (EB 10, 1978)

Which one of these opinions comes closest to your own on the future elections
to the European Parliament?

–   It is an event with important consequences which is certain to make Europe
    more politically unified.
–   It is an unimportant event because the national governments will not be
    bound by the votes in the European Parliament.

Some of the respondents likely have a pre-existing personal opinion, even if it
is a confused one, on the election of MEPs with direct universal suffrage. But how
many among them have asked themselves the question in these terms, or based on
the alternatives suggested? This issue of the adequation between the informational
elements given by the pollster and the respondent's spontaneous disposition to
express an opinion is also raised when we consider the choices of answers offered and both the polarised and precise character of the possible answer options.
The conception of the question-answers group tends to place the respondent in an
unusual situation of choice, sometimes even unreal, as it is very far from common ways to understand to societal or political problems. Hence, the situation
cannot be compared to pre-election polls, whose relative predictivity has legiti-
mised the validity of all political opinion surveys. The reliability of pre-electoral
polls increases as the electoral campaign develops,[7] as the political projects and

---

7.   Especially in national elections, campaigns induce a general upsurge in interest for politics (Bennett 1988).

the competing personalities come into focus, and especially as the moment when the voter will effectively have to make a personal choice draws nearer.[8] But with the exception of rare situations, such as the organisation of referendums on the ratification of a constitutional treaty or the election of MEPs,[9] political Europe is a rather remote subject, even foreign to the preoccupations of most social actors. The fictional character of the theme and of the method of questioning can only be heightened when the respondent is asked to react as if he or she were a policy-maker.

Excerpt 2 (EB 3, 1975)

Taking into account the great problems facing your country at this time, which of these three ways would you prefer to solve the problems?

– National independence
– Inter-governmental cooperation
– The political unification of Europe with election of a single Parliament evolving quickly into a true European Government.

Excerpt 3 (EB 63, 2005)

From the following list of actions, could you tell me what should be for you, the three actions that the European Union should follow in priority? (Max. 3 answers). (List: Fighting illegal immigration/Asserting the political and diplomatic importance of the European Union around the world/etc.)

Aside from the biases I have pointed out (lack of realism of the injunction to provide an opinion, shift from expected social roles towards role-playing), this type of solicitation directly mobilises a vocabulary and concepts borrowed from political or legal analysis. Yet, only part of the population uses schemes of con-ceptualisation of political subjects that directly refer to explicitly political catego-ries of understanding and judgement. Indeed, the propensity to have recourse to 'political principles' (Bourdieu 1984) to judge political questions is distributed neither equally nor randomly in society. It is correlated with the level of education, social status and occupation. Individuals who are weakly politicised and have lit-tle educational capital tend to rely on 'ethical principles' to produce their political opinions, in the sense that they refer more to 'common sense' and domestic moral-ity (Bourdieu 1984). EB questions, which are built around an explicitly political terminology and theme, therefore run the risk of confronting respondents with an

---

8.   Polling voting intentions amounts to questioning citizens on a choice they will effectively have to make, in a role – that of voter – that is familiar and that they acknowledge to be theirs. The realism of the solicitation increases near the day of the vote, when the choice will inevitably become concrete through one of the following actions: abstain, vote blank or vote for a given candidate or party (Berelson *et al.* 1954).

9.   These elections are characterised by low turnouts and low level of mobilisation during campaigns where national political issues prevail (Bélot and Pina 2009).

unrealistic request which hinders the sincerity, the consistency and the stability of their answers. There are significant chances that some respondents will only make a choice in order not to lose face and not to break the fleeting 'pact of the survey' that links them to the pollster,[10] not to mention the many risks of misunderstandings between the question as it was conceived and worded by the pollsters and as it is understood by the pollees (Gaxie 1990). The degree of misunderstanding of the questions – and of their specifically political implications – and the feeling of incompetence that respondents may experience facing such solicitations cause biases that are all the more significant as Europe is generally perceived as a remote and complex topic.

Generating and interpreting opinions on Europe: the Eurobarometer's induced and topical biases

To a large extent, the EB's credit derives from the rigour and the scientific apparatus of its methodology. Since the programme was launched, the Commission has added 'technical specifications' to the reports, where the survey methods and conditions are briefly outlined (institutes in charge of administering the questionnaire, number of respondents per country, etc.) The instrument's reliability and objectivity are asserted through the ostensible compliance with the canons of scientificity: the method is openly exposed; guarantees are provided on the independence and competence of the authors and of the subcontractors; and in a more recent development, the margins of error of the results are also made explicit:

Excerpt 4 (EB 62, 2004)[11]

In all countries, gender, age, region and size of locality were introduced in the iteration procedure. [The process of 'weighting' for the calculation of EU averages is explained.] Readers are reminded that survey results are estimations, the accuracy of which, everything being equal, rests upon the sample size and upon the observed percentage. With samples of about 1,000 interviews, the real percentages vary within the following confidence limits:

---

10. According to Alain Garrigou, there is a 'pact of the survey' (in French, 'pacte de sondage') whereby 'the pollee poses and conforms to the duty of opinion' and 'pollsters first have to reconcile hardly compatible constraints: ask questions that the authors of the poll ask themselves to pollees that might not have considered these questions' (Garrigou 2006: 47).

11. Strictly speaking, confidence intervals are only valid within the framework of the probabilistic method, i.e. for strictly random samples. Yet, the EB initially worked with 'national representative samples drawn up by quota' (EB 1, 1974), and now relies on a sample design with several levels of weighting, presented as a 'multi-stage, random (probability) one' (EB 69, 2008), but which departs from the probabilistic method.

Observed percentages	10% or 90%	20% or 80%	30% or 70%	40% or 60%	50%
Confidence limits	± 1.9 pts	± 2.5 pts	± 2.7 pts	± 3.0 pts	± 3.1 pts

These explicit signs of scientificity can be interpreted by readers of EB reports as tokens of 'scientific' credibility,[12] and attest to the validity of the data and of their analysis. But beyond the ostensible compliance with statistical rigour, the EB survey system has biases related to the processes used to generate answers and to interpret data. The first bias classically concerns the intelligibility of the questions. Indeed, as Madeleine Grawitz pointed out, opinion polls 'obviously depend closely on the interviewees' answer possibilities' (Grawitz 2001). 'Answer possibilities', however, can be understood in at least two ways: first, as the latitude granted to the respondent by the degree of orientation (or polarisation) and the more or less limited number of answers. Then, as the comprehensibility of the question-answers groups, which hinges on the wording (clarity of the formulation and of the terms) and on the social significations of their content (readability of the individual and/or collective stakes raised by the question). The problem of the latitude of possible answers leads us to study its potential effects on the distribution and therefore on the structure of the results, which is crucial in statistical interpretation. The problem of the ambivalence of significations, on the other hand, suggests evaluating the social range of the intelligibility of the problems raised by the questions, and therefore questioning the nature of the responses obtained.

Before I delve deeper into these issues with EB surveys, I want to briefly discuss the distinction – in terms of method and effects of the method – between opinion polls on politics and polls on everyday behaviours (habits, material or symbolic consumer practices, education, etc.), on the perception of public objects (image of a public figure, a party, popularity of a brand or institution) or social problems which the respondents feel personally concern them (purchasing power, security, etc.). EB surveys combine these different categories, but here their affiliation with the first category will be considered. In principle, political opinion polls do not differ from others in any way: they collect, classify, compare judgements, attitudes and subjective perceptions according to a method that precisely aims to calibrate and normalise these subjective opinions – hence, to deprive them of their personal, singular character – in order to be able to code them and statistically process them. This depersonalisation is the price to pay for the comparability of the data collected. In order to achieve it, questionnaires often exert a certain degree of symbolic violence on the respondents, through the overly academic character of their questions (technical vocabulary, politicised questions) and the extreme standardisation of the answers offered (polarised and limited choices). Then, by

---

12. Arthur Bowley, the inventor of the measure of confidence intervals, 'has made of imprecision, of the margin of error, a respectable, clean object, no longer shamefully hidden in the bashful silence of error' (Desrosières 1993: 275).

imposing such solicitations, in strictly identical terms, to respondents who are unequally endowed with the competence to express opinions on political subjects, this type of survey is ultimately more likely to measure (with an inappropriate tool) the interviewees' level of political literacy[13] than to find out how their points of view on the question asked are constructed and why they are expressed. In the methodology of opinion polls, this bias is inevitable (due to the requirement for comparable data), but it can be kept in check by wording question-answers groups less technically or emphatically, by introducing open-ended questions or by giving the possibility to give so-called spontaneous answers, so that the principle of uniformisation does not cause a laminating effect (opinions are crushed and silenced) or a ventriloquism effect (the opinions collected are purely artefactual). In this case, it depends on the level of political formalism of the instructions given to respondents. Do EB surveys capture the way the respondents perceive the issues and challenges of the EU, or do they inadequately measure their level of European literacy? The following excerpt provides some elements to answer this question.

Excerpt 5 (EB 42, 1995)

For some time there has been talk of a 'Two speed Europe'. This means that some countries would be ready to intensify the development of a common European policy in certain important areas, while other countries would not. Please tell me, for each of the following countries, whether or not you see it as being ready to intensify the development of a common European policy in certain important areas. [List of Member States]

This question, which I have picked among many similar ones, attests to the explicitly political character of EB questions. Admittedly, the phrase 'Two speed Europe' is explained somewhat didactically to the respondents.[14] Yet, in order to be able to formulate informed answers to such questions – i.e. being aware of the political issues involved and being able to take a stance on that basis – respondents require a pre-existing knowledge of the problems raised by the institutional situations mentioned and a structured vision on the alternative positions or solutions available in the debate. Overall, on such a political question, the likelihood of collecting an actual opinion depends not only on the comprehension of the question's terms and concepts, but also on the knowledge of European institutional mechanisms (here, the Member States and their respective stances vis-à-vis Community integration). Hence, simplifying the wording does not fully solve the problem of the intelligibility of the question-answers groups.[15] Indeed, with such questions,

---

13. The term literacy emphasises the evaluative dimension – testing the level of academic knowledge – of such a set-up (Cheveigné 2004).

14. Without, however, dissipating the ambiguity of the question: for French respondents, the phrase 'two speed' has rather negative connotations and is likely to be perceived as a metaphor of *de facto* inequality in the access to certain rights and services.

15. Such simplification can amount to euphemising or even denying the political controversies related to a European issue by offering a depoliticised vision of the issue.

the problem of intelligibility is twofold; it is both linked to the specifically political nature of the issue raised and to the somewhat esoteric character of European political affairs. In addition to the bias induced by the means used to generate 'opinions' (politicisation of political questions), there is another topical bias linked to the material, cognitive, and symbolic distance that generally separates respondents from EU realities, as the few studies relying on qualitative material show (Bélot 2000). Reasons that can explain this confused relationship towards Europe include the feeling of geographic and 'affective' distance from Brussels, the originality and the impersonal character of the mechanisms of EU decision-making, and its changing borders. This confusion manifests itself through the interviewees' difficulty to assign specific responsibilities to the EU in terms of public action.

Questions that are explicitly about the EU and its functioning are perceived almost as academic tests of knowledge for which the interviewees almost always feel insufficiently qualified. This dimension of the relationship to political Europe is confirmed by the results of qualitative surveys financed by the European Commission in the past few years. These studies have relied on focus groups, and their results very clearly contradict the opinion trends traditionally observed by the EB.

Excerpt 6 (Qualitative EB, *The European Citizens and the Future of Europe*, May 2006)

[There are] admission[s] of ignorance of the process perceived as complex and difficult to understand. Judgements requested from respondents on the functioning of the Union are therefore very rarely backed up by known facts. Participants from several groups for that matter state right away that they are unable to voice a well-founded opinion. Without having much clearer views, respondents from numerous other groups have rather negative impressions, with the concept of complexity, opaqueness, slowness of processes or low efficiency...

As they give interviewees more opportunities to express themselves, these qualitative studies collect opinions that are rather different from those generated by closed-ended questionnaires and highlight the feeling of lack of knowledge on European institutions. The quizzes included in EB questionnaires in the past few years have actually confirmed this point:

Excerpt 7 (EB 67, 2007)

For each of the following statements about the European Union could you please tell me whether you think it is true or false? [EU answers]

	True	False	DK
The EU currently consists of fifteen Member States	23%	**57%**	20%
The members of the European Parliament are directly elected by the citizens of the EU	**45%**	35%	20%
Every six months a different Member State becomes the President of the Council of the European Union	**49%**	25%	26%

NB: Correct answers are in bold

For the authors of the EB surveys, these responses work as indicators of the re-spondents' 'objective knowledge' (or 'actual knowledge'). Despite the shaky logic of the testing system,[16] this 'quiz' shows the high rate of incorrect answers and the very high rate of 'Don't Know' answers to questions on basic institutional mecha-nisms. For several years, the EB questionnaire has also included a solicitation for a self-assessment of the interviewee's knowledge on the EU, which is taken as an indicator of 'subjective knowledge'.

Excerpt 8 (EB 63, 2005)

Using this scale, how much do you feel you know about the European Union, its policies, its institutions? (Scale from 1 (know nothing) to 10 (know a great deal)) Results [EU]: Know (almost) nothing (1–2): 19%/Know a bit (3–5): 51%/ Know quite a bit (6–8): 27%/Know a great deal (9–10): 2%. The average level of subjective knowledge of European Union citizens is 4.5.

These results are also debatable[17] but the general tendency of the answers (sta-ble for a decade) confirms a widely shared feeling of lack of knowledge on how the EU works. Several types of results converge on this point, which calls into question the actual properties of the EB data. When 70 per cent[18] of respondents say that they only know 'a bit' or 'nothing' about the EU, questioning the sincerity and the consistency of their responses to the remaining solicitations of the ques-tionnaire is not illegitimate.

The internal analysis of the EB instrument thus shows that the conception of political questions introduces various biases. The lack of realism of the solici-tations, the politicisation of the questions, the socio-centred character of the in-structions (which follow the conceptualisation and the vocabulary used by the pollsters and those who commission the polls), and, lastly, the social resonance of the European object produces raw data whose sociologically debatable char-acter cannot be overshadowed by the sophistication or the rigour of the statistical treatment applied in primary and secondary analyses.[19] The analysis of opinions on Europe does require recourse to quantitative methods for an initial outline – making out general trends, regularities, identifying paradoxes – before going into more in-depth sociological investigation (Zalc and Lemercier 2008). But both the promoters and exegetes of EB data grant them much more value than merely pro-viding an overview on relationships towards Europe. Displaying a genuine instru-

---

16. Nothing tells us that the respondents who have chosen the correct answer to the first or the third question actually know the accurate answer.

17. To evaluate their own knowledge of a given subject, interviewees always refer to what they think is a sufficient level of knowledge. Yet, the respondents also have different yardsticks according to their social properties, nationality, or to their country's date of accession to the EU.

18. This number is obtained by adding up the proportions of respondents who evaluate their own knowledge between 1 and 5 (see Excerpt 8).

19. On the problem of the reliability of data from international surveys see Adam 2008.

mental positivism (Bryant 1985), they view it, or feign to view it, as the numerical expression of European public opinion; the statistical and rationalised version of its concrete reality.

The monopolistic market of European polls

While opinions on Europe exist independently from the polling instrument that records them and may constitute a European public opinion (henceforth EPO), the latter is first and foremost comprised of what the EB measure, to paraphrase George Gallup's famous assertion. Apart from a moving and composite phenomenon investigated by sociologists and philosophers (Ferry 2006), the EPO appears as a social and political reality mostly in the form of a normalised designation of a statistical assembly of attitudes recorded through polling. In this perspective, it can be seen as the 'product of a conventional process' that manufactures shared attitudes through extrinsic equivalences[20] and therefore provides European leaders with a concrete reality which can be used in their interactions (Desrosières 1993: 7). Indeed, for more than thirty years, the EB has performed a double process of substantialisation and pre-emption over the EPO. The very first EB-labelled survey presents the programme as a means to 'follow the trends in *European public opinion* with regards to Community activities, particularly the areas of most interest to the public' (EB 1, 1974, my emphasis). The idea of a EPO is now so naturalised that nobody even seems to think about debating whether it has any foundation. Based exclusively on EB results, academics claim that 'Europeans support the Europeanisation of public power because they doubt the skills of their State in the context of globalisation' (Reynié 2008: 11), or that 'the fact that more than half of Europeans express some form of identification with Europe, even if usually secondary to the national or regional identifications, is indicative of a proto-European society layered over national and subnational societies' (Diez Medrano 2008). Opinions collected by sample and interpreted by the EB commands so much credit that nothing, even actual elections, seems to be liable to challenge it. While, sociologically speaking, it is difficult to claim that the EPO is – or is not – what the EB polls measure, the EB-EPO equivalence is considered as self-evident and never called into question by the principal users of the Commission's surveys. The instrument gives form and intention to the EPO and, in so doing, proves to be very useful to all actors interested in the Europeans' attitudes and opinions, including political leaders, specialised journalists and scholars. The transformations undergone by the EB programme since its inception reflect the instrument's progressive instrumentalisation quite well.

---

20. Responses to a question on positive or negative feelings towards Europe are taken as indicators of support for political unification; those on the modalities of election of MEPs as indicators of attachment to European Parliament.

From an experimental feedback tool...

On the market of trans-European polls, the EB holds a seldom challenged monopoly position, the only exception being the four waves of the European Values Survey over the last thirty years: 1981, 1990, 1999, 2008. This position is maintained by a powerful institution (the European Commission), which funds, orders, controls and regularly publishes a state of opinion of which it is both the guarantor and the driving force. The first reason for this situation, of course, lies in the difficulty and in the means required to simultaneously collect, analyse and compare opinions of twenty-seven national populations. By publishing EB reports and then making them available online free of charge, the European Commission has managed to turn its polling programme into an ideal database for students, journalists or researchers working on the subject.[21] In Europe's current institutional configuration as in less democratic regimes (Rowell 2005), the fact that only politicians are in charge of measurement instruments that allow the definition and handling of a 'social reality' is problematic, especially when said instruments explicitly borrow from science their supposedly apolitical truth in order to make their analysis of that reality indisputable.[22] Since its inception in 1958, the European Commission has progressively come to rely on increasingly sophisticated tools of management of the public space and opinion, justified through the imperative of counteracting its deficit in popularity and legitimacy, pointed out by observers (Marquand 1979) and MEPs beginning in the late 1970s. The EB, created in 1973, has played an increasingly important role in this instrumentation and, like all tools of government, has experienced and been transformed by the tensions, priorities and beliefs of the institutional actors in charge of it.

The development of a semi-annual polling programme backed by the Commission was initially conceived as a 'feedback tool' allowing European decision-makers to be informed on the state of opinion on Europe through regular and longitudinal opinion surveys conducted in all Member States.[23] In a Community born from diplomatic negotiations, built on technocratic processes, with support from national parliaments but no popular consent, this was a way to get a feel for the attitude and the support of European populations towards the integration process, in the absence of electoral consultations and recognised opinion brokers. The EB's early stages were tentative and the success of the endeavour was uncertain. It was initially a marginal, even precarious experiment: not only is this shown by the

---

21. Most of the nearly seven hundred EB surveys (including seventy-one Standard EBs, 231 Special EBs, 281 Flash EBs and fourteen qualitative studies) are available on the EU's official website (europa.eu). Questionnaires and part of the raw data are available on the website of the Mannheimer Zentrum für Europäische Sozialforschung (http://www.mzes.uni-mannheim.de) and the Inter-University Consortium for Political and Social Research (Ann Arbor, Michigan).

22. A report from the Bureau of European Political Advisers to the President of the Commission, based on EB and Eurostat data, is significantly entitled 'Europe's social reality'.

23. MEPs asked for regular trans-Community polls in the February 1972 Schuijt Report.

status of its founder Jacques-René Rabier,[24] but also by the lack of institutional re-sources (an office and a secretary) and the amateurism of the first EB reports. The first eleven reports were introduced as 'Working document for the Commission of the European Communities'; they were typewritten, with many typos and incor-rect table borders. Conducted by the French polling institute IFOP using the quota method, these polls are retrospectively striking in terms of their freedom in the wording of the questions, their analysis, the inventiveness of the indicators and the scientific reflexivity on display. For instance, the following remarks were made on the possible methodological effects related to the very principle of soliciting an opinion on whether more or less Europe was needed:

Excerpt 9 (EB 1, 1974)

There are two possible explanations for the fact that what the Commission is doing is now considered insufficient and it is difficult to choose between the two at the stage reached in the analysis. This critical reply may be a stereotype by which the public expresses its feeling that 'the Government never does enough'.

While they may seem entirely justified, these considerations on the effects of the method of questioning – and their tendency to artificially manufacture favour-able opinions towards Europe – progressively disappeared.[25] Likewise, the first EBs included questions whose theme and wording soon came to be perceived as 'unnecessarily controversial'.[26]

Excerpt 10 (EB 3, 1975)

If you were to be told tomorrow that the Common Market was to be scrapped, would you feel: Very sorry/indifferent/Relieved/Don't know?

Excerpt 11 (EB 6, 1976 and EB 21, 1984)

This is a list of the countries belonging to the European Community (Common Market). (Show CARD). Among these countries of the European Community, are there any, including your own, you would prefer not to be in the community? Which ones? (Followed by a list of the ten member countries)

---

24. Formerly Jean Monnet's Head of Cabinet at the High Authority of the ESCS, he was forced in January 1973 to surrender his position as Director-General of the Press and Information Service to an Irish official. He was put in charge of the conception of a European polling programme as 'adviser' (which did not entailed managing an administrative service or implementing policy).

25. However, the questionnaires' 'contamination' effects (Lau *et al.* 1990) – personalisation or politi-cisation introduced by the enumeration of 'political' questions and questions related to the social and economic context – remained numerous in the EB after this initial period.

26. According to a senior DG Communication official (interview with the author, May 2007).

Excerpt 12 (EB 3, 1975)

Would you, or would you not, be willing to make some personal sacrifice -for example- pay a little more taxes to help bring about the unification of Europe? Very willing/Fairly willing/Not very willing/Not at all willing/No reply.

Results [EC]: Very willing 5%, Fairly willing 21%, Not very willing 24%, Not at all willing 43%, No reply 7%.

The greater publicity and media visibility of the results led to a transformation of the EB reports, both in form and content. With regard to form, in the 1990s, the reports as material and then virtual objects (on the Internet) resembled products delivered by marketing and polling institutes to their customers: they were printed in colour on glossy paper, with a recognisable graphic charter and layout, and the main results were projected onto maps, etc.[27] In terms of content, results were now presented as sound, and doubts or scientific discussions on possible invalidating points were no longer mentioned. The questions likely to reveal or feed tensions between Member States were removed. Beyond the directness, even the brutality of their wording, the questions on scrapping the Common Market and personal sacrifice were also progressively removed because their results contradicted the fundamental measure of support for the EU. The latter is traditionally in the majority among respondents, even though only one out four respondents is very or fairly willing to accept sacrifices for the unification of Europe. Faced with the perspective of 'scrapping' the Common Market, more than a third of respondents chose 'indifference', and a sizeable proportion (13 per cent in 1975) went for 'relieved'. The desire of being part of Europe is contradicted by the 'indicator of tension': many German (33 per cent), Luxembourgian (38 per cent) and French (41 per cent) respondents preferred Great Britain to be out of the Community; 47 per cent of Danish and 28 per cent of British respondents excluded their own country (EB 21, 1984).

As the years passed, even though respondents mostly feel incompetent, indifferent,[28] badly informed and not interested in being informed on European politics,[29] results favouring unification have been more systematically highlighted. Since it proposes a restricted number of responses, the EB survey system concentrates and polarises the distribution of responses, with remarkable rates for variables that would not otherwise be salient or significant. This is the case for the measure of support for unification, trust in the European Parliament or the wish to have the EU's competences extended to other fields. In 1975, during an

---

27. This evolution matches the end of the EB's 'Stoetzelian' period; since its inception, it had been managed by the IFOP and Faits et Opinions polling institutes. In 1989, INRA, a European consortium of opinion research and polling institutes, won the framework contract for the Commission's opinion polls.

28. The EU is at the bottom of the list of subjects treated in the media to which respondents 'pay attention' (EB 52, 2000).

29. A majority of respondents consider that the press (51per cent) and television (50 per cent) give 'sufficient' and 'objective coverage'.

era defined as one of 'permissive consensus', the distribution of responses to the question 'All things considered, are you in favour of the unification of Europe, against it or indifferent' reveals the respondents' low level of involvement: 35 per cent were 'very much in favour', 34 per cent were 'somewhat in favour', 15 per cent were 'indifferent', 5 per cent were 'somewhat against', 4 per cent 'against' and 7 per cent 'Don't know' (EC Results, EB 3, 1975). While the official interpretation given consists in adding up the first two percentages to claim that 'seven out of ten interviewed (69 per cent) were in favour of the unification of Europe' (ibid.), undetermined ('indifferent') responses, ones that entail less involvement from the respondent ('somewhat...') and negative responses add up to 58 per cent of the overall number of respondents, without taking into account 'Don't know' answers. Probably for this reason, questions were progressively rewritten in more polysemic terms, with less involving wordings, and only offering one possibility for an in-between or neutral response, thereby reducing the gradation and the dispersion of the results. Hence, the politically very sensitive question held as an indicator of support for the unification process requires respondents to assess their country's membership of the EU as a good or bad 'thing'. The removal of the phrase 'political unification' and the undetermined, vague character of the term 'thing' might contribute to neutralising the politically involving character of the question. Similarly, the reduction of the number of answer possibilities limits the fragmentation of the responses, which would emphasise the ambiguity and even the fragility of the support expressed.

Excerpt 13 (EB 70, 2008)

Generally speaking, do you think that (OUR COUNTRY)'s membership of the European Union is: a good thing/neither good nor bad/a bad thing/don't know? Results [EU]: A good thing 53%, neither good nor bad 27%, a bad thing 15%, don't know 5%.

Generally speaking, the strategy of presentation of the results aims at downplaying the importance of negative, neutral responses and non-responses. Since the 1990s, the results judged by the authors of the reports to be the most significant are presented to the reader as map projections and bar charts, which never concern marginal values, 'negative' results, distant or qualified responses (Lehingue 2007c: 54 ff.). Behind this very selective presentation of the results, early on, a number of researchers pointed out the relative weakness of very favourable opinions towards the EU, and the importance of a form of 'benevolent neutrality' for Europe. (Percheron 1991). The statistically sizeable proportion of rates recorded for all low involvement responses is sociologically significant: it provides an indication of the social and symbolic distance between pollsters and respondents as well as between respondents and political Europe. This presentation of the results shows that the feedback tool has progressively become an instrument of political expertise, whose data are oriented by techniques of generation and valorisation facilitating the control of publicisation effects – a well-known and recognised mechanism of production of EPO, used both to organise the Union's 'governance' and to exhibit European democracy as the Commission's leaders conceptualise it.

... to a governance instrument

The Commission's official documents now present the EB as a 'governance' instrument,[30] capable of revealing citizen expectations to European decision-makers. Indeed, it is perceived as a tool to discover the dispositions of particular social groups towards Community initiatives, to help make informed decisions, to structure the political agenda and to devise communication plans. The analysis of the Commission's official documents on communication policy clearly indicates such use of EB surveys by the EU's institutional partners (college of commissioners, the Commission DGs, the Press Service of the European Parliament, the Member States' communication services).

> Before funds of European messages can be developed on major issues, an in-depth analysis must be carried out of public opinion in the Member States. The European Commission has the necessary experience and capacity at European level to do this. Eurobarometer, and the opinion polls and qualitative studies which it draws on, enable it to develop this perception on a consistent and regular basis. [...] This cooperation [with Member States] should make it easier to meet the expectations and needs of ordinary Europeans more effectively. The development of this information monitoring capacity – which could take the form of a web-based network linking all the partners involved – will thus provide a framework in which to formulate the messages needed for each topic or information campaign.
>
> (European Commission,
> An information and Communication Strategy for the EU, 2002)

As such documents must be made public in Europe, 'information monitoring' of opinion is presented as a service to citizens. But this rhetorical smokescreen hardly conceals the instrument's political instrumentalisation.[31] Since its inception, the EB has proved to be an efficient tool to assess political leeway for Community action. As early as EB 3 (1975), the attitude of respondents towards the possibility of having MEPs elected by direct universal suffrage was studied. This question was systematically asked until the effective introduction of the reform. The same goes for the introduction of the single currency, the European passport, European diplomacy, a European Olympic team, but also for the harmonisation of labour laws, of social contributions or the idea of European protectionism. The themes of Special EBs and the Flash EBs have signposted the transformation of the feedback tool into an instrument of political governance most often in the service of the Commission's projects.

---

30. The Commission's White Paper on European Governance (2001), which itself involved an EB survey, emphasises continuous polling as a governance instrument.

31. According to Max Weber, in democracy, more than in other types of government, 'the fact that the chief and his administrative staff often appear formally as servants or agents of those they rule, naturally does nothing whatever to disprove the quality of dominance' (Weber 1978).

Keeping in mind that the Commission embodies and defends Community interests against national objectives and resistance from the States, we may have another perspective on the undoubtedly political role of the EB's publication and mediatisation in institutional power relations, i.e. in Commission-Parliament-Council relations. Ostensibly constructed as the faithful and objective (and scientific, therefore undebatable) reflection of EPO, the EB reports are meant to provide evidence of the social demand for 'more Europe', which can be generated artificially,[32] even in unfavourable European contexts. Even though they expose European citizens' confusion and lack of knowledge on Europe, qualitative studies are also used to support the diagnosis of public support for political integration: a qualitative EB claims 'that strong expectations remain towards the European Union can be clearly seen when asking the respondents about the Union's goals and the priority objectives which they would set for it' (The future of Europe, May 2006). The EB is also now considered as one of the main resources of the participatory turn in European communication, aiming at setting the 'listening process' as one of the Commission's new legitimating principles. Since 2001, the Commission has claimed it wants to 'draw more systematically on feedback from citizens' in the conception of European policies.

> The research function will be the fundamental element of the 'listening process', through the analysis of Eurobarometer and other survey results, as well as media [...] monitoring.
>
> (European Commission,
> Action Plan to Improve Communicating Europe, 2005)

The opinion manufactured by the EBs works both classically as a 'legitimating principle for political discourses and actions' (Champagne 1990: 42) and as a means to assess opportunities and clear paths to develop Community initiatives. Some Colleges have used EB more systematically than others. The Delors presidency (1985–1995) was a period of intense development and exploitation of opinion polls by Commission services, before a relative decline during the Santer and Prodi Commissions. Since the introduction of the first Barroso Commission (2004), there has been a surge of interest in the EB, mainly linked to the overhaul of the EU's communication policy. After the rejection of the constitutional treaty, the White Paper on a European Communication Policy (2006) announced the launch of 'a special series of Eurobarometer polls [...] to provide the best possible data for analysis' and went on to explain that:

> In modern democratic societies, policy-makers devote a great deal of attention to analysing public opinion, using tools such as opinion polls and media

---

32. Not to mention the orientation of questions such as 'The nine countries of the EEC are together dealing with a number of shared problems. Here is a list of them. Could you please tell me which one of these problems is the most important at the present time? And which is the next most important problem? (EB 1)

monitoring. The importance of these tools has increased in parallel with the tendency for citizens to withdraw from traditional politics (joining political parties, voting in elections, etc.). European public opinion is complex and diverse, reflecting different national perspectives. Understanding it therefore poses a particular challenge. The European Commission has been a front runner in developing modern tools – such as the Eurobarometer surveys – for analysing European public opinion.

(European Commission,
White Paper on a European Communication Policy, 2006: 10)

In addition to its expertise, the instrument is now also presented by the Commission and other institutions[33] as an instrument for listening to citizens and interacting with them. The 'State' polling programme has progressively turned into a democratic artifice thought to be capable of bridging the gap between political Europe and European citizens.

Conclusion

It does not seem that the scientifically debatable character of EB data on political opinions or the instrument's blatant instrumentalisation are likely to slow the dynamic of its extensive and multiple uses. Most discourse and studies on opinion trends and European values, after all, very closely depend on the data built and published by the Commission (see Chapter 1 in this volume). This situation of excessive, sometimes exclusive, dependence on a political instrument raises a number of ethical and methodological issues. Researchers who conduct secondary analyses of the EB database are generally willing to admit its imperfections, but rarely acknowledge its institutional origins. Hence, Pierre Bréchon concedes that the EB, like other major international surveys (European Values Survey, World Values Survey), provides 'fragile' data, which 'are not as refined as qualitative data', and that some of its indicators are 'in some respects simplistic' (Bréchon 2002). But he argues in the EB's favour in terms of necessity (the EB, he says, provides invaluable and irreplaceable services in furthering scientific knowledge) and, especially, scientific rigour (the sophistication of the secondary treatment is seen to rectify the data's genetic biases). Usefulness ultimately prevails over the data's intrinsic weaknesses. Such arguments are rather common among consumers of international surveys and tend to neglect the key discussion of legitimate scientific objections to their use, for instance on sample representativeness[34] or the

---

33. See the European Parliament's report on the period of reflection (A6–0414/2005), 2005.

34. The random sampling technique relies on the ability of the people drawn at random to respond to the pollsters, but members of some segments of the population (single, elderly, less-educated, unemployed persons, etc.) more rarely agree to participate in surveys (Bon 1991: 193). The reputedly significant proportion and the social profiles of those who refuse to participate in EB surveys are never made public or discussed.

political role of EB results. Similarly, the question of whether EPO is an extrinsic reality to the instrument that measures it is seldom raised.[35] The systematic lack of regard for these issues is likely related to the forms of institutionalisation of the instrument which, since its inception, has resulted from close and permanent co-operation between Community agents schooled in social science,[36] specialists of survey research and polling institute professionals (Aldrin 2010). Books (Inglehart and Reif 1991; Bréchon and Cautrès 1998), workshops and conferences[37] on the EB are traditionally presented as a publicised moment of this process of copro-duction of expertise on EPO, to which each category of partners brings their own specific legitimacy: institutional and political legitimacy for senior officials and commissioners, professional and technical legitimacy for pollsters, and scientific and academic legitimacy for researchers. To a large extent, this state of affairs explains that the instrument is perceived as an oracle and elicits so little critical discussion.

---

35. Symptomatically, in their insightful synthesis of studies on European opinion, Céline Belot and Bruno Cautrès only mention this in the first footnote: 'The idea that there is such a thing as a 'Eu-ropean public opinion' is eminently problematic. [...] Nevertheless, since European institutions consider Eurobarometer data to be the expression of a European public opinion, and since they take into account their results when they define policies, it ensues that European public opinion actually exists' (Belét and Cautrès 2008: 153).

36. Jacques-René Rabier's successors, Anna Melich and Karlheinz Reif, were academics specialised in public opinion.

37. See the conference '35th anniversary of Eurobarometer. Understanding European public opinion', organised in November 2008 by the Commission's DG Communication (www.eurobarometer-conference2008.ec.europa.eu).

chapter three | methodology of the project

Daniel Gaxie and Jay Rowell

In spite of the extensive bibliography dedicated to the attitudes of ordinary citizens towards European construction, much is still unknown. One of the most significant gaps results from the under-estimation of the diversity of attitudes towards Europe. Likewise, research, so far, has largely failed to explore the motives and reasons which lead citizens to express either positive or negative judgements on Europe. Many correlations between European attitudes and a number of 'variables' have been assessed, but establishing a correlation does not amount to providing an explanation. To effectively analyse citizens' dispositions towards Europe, it is necessary to get a better grasp of their perceptions and their subjective evaluations. These perceptions vary according to both the national context and socio-demographic characteristics. To explain the effect of nationality, scholars often put forward culturalist hypotheses (see Chapter 1), which are hardly compatible with the diversity of attitudes between the various categories of the population in each country. Hence, more in-depth comparisons are needed in order to take national specificities – but also convergences – into account. In the same way, more precise information is necessary if we want to better understand how socio-demographic characteristics predispose people to having particular visions of Europe.

Research questions and hypotheses

Most analyses of European attitudes are carried out by statistically processing formally identical answers to closed-ended questions. The comparability of answers collected in different national and social contexts cannot however be taken for granted. The illusion of an immediate comparability of quantitative data relies on a form of nominalism which presupposes that in spite of their differences, interviewees attribute an identical signification and importance to questions asked and answers given. Such a methodology also implies that all the interviewees could have answered the question with their own means if the answers had not been suggested to them; the hypothesis being that the interviewees respond with the same discursive register as contained in the questions. Similarly, it is assumed that most citizens are capable of expressing political views on the main issues of European construction.

We started from different research hypotheses. In contrast to the general assumptions made in the specialised literature, we think that the European attitudes and opinions of citizens are diverse. We are not only referring to a divergence of views – favourable, critical, or composite – towards the EU. Political science has long established that citizens are unequally informed on public affairs and unequally interested in political subjects.[1] Several decades of research have shown that citizens are unequally at ease when giving opinions on political questions, especially on those that are more abstract.[2] There is no reason to think that these well-established results do not also apply to European political issues. Arguably, they might apply to this field all the more as there is no purely European space of political transactions, and little mobilisation and media coverage on European issues.

Standardised surveys ask representative samples of the population to express themselves on many EU-related subjects. Their authors consider it self-evident that all citizens are capable of expressing themselves on often complex questions. The low percentages of 'no answer' responses generally observed seems to prove them right, at least if we ignore the fact that this is largely due to the use of closed-ended questions. On the contrary, our initial hypotheses relied on the consistent results from countless studies, which established that the familiarity with political questions and the consistency of political opinions are mostly weak, and that they vary greatly according to the level of education, social position and gender. However for the last twenty years various research trends have emphasised the idea that citizens are not completely helpless when it comes to expressing themselves on unfamiliar political issues. One hypothesis is that citizens use cognitive 'shortcuts' and heuristics (Popkin 1991; Sniderman *et al.* 1991; Lodge and McGraw 1995; Lupia *et al.* 2000). Until now these research perspectives have been almost totally neglected by European Studies. We know nothing or nearly nothing about the cognitive tools that citizens mobilise to form an opinion – when they have one – on European subjects. Diverse studies have also highlighted that the understanding of a question or of a situation can result from various transpositions, translations and distortions, but these research perspectives are also ignored by most studies on European public opinion.

These research traditions suggest several main research questions. To what degree are the various categories of the population capable of stating an opinion on the issues of European public debate (for example on the construction of a political union, the reinforcement of European integration, the democratic deficit in the Union, or services of general interest)? If the citizens have an opinion on these questions, how firm and coherent is it? What cognitive instruments of evaluation are used to produce an opinion? Are opinions the expression of structured attitudes? For what reasons are the evaluations of European construction positive or negative? Do the opinions expressed rely on specific instruments of evaluation, which are mobilised in specialised political debates or are they produced from different instruments which still need to be defined? To what extent are the survey questions on European political issues understood? Is the phrasing of the questions understood or, on the contrary, can we observe misunderstandings?

It has also been long established that the attitudes of the citizens – especially

---

1. See the results of surveys carried out since the 1940s, notably Lazarsfeld *et al.* (1968) and Campbell *et al.* (1980).

2. Converse (1964) and, more recently, Zaller (1992) are two of the most frequently cited studies.

the less politicised ones – towards politics still depend on the saliency of the issues (Nie *et al.* 1979). After the establishment of free movement and a common market, the Euro, the increase of the number and scope of directives and regulations, the enlargement to new member states, the debate surrounding Turkey's accession, or, in some countries, the controversies sparked off by different referendums, we can also think that the EU or the politics and the decisions of the EU have become more familiar to certain segments of the population. The analysis of the relationship to European construction therefore has to take the experience of Europe into consideration, i.e. the extent to which each individual is personally (or indirectly, through their social circle) confronted by realities that are European or perceived as such.

Methodological choices

These questions influenced our methodological choices. One of our goals was to see what citizens think of when asked for their opinions on 'Europe' and the EU, and to observe the instruments of appreciation they mobilise to formulate their judgements. We did not want to assume that they all have a general view on the European Union and that they are capable of expressing political points of view on its evolution. On the contrary, we thought that different citizens relied on varied orientations and background information to formulate their opinions. We therefore began by asking very open questions on the overall perception and judgement on 'Europe'. The objective was to let the interviewees freely develop their views, in their own words, without suggesting any answers. Thus, we wanted to be able to observe the categories and, beyond, the cognitive instruments spontaneously used by the interviewees, the arguments they put forward and the elements of perception of European realities they mobilised. For this it was necessary to rely on semi-structured interviews rather than closed-ended questionnaires.

The interviews such as those which were carried out in the framework of this study are said to be 'in-depth', first because they generally take longer to conduct than questionnaires and secondly because open-ended questions force the interviewee to form their point of view using their own means, without being able to 'cling' onto suggestions. As they are more flexible, during in-depth interviews it is also possible to follow up, which allows the interviewee to develop or clarify a point of view. The association of ideas can reveal certain background aspects of perceptions and judgements that are not explicit in what is said. But the interest of conducting in-depth face-to-face interviews does not only lie in the content of what is said or suggested by the interviewee, but also in the modalities of their discourse. One can observe hesitations, pauses, reactions of embarrassment, intonations, modulations in speech and changes in body language. An opinion may be considered differently when it is given with a shrug or in a weary or hesitant voice. Like questionnaires, these interviews can, in some cases, confront interviewees with issues that they have never previously encountered. The risk of producing an artefact, which we discuss further on, is significant in studies of themes that are not part of most citizens' preoccupations or everyday conversations. Closed-end questions raise methodological difficulties partly because the interviewees who do not have a personal opinion on a certain question are inclined to seize any suggestions in order to save face and to hide their embarrassment, while, failing to prevent it, open-ended questions can help reveal the presence of such an imposition. When interviewees have to formulate answers themselves, it is easier to notice that they do not have a firm opinion on certain topics because of their hesitations and reactions.

Because certain fractions of the population are not very familiar with European subjects, their reactions to the survey and to the questions are, in some cases, as revealing as their statements themselves. Interviewers were given instructions to transcribe as accurately as they could, not only the interviewees' discourse, including any blunders, repetitions, incomplete sentences, language mistakes and informal phrases, but also pauses, hesitations, and noticeable gestures. However, regardless of the amount of care put into this work, the transcript will only include part of the relevant information. As all the interview transcripts were made available to all team members, the authors of the chapters in this book worked on interviews that they had not always carried out themselves. They might have misinterpreted an interviewee's discourse or ignored certain non-verbal reactions, which might not have been indicated. At the same time, all of the authors conducted interviews, which made them aware of these difficulties.

The objectives, the organisation and the conduct of the interviews

The interviews were conducted based on a template inspired by our theoretical research hypotheses. Most of the template applied to all countries, but certain questions were adapted to national contexts. The interviewers began by asking the interviewees if 'Europe' evoked anything either positive or negative to them. The objective was to reveal the existence and the orientation of possible attitudes. Subsequent questions focused on the elements of perception mobilised, before moving on to more precise themes such as the Euro, free movement, the Schengen Agreement, enlargement, the possible accession of Turkey into the European Union, competition policy, the question of public services, and, in the French case, the directive on services. In addition to documenting attitudes, the objective was to also clarify the level of information of the interviewee without directly testing their knowledge. For example we asked what the interviewee thought of the Schengen Agreement in order to see if they had heard of this expression and if they knew what it meant. If the person replied that they did not know what it meant, or said that they had heard of the name but that they no longer remembered what it is about, the interviewer provided cues before asking the same question again. Thirdly, the interview was based on experiences of Europe. The objective was to observe if and how each interviewee had encountered 'European' realities – or realities perceived as 'European' – in their educational, professional, family, religious, union or associative experiences or in their hobbies. These questions revealed specific information on the interviewees' biographies, social characteristics, participation in civic activity, living conditions, positions and social status. The interview then focused again on the interviewee's level of information, and aimed at clarifying whether or not the person felt well-informed on European subjects, and finding out what exactly they had trouble understanding. They were then asked about their usual sources of information. We also used questions from the Eurobarometers concerning the level of confidence in the European Parliament, the Commission and the Council in order to test the degree of familiarity with these institutions. The fifth phase of the interview was devoted to the votes during the European elections and the 2005 referendum for interviews carried out in France. The goal was to see if the interviewee had political preferences and if these preferences were coherent with European attitudes. The interview finished with a few questions on some of the big political issues of European construction. Using some of the wording from the Eurobarometer surveys, we asked the interviewees to give an opinion on political Union, on the reinforcement of integration, or on the democratic deficit. The originality of the approach consisted in asking the interviewee to specify the motives behind their answer, which often led them to clarify what they understood by 'political Union', 'integration', or 'democratic deficit'. We were thus able to observe if and how these standard questions of public debate were understood. Again the objective was to see to what extent positions on European political issues are understood and mobilised by various categories of the public and to what extent their (eventual) attitudes towards Europe are structured by or around views on these issues.

The composition of the samples

Since we started with the hypothesis that attitudes towards Europe are multiple, it was necessary for us to be able to observe this diversity. This meant diversifying the sample as much as possible: men and women of different ages, places of residence, levels of education, income, profession, experience of Europe, engagement in associations, religion, unions or parties, level of politicisation and political orientations. As is generally noticed in this type of survey, interviewers had little trouble connecting with people who are socially close to them, generally belonging to the middle or upper middle spheres of the social space. It was necessary to make a greater effort to connect with interviewees from the upper and especially lower classes. The latter turned out to be the most difficult to reach and it was particularly hard to convince them to talk about certain subjects which are very remote from their everyday preoccupations. Many interviewees could not understand why we would be interested in their opinions on such subjects. Some shrugged to express their incomprehension. Those who agreed to venture into such unknown territory tended to interpret the questions as a knowledge quiz. Certain interviews were just as painful and difficult for the interviewee as for the interviewer. To compensate for the difficulties of reaching different categories of the public, we sought help from members of the interviewers' social circles, including numerous students who took part in this project. Thanks to them and to the combined social capital of the relatives, friends, neighbours, acquaintances, we managed to put together relatively diverse samples. When a person is asked by someone close to him or her to participate in an interview, it can be difficult to say no. We were thus able to meet men and women who without a doubt would never have accepted to take part in an interview on such subjects if it had been carried out through ordinary methodological principles, such as anonymous telephone surveys. This was an opportunity to listen to people whose attitudes, reactions and opinions are seldom considered and analysed in the social sciences.

Our samples were composed in both rigorous and pragmatic ways. They are rigorous in the sense that the choice of interviewees was guided by several questions and theoretical hypotheses, relying on a solid scientific literature. Throughout the study, we regularly evaluated progress in order to locate the gaps and to clarify the types of people whose reactions needed to be further explored. At the same time, our samples were composed of acquaintances, friends and relatives of collaborators. Some of the interviews were conducted by experienced researchers, but some were carried out by students as a part of their training in survey techniques. The results are therefore unequal and some interviews were difficult to use.

Relationships between interviewers and interviewees

As we have pointed out, the empirical material was accumulated by relying on the acquaintances, encounters, initiatives and recommendations of the interviewers and of their social circles. In many cases, the interviewer did not know the interviewee before questioning them. In other cases, they interviewed someone who they knew, or even someone very close to them. This choice contrasts with a certain orthodoxy in which the conditions of the interview should be formally identical and interviewees and interviewers should be complete strangers in order to guarantee the strict neutrality of the survey. Our experience has led us to question these methodological premises. Every interview unfolds in a specific configuration which inevitably affects the result. There is no interview situation without a 'bias' and without interference due to the context of the encounter, the questions asked and the relationships established between the interviewers and the interviewees, according to their positions in the social space. Therefore, attempting to neutralise the effects of the interview situation would be vain, as they cannot be ignored. It is undoubtedly preferable to try to spot the effects produced by each particular interaction and to take them into account when interpreting the results. Whether the interviewer and the interviewee are familiar with each other or not, there are advantages and disadvantages, which may partially overlap or differ. On a subject like 'Europe', there is nothing embarrassing to conceal or to hide from somebody one may encounter in other circumstances. One of the main drawbacks of the interview between friends or relations is the complicity which sometimes exists, and which may prevent them from elaborating on points that appear self-evident. On the other hand, an advantage of this type of interview is the confidence that can encourage straightforwardness: the interviewees may have to acknowledge their lack of information on the issues discussed. Even more so, one of the most interesting advantages of the interview carried out between friends or relatives is that the interviewer can assess whether the opinions expressed by the interviewee in this formal situation of a recorded interview match their usual views or not. In standard opinion surveys, the interviewer is not capable of knowing whether the recorded reactions differ or not from the way in which the interviewee reacts in other circumstances. The specific effects of the survey situation are therefore more difficult to take into account.

The representativeness of the samples

Quantitative surveys relying on closed-ended questions with what is presumed to be a representative sample are considered 'standard' methodology in normal science. To some extent, all research is more or less explicitly evaluated by this yardstick. The Concorde programme also departs from this standard methodology in this regard. The objective was not to form 'representative' samples of the populations of the five selected countries. Our samples are not representative in the statistical sense of the term, which prevents us from drawing any quantitative general conclusions. Thus, as is usually the case, in spite of our efforts, the lower class are under-represented whereas holders of academic degrees are over-represented. For this reason, we cannot assess the frequency of the phenomena that we analyse. We can, for example, describe the different levels of information on European questions but we are unable to say what percentage of the population can be characterised as having a particular level of information. But while our samples are not representative, they are sufficiently diverse to allow us to observe, describe and to attempt to explain contrasting attitudes. Thus, our methodology is adapted to our research objectives. Likewise, although our samples are not representative in the general sense of the term, the number of people questioned – including the under-represented categories – is sufficient for the results to hold a satisfactory degree of validity.

The analysis of the interviews and the nature of the results

In order to formulate general propositions on the description, the understanding and the explanation of attitudes towards Europe, we continuously tested our analytical framework with the individual cases. By repeating such observations, we were progressively able to locate similarities and differences between individuals and to establish general types. Every interview is a particular case, but the comparison of these particular cases allows for the progressive identification of several invariants, as well as more or less marked deviations from these invariants. Each particular case is made up of a number of characteristics in terms of opinions, attitudes, practices, experiences and individual properties that are shared to various degrees by groups of particular cases. This individual and collective dialectic is the basis of empirical generalisation founded on qualitative material. The comparison between individual cases, guided by our research hypotheses, allows the progressive emergence of characteristics which define the general types. The typifications proposed in this book link perceptions of 'Europe' with representations, opinions, practices, experience and social characteristics. They are based on instruments of observation which evidently entail limitations (like all instruments), but which also allow more detailed reconstitutions of the individuals' subjective representations than when using closed-ended questions. These subjective representations are presented in a typified and stylised form. They are linked to types of practices, experience and social properties. This articulation of 'subjective' and 'objective' aspects provides explanations of attitudes toward Europe (in a given national context, at a precise time) that seek to go beyond the epistemological alternative of understanding and explaining.

The question of the 'validity' or solidity of the results

As the methodology used allows for more in-depth analysis than closed-ended questions, we can better grasp the complexity of attitudes towards Europe as well as the many factors which shape them: this is one of the main advantages of qualitative surveys. These results, as we have said, are presented as ideal-typical descriptions. Their solidity is based on several elements. The first element is the relevance of the system of hypotheses and its progressive refinement. The second one is the quality of the confrontation between this theoretical framework in constant evolution and the results of each empirical case. On the one hand, the research hypotheses structure the analysis, the description and the characterisation of each particular case. At the same time, every interview conducted and interpreted feeds back into the hypotheses, which are accordingly readjusted.

As in quantitative surveys, but in a different way, the quality of the empirical investigation depends on the quality, the number and the diversity of the observations. In the case of the interviews, this quality depends on how the interview template fits the theoretical framework, and on the capacity of the interviewer to comply with the template and encourage the interviewees to develop their answers. The difficulty resides in getting the interviewee to deliver the maximum amount of information relevant to the hypotheses. The number and the diversity of the interviewees are decisive for various reasons. Insofar as the concrete empirical cases are never exactly identical and deviate more or less from stylised typifications, increasing the number of cases provides more opportunities to elaborate and specify appropriate typifications. But just as much as the number of interviewees, their heterogeneity is essential in a survey on the variety of opinions and attitudes. The interviewees should be sufficiently diverse (in respect of the properties relevant for the explanation of the phenomenon studied), so that no particular type of attitude is ignored. Provided that the conditions of the survey and of the analysis are rigorous, the diversity of the interviewees prevents the researcher from unduly generalising conclusions which only apply to a sub-group, and leads him to make all the necessary distinctions between types, subtypes, variants and intermediary cases.

As in quantitative surveys, again, but again in a different way, the number of observations is therefore one of the criteria of empirical rigour. We know, however, that the increase in the size of the sample tendentially yields declining empirical returns. It is therefore in each case necessary to reach a compromise, on the one hand between the time and the means available, and, on the other hand, the compliance with the accepted empirical standard. In the case of the qualitative surveys, it is the saturation of the procedures of description and typification which indicate that a satisfactory level of quality of observation has been reached. When one observes that additional interviews no longer allow the diverse typifications to be refined, this is a sign that a (temporary) foreclosure of the empirical investigation can be safely decided. In this sense, most of the results presented in this book have a reasonable degree of validity. But even if they are reasonably solid, the results of a qualitative survey (like those of a quantitative survey) remain necessarily tentative. They are for example likely to be amended by new empirical elements, for example when the survey procedure is improved, or when new types of cases are considered. The social and political context can also evolve. We can clearly see, for example, how the Euro hugely affected the attitudes of certain categories of the public. Finally, because they always depend on a theoretical framework, the results obtained at a certain time can be questioned by new questions or hypotheses.

Contrary to what is usually assumed, qualitative surveys are not less rigorous than quantitative surveys; rather, their rigour assumes different forms. Insofar as methodological rules are respected, the size of the samples – smaller than those of the quantitative surveys – does not necessarily hinder the contention of grounded generalisations. The greater precision and detail compensates for the impossibility of quantifying. But statistical results are after all only one of the types of results that social science can offer.

The question of the publication of the elements of empirical validation

There is, however, a difficulty that remains, related to the constraints of publication rather than the research method itself. The results of the survey are based on a progressive back-and-forth between the research hypotheses and the empirical investigations. The rigour of the approach and the (always relative) solidity of the results are based on the quality of this continuous confrontation. But, like every written account of a survey, this book provides the 'final' state of the analysis, without being able to reproduce the stages, the uncertainties, the hesitations, and the reasons, notably empirical, which led to adopting a given explicative position rather than another one.[3] The interview excerpts that the reader will find in these chapters do not have the status of 'evidence'. In order to provide 'evidence'[4] it

---

3. The impossibility of providing the reader with all the information necessary to assess the validity of the method and of the 'results' is not specific to qualitative surveys. Quantitative surveys are assumed to provide all the required elements to validate their conclusions, but in general we know very little about the conditions of the selection of interviewees, the sampling bias, the conditions in which the interviews were conducted, the interviewees' reactions, their understanding of the questions, the modalities of their answers, the uncertainties in coding, etc. Often, the apparent objectivity of statistics appears to give credit to the validity of the results. In reality this supposed validity is based on the belief and the confidence in the validity of the research operations, based on a more or less unanimous consensus in the academic community.

4. 'Evidence' is used here in a metaphorical manner in order to simplify the expression and to

would have been necessary to not only publish all of the mobilised empirical material in this research programme (more than 10,000 pages of interview transcripts!), but also to describe the entire process of the analytical treatment of these materials, which is obviously impossible. The possibility of controlling the results presented does not reside in the publication of empirical 'evidence', but rather in the description of the survey and analysis procedures which would make a Popperian exercise of refutation possible. The empirical material presented in this book, notably the interview extracts, are illustrations. They were not chosen to produce a reality effect, but to allow the reader to get a 'sense' of how the attitudes towards Europe are expressed. The empirical illustrations were chosen because of their pertinence (within the limits of the constraints imposed by publication costs). It is, for example, because some interviews reveal certain aspects of European attitudes in a form close to ideal-types that they were chosen to display the empirical bases of the descriptions and explanations put forward. The interviews mentioned only make up a small part of those which were taken into account in the analysis. Most of the interviews carried out are not mentioned in the work for various reasons. Some of them turned out to be of little use because the interviewer was unable to get the interviewee to express himself in a pertinent way. Many provided pertinent information, but in a less 'illustrative' way – i.e. in a less typical way –than the interviews which were used. Others were also pertinent, but redundant.

A comparative programme of research

As it had potential to provide a broader outlook, the comparative approach immediately appeared to be suited to this project. It is often assumed in the specialised literature that nationals from various member states of the EU have a particular vision of European construction, relating to the specificities of their national history and the particular conditions of their country's involvement in the European integration process. In addition, information on Europe is filtered and interpreted within the context of political competition and media spaces which remain strongly structured by the national framework. Some 'European' themes can be amplified and turned into political issues in one context, and remain invisible in another. We see that the salience and the understanding of 'items' in a questionnaire administered in several countries necessarily vary according to the national context, which raises the question of the comparability of the answers obtained. The comparative method appeared to be necessary especially to understand and explain the role of national context and its articulation with other factors.

The very abundance of information provided by the qualitative surveys makes the comparative process difficult. The limited standardisation of procedures, the variety of reactions to the open-ended questions, the time needed for conduct-

---

facilitate communication. From an epistemological point of view, for several reasons that we cannot discuss here, social science cannot provide 'evidence' in the sense of a 'justificationist' philosophy of knowledge.

ing and transcribing the interviews, the difficulty in analysing all of the material gathered, prevent the survey from being carried out in all EU member states. But the difficulties in collecting and interpreting the qualitative material produced in different national contexts suggest a few blind spots in international quantitative surveys which rely on ready-made comparative instruments.

The comparative approaches which rely on databases such as the Eurobarometer are based on the premise of a universal and uni-vocal character of the mobilised political categories. One of their blind spots is the problem of the status of a point of view that is supposedly neutral and at equal distance from different contexts. Such premises are hard to sustain. Individual researchers – or even a research team – can hardly control the political situation, linguistic nuances and the range of political significations of national contexts. The differences between national contexts are explained in this type of study by sweeping generalisations (for example, the conviction that members of countries that benefit from European funds are in favour of European construction), or by culturalist interpretations based on the 'compatibility' between European and national values (for example, the supposed importance of national sovereignty or the experience of a federal state, believed to make European construction more familiar). Such *ad hoc* interpretations reproduce and reify various clichés on national cultures, but most often without the support of empirical means to ensure their relevance. The statistically significant correlations produce an impression of scientific rigour. However, these correlations are abusively extended to haphazard causal interpretations encompassing twenty-seven national contexts, which can never be satisfactorily covered by a single researcher or small research team.

Our survey is based on the principle that comparison is always asymmetrical. On the one hand, the researchers are socialised in a linguistic, social, national and specific scientific context. They are predisposed to transfer familiar categories of thought and frames of reference to other contexts. Comparison always begins in this way, by determining a standard for classifying empirical observations in multiple contexts on a scale going from the identical to the most different.[5]

Our research is based on a tradition of research, developed in the United States and in France, on the socially-differentiated capacity of appropriation and production of a discourse on politics. This approach was transposed to European questions in a French context, and then in other national contexts. To ensure the comparability of the results, it was necessary to ask sometimes identical and sometimes different questions according to the contexts, by respecting a survey protocol of semi-structured interviews, in order to determine the range of possible social and national specificities relative to the meaning of the same terms and to the registers of the answers.

---

5. As Jocelyne Dakhlia (1995: 44) writes, 'The intuition of an analogy, the idea that a phenomenon of the same order can be observed on both sides of a (cultural, political or religious…) border, is necessarily based on an annexationist approach. Whether one eventually concludes that there is identity or difference, the goal is always to test the conformity of an object that we know less, or little, or not, with an object that is already known'.

Two safeguards were introduced to control the effects of the 'annexationist' logic of the project. The first consisted in closely associating the specialists of each country at every step of the project. In order to avoid the pitfalls of a 'ventriloquist comparison',[6] the questionnaire was adapted to each context by the inclusion of specific questions on 'European' issues particularly prominent in 'national' public debates (for example, in France with the Bolkestein directive or the 'Polish plumber' controversy, and in Germany on Turkey joining the EU, and in Poland with reference to Christian foundations of Europe in the preamble to the European Constitutional Treaty). The second safeguard consisted in cross-checking empirical material. This enabled us to shed light on a number of blind spots in the initial theoretical framework built around the French case and to test its more general validity. This assumed asymmetrical approach differs from secondary analyses of international databases where work hypotheses, questions and the survey protocol are settled before the survey actually begins, which makes it impossible to adjust the theoretical framework in light of the fieldwork. On the opposite, our reflexive comparison produces leverage effects; the basic theoretical framework can be refined and new questions can be included.

Such an approach is meant to address two sources of fragility of comparative knowledge due to insufficiently reflexive uses of international databases. By considering comparison as a necessarily asymmetrical and progressive process, we attempt to take into account the inevitable national dimension of language and cognitive schemes. We were able to compare the French context of the initial analytical framework with other countries both by sharing provisional results at each stage of the survey, and by including researchers from the different countries in our team. The latter brought their knowledge of specific national contexts and questioned a number of French-centred biases in the initial research hypotheses. We have also attempted to bridge the frequent gap between the survey material available and often culturalist and intellectualist interpretations put forward in international comparisons. Qualitative methods turn out to be suitable to question common assumptions on the national specificities of representations of Europe. We know, for example, that German federalism or the complex relationships to national identity are often presented as a cognitive frame, explaining the relative consensus on the EU in Germany. The interviews provide the opportunity to confirm the effective presence of such arguments and to list the limited segments of the population who are likely to appropriate such references.

As it developed, our research, which was initially limited to France and Germany, expanded to include Poland, Italy, and the Czech Republic. However, resources were limited and survey conditions were not identical in all countries. The survey began in France in 2006 with in-depth interviews and it ended in early 2009 (based in Paris and Strasbourg). For several years the political science

---

6. This phrase coined by Patrick Hassenteufel (2000: 18) refers to 'cases where comparison is only there to validate a hypothesis without other hypotheses being taken into account. The researcher does not let the comparison speak, he makes it speak, or rather he speaks in its place.'

research team of Amiens University (CURAPP) repeatedly interviewed a small sample (N=24) in order to observe their relationship to politics and any potential change that might occur due to current events, for instance during electoral campaigns. The CURAPP researchers introduced some questions on European issues from 2007 onwards. The survey was carried out in Germany from Berlin and Strasbourg. As few of our interviewers were able to conduct these interviews in German, the German sample was smaller than the French (132 and 332 interviewees respectively). The choice of the three other countries was dictated by practical considerations and by our research hypotheses. Ondrej Novotny joined the Concorde programme in order to develop his own research on employees of Czech industrial companies. Due to his own scientific objectives and financial resources, his sample is less varied and smaller (N=44) compared to other countries. The Turin University team received funding in late 2007 to start conducting interviews in Italy. In this case too, due to time and budget constraints and the small number of interviewers, fewer interviews were conducted than in France and Germany (N=60). In Poland, the survey began in early 2008 and 100 interviews were completed. The extension of the number of countries concerned by the survey benefited our theoretical framework. Indeed, while Franco-German comparison included two countries with contrasting national histories and political systems and different levels of politicisation of European issues to be compared, both are 'big' countries and have been involved in European construction since the earliest stages. By including Italy and especially the new member states, we were able to study issues which had not been considered initially, for example the possible effects of political defiance, the duration of EU membership, the legacies of Communism, the effects of economic and political transitions, or the opposition between 'big' and 'small' European countries.

Attitudes or artefacts?

With the proliferation of opinion surveys, the possibility of interviewing samples presumed to be representative of a given country on European questions seems to be self-evident. However such surveys raise thorny methodological problems. Very few sections of the public are really interested in European questions and are well informed. In our efforts to question people belonging to all social categories, we faced many refusals, but also managed to interview many people who rarely or never have the opportunity to discuss the subjects mentioned in the interview. Therefore, their answers have an ambiguous status, since many of them have no existence in the social world outside of the context of the survey. Some of the attitudes towards Europe recorded are therefore based on material whose status is close to that of a survey artefact. This is especially a problem for categories that have little information on political questions and are not specifically concerned by the activity of the European Union institutions. In addition, the problem varies according to the topic. Some European realities have become 'familiar' ('salient') in the eyes of the entire public. Thus, even members of the fractions who are the most unfamiliar with political debates on European questions 'know' the Euro and have had the opportunity to discuss it, however briefly. All reactions recorded during a sociological interview should therefore not be considered as survey artefacts. As European construction has developed, it can be argued that this artefactual aspect of surveys on European questions has somewhat declined, even if it remains very important for many subjects.

Survey artefacts and social realities

The difference between a survey artefact and a social artefact should be emphasised. Samples of citizens from member states of the European Union are regularly questioned on a wide range of European topics. For instance, a deliberative poll was organised in Brussels in October 2007 and the organisers celebrated the emergence of a 'European public sphere'. Such deliberative polls, as well as traditional opinion surveys, are used in various ways and produce political effects. On a broader scale, various referendums were organised in some countries on issues related to European construction. In the French case, the interviews show that the 2005 and even the 1992 referendums left traces, however confused and limited. These traces tend to fade away with time, but some of them remain, especially within politicised sections of the population, but also, more surprisingly, and occasionally, in less politicised sections.

Since the public is requested to give an opinion on European questions, it is not sociologically illegitimate to try to 'experimentally' reproduce situations where citizens of all social status are asked for their opinion. In particular, the ways in which various categories of interviewees understand the questions asked and respond to them, or the degree of conviction of their answers are avenues worth exploring.

Opinion surveys, qualitative or quantitative, try to collect opinions on European issues from people who are effectively unequally interested in and informed about them. This makes it difficult for surveys to identify the fractions of the public which are actually mobilised. This is why we have tried to observe spontaneous forms of citizen mobilisations. The aim was to study the reactions towards Europe expressed in the individuals' social activity without being provoked by an opinion survey or an interview. Hence, some members of the team studied readers' letters to newspapers on 'Europe', email addressed to members of parliament, or answers to online questionnaires on the websites of federalist organisations. The aim was to observe and to describe the characteristics and the opinions of truly mobilised fractions of the public. This section of the project was carried out in France, but was not possible to duplicate in other countries. Nevertheless, we chose to present its main results in this volume insofar as they confirm some of the more general results.

The effects of context and collective interviews[7]

A survey records the perceptions, representations, opinions and reactions of a person questioned in the particular context of an interview or of a questionnaire. The risk is to hastily consider that the opinions collected within this specific framework are the 'authentic' opinions that the person interviewed would express in any circumstance. If we try to deduce underlying attitudes from what is observed, we risk confusing a free-standing attitude to Europe with an attitude that is revealed in a particular and somewhat artificial circumstance. This methodological issue is less of a problem when the survey is conducted following a process of social mobilisation. In that case, the opinion of some interviewees is to some extent the product of the mobilisation, rather than of the survey situation. In other cases, we cannot assume that the reactions recorded during an interview would be identical if they were expressed in a different context. This is why fifty-four collective interviews (focus groups) were also conducted during the Concorde programme, first in Strasbourg and then in Paris between 2006 and 2009.

These focus groups help us observe how various participants react and debate amongst themselves on themes proposed by a moderator. While this system has an artificial aspect, it allows for the observation of discussions as they unfold and record spontaneous opinions, arguments, and conceptualisations of the interviewees.[8] Because the presence of the interviewer is less intrusive and an interaction between 'peers' is taking place, the technique can create situations that resemble ordinary conversations between acquaintances. Discussions can flow more 'naturally' (Stewart *et al.* 2006: 41 ff.) than those recorded in an interviewer-interviewee relationship.

These collective interviews were used as an instrument to put our research questions to the test. The goal was to see if the attitudes towards Europe were likely to evolve within the context of the interaction. They were, however, only conducted in France and do not cover a sufficiently varied sample of the pertinent categories. Still, thanks to them we were able to observe the way in which the interviewees go about 'holding an opinion' on Europe throughout an interaction that is more natural than an interview.

We see, for example, how each of the members of a group of seven blue-collar workers contributes to the definition of a shared framework. One of them mentions the entry of the 'Eastern European countries' into the EU and their effect on the economy. Another one puts forward the problem of 'relocated factories'. A third person claims that France's 'no' vote in the 2005 referendum is 'the proof that everybody understood'. Cooperation is not only informational or lexical. These mutually reinforcing comments demonstrate the force of conforming group pressure – especially as participants already knew each other – in this

---

7.   Philippe Aldrin has suggested some of the remarks made in this section.

8.   According to William Gamson (1992: 17), 'the greatest advantage is that it allows us to observe the process of people constructing and negotiating shared meaning, using their natural vocabulary'.

case, echoing a more general critical discourse of low wage-earners on Europe (relocations, higher prices caused by the Euro). In such cases, the method seems to favour the construction and the affirmation of a collective position. In contrast, the group interviews carried out with a more heterogeneous group tend to provide less clear-cut results. In the absence of an implicit agreement between participants, the exchange of opinions is often more chaotic and the multiple interruptions and digressions obscure the expression and unfolding of opinions (Delli Carpini and Williams 1994).

This material is only rarely used in this book. The focus group technique was only experimented in the French case, and therefore has no comparative dimension. As this new methodology requires further development to control its biases, our results are tentative at best and more work will be necessary to fulfil its potential.

chapter four | types of attitudes towards europe

Daniel Gaxie

The ideal types presented in this chapter stylise the different dispositions of citizens towards European construction. The attitude of each European citizen can be situated in a complex space comprising several dimensions (mainly: a more or less favourable, hostile, ambivalent, or undetermined attitude; the experience of 'European' realities, the degree of practical familiarity with Union policies, decisions, regulations or grants; the level of information on European issues, and the degree of familiarity with political debates on Europe). This chapter defines the types of attitudes which can be observed within this space.

The approach adopted here partly converges with Weber's methodology in *Gesammelte Aufsätze zur Wissenschaftslehre* (1922). As with Weber, the types of attitudes described here are representational constructs, which take into account opinions, reactions, practices, events and characteristics expressed by interviewees or inferred from their discourse. This process articulates a wide spectrum of phenomena which can be observed in a more or less diffuse or isolated manner. The characterisation and the description of types rely on the selection of the most salient phenomena. The constitutive traits of a type of attitude may appear in many empirical cases, and sometimes in a few, but they are only considered as a typical element if they can be observed as such. These ideal types, which are progressively constructed, rarely appear in their purest form in a given case. Each interviewee is a specific case, and is more or less close to one (or sometimes several) of the ideal types constructed through empirical observation. Ideal types are meant to analyse and situate individual cases. Conversely, the distance between individual cases and ideal typical constructions also allows for the testing of the relevance of progressively constructed types. When an empirical case appeared to be too remote from all existing types, an additional type or a variant of an existing ideal type was developed.

Ideal types are nodes, to which most individual cases can be linked to some degree, in their pure form or as a variant. However, it has proved difficult to link some individual cases to a single ideal type: either the conditions of the study have not allowed us to gather enough information, or their composite characteristics have forced us to link them to several ideal types.

Unlike in Weber's approach – at least the one he seems to advocate in his methodological writings – the ideal types of attitudes presented here are not the product of the analyst's rational imagination, but are rather built on systematic observation, and were progressively constructed by comparing specific cases with the initial tentative ideal types. Even though Weber occasionally distinguishes logical and empirical ideal-typical constructions, he mainly conceives his ideal types as hypothetical-deductive models based on a number of presuppositions. Hence, he repeatedly claims that these ideal types are 'utopias' understood as ways to question reality rather than as explanatory hypotheses. The ideal types presented here are not 'utopias', but empirically grounded descriptions of the diverse attitudes of ordinary citizens towards European realities. Even though each individual attitude is unique, observation reveals that certain individual cases have common traits that distinguish them from other groups of cases. The ideal types presented here are a stylised description of several groupings of concrete empirical cases. Similar to those outlined by Weber, their goal is to describe, understand and explain. They describe insofar as they consist in identifying characteristic traits. They serve to understand, as they rely on in-depth observation of subjective perceptions and mobiles, as well as cognitive instruments of appreciation used by categories of citizens to develop, express and justify their judgements on Europe. Lastly, they serve to explain insofar as the description of ideal types includes individual conditions (life stories, socialisation, family, academic, professional and activist histories, social and professional conditions, positions and situations, social, religious, ideological, union, political and associative backgrounds) and contextual conditions that influence perceptions and evaluations of Europe. This methodology was developed within the framework of the in-depth analysis of interviews conducted in France. The conclusions of this chapter, and of other chapters in this volume, put the results collected in the French context to the test of comparison, by identifying the effects of national contexts on the attitudes of Europeans towards Europe.

Synoptic involvement

A first type of attitude towards European construction can be defined as synoptic involvement. The interviewees linked to this ideal type have in common their involvement in European issues, and the fact that they have an overarching view of them – a political one, in the sense that their arguments echo the ongoing debates on Europe in politics and the media. This specific type of attitude is characterised by the existence of relatively firm and elaborate orientations. These interviewees are the only ones who may have general attitudes on European construction that are politically structured. For instance, when they express a judgement on the Euro, they do not think, or do not only think about its (assumed) effects on their personal situation, as other categories do. Their position is general and includes macroeconomic issues (the Euro limits the effects of the increase in oil prices, it prevents the country from having to devalue its currency) or political ones (the Euro strengthens the EU's role in the world, it is managed in an undemocratic manner by the central bank, it favours industrial outsourcing). What characterises their attitude is the expression of a global, synoptic point of view on certain issues of European construction, reflecting the issues and language of debates in various national or supranational arenas. These structured, political orientations can be positive, negative or uncertain.

Those who express positive synoptic orientations are the core group of supporters of European construction. Some discuss it with enthusiasm: it appears necessary and even thrilling to them. Europe is seen as a great adventure and a great hope. In the French case, the positive vote to the referendum on the European constitution was considered as self-evident, and the rejection of the treaty highly disappointing. In these categories, some spontaneously refer to their own European identity.

The reasons for their support are numerous. Those who have personal or indirect experience of the war put forward the argument of peace and reconciliation. Others emphasise the necessity of union between countries who have become too small to face the major world powers. Many are satisfied that borders have been opened, that circulation has become easier, and that closer relationships between populations are possible. Many of those who hold positions in private companies applaud the benefits of the open market, the opportunities to develop exchanges and investments, and the resulting increased welfare. Despite what some authors claim, it is difficult to say whether these economic considerations refer to their own situation, to that of their country or to Europe as a whole, as we may see with a French financial manager, graduate of a prestigious business school and son of an engineer in a major industrial company:

> [Europe is] rather positive, on the one hand, from an economic point of view, because economic liberalism provides the opportunity to develop relationships with many countries... get access to new markets... for richer countries, it's the possibility of being able to invest in new countries, [and for others] it's an opportunity for development. [...] Europe as such doesn't have the place it should have on the international stage. To me, it's an economic zone that works; well, it could work better from a... I don't know, from a political, military point of view, etc., it's clearly not a major force at this point.

We may thus observe that members of this group do not only express economic preoccupations. Some arguments frequently put forward (peace, closer relationships between populations, democracy, possibilities of 'modernisation', the idea that European countries will only have influence at global level by working together) are important in their perceptions but are not often considered by most observers of European attitudes.

Some of those whose attitudes towards Europe are marked by this type of synoptic involvement express negative views. Their arguments are also varied. Some lament standardisation and the disappearance of national cultural differences. Others complain that Commission technocrats decide, that the European Parliament has few powers, or that the European Central Bank is unaccountable for its actions. Many blame Europe for outsourcing and claim that EU enlargements are responsible for lower wages.

The criticisms expressed by these interviewees also rely on general political considerations. Left-wing interviewees attribute lower job security, a decrease in purchasing power and the dismantling of public services, labour regulations and social benefits to the neo-liberal dogmatism of a mercantilist Europe. Right-wing interviewees see the EU as a Trojan horse for globalisation, multinational firms and the United States. Freedom of movement is said to open borders to uncontrollable migrations. The ongoing construction strives to destroy nations to impose the neo-liberal model against the will of the people. For them, nations remain a fundamental reality, with their own visions and interests. Hence, a European people cannot exist.

Again, the justifications given for these critical attitudes are not always reflected in the most frequent explanations of European attitudes. The argument of negative economic consequences induced by integration is effectively emphasised and seems to echo the so-called utilitarian hypothesis. But these interviewees rarely use their personal situation to justify their stances. In a typical manner, a young engineer deplores the threats on protective labour laws, although she is a civil servant and her status guarantees her employment. It seems that these fractions of the public are loath to root their judgements on personal considerations and make it a point to express a general point of view. It is also because the arguments of these interviewees are relatively complex and nuanced that their point of view is rarely black or white. In some cases, favourable and critical judgements are so intertwined that it is difficult to decide whether a point of view is mostly positive or negative (see Chapter 5). Those portrayed as Eurosceptics in the literature are often eager to call themselves 'pro-Europeans'. People who denounce the EU's 'liberal' orientations generally point out that they are not hostile to 'Europe' in general, only to Europe as it is. They call for the advent of a 'social Europe'. Likewise, the staunchest right-wing opponents of the EU claim to be part of the 'European civilisation' and argue in favour of a Europe of nations or a variable geometry model of European integration. At the present point in the integration process, few are radically hostile to every aspect of Europe in these categories. Critical points of view cannot be analysed in a substantialist manner, as expressing a fixed, unwavering ideology. They are changing judgements, built in opposition to a European orthodoxy, and encompassing key contextual dimensions of several decades of European construction.

Beyond the globally positive, negative or composite character of their attitudes, these segments of the public share a number of typical properties. They are relatively familiar with European issues: for instance, they know what the Schengen Area is. In the French case, because of the 2005 debate, they have, of course, heard of the so-called Bolkestein directive. Some are surprised that we even ask such a self-evident question. In the German case, they are well informed about the ratification process of the Lisbon Treaty. They know and use (with varying degrees of accuracy) certain technical or political terms of European debates (Federation, directives, Rome treaty, social or political Europe, subsidiarity). They discuss European issues with ease, and spontaneously elaborate on them. It is only with these interviewees that some of the most 'political' questions of opinion surveys such as Eurobarometer can be asked without too many difficulties. Typically, a high-ranking officer at the Agency for Continuing Adult Education (Agence de Formation Professionnelle des Adultes) does not even wait until the end of a question on 'Europe's democratic deficit' to say that he is in complete agreement and launch into a critique of the voting system in European Parliament elections. During the interview, he develops views on Europe's Christian roots, on 'political Europe', which he opposes to an 'enlarged single market', Schengen and border protection, 'Europe with twenty-seven countries, which cannot have the same rules as with fifteen', Europe and liberalism, 'the geopolitical problem raised by Turkey' and the 'tragic absence of Europe in the Balkan wars'.

In this group of interviewees, we met people who actively seek information on European subjects and have for instance read at least a few passages of the constitutional project. These active dispositions are related to the tacit feeling of being able to express a point of view. Members of this group can admit to occasional shortcomings, but do not express the general feeling of incomprehension that is perceptible in other categories. However, these well-informed fractions of the public are less familiar with European questions than with other subjects. Sometimes, they mention their difficulties in grasping certain aspects of the functioning of the EU, notably the role and powers of the main institutions. Some themes of the public debate, for instance the question of democratic deficit or political union, may elicit reactions of perplexity and incomprehension when they come up in the interview. These shortcomings, however, do not threaten the tacit feeling of competence (in the jurisdictional sense) that characterises these interviewees.

In these fractions of the public, relatively elaborate political expectations are expressed, such as harmonising social contributions, taxation and labour laws to avoid 'social dumping'; 'political', 'social' Europe or Europe 'for employment'; reinforcing the capacity for military intervention, fighting pollution, tax havens; or the United States of Europe.

Interest in European issues is part of a broader interest in politics. These categories follow diversified and sophisticated media. They express firm and developed general political preferences, which often come with various forms of distrust in political parties and political games. These attitudes towards European construction can be considered as politically structured, because they derive from diversely oriented general political convictions. These interviewees, however, do not only stick to repeating the discourses of certain opinion leaders. They are able and often eager to express 'personal' points of view. On occasion, they refer to what they have read or heard, but they are also able to elaborate personal opinions. It is because these opinions are the products of similar schemes of appreciation that they are close, both in form and content, to positions expressed by political organisations.

Another distinctive feature of this synoptic involvement is its reliance on personal experience of European realities. This experience is first and foremost intellectual. Members of this group are eager to talk politics with friends and relatives, and they discuss European issues quite 'naturally', even if not very often. In a typical manner, an interviewee mentions that he discussed the Schengen Area with a policeman he knows, and recalls a conversation on structural funds with a taxi driver during a stay in Portugal. This intellectual experience can also be academic. Memories of high school or more specialised knowledge acquired during studies in law, economy, history or politics are used to express points of view. Others whose studies were shorter have acquired information through political, union, or associative activities.

For most of these interviewees, this experience of Europe is predominantly academic, political and intellectual. In other cases, synoptic involvement in European issues also ties in with more practical experiences, for instance in a work or associative context. The example of a consulting firm manager who is a staunch supporter of European construction, to the extent that he claims, 'Europe is my country and France is my region', is symptomatic. He has offices in Paris, London and Porto and resides in the south west of France. He explains that he feels at home whenever he goes from office to office. Members of these categories travel and speak one or several foreign languages. They have regular contacts with friends, customers, commercial partners, colleagues, voluntary workers in associations or religious organisations in several countries. They may have experience of European institutions, policies, decisions, norms and controls. A statistician working for the Organisation for Economic Co-operation and Development (OECD), for instance, has professional relationships with her Eurostat colleagues. A very 'pro-European' judge explains that he plays a part in implementing European policies, since he has placed appeals against deportation orders given by prefects to illegal migrants.

In this field as in others, experience structures perceptions and those who face European realities in everyday life are likely to identify other realities in these perceptions as they encounter them.

Lastly, this specific type of attitude towards Europe is characterised by the backgrounds of the persons in question. Synoptic involvement is mostly found in the upper and upper middle regions of the social space. So-called Eurosceptic political positions thus mainly exist in social categories that are rather remote from the xenophobic, authoritarian and intolerant working class milieus where they are assumed to be socially rooted. The relatively high level of information, regular participation in conversations on political subjects, use of sophisticated media, practice of foreign languages are related to a high cultural and academic level. Those who experience Europe in professional contexts or during holidays are mostly high- or mid-level managers. But synoptic involvement can also sometimes be observed for men and women whose academic level and social position are significantly lower. They rely on substitute forms of cultural capital, often accumulated during a career as an activist or voluntary worker in associations, youth organisations or unions. This substitute capital can also be acquired in primary groups, for instance families, or through contact with relatives whose level of cultural capital is higher.

The segments of the public with synoptic attitudes towards Europe are both similar and different. They are similar insofar as they share all the typical traits previously listed, especially belonging to the upper or upper middle spheres of the social space, or possessing a substitute cultural capital. But they are also opposed on various points, such as favourable or hostile orientations towards Europe. It appears that these opposed synoptic orientations correspond to distinct positions in the upper or upper middle regions of the social space. The most fervent supporters of European construction belong to upper or middle categories in private companies, independent or intellectual professions, or civil service, and they often hold positions of power. They are the clearest beneficiaries of the existing social and economic order and are likely to have a positive outlook on a variety of issues, including European construction. In such cases, more than direct benefits, this confident relationship to the social world orients perceptions of Europe, not as explicit arguments, but rather as a general background for discourse. Some members of these groups also have extensive and positive experience of Europe. They have gained through Europe and some even say so explicitly. This situation reinforces their predispositions to have a positive perception of Europe, even though the benefits that they have drawn from it or that friends and relatives have drawn from it are not explicitly mentioned to justify such a positive perception. It is possible to be 'for Europe' without necessarily being a 'beneficiary of Europe', but those who are for Europe tend to be 'winners' in the social interactions in which they partake.

Subtly different backgrounds can be observed for those whose attitudes towards European construction are more critical. They also belong to the upper or upper middle regions of the social space, but generally hold lower and less prestigious positions. They can be found for instance in the public sector or in intellectual circles. Some mention their negative personal experience of European policies, regulations or decisions to justify their reservations. In other cases, more indirect and general reasons prevail. Typically, an engineer in a computer company, rather critical about Europe, explains (with a barely perceptible hint of bitterness) that in his company, there are managers with or without personal assistants and that he belongs to the latter category, because he went to a less prestigious school than other managers. Obviously, there is no direct causal link between his high but relatively subordinate position in his company and his attitude towards Europe. But his particular position has effects on his world view, and accordingly on his relationship to Europe. His arguments are not based on his situation, but his situation affects the arguments he selects, even though they might not bear any direct relation to it. Likewise, a university professor of fine arts expresses rather radical left-wing views on various subjects, including European issues. He blames the European Commission for always trying to favour the private sector, 'whose goal it is to make money'. He adds that since the 1970s, directives have been adopted 'at the European level, at the European Commission level, asking that health, education and other public sectors be handed back to the private sector... liberalised, [given back] to the market'. Even though he does not refer to his personal situation and does not express fears for himself, it is based on his position as a civil servant, professor and intellectual that he perceives European construction as negative for public sectors, social policies, education, culture and intellectual values.

Remote evaluation

A second ideal type of attitude towards Europe is that of 'remote evaluation'. Members of this group are convinced that Europe does not have anything to do with them, that it is too complicated for them, devised by and for the powerful from which they have little to expect but more problems. According to an employee in a bakery: 'Europe might be good, but for others. The Euro does help with travelling, but we don't travel anyway'. Distance towards Europe is also expressed by a secretary in a ministry through a sense of indifferent incomprehension: 'Europe is impossible to understand!' She has no idea of what the European Parliament or the Commission is, and she adds that it does not interest her. These interviewees do not know what the Schengen Area is and have never heard of the Bolkestein directive. European issues and other general political themes are not among their conversation topics. This can be observed when a 27-year-old construction worker is asked whether he sometimes discusses politics or European issues:

– Politics... let's say it's not really my cup of tea, right? Well sometimes it happens... I remember when Sarko[zy], he set up his speed cameras, right, we talked politics a bit with colleagues, and we all agreed that this was just a bunch of bullshit... to make money off ordinary people once again... no, otherwise I don't talk politics with my mates.

– And European questions?

– Europe?! We don't give a damn about Europe... so, well... no, I never talk about it, it's the older guys who tell us... the Euro is messed up, all that.

For these interviewees, exposure to the media is limited to media that offer little coverage on political issues, and even less on European issues. A worker in a slaughterhouse explains for instance that he reads 'the local paper, on what's going on in the area, what's happened, to see if there were any accidents'. He regularly watches the evening news, but European issues are an example of subjects he is quick to avoid. Likewise, the construction worker relates his reaction when he received the constitutional text in 2005: 'this constitution, right, I've never seen such bullshit before, those guys send us a huge book, impossible to read! You've seen it? Honestly I tried five minutes, and then I dropped it, it's completely incomprehensible'. These interviewees often claim to be badly informed (see Chapter 9), but they immediately add that this is because they have no interest in the subject. They readily admit that they do not know and understand much about Europe and that these political subjects fly over their heads. They are generally puzzled when asked about their opinion on subjects of European political debates. Some stare at the interviewer with eyes wide open. Others repeat the question with a worried tone and answer that they 'don't know about all this!' Others attempt to save face and improvise an answer without much conviction. A question on the democratic deficit, for instance, might elicit comments on the State's budget deficit or the declining birth rate due to a confusion between democratic and demographic. Because they do not comprehend the meaning of the question as it is asked, in the terms of the political debates, these interviewees often express themselves on subjects they have entirely misunderstood. The reaction of the construction worker when asked whether he is for or against European construction is in this sense revealing:

European construction... well... anyway... in my company, I haven't heard about that... European construction... Well, if they do something for construction I'm in favour of it, for once it's for the workers... well... construction... what kind of construction actually? I know French construction a bit, I can tell you what we do in France in the construction sector but at the level of Europe... I didn't know they did stuff... I'd be in favour of it... we'll see how they want to do it.

A Eurobarometer question on trust in the institutions reveals the same kind of discrepancy between the meaning given to the question by the interviewer and the interviewee. The same worker, for instance, answers that he tends 'not to trust' [the European Parliament], and when asked why, he explains: 'Well, I don't even know who those guys up there are, what they do... So I don't trust them'. When asked their opinion about political subjects, for instance Turkey's accession to the EU, responses (if they exist), are often given without much conviction, because 'we're not the ones in charge'.

It is also because these interviewees have a limited experience of Europe that they rarely discuss it. They seldom travel, do not speak foreign languages, and have few opportunities to meet citizens from other EU countries. They do not think that the EU affects their personal lives, except for the Euro and certain subjects of preoccupation for which they hold Europe responsible.

Negative remote evaluation

Some members of these fractions of the public express very negative judgements on Europe. Various criticisms, always vehement, are justified by the interviewee's personal situation and experience. A worker in a poultry slaughterhouse claims:

It's Maastricht's fault, we don't have the same advantages... everyone thought we'd get the same as the other countries [actually] we lose money... For 1,000 francs, you used to get a full shopping cart, good stuff, right [his wife confirms], now for 150 Euros [the equivalent] your shopping cart is half empty.

Similarly, it is because she attributes the difficulties she is facing to Europe that a 57-year-old woman of West Indian origin, who works as a secretary in a ministry, has very negative perceptions. She complains about rising prices and her difficulties to make ends meet. She is very unhappy with her housing situation; several requests for public housing have remained unanswered. When asked if she sees something positive about Europe, she answers: 'no, no, to put it a bit coarsely, it's bullshit as far as the people are concerned'. She criticises the possibility of moving more freely from one country to another:

Before, when there were borders, you had less openings, less risks, you were safer than now that everything is open. People come to get stuff in France... you're never entitled to anything, a flat or anything else... the others, they come straight from Bab El-Oued, they get everything.

This type of negative evaluation is remote. These interviewees do not have an elaborate vision of Europe's responsibilities. Their imputation is uncertain and probably partly results from the context of an interview on the subject. Critical attitudes are based on links made between Europe and the multiple problems they

confront in daily life. But in contrast with certain utilitarian assumptions, imputation to Europe is uncertain, confused, and partly an artefact produced by the
interview situation.

Judgements on Europe are also contaminated by expressions of defiance towards political leaders, considered to be responsible for the interviewees' difficulties. Europe 'is politics' and hence something from which one cannot expect
anything positive. Such condemnation of Europe is not part of a structured and
developed vision. As these interviewees have a very vague perception of Europe,
their negative reactions should not be interpreted as the expression of an informed
analysis of the European institutions' orientations. For instance, for the poultry
slaughterhouse worker, the French have lost a lot with the Euro because 'in each
country, the Euro isn't at the same price for everybody yet... if the Euro went
down [in France] to 3.30 or 3.40 francs as it is in other countries... our lives would
be a lot better'. When these interviewees talk about Europe, they generally do not
refer to the EU. The secretary in a ministry explains that Europe brings to mind
'France... and the surrounding countries'. While they often complain about the
Euro or immigration, they have no notion of the circumstances and procedures
that have led to the adoption of the Euro or EU enlargement. Even though they
denounce situations which (partly) result from the developments of European construction, they are not necessarily able to make such causal links themselves. Their
indictment may actually indifferently concern situations where such a link can
exist (from the point of view of an informed observer) and others where there is
no such link. The secretary complains about the Euro, but also about her rent, her
taxes, the TV licence fee, or cuts in the reimbursement of medication. She is not
preoccupied by migration within the EU, but by the arrival of 'people who come in
from Bab El-Oued'. If some members of this group deplore the fact that foreigners
are able to settle in France, it is not because of an elaborate ideological vision or
fears for their identity. It is not immigration or even the attribution of a number
of supposed advantages to foreigners that are denounced; rather, it is the fact that
the French (that is to say, themselves) do not have priority. The invocation of the
nationality criterion is a resource for justification more than the expression of a
politically formed view. Tellingly, the secretary in a ministry, who is herself West
Indian, berates the 'West Indian' and the 'African woman' in her building; they do
not work and 'go to the town hall to have their rent or electricity bills paid'. She is
fine with 'enlarging in the right direction, but it doesn't have to be the same ones
who pay and then can't make it themselves'. She adds that it 'would be better to
help out the French before the foreigners... even though, myself, I feel French
without really being French... because my skin is black'. This is a specific case,
as these interviewees answer that they feel 'French', and not 'European', when the
question is asked, and some do so spontaneously. These expressions of identity are
mostly associated with nostalgia for better economic times and the denunciation
of a present situation perceived as particularly negative. Defensive, rather than
vindictive, they are the expression of a general sense of unease rather than part of
an ideological attitude towards Europe, as it is the case with fractions of the public
who express a politically developed judgement. From this standpoint, the attribu-

tion of nationalist, xenophobic or authoritarian connotations to such expressions of identity amounts to over-interpretation.

These segments of the public rely on arguments against Europe which may have political undertones, but are not expressed in an abstract register. To them, Europe is related to political considerations that are outside their preoccupations, that they are wary about and keep at a distance. A pattern of political thought cannot be attributed to interviewees who are dismayed when asked to adopt a general point of view. The slaughterhouse worker remains silent when asked if he thinks it is preferable to introduce competition in the rail and mail sectors. When the interviewer tries to provoke a statement by asking if prices would decrease, he answers with his personal experience: 'Yeah, you could hope they will... but well, I don't think it's too much, either... I see, myself, my daughter, for a round-trip to Paris, she pays 50 Euros'. These fractions of the public express harsh judgements on Europe, but their appreciations are not politically oriented and not easily mobilised in political competition. Many did not vote in the 2005 referendum, often because they were not registered or because they have stopped voting altogether. Others claim to have voted negatively, not necessarily because of the grievances they express towards Europe, but because they were turned off by something they happened to read on a page of the Constitution project, or because they wanted to send a message to national political leaders. These interviewees seldom express political preferences. Some claim that 'left and right are the same, it doesn't make any difference'. Others have some sympathies, but fragile ones, often focused on specific persons, and sometimes somewhat contradictory. This type of attitude towards Europe is thus not articulated with general political opinions or identifications with a party or a politician.

This negative remote evaluation of Europe can be observed in the lower regions of the social space. It is related to a situation that is characterised by little cultural capital, devaluated or non-existent diplomas, employment with low qualifications, often difficult working conditions with no career prospects, experience of unemployment and job instability, or fears about job security, limited income, the experience of deprivation, and holding subordinate positions at work. Arguably, the criticisms are most intense in the fractions whose situation is tense, that is, those who have known better times or who have enough to hope for something better but few prospects, rather than those who are the worst off.

Non-negative remote evaluation

In the same lower regions of the social space, less negative opinions can also be observed. Some say they are unable to say whether Europe is something positive or negative, because they 'haven't looked into it'. A 40-year-old woman, working as a secretary in an occupational health centre, first remains silent when asked if Europe is positive or negative to her, then eventually says that 'it can be both'. When the interviewer asks her whether the positive or the negative prevails, she is unable to choose. Others have a vaguely favourable attitude, but without clear reasons. A 20-year-old salesman in a sports shop explains that Europe, 'it's positive, because otherwise we wouldn't have gone that far, they wouldn't have continued'. In these cases too, Europe is evaluated in light of its repercussions on personal situations. However, for these fractions, the evaluation is not negative or not very negative. They are willing to concede that Europe is something positive or at least that it is an aspect of reality about which there is not too much to complain, even though or because they feel that it is not their concern. The young salesman, for instance, explains that 'if they do it, it's because it's good. Is it good for me? Probably'.

On more familiar subjects, these interviewees tend to minimise the impact of elements generally described as negative in their social circles. They share the opinion that the introduction of the Euro has led to rising prices or that citizens from certain European countries take advantage of freedom of movement to work in France, but they do not seem to attribute a lot of importance to this. A 43-year-old secretary, who has been on unemployment benefits for a long time and is taking part in a continuing education course at the time of the interview thus says:

> I think at the moment, maybe people come and work here, they're getting paid less, that's what you hear... But I tell myself it can't go on like this... I think not everyone is going to leave their country to come and live here.

Unlike those who react negatively, these categories do not have the feeling of being personally prejudiced. Opinions are expressed tentatively, but the non-negative result of the evaluation prevails, summed up with the recurring phrase: 'it doesn't bother me!'. The young salesman explains that 'personally [Europe] doesn't really affect me, except the Euro, there's nothing concrete for me, apart from the Champions League'. To him 'Europe is only useful on the financial level' and 'everything that has to do with the economy, it doesn't affect me... a lot of people think the same as me... they don't see what it's going to bring them'. When asked if the enlargement of the EU to the East is a good thing, he asserts his cognitive and statutory incompetence: 'I don't know, I only have the Bac [high school diploma], but surely there are positive aspects to it'.

The backgrounds of those who express these non-negative remote evaluations on Europe are close to those of segments of the public whose reactions are more critical. In both cases, they are men and women who hold low or lower middle positions in the social space, with most of the characteristics and consequences this implies. The only observable specificity is their relative satisfaction with their own situation. The salesman quoted above explains that his dearest wish has come true: he has left school. He says he is happy to make a living and satisfied with his job, which is 'going well'. He is also happy with his salary because he lives with his parents and has 'no expenses'. A secretary in an occupational health centre is married to a joiner. They have two salaries, and are the owners of their house. Although they are not well off, they do not experience any serious financial difficulties, and this contributes to their serene outlook on the repercussions of the introduction on the Euro on prices.

Limited involvement

Limited involvement is a third type of attitude towards Europe, based on an intensive but bounded experience. For these interviewees, Europe is immediately identified with precise and familiar activities of the EU. This type of attitude can for instance be typically observed among farmers, fishermen, hotel and restaurant owners. The everyday life of a 41-year-old farmer, holder of a professional baccalaureate, is constantly affected by European regulations, which he discusses at length: 'For instance you have specifications to follow on storing phytosanitary products for wheat processing... European directives that have been introduced... on the identification of the animals... also directives on veterinary products, with traceability...' He explains that for a farm like his, the Common Agricultural Policy represents 80 per cent of the income. He receives a bonus for each cow, within the limits of a quota. He also has to submit to closely-monitored quotas on milk production: 'if you produce more you're punished'. The inspections and the sanctions weigh on him, even if he believes he is among those who have managed to modernise enough to face them:

> They can call me on Monday morning at nine and tell me, hey, we're coming Tuesday morning to inspect your farm, get your documents ready... now we have software for all that, but of course, the guys who are 50, 55 years old...

This intensive experience is however a limited one. Members of these categories seldom travel, speak foreign languages or have contacts with citizens from other countries. What matters to them is the effect of European regulations on their personal situation. Hence, a dairy farmer from Normandy warns the interviewer when she asks him to give positive or negative thoughts about Europe: 'I'm going to talk to you about agricultural stuff a lot because that's what I know about, it's my field'. Europe is perceived positively when the personal experience of European realities is itself positive, and vice versa. Accordingly, for a 53-year-old man who owns and manages a hotel-restaurant in Brittany, Europe is a 'catastrophe':

> The VAT [the decreased VAT rate], we couldn't get it [at the time of the interview] because other countries... etc. I think it's hard to manage things with ten countries to begin with, so with twenty-five it's impossible. It's a huge aberration. For the hotel business, economically it was a catastrophe... with the VAT, we lose 15 per cent of our income.

But his judgements on Europe also rely on his more general experience of the social world. This is demonstrated by a strong dislike of administrations:

> Technocracy is everything I hate, all this administration that one day can grab us by the ear and make us close shop, it's almost like they have a right of life and death over small businessmen like us, who can lose everything.

Hence, both his experience of the norms and controls introduced by European directives and his hostile dispositions towards the intervention of the State and its agents predispose him to associating Europe with increased controls that penalise those who respect the rules:

Europe is crazy, because you have hygiene, customs, fraud, the hotel rankings with the stars... it's a good thing that establishments have to follow the rules, that there is safety... in France we've played the game, but... in the new countries that are coming in, it's not the same thing.

These positive or negative assessments do not exclude contrary appreciations, either on familiar subjects, such as the Euro, or on certain relatively accessible general questions, such as Turkey. But such considerations are implicitly perceived as secondary. Hence, the dairy farmer from Normandy has a 'rather positive' vision of Europe but also expresses several critical views. It appears, however, that he does not feel as strongly about the fact that the agricultural world has 'profited' from Europe and his critical reactions on other subjects. For instance, he is hostile to the accession of Turkey, but he also tacitly considers that his opinion does not matter greatly: 'I'd be categorical, it'd be no for me, but well, yeah, that country, I don't see it in Europe [but] if we have to take 'em, we'll take 'em, right? [laughs]'.

These fractions of the public thus express firm positions on subjects that particularly matter to them and have a looser relationship to other issues. They show no embarrassment or regret in admitting their incomprehension on the general functioning of European institutions when asked how much they trust them. The dairy farmer answers, 'I know what I want to know' when asked if Europe is complicated for him. These interviewees have their own information channels and are well informed on subjects that concern them directly. Farmers, for instance, receive documents on European regulations put together by their unions, and they may attend training sessions organised by chambers of agriculture. But as far as general information is concerned, they have a restricted use of unsophisticated media, that is, in most cases of a local or regional newspaper.

These interviewees show interest in European issues, but not in a synoptic manner. Their relationship to Europe is based on an assessment of its repercussions on their situation, as in the case of remote evaluation, but here, the imputation is based on specific, close and informed relationships with European policies and institutions. Their attitude towards Europe is structured (positively or negatively). They express firm personal points of view, based on particularly salient elements of appreciation, as their economic situation and professional future are at stake in the orientations of European institutions. Their points of view are likely to be politically mobilised. This is another element that differentiates these interviewees from those who keep their distance from European issues. Farmers whose perception of the common agricultural policy is positive voted 'yes' in the 2005 referendum, as the dairy farmer from Normandy explains:

In our profession, we don't have a choice... I don't think the French state has the resources to subsidise agriculture the way Europe does... then, in the long term, are we going to get as much as support as now? If more of us have to get our share then maybe it'll be different.

But if their attitude is structured by the judgements they express on sectoral policies, it is generally not linked to general political orientations. Once again, mainstream academic literature does not explain this specific type of relationship to Europe well. Neither 'identity' (national or European), nor ideological or political values or party preferences motivate and explain the European judgements of these fractions of the public. To some extent, their judgement might be described as 'utilitarian', with the caveat that it is based on personal experience and limited to this experience. Hence, the criticisms formulated by the owner of the hotel-restaurant from Brittany should not be interpreted as the expression of a classically 'Eurosceptic' point of view.

This specific type of attitude can be observed in categories of the intermediary regions of the social space that are particularly concerned by European regulations. Like other intermediary social categories, their cultural level, except for a few cases of political, union or associative engagement, does not predispose them to be interested in general European political issues. Their specificity resides in their close relationship to certain EU policies or decisions. As we have established, this involvement is based on the evaluation of the effects of European policies on their personal situation, but also on a more general attitude towards the social world. The experience of the norms and controls tied to the common agricultural policy can lead to diametrically opposing judgements according to one's economic situation, and beyond that, the assessment of one's own position and perspectives. The case of a farmer who lives and works in the region of Angers, for instance, is typical of a position in the social world that predisposes him [at the time of the interview] to optimistic general anticipations, and correlatively, to positive appreciations of European construction. He points out that he manages his farm 'like a business… we're dealing with 300,000 Euros of yearly turnover'. He speaks proudly of the two computer programmes he uses. His vision of the world is informed by the conviction that he owes his success to his personal merits: he thinks that 'you get what you deserve' and is proud of his quality of life.

Symmetrically, the negative judgements on European norms expressed by a 42-year-old winegrower, president of a cooperative in the South of France, are based on critical dispositions that are explicitly articulated with a more fragile economic situation. He works on a 'small vineyard… average… rather small, about 30 hectares, it's not that much'. He feels like he is facing competition from all the countries of the new world and even from the 'Eastern-European countries' – he fears that 'they're going to swallow us whole'. He regrets having to 'deal with more and more constraints, inspections… and I'm telling you, the problem is that we're not industrialists, we're winegrowers, we're almost craftsmen'. He was 'against Europe, at first, because I think if we open the doors, we sacrifice our agriculture'. Also, 'in the wine sector, we're the ones who get the least European funds'.

Restricted general involvement

The last ideal type of attitude towards Europe can be defined as 'restricted general involvement'. Members of this group refer to their personal experience – for instance, of the Euro or the abolition of border controls – but they also express a general point of view, which distinguishes them from the more uniformly 'privative' judgements of more distanced fractions of the public. These general points of view also have several features that differentiate them from synoptic political appreciations. These interviewees often have difficulties in expressing their points of view. A plumber from the west of France, for instance, claims that 'Europe is something positive' but adds that he is 'not able to say why'. The arguments used to justify their judgements are rather vague, and their very conception of Europe is nebulous. More than the EU, these interviewees often refer to 'all the countries, a whole environment of neighbouring countries' (France, M, 64, retired site manager). Some points of view are predominantly positive or negative. In other cases, favourable and critical arguments are so closely intertwined that it is impossible to make out a general orientation. Some actually admit that they are unable to choose. These interviewees often rely on 'common sense' appreciations or ethical judgements, which are often tentative, sometimes improvised, and express half-hearted convictions.

Many of those who have positive perceptions of European construction offer variations around the saying 'Union is strength'. They explain that individually, European countries have become too small and that they have to join together to face China or the USA. Others build arguments around the fact that citizens from different countries should have closer relationships and understand each other more. To a 25-year-old woman who teaches physical education, Europe is:

> The idea of union, exchanges, different cultures, a grouping of people who like each other, right? The idea of being able to travel, to cross borders almost without having anything to show... it's interesting and enriching, too... [and then] the idea of all of us getting along... it's nice, right, intellectually.

The argument according to which Europe allows less developed countries to catch up is also put forward. To a young actress Europe is 'reaching out to countries that are not very wealthy, and it brings us diversity in return'.

Critical arguments mirror the positive ones. Some lament the loss of independence, such as this retired social security employee: while unable to 'go into much detail', she thinks that there are 'too many directives, we're too bound, we have to put up with too much, we're not independent enough, Europe decides everything'. Others fear a loss of identity: 'We lose some of the countries' history, there's a loss of identity with the currency and other things that are lost. I feel French first and European second; Europe is too far for me to identify with spontaneously' (France, F, 21, unemployed, studied theatre). A third grievance lies in the feeling of being disadvantaged in comparison to citizens from other countries who do not follow the rules, profit from a more favourable Euro, or from business outsourcing, and can come and take jobs by accepting to be paid less. As the retired site manager explains: 'my purchasing power decreases everyday, while theirs rises and I'm going to go down so that they can meet me on the way up'.

Unlike synoptic involvement, current political debates have little impact on this type of relationship to Europe. Only a faint and simplified trace of political issues can be found: for instance, a 25-year-old man, who studied accounting and management for two years at university and works as a communication trainer: 'It shouldn't be just an economic policy, it has to be social too'. These interviewees experience difficulties in giving their opinion on the main issues of European construction. They accept to express themselves on political subjects more easily than the more distanced fractions, but unlike the most politicised categories, they hesitate in their answers, remain silent for a long time, and tend to transform the meaning of the question when they eventually answer. Asked about the development of competition in Europe, the physical education teacher initially says that she does not really know what to answer, and expresses her embarrassment by invoking contradictory considerations. She does not get involved in the debate on competition in public services and, as she says herself, cannot 'go any further' than her privative consumer experience when asked if she thinks that Europe has changed something 'in terms of the post office and the EDF' [national electricity company]:

> The post office... well, I just slip letters into the mailbox, right... EDF? I've never really given that much thought... as long as I have electricity, I'm all right. I suppose EDF can get cheaper electricity from other countries now.

These difficulties in expression are partly due to the lack of grasp of specialised language, as can be observed when the communication trainer discusses the question of European integration: 'when you make choices, let's say social or economic choices in France, if it's not validated by Europe, you're, uh... it's Europe that wins and we don't have a say in it anymore'. Misunderstandings are often observed when interviewees are questioned on the main European political issues. To the physical education teacher, there is a democratic deficit in Europe because:

> It's like in the world, the more powerful the country is, the more they'll listen to it... well, like everywhere, you've got the powerful ones who have power and those who are a bit less powerful; so in that sense it seems to me that democracy between countries is a bit... fading, right?'

Their relationship to Europe mirrors their more general relationship to politics. They do not discuss these subjects regularly with their friends and relatives, especially when they have a European dimension. They consult unsophisticated media (generalist radio or TV news, popular or regional newspapers). These interviewees also have a limited experience of European realities. They seldom travel in neighbouring European countries and when they do so, it is mainly for leisure. They are not proficient in foreign languages. These interviewees feel that European construction is a source of major transformations that they perceive positively and/ or negatively, but that hardly affect them personally. When asked how and when she encounters 'Europe' in her everyday life, a young woman can only mention safety regulations on toys and bike helmets. Another talks about the instructions written in several languages on product boxes and citizens from other countries who buy houses and become her neighbours. Several interviewees discuss school memories, including visits of the European Parliament. Others experience Europe by proxy and refer to their relatives' experiences. A woman mentions the agricultural policy because her brother, who is a farmer, often speaks about it. She also mentions her nephews, who have set up a furniture factory in the Czech Republic. As previously noticed, the physical education teacher expresses an attitude that is both favourable and uninvolved when she exclaims 'Europe is a nice concept, intellectually!' Her judgement on the Euro, similarly, is positive but has tacitly little impact: 'it's good… it makes everything easier, it's true [that] at our level it's just for travelling'. She occasionally makes efforts to seek out information, but she feels unable to fully understand things: 'I feel like I don't know anything about Europe… like I don't have any concrete, objective information, I don't really know what it's about, I don't know what's at stake'.

Interviewees in this group have an intermediary level of information. They are less familiar with European issues than in the 'synoptic involvement' type, but more informed than those who are characterised by their 'remote evaluation'. Indeed, they often claim to 'know' about the European Parliament, even if they only 'know' that it is 'based in Strasbourg'. On the other hand, they are often confused as to the role of the institution. According to the physical education teacher, 'they exchange points of view about things that are going on in different countries… they propose stuff that you have to vote or not… I can't tell you more than that'. Similarly, the retired accountant draws on the few elements he has at his disposal to discuss the European Parliament, for instance French MEP's absenteeism; but looks embarrassed when asked how much he trusts the Commission: 'so, then, what's the difference? Wait, the European Parliament and the Commission… [long silence], isn't it Giscard who… is responsible for… the Parliament? Or the Commission?' Asked about the Council, he completely surrenders.

These interviewees feel insufficiently informed, but they also add that they do not seek out information actively because it is very 'obscure' anyway. They complain about not being able to distinguish the roles of institutions they have heard about. They wonder about decision-making mechanisms, because they have heard somewhere that decisions are taken with a majority and, at the same time, that treaties are ratified unanimously. They lack the reference points that are available to them for national institutions. For some, this incomprehension may foster negative perceptions. As a nurse explains: 'the fact that Europe has more weight on the economic level, maybe it's true, but I'm not sure, it's all very politicised, it's true, I think I don't know everything, and since I don't know everything, I'd rather be against it'.

The attitudes of these intermediary interviewees have paradoxical and contradictory features. They express relatively structured points of view on Europe, which are not always mobilised politically. This is clear in the French case, since some of those who claim to be in favour of Europe no longer remember their vote, did not vote or did not approve the European Constitution treaty in 2005. Their positive or negative judgements are not reducible to *ad hoc* reactions to an interview, but are accompanied by a strong feeling of incompetence and a difficulty in justifying their viewpoints. They occasionally overcome these contradictions by adopting an attitude of withdrawal and delegation, like this 26-year-old actress, holder of a Master's degree in psychology:

> It's very obscure… that's why people are not interested… actually, it's like when there's a European decision, it's not something you can debate… when you don't know what's going on, well… I don't really worry about that and unconsciously, I let them take care of it, it's their job, it might seem like blind trust, but I don't feel like I have a choice.

Although they cannot fully express first person judgements on European issues, members of this group sometimes rally behind the authority of someone whom they trust: friends, relatives or political leaders. The retired accountant thus explains why he voted 'yes' in 2005:

> We followed the pro-Europeans; Chirac was in favour of it, well, he's our president, most of the PS were in favour of it, the UMP too, well, we trusted all these people… you think, well if the leaders themselves think it's a good thing…

Such an example shows that it is mostly with these interviewees (and not with the entire population) that party preferences are likely to orient European attitudes.

This attitude of restricted general involvement towards Europe can be generally observed in members of the intermediary regions of the social space. They have an average or above average cultural level. They may have a Baccalauréat, a technical diploma, or university degrees in specialities which do not predispose them to take interest in the issues of European construction. Such cultural capital allows access to generalising points of view, but does not predispose its holders to the informational investments of the more involved segments of the public.

But while these intermediary interviewees share the same type of attitude, they also express diverging appreciations of Europe. It is often difficult to explain these divergences because these positive and negative appreciations are frequently intertwined, and consequently, in some cases, a general orientation on Europe is impossible to discern. Some elements of interpretation can however be observed. For instance, the judgements on Europe of some of these interviewees are oriented by general anticipations related to the individuals' own situation. In a typical manner, a 26-year-old woman working in an active international bank proudly explains that her company has developed a 'corporate function' to coordinate the actions of their branches and share 'best practices'; her general outlook on the world predisposes her to optimistic views. This predisposition also informs her vision of Europe, insofar as it leads her to minimise the difficulties and only consider aspects perceived as positive. Conversely, a 23-year-old fashion designer, who works in a company that sells textile products to central purchasing agencies, expresses the feeling of being 'in a dead end'. Her company's production has been relocated to Morocco. She has to deal with the demands of her customers who seek the cheapest possible products. Sometimes, they do not buy the models she presents to them and she sees her models in shops a few months later. Her general pessimism rubs off on her perceptions of Europe. With a friend who is in the same professional situation, they repeatedly express reservations during a collective interview with others who – including the bank employee – express points of view in favour of integration. She strongly approves when her friend eventually explains the reason for these reservations: 'that's the problem with Europe, for the jobs we have, the borders should be closed, we should work with European countries instead of going to China, we can't manage in France, too much competition'.

Types and variants

Let us remember, at this point, that attitudes towards Europe described here are ideal typical constructions and that concrete empirical cases are more or less close to these ideal types. Furthermore, variants of certain types can be observed.

Hence, interviewees considered in the type of synoptic involvement express a general point of view that is based on a number of political considerations. Some interviewees who have a more developed experience of European realities, for instance because of their profession, introduce practical considerations into their judgements. Conversely, the attitudes of those with less direct experience of Europe tend to express themselves intellectually and/or politically. Two variants of synoptic involvement should thus be distinguished: on the one hand, a synoptic involvement in which arguments drawn from experience are mobilised in support of general judgements; on the other, a predominantly 'political' or 'intellectual' synoptic involvement. The latter variant is quite frequent in categories whose experience is often limited to university courses. Those who are not in touch with European issues or have had little exposure to Europe during their studies display uncertain reactions that tend to resemble intermediate attitudes. In such cases, the information level, interest in European questions (and general political questions) and the ability to express developed points of view tends to be weaker and further away from the properties of the synoptic involvement ideal type.

It is also useful to point out, again, that ideal types describe 'nodes', or points of relative concentration in the space of European attitudes. Some empirical cases can be rather far away from these nodes. Such is the case for those who have characteristic traits that match several types of attitudes. Attitudes of the politicised members of intermediate categories who are directly concerned by European policies can be articulated with more developed general political expectations and resemble a synoptic attitude. This dissemination of empirical cases around an ideal type, but with some distance from it, is probably more frequent in the case of restricted general involvement. Because it is an intermediary type, the empirical cases that can be ascribed to it are more likely to be affected by properties associated with other types of attitudes. This can be seen, for instance, in the case of a 51-year-old woman who teaches German in a secondary school. Her attitude towards Europe shows most of the typical features of restricted general involvement. Her favourable judgements are based on very characteristic ethical considerations: Europe 'allows us to widen our horizons a little bit, to open up to others', it reduces 'the petty spirit of the French border', it is 'rather likeable, more human'.

But other appreciations are more in tune with themes of political debates: 'Europe is democracy, respecting human rights, liberal economy'. Her German origin, the fact that several relatives married citizens from various European countries and her job as German teacher gives her more experience of Europe than is usually observed in intermediary interviewees. As she points out, with humour: 'Europe is in my blood anyway'. But while these features show similarities with interviewees who are politicised and involved in European issues, others differentiate her from them, such as her insistence on repeating that she is 'not really aware of what's going on' and that she 'doesn't have enough knowledge on this'.

Attitudes in context

Lastly, the types of attitudes towards Europe that have been described, were observed through interviews, which may elicit fragile opinions in fractions of the public who are only weakly mobilised by European subjects. Insofar as the opinions expressed are more structured, they rely on various salient points, some of which are shared in countries studied in the framework of this research, while others are specific to one or several of them. In the French case, remnants of the experience of the constitutional treaty referendum are (to various extents) present in some interviews. More or less confused traces of debates on the 'Bolkestein directive' or the 'Polish plumber' controversy can be observed. Most Polish interviewees ignored the existence of this directive project, but were more familiar with the Schengen Area, due to the frequency of economic migrations in the country. The question of the enlargement to Central and Eastern Europe countries and Turkey appears more frequently in interviews conducted in Germany, even if these themes are treated differently depending on the type of public. The Turkish question is formulated in terms of personal experiences with neighbours or colleagues by lower or intermediary interviewees. They tend to express judgements on the Turks they know, who are described as 'hard-working' or 'welfare recipients taking advantage of the system'. In politicised fractions of the public, the accession of Turkey is discussed in relation to issues such as democracy, women's rights, religion, or the state of the economy.[1] The impact of the Second World War is also often taken into account, albeit always in diverse manners, in the judgements of German interviewees.

Attitudes towards Europe are the product of a convergence between individual dispositions and national contexts. These dispositions are the result of socialisations which vary according to social status, economic situation, cultural levels, occupation, membership in unions, associations or religious organisations, family status, personal history and many other elements. They are relatively stable and contribute to structuring attitudes towards Europe. This individual structuring of attitudes is complemented by various factors related to national socialisation. One of the most interesting benefits of the comparative analysis is that it shows

---

1. My thanks to Nicolas Hubé for bringing these points to my attention.

a number of background elements on the formation of attitudes that generally remain invisible as they are self-evidently shared by citizens of a country. German
'synoptic' interviewees distinguish themselves from their counterparts in other
countries through their frequent reference to the issue of federalism and subsidiarity, or through the comparisons they introduce between the European Court
of Justice and the Constitutional Court of Karlsruhe. Likewise, some Czech and
Polish interviewees fear that the EU will favour the domination of 'big' countries
over 'small' ones,[2] whereas such arguments are absent in the interviews conducted
in Germany, France and Italy. Most opinions given in these countries are the expression of a tacit point of view of people who do not see any reasons to fear
cooperation with other States.[3] The blossoming economic exchanges in the single
market elicit varied appreciations depending on profession, sector and national
origin. Relationships between economic agents from the east and the west of the
Union are for instance tacitly and widely considered as relationships between
high-wage and low-wage economies. This assumption makes certain German or
French workers fear their company's relocation or the arrival of workers ready
to accept lower wages, whereas their Czech and Polish counterparts embrace the
opportunities for mobility. Some German and French businessmen have a positive
outlook on the possibility of investing in these countries, whereas Czech employers may lament the impossibility of competing on an equal footing with more powerful Western companies. The specificities of national frameworks for evaluating
Europe thus depend on the position of each national group in various political,
economic, or other configurations. These position-related specificities produce effects that mirror those induced by positional properties in the 'internal' order (for
instance employer vs employee, entrepreneurial agriculture vs small farms). They
are also the product of specificities of certain countries or groups of countries.
Thus, the arguments of the politicised segments of the public echo more or less
closely stances taken by political representatives. From this, we can infer that each
party system, notably characterised by commonly-exchanged arguments and the
existence or absence of critical points of view – left-wing or right-wing – is an
aspect of the national context that is likely to inform perceptions of Europe. This
constitutes one of the avenues for interpreting the – ultimately rather small – differences between situations in France, Germany and especially Italy,[4] where political criticisms of European construction have less impact as they are less audible
in the public space. Party-influenced points of view do not however concern the
whole public, as many members of lower and intermediary categories have little
awareness of the political debates on Europe.

These national contexts of perception and evaluation of European realities are

2.   I owe these observations to Dorota Dakowska and Ondrej Novotny.

3.   Only in circles of French sovereigntist activists or sympathisers were fears of a German domina-
      tion over Europe expressed.

4.   One of the main results of the study conducted in Italy by Giuliano Bobba and Alfio Mastropaolo
      is the relative absence of critical points of view on the EU.

defined historically. It ensues that attitudes towards Europe are structured at a given time in history and through a collective experience of European construction (see Chapter 6). Again, some light can be shed on this background element by comparing contrasting national cases. For instance, some Czech and Polish citizens consider that the EU is one of the empires under whose rule their nation has had to live during its history, just like the USSR, and that like other empires, it is bound to fall. Such a possibility is never mentioned in France outside of very small circles of close sympathisers of marginal nationalist movements. The long-standing membership of France in the successive European communities and the European Union's increasing institutionalisation seem to foster diffuse beliefs in the irreversible nature of the ongoing processes. Conversely, these processes appear reversible to some of the Czech and Polish interviewees, whose experience of Europe is evidently different, if only because of its shorter duration.

But when attitudes towards Europe are expressed within the framework of an interview, they are also informed by the very context of the interview. This is especially visible in collective interviews. The various types of attitudes described in this chapter also appear clearly with this methodology. But the context of a rather free discussion lasting one or two hours can introduce certain inflexions. The most notable one is a (limited) tendency towards the elevation of the group members' level of information through an effect of shared knowledge. In a few rare cases, a tendency towards shifting from one type of attitude to another can be observed – for instance, from an intermediary attitude of restricted general involvement to a more politicised involvement.

In the setting of collective interviews, such changes are effective but limited, insofar as they only concern a few individuals and only occur in specific configurations. When a collective interview brings together participants whose information level and interest in European issues are low, no change is observed in their attitudes. This is also the case when the familiarity levels of the participants are too diverse. Significant changes are mostly observed in specific configurations, for example when a well-informed person provides elements of thought to participants who have dispositions and abilities to appropriate them. Further research will be necessary to study these dynamics, which do not question the validity of the list of types of attitudes proposed in this chapter. However, they suggest that if major contextual changes were to occur – for instance a long campaign raising awareness and fostering debate as part of a referendum on European issues – the distribution of types of attitudes in the various categories of the public could be significantly altered.

German specificities

Nicolas Hubé, Jay Rowell

This short text outlines the specific features observed in German interviews compared to the ideal-types defined in this chapter. We initially set out to study the differences in the structuring of the interpretative discourses on the EU in the national public spaces to see if, and how, these differences can be observed in the interviewees' discourse.

Unlike Poland and to a lesser extent France, there is a relative consensus on the positive aspects of European construction among German political and media elites, as well as among intellectuals. Yet, this general consensus has not stopped the expression of a slightly more critical relationship towards European construction since the end of Helmut Kohl's mandate – for example discussions on the German contribution to the EU budget, fears about the lack of budgetary rigour in several countries in the Eurozone, criticisms levelled towards agricultural policy, reservations on Turkey's application to accede to the EU. In the vote on the Constitutional Treaty in the Bundestag on 10 May 2005, the major parties represented confirmed their general support. Yet, a few dissenting voices were heard: there were twenty-three negative votes (of which twenty were by members of the Christian Social Union of Bavaria (CSU, right-wing) and three were by members of the Party of Democratic Socialism (PDS, now merged into the Left Party, radical left-wing)) and two abstentions from social democrats. The PDS's argument was based on two aspects. First, the treaty confirms the EU's military orientation, and some interviewees (not always close to the PDS) do indeed develop a discourse on pacifism. Secondly, a lack of respect for the people is denounced: they criticise the choice of holding the debate only in the Bundestag. The CSU's argument is also focused on this last issue, but also includes the theme of the accession of Turkey, which they strongly oppose, as well as the lack of reference to religion, because 'without God, Europe is promised to the devil' (Weiland 2005).

Despite these differences in the structuring of the political and media discourse on the EU, favourable, unfavourable, ambivalent or indifferent postures can be found in similar proportions to the French case. While a pro-European discourse prevails in the public space – although it has a very marginal role in political debates (Garcia and Le Torrec 2003; Sievert 1998; Seidendorf 2007) – Germans do not appear to support Europe more than their French counterparts. The only major figures associated with a profound European engagement are Helmut Kohl and, to a lesser extent, Daniel Cohn-Bendit. The aspects perceived as the most positive are broadly the same as in France: a sense of enthusiasm about Europe, not so much as a political entity, but as a space for tourism and work; the general idea expressed being that Europeans are becoming closer.

All the types of relationships to the EU described by Daniel Gaxie in the French context are also observed, but sometimes arguments are specific to the German case. The proportions of cases that can be linked to specific ideal-types are slightly different, probably due to the differences in the composition of the sample: fewer interviewees with a limited involvement (farmers, fishermen) and fewer members of the working-class. Unsurprisingly, the sociological properties tend to be similar for each ideal type.

Specific arguments

Several elements that differentiate the German case can be identified in terms of the *arguments mobilised* by interviewees to express their points of view. First, the question of *enlargement* appears early on and 'spontaneously' as a focus of discourses on Europe. Enlargement is often perceived as the introduction of competition from Eastern workers on the job market, threatening wages and security. Such considerations often rely on news stories. Among interviewees who are interested in politics, who work in industries facing risks of relocation or union members, the mention of enlargement elicits a quite spontaneous and often quite sophisticated discourse on business relocation and its mechanisms (taxes, manpower cost, subsidies, and movements of capital). While European policies are not the only ones blamed for this risk (which is sometimes perceived as an inevitable consequence of globalisation) and the Bolkestein directive is never directly mentioned, we can observe that these interviewees develop themes and examples mobilised since the early 1990s around the theme of Standort Deutschland,[5] transposed to European issues: free movement of capital, enlargement, gaps in living standards and wages. These questions are also present in more working-class circles, but then tend to be expressed in terms of direct experience, or experience of a friend or relative (wages in the sector of employment such as construction or industry, shopping in Poland) or media reports (stories on the 'Russian mafia', illegal immigration, the Nokia scandal). More generally, the theme of enlargement is discussed along an East-West cleavage, which is superimposed on a rich-poor divide. While some members of the upper classes defend an economic liberalism that benefits everyone, most German interviewees worry about lowering standards – wage pressure, the decline of the Welfare State, or the cost of helping less advanced economies catch up in the East or in Turkey. Lastly, interviewees from the ex-GDR – only them – rely on the experience – and the disappointments – of economic modernisation in the new Länder to build a discourse on the expected effects of the European continent's 'unification' for them or for Germany.

Turkey tends to be mentioned more spontaneously in German interviews than in the other national samples due to the presence of a large immigrant Turkish community living in Germany since the 1960's and the centrality of the question of integration in national political debates. This theme is discussed *both* as an everyday issue and as a general illustration of the problem of European borders. Judgements of the Turkey issue may sometimes be related to relationships with their neighbours for intermediary or interviewees with a distant relationship to Europe. 'Turks' are a perceptible 'reality' (they 'build houses' or 'buy shops').

---

5.   This debate, which appeared in the early 1990s, thematises the problem of deindustrialisation and the loss of competitiveness of German industry.

They are 'hardworking' and/or 'freeloaders': these considerations inform the interviewees' stances on whether Turkey should access the EU. In more general points of view, Turkey is more classically related to the themes of human rights, democracy, women's rights, religion, mentalities or the economy. Synoptic viewpoints are mainly supported by considerations on human rights, economic considerations, geo-political discourses or historical references, whereas interviewees with a restricted general involvement tend to mobilise cultural or religious issues, discussing the Islamic headscarf, forced marriage, or vague references to democracy and poverty.

The weight of history is also a dominant theme in the German case. While some educated members of the sample effectively link German guilt and a historical responsibility leading to a post-national stance, in other interviews Europe is seen as an instrument to weigh on world affairs: 'Europe is a way for Germany to make itself heard'. But this general argument is counterbalanced by others expressing the feeling that German guilt is instrumentalised by European partners: 'We Germans cannot have our say on anything since World War II'. Interestingly, the experience of the war is sometimes extended to all Europe (war has made Europeans more prudent, more pacifist) and used to justify both a shared European identity and a political necessity of protection against other 'aggressive' major powers that did not have the same historical experience: 'We know the war and we have an approach that is different from the Americans. Maybe we are more prudent, more careful' (G, F, 52, university degree, housewife).

Missing arguments

One of our initial hypotheses, based on a widespread intellectual discourse in Germany on the Germans' relationship to their currency, consisted in a specific relationship to the Euro, and by extension towards the EU. Yet, there is virtually no trace in our interviews of the supposed attachment to the Deutschmark leading to a sceptical view of the Euro, the fear of inflation thought to be a part of the German psyche since the time of hyperinflation or the importance of monetary sovereignty. Germans formulate the same types of criticisms and/or appreciate the Euro in the same terms as French interviewees.

The debate on the EU's social dimension (or lack thereof) is relatively present in the French corpus. Interestingly, this question, which is seldom discussed in the German public debate, is very infrequently present in German interviewees and is almost never mentioned as such in answers to questions on the fields in which the EU should be more active. Interviewees only draw up a link with social Europe when discussing the (national) consequences of the opening of borders and the enlargement to the East, as stated earlier.

Synoptic variations

Lastly, several arguments specific to Germany and to the ideal type of synoptic involvement can be observed. Interviewees make a distinction between the EU and Europe (Europa), or even for some, the European Communities (EG). In these interviews, the *subsidiarity principle* (or European federalism) tends to be spontaneously mentioned – either to regret that it is not developed enough or to express support for this system and its use at the European level. Several interviewees compare the Court of Justice of the European Union to the Karlsruhe Constitutional Court. Typically, a corporate lawyer says: 'I am a strong supporter of the subsidiarity principle: everything that cannot be handled at our level should be handled over there'. This discourse, which describes the European political order as a prolongation of German federalism is also the prevailing discourse of the elites. In other types of attitudes (in particular restricted general involvement), federalism is mobilised as a system of interpretation of the EU in less sophisticated and more metaphorical ways. For example, based on the great political and cultural diversity between Länder, which are seen as problematic within a single political system, some interviewees claim that the same difficulties, yet more acute, face the cohabitation of twenty-seven European countries in one political entity.

Similarly, only synoptic interviewees are aware of the contents of the EU treaties, of the French and Dutch 'no' votes, of Merkel's involvement in the Bundestag's ratification and of the debates on the then ongoing ratification process in other countries. Indeed, unlike in France, where the referendum produced a few politicisation effects, the Lisbon Treaty and surrounding debates have had a much more limited echo in Germany. In this ideal type, Europe is also the object of a general discourse on the *'globalisation' process*, in positive terms (protection, unity against other powers) or negative terms (lowered social standards).

The *common foreign policy* is presented as a necessity (and more rarely as a positive goal to achieve) to face other major world powers: the United States and China are most often cited, followed by India and Russia. The latter is also more present in German interviews than in the French sample, and is portrayed as a rival power or partner of the EU, or as country that exports its crime.

Finally, Europe is considered by a vast majority of interviewees (including those who have firmly positive attitudes) as '*too bureaucratic*' (or, over-regulating, cut off from the real world, dealing with unimportant details, inefficient, wasteful or not open enough). This is the main negative point that is spontaneously mentioned at the beginning of most interviews. But in synoptic postures, these criticisms are supported by a number of diverse and in-depth arguments with precise examples, for instance on the shape of cucumbers or the pasteurisation of cheese. These interviewees also focus their criticisms on the institutional space: they speak of the Commission or the Parliament and not of Brussels or the EU in general, and develop arguments to explain or sometimes minimise this 'bureaucratic drift'.

Italian specificities

Giuliano Bobba

An initial observation is that all the ideal types identified in the French case are also relevant for the Italian interviewees: synoptic involvement, limited involvement, restricted general involvement and remote evaluation are all present in our sample.

However, an important difference should be pointed out regarding the appreciation of Europe. Whereas in France, it is possible to distinguish a positive, negative or ambivalent point of view for most ideal types, in Italy, there is a more limited range of variations and non-negative (positive or ambivalent) points of view prevail. While critical positions are found, as in France, these criticisms are not unilateral in most cases. Critical attitudes are concentrated among interviewees close to the remote evaluation ideal type. These interviewees generally have little cultural or political capital, or are sometimes experiencing downward social mobility. In these cases, their rejection of the EU is neither based on direct knowledge of the EU, nor on professional or personal experiences; rather, it is an expression of a general refusal and mistrust of any form of government and control. When a strong opposition to Europe is observed, it often relies on anti-political arguments: the interviewees refuse Europe as they would refuse politics in general and the national political personnel and institutions.

In other ideal types, there is a less noticeable cleavage between negative and positive orientations. As in other European countries, judgements on Europe can be severe, but they rarely express a radical rejection. Favourable preconceptions of Europe are a common feature of the Italian sample, which distinguishes it from the French one. These favourable preconceptions can be explained by three Italian specificities: the lack of a critical party discourse on Europe; the lack of a public debate on European issues; the widespread perception of a dysfunctional Italian state.

The lack of a critical party discourse on Europe

To various extents, Italian parties all support the EU. In public discourse, Europe is never accused of being the cause of any specific problems. It is rather the opposite in that there are rather positive perceptions of the EU, even if some European obligations are not always welcomed in political circles, especially on the right. The analysis of the most recent electoral programmes (2009 European elections) shows that the Partito Democratico (PD, centre-left) is the most favourable to Europe, which it considers as a 'natural' opportunity for development. Silvio Berlusconi's party, the Il Popolo della Libertà (PDL), on the other hand, sees it as a 'necessary constraint'. The Northern League considers it as a functional expedient for its political projects, whereas the radical left views it as a space to develop social movements across national borders. The absence of openly critical political entrepreneurs may be one of the reasons why no globally negative judgements are observed in interviewees who are politicised or familiar with European realities. They rather express neutral or more favourable positions towards the EU which are often superficial and based on a rather vague form of consent or utilitarian calculations.

Somewhat paradoxically, even in the context of the absence of negative party discourses, non-favourable attitudes are mainly related to the interviewees' political and ideological orientations. Critical sentiments are expressed not against Europe itself, but against the general orientations of the integration process. This point of view is frequently expressed by left-wing or centre-left voters, who oppose the priority given to the economic dimension and to neo-liberalism, even if they also acknowledge the need for social integration and unification of the continent's populations. Right-wing voters seem less eager to criticise the EU. When they do, they use nationalist or sovereigntist arguments which on very rare occasions lead them to reject the EU radically.

Overall, we have observed anti-European arguments, but they are not part of a coherent general vision of the EU. Certain aspects of the functioning of the EU are criticised, but not the EU itself. The aura of Europe in general seems to produce immunisation effects.

The lack of a polarised public debate on Europe

In the past few years in Italy, there have been no major debates on European issues, as they occurred in France on the 'Bolkestein directive' or the referendum on the Constitutional Treaty. The Italian Parliament ratified the treaty. Political parties and the media have not been at odds on the Constitution; rather, they have tried their best to assert their faith in Europe. The opening up of borders to new Member States from Eastern Europe became an issue in the media and on the political agenda after a few criminal cases were blamed on 'Romanians'. Especially thematised by the right, this question was first treated as a matter of immigration and public order, having to do with Romania rather than the EU. When the European Commission and some MEPs stigmatised Italian decisions as 'anti-immigration measures', the government accused the European Commission of preventing them from 'doing something about these crimes by expelling their authors, because [the criminals] are European citizens'.[6] Europe has become both a 'necessary constraint' and a scapegoat to explain the inefficiency of the policies aimed at regulating immigration and punishing crime. While the 'Polish plumber' was the object of a wide-ranging debate in France, the 'Romanian' issue was dealt with as a problem of (national) public order. The solutions proposed have not targeted European institutions, but rather bilateral relations between Rome and Bucharest. Similarly, regarding the arrival of immigrants from the other side of the Mediterranean in Sicily, the government did invoke 'European solidarity', but neither politicians nor journalists defined the question as 'European', and there was no 'European'

---

6.   Roberto Maroni, Interior Minister, 23 March 2009.

dimension in the debate on the subject.

This lack of a cleaved public debate on the European integration process is a possible explanation for the low number of occurrences of unilaterally negative judgements among interviewees who can be classified in the types of attitudes of synoptic, limited or restricted general involvement. The relative consensus on European issues between political leaders and journalists has been an obstacle to the diffusion of 'negative cognitive shortcuts', which allow certain citizens of other countries to form their opinion on these complex subjects. The reinforcing of individual opinions (Klapper 1960) cannot occur and heterodox opinions (Neumann 1986) remain isolated and lack authority and social legitimacy.

The perception of a dysfunctional Italian state

The Italian state is frequently criticised for its inefficiency. These criticisms are found in nearly all interviews. When this sentiment does not lead the interviewees to reject the entire ruling class – as in the case of some respondents corresponding to the remote negative evaluation ideal type – it encourages them to see Europe as an opportunity for improving governance and living standards. Asked about the effects of EU public policies on the quality of Italian public services, an engineer replies:

> If these issues are dealt with at the European level, it will allow us to improve. In Italy, we have no choice but to improve on many aspects. For instance... if the question of transportation becomes European, things will improve in Italy. Otherwise nothing will change.

In other cases, Europe is perceived as a counterweight to the State's inefficiency. A university lecturer in psychology explains that:

> Given the often critical and problematic situation in Italy it seems to me that [Europe] is a sort of guarantee [...]. In Italy things are not going well, there are problems, but we are part of Europe, and thus, the situation cannot be worse than if we were alone. That's how I see it [...]. It's like having an additional controlling organisation... that kind of controls each State's affairs [...] So I consider Europe as an organisation that is able to curb and remedy our country's woes.

The feeling of disorganisation also elicits derision. The more absurd aspects of the Italian system and the (real or imagined) virtues of Europe are opposed, for instance by this unionised worker, a left-wing voter:

> If the Italian government makes a law, it has to proceed through the European legislation, and that this law changes some aspects of my everyday life, who should I thank, Italy or Europe? [...] The answer is simple: if the law is a good one, I say 'Thank God Europe is there and Italy has to accept it'. If the law is bad, I say 'Damn Italy!'

Polish specificities

Dorota Dakowska

As in other European countries, in the Polish sample we have found attitudes that broadly match the main ideal types presented by Daniel Gaxie in this chapter. Let us however mention here a number of specificities observed in Polish interviewees, which complement, and sometimes nuance the ideal typical characterisation of these attitudes.

The observation according to which interviewees with a *synoptic involvement* use the word Europe to refer to the European Union should be qualified here. The distinction between 'Europe' (in the geographical, cultural sense) and 'European Union' (the Community, based on economic integration and a number of sectoral policies) seems to be more pronounced in the Polish case than in France, where uses of the two terms are often blurred or interchangeable. As in Germany, the ambivalent phrasing of questions about 'Europe' often leads the more educated interviewees to ask for clarification. Due to this widespread semantic distinction, interviewees from all categories speak about the 'Union', which makes playing with the polysemy of the term 'Europe' more difficult.[7] The experience of belonging to the Eastern Bloc and the recent character of the accession to the EU are likely to contribute to encouraging such a distinction (see Chapter 6).

Furthermore, the salience of political issues varies depending on the countries studied. Some of them do not have a direct echo in Poland, when others, less generalised in France, are omnipresent in Poland. For instance, the awareness of the Schengen Area, which is linked in the French case to synoptic involvement, cannot be considered as a determining feature of this type in Poland, where many interviewees are able to identify the principle of free movement of persons within that space because of the media coverage of its extension to Poland at the time of our research. This can also arguably be explained by the widespread awareness on the modalities of crossing borders related to pre-1989 restrictions. Conversely, the Bolkestein directive, publicised in France during the debate on the constitutional treaty, remains unknown in Poland, even within the most informed fractions of the population.

In a sample of 120 interviews, very few can be related to the ideal type of *limited involvement*. 'Precise and familiar activities' of the EU are admittedly mentioned by farmers, a teacher interested in youth exchange programmes, and by a truck driver. Yet, these interviewees rarely limit themselves to these observations; they answer other questions with a positive or negative investment. Hence, a 59-year-old farmer claims to be very satisfied with the small European funding that enabled her to 'save' her farm. Asked about the Schengen Area, she replies that it is 'really good' that 'those who travel' can move freely. The small propor-

---

7. We should also point out that interviewers, because of this common distinction, tend after the initial questions on 'Europe' to mention the European Union in the questions more explicitly than in France.

tion of interviewees focusing on a specific aspect at the expense of the others could be related to the fact that in this new Member State, categories who are very dependent of European funds – and whose professional socialisation is conditioned by their ability to deal with the standards used in their sector – do not have the same weight as in France.

Among the interviews that can be related to the ideal type of *remote evaluation*, when answers are articulated negatively, the judgement is not clearly focused on the EU: often, a broader distrust towards politics and a critical evaluation of the interviewee's personal (often material) situation are then expressed. A homeless mother (31, holder of a vocational certificate) has little to say on the EU: the only change she has perceived since the accession are renovations: 'there's money, they're renovating the houses, near where they live, near the town hall', but mostly she regrets the absence of social housing and the fact that 'it's everyone for himself'. The relative visibility of the effects of accession could, however, explain why some politically disinvested interviewees, close to the 'non-negative remote evaluation' category, do not systematically give up on trying to answer questions about Europe. Among these interviewees, some are able to list reasons why the EU (or the accession of Poland to the EU) seems like a positive thing for them. A retired waitress spontaneously mentions funds received by farmers, the construction of roads, better living conditions. Yet, she still manifests her feeling of being incompetent during the entire interview, says she does not feel concerned by the EU and also perceives negative elements (she is unenthusiastic about the prospect of opening up foreign markets to workers from new Member States, because according to her, 'there should be work in Poland').

As for *restricted general involvement*, enunciations that can be traced back to this type of attitude are numerous and varied. In several interviews, answers are general, often hesitant, and they have an ethical orientation. But the fact that these answers are uncertain, vague and far from categories based on the political or sectoral dimension of European construction is not the only distinguishing feature of the interviews in this intermediate category. There are also answers which, although they remain general, do seem invested and even informed, without necessarily reaching the sophistication of the information levels, contents or the ease of synoptic interviewees. A 53-year-old worker explains the reasons for his opposition to Turkey's accession to the EU: he mentions interests that diverge from those of France and Germany in the industrial and agricultural sector and expresses fears about the return of 'two clans' in Europe. The possession of a substitute cultural capital (wife or children having completed university studies, trade union engagement) seems to play a role for some of the interviewees that are close to this 'strong' variant of general involvement.[8] Several main reasons can be put forward to explain these variations.

---

8. Arguably, their socialisation within a communist regime and their experience of mass protests in the 1970s and 1980s might have contributed to the politicisation of some groups of workers.

The salience of the accession issue in the public space

The context and the dynamics of the political and media construction of the European issue during the debate around the accession to the EU (a matter of controversy from the beginning of the accession negotiations in 1998, being particularly intense during the 2003 referendum, but still present at the time of our research) partly explains the stances observed in Polish interviews.[9] Generally, Europe is seen through the prism of the recent accession or of the systemic transformations, depending on the appreciation of these events' importance in the interviewees' life stories. These contextual factors explain the relative reactivity of Polish interviewees on questions about Europe, even though their information levels are not significantly different from those of other European citizens. Whether the evaluation is positive or negative – often, both are combined – many interviewees are able to identify the effects of accession in their everyday lives.[10] In the words of a market seller, with a secondary technical education: 'Everything moves so fast, it's crazy. Actually, it's not over there that it's changing, it's here, in Poland, that everything is changing'. The EU appears as a means to travel, to work abroad, 'an opportunity for young people'. But the opening of the borders also triggers fears about organised crime or the exodus of skilled workers. The perspective of introducing the Euro elicits numerous reservations. Seen as a factor of development, the EU is perceived through its concrete achievements: roads, bridges, training programmes. Conversely, some interviewees mention closing factories or foreign companies which send their profits to their home countries. Overall, social problems (unemployment, low pensions) are rarely blamed on the EU – they tend to be attributed to the Polish government.

Catching up with the West: 'back to normal' or lingering inferiority?

In contrast with the Communist past, 'when we were second-class citizens', as a worker puts it, the accession is experienced by some interviewees as a historical revenge; going 'back to normal': 'now we feel like normal Europeans and we want to be treated normally'. This normality entails the aspiration to enjoy the same rights (or even the same living standards) as citizens of Western Europe. Yet, the fear of being considered as 'second-class citizens' in the enlarged EU is frequently voiced by interviewees, especially those from the lower social categories – as observed in phrases such as 'I live in the Third-World', 'we are not on the same footing' or 'the Poles will always be treated like someone's nigger'.

---

9. The long-standing debate on Europe, historically conceived in terms of a modernity/backwardness dichotomy, already tended to associate Europe with the West; the debate on the accession to the EU was partly based on those topoi (Horolets 2006).

10. Regarding sources of information, those who are not interested in politics may mention mediators, such as a village priest who encouraged farmers to overcome their wariness and apply for European funds.

The EU as an arena of power

The perception of the EU is generally ambivalent. Many interviewees see the EU as structured by a balance of power where the largest, most powerful states, the oldest members of the Community, have the upper hand. To them, Poland is a politically weak, economically backward country, and runs the risk of having to enforce unfavourable decisions. European standards tend to be seen in a negative light. Yet, the EU's hegemony can also be interpreted as an opportunity to make up for the shortcomings of national public policies. As in the Italian case, several interviewees hope that the EU is going to 'force' the Polish state to tackle social issues, care for the environment and improve public services.

These observations reveal the importance of context in the structuring of attitudes on Europe in interviews. In the Polish case, the effects of accession and of the related media coverage as well as the experience of the regime change seem to play a key role. Other contextual effects inform their reactions: at the time of the study, the Polish economy was relatively spared by the financial crisis, and the low inflation and worse-case scenarios imagined by a number of parties before the accession had not occurred. These factors have contributed to the often positive orientation of the arguments; they shed light on appreciations such as this one, from a young Warsaw jurist, who in 2003 had voted against his country's accession to the EU: 'The sky did not fall on our heads.'

chapter five | for or against the eu? ambivalent attitudes and varied arguments towards europe

Dorota Dakowska and Nicolas Hubé

In this chapter the intention is to question the commonly accepted claims that attitudes towards Europe are ideologically coherent. From this perspective, representations of Europe are thought to be part of an organised system of ideas and beliefs, and are based on a clear opinion of the political process of European construction. A few scholars have sought to understand what 'Europe' means for individuals and to find out what cognitive instruments they use to grasp it (Bélot 2002; Diez Medrano 2003). However, for most authors, citizens' attitudes usually fall into one of two binary categories: support or rejection of European integration in general (Eichenberg and Dalton 1993; Szczerbiak 2001; Bielasiak 2002) or of specific European institutions and policies (Hooghe 2003; Schoen 2008). One of the essential political and scientific questions involves trying to solve the enigma of negative opinions towards the EU. Numerous studies have attempted to find out 'what part of public opinion [...] refuses the historical evolution' (Cautrès and Denni 2000: 324) of European integration. Others have asked to what extent these opinions are linked to the electoral success of 'populist' or 'extremist' parties (Kitschelt 1995; Taggart 1998). The gap between European debates and the national political game is most often assumed to lead to a divide between 'integrationists' and 'sovereigntists', to a polarisation of voters on European questions (Schmidt 2006; Conti 2007), as well as to a politicisation of European issues (Hooghe and Marks 2009).

Generally, the authors test and compare the 'weight' of a number of arguments from which they deduce reasons to be for or against European integration, without trying to establish if they are 'significantly adequate' (Passeron 2006: 159). Yet, for at least three reasons, this quest for singular and unilateral explicative arguments is heuristically weak. First, social agents use different types of arguments. Secondly, the justifications do not have the same degree of salience. Lastly, not all the arguments have the same status; they can be developed, informed and structured in different ways.

In this chapter, the thesis of a homogenous and uniformly structured orientation of attitudes towards European integration and EU public policies is questioned. Our ambition is to account for the diversity of arguments and the ambivalence of attitudes towards Europe. We argue that not all attitudes are politically structured. In the process, we will question the widespread academic interpretation of a division of citizens into two clearly identifiable groups: Euroenthusiasts and Eurosceptics – a categorisation that is more normative than explanatory. Conceived as a political label used to refer to party political games in the British context during the 1980s

(Harmsen and Spiering 2004), the notion of Euroscepticism appealed to academics looking for a means to classify European parties (Taggart 1998; Szczerbiak and Taggart 2008) and its use prevailed among political actors (Lacroix and Coman 2007).[1] Studies of Euroscepticism analyse the criticisms of the EU as an essentially political opposition. Our research questions the validity of this assumption, showing that not all attitudes are politically (related to political issues and games), or ideologically structured (based on a set of coherent values). In some cases, the opinions collected may reflect a more general judgement on politics, whereas in other cases they may reveal the interviewee's feeling of incompetence. Despite the assumptions formulated in most of the academic literature on a cut-and-dried line of demarcation between sceptics and enthusiasts, attitudes towards Europe are often ambivalent, of varying intensity and based on diverse elements of appreciation.

First, we will see that social agents interviewed on Europe express themselves on different issues, which can refer to European integration, but by all means not always and exclusively. Attitudes towards Europe appear as polymorphic and diverse. They are ambivalent with regard to the general appreciation of Europe, and diverse in terms of the identification of what Europe represents. The arguments, which are of an unequal intensity, can be scattered, limited or panoptic. Secondly, we will focus on the ambivalence of attitudes, and the resulting difficulty in definitively categorising citizens as either for or against European integration. The arguments that can be identified to systematise the construction of structured judgements on Europe do not obey a privileged mode of justification to the detriment of others. By shedding light on the content and the social conditions of the production of this discourse, we reveal the difficulty in classifying these attitudes along a politically structured line or according to an exclusive explanatory logic.

Beyond false assumptions: a multiform Europe

The starting point of the analysis of attitudes towards the EU often consists in analysing the answers to binary questions such as 'Are you for or against European integration?' 'Is EU membership a good thing for your country?'. Whether the interviewees understand these complex, esoteric terms and give meaning to them is not considered. In the first section of this chapter, we will investigate how attitudes are structured and according to which elements of appreciation. More precisely, we will see that interviewees attribute varied realities to Europe that they do not necessarily associate with the European Union. Depending on their personal situation, they invest their answer with a varying degree of intensity. In order to better grasp the mechanisms of construction of the meaning given to European issues, it is necessary to study the cognitive shortcuts that are mobilised as well as the available individual experiences or discourses on which interviewees can rely.

---

1. There is a long list of studies on Eurosceptic parties; for a critical synthesis of this research see Crespy and Verschueren, 2008 or Fuchs, Magni-Berton and Roger 2009.

Distinguishing judgements on Europe from attitudes towards European integration

Europe and European integration are not always the same thing in the minds of ordinary citizens.[2] This is firstly due to the ambivalence of the term 'Europe' itself, deliberately retained in the Concorde study in order to observe the interviewees' universe of representations.[3] The terms 'European Union' and 'Europe' are not synonymous in all contexts. Some interviewees do not make a difference between the two terms; for others Europe is associated with a geographical continent or the 'birthplace of civilisation', whereas the European Union is associated with public policies and Community institutions. Asked whether the EU suggests negative associations to him, a Polish shop owner replies: 'The Union, no. Europe, yes.'

Confusing attitudes towards Europe and attitudes towards the EU is ignoring the fact that the interviewees understand the very terms of the 'European integration' process very differently. Academic and Eurobarometer surveys usually assume that these terms are self-evident (Diez Medrano 2008), which is far from being the case. In the French context, for instance, a common term of the political debate and academic studies is assumed to be known by all: 'European construction'. When we include this term, largely used by Eurobarometer questionnaires, in our qualitative, open-ended survey, the results are often striking. Although many interviewees express their incomprehension or remain silent when this term is mentioned, several French interviewees attempt to produce an artificial response to a question that is unfamiliar to them. A number of interviewees rely on exercises in style to try and define the term. Some use a metaphor – 'Ah…construction [sighs] that sounds arduous, like construction, actually. Brick by brick – Yes…why arduous? – Well because there are always discussions… tweaking… tweaking…' (France, F, 70, housewife, married to an engineer) – or acknowledge the limits of such an analogy – 'Well, that's got nothing to do with building! [Silence] If I'm for Europe, then I'm for European construction…when it comes down to it [sighs] what is European construction? Well it's constructing Europe, making it better than it is now' (France, M, 55, plumber); 'I am against it. In the same sentence, "construction" and "European", I can't have them; they don't fit together. In my opinion Europe does not construct anything. But anyway, I don't know any of the positive sides of Europe' (France, F, 22, café manager). For others, European construction is linked to a divide between 'them', the elites/European institutions, and 'us', the population – 'Well they should organise themselves a bit you know. Yeah, I don't know, not just several countries getting together, they should organise themselves…' (France, F, 24, nurse). The term can also be interpreted in geopolitical terms, as this retired magistrate does:

---

2. From a political and historiographical point of view, the process itself is a source of confusion and controversy even for those who are directly involved (Gillingham 2003).

3. For a more precise analysis, see Chapter 6.

> To me, it's a big whole, to weigh in the balance against the United States or the Soviet countries, all of those big countries… or even China which is emerging […] Because France alone, it's just a small country. This is where you see that European construction is interesting.

European construction is thus the subject of all sorts of interpretations and reinterpretations (Joignant 2007), onto which personal expectations, elements of knowledge on European institutions or relationships to politics in general are projected. The cognitive shortcuts used by the interviewees to answer this type of question have little to do with the concrete institutional or political manifestations of European integration.

More generally, Europe – like other political objects – is related to a feeling of 'political competence' (Gaxie 2007). Questions on the EU, often perceived as esoteric, produce an effect of symbolic violence on the more socially and politically disadvantaged persons. To them, the EU appears as an undifferentiated reality, which exists outside of the realm of their preoccupations. 'The EU is remote, it's not real', claims a 45-year-old Polish cleaning lady.

> About the Union, well in general it is a subject I don't know much about, I don't understand it, I don't know it. I know one thing: that the Union is a group. A group with a few poor and rich States in it. And I only know that nobody has ever given anything out for free and to me, the Union in the physical sense, the Union, it hasn't given me a thing […] To me, the Union, it's simply nothing.
>
> (Poland, F, 60, nurse)

More complex than national politics, the EU appears as remote and elicits incomprehension among lower class respondents. This distancing effect can also be observed in individuals with high educational attainment and social status, who often quickly run out of arguments during the interview. A French designer for instance told us: 'Each time you ask me a question, I don't understand it' (France, F, 47, graphic designer in an advertising agency).

Europe (or the European Union) is a complex subject, with few cognitive shortcuts available for most interviewees. Even those who have an everyday experience of the EU – for example those who deal with European funds – may express a feeling of distance from European realities. A young graduate working for the Agency for Restructuring and Modernisation of Agriculture in the east of Poland, who manages paperwork related to agricultural funds, expresses a feeling of incompetence throughout the interview. Responding to a question on upcoming EU enlargements, she exclaims: 'Oh gosh… these questions! Sure the EU has to grow. I think that it's also a chance for other countries, including the smallest ones.' On Turkey, she gives up: 'Oh my God, I'm not the one you should be asking about this, I don't know much about it. Sure, let Turkey join!' This distant relationship, linked with a general lack of interest in politics, is not compensated by a technical familiarity with her Europeanised sector. Such an example, among others, questions Inglehart's cognitive hypothesis (1970), which posits that the general trend of longer schooling creates a capacity for abstraction conducive to a positive reception of the European integration project.

Contingent and context-related attitudes

The results of our qualitative survey show that 'Europe' is a flexible notion. It can suggest references to precise EU directives as well as realities that are remote from Community policies. Interviewees use extremely diverse arguments. Moreover, their attitudes are not necessarily lastingly structured. On the contrary, the arguments put forward by the interviewees – who express themselves on subjects that are often distant from their everyday preoccupations – often depend on the salience of an argument circulating in the public debate at the time of the study. Because of the polarisation of public debates in the accession period, numerous better-educated Polish interviewees, holding intermediate or high social positions, are capable of retracing the evolution of their opinions on the EU. Due to the high level of media and political attention on the accession issue at the time of the study, European standards and regulations are mentioned – not necessarily in a technical manner, but with a personal investment by wider fractions of the population than in France or Germany. For instance, many pensioners, even though they are not directly concerned by industrial policy, mention the production quotas that lead some factories to close down. The ways a farmer or a pensioner criticised the closing of a sugar refinery are quite similar even though neither was personally affected by this decision. However, for one farmer, this event is an isolated criticism which does not dent his overall positive attitude towards accession, whereas for the latter, the factory closure confirms his negative vision of the EU. An 80-year-old nun criticises the quotas imposed upon Polish fishermen. This type of opinion expresses a more general worry towards what is perceived as a diktat of the European Union, more than an informed opinion or a reflection related to her own situation. The fact that older interviewees are sensitive to the impact of the EU's regulating pressures undoubtedly shows that these pressures are added to the perceived effects of the systemic transformations of the country, which may be judged negatively. Furthermore, citizens in Poland can mobilise such examples on EU regulations because the national media (and particular TV news) devote space and time to covering the 'absurdity' of certain European standards, such as the EU regulations on the size and shape of carrots. The same phenomenon can also be observed in Germany, when the tabloid newspaper *Bild* (12 million readers), denounced in 2007 an 'absurd' European directive on cable cars, which is mentioned in some interviews conducted at the time.

The terms 'Europe' and/or 'European Union' elicit associations that may be heterogeneous, but still identifiable, as well as specific ascriptions. For some interviewees, the image of the founding myth of the EEC (peace) spontaneously comes to mind. This is the case for a young Spanish teacher in the Paris area, of Greek origin, for whom Europe 'is about roots, let's say. It's the idea of finding a way to unite countries to prevent them from beating each other up. So that's really it: how Europe was born'. This argument is put forward more often by the older generations. It may be related to the Franco-German 'couple' and to the former rivalry between the two countries: for a parish priest in a small village in Brittany, who lived through World War Two, Europe 'is Germany'. Several other interviewees refer to the idea of unity, of 'getting together', or even of 'solidarity'. Europe is thus basically related to an idea of living together, and to a place or a territory.

Because Europe affects the everyday experiences of individuals, virtually no 'non-attitudes' (Converse 1964) towards Europe can be observed. It appears possible to identify a limited set of supporting practical elements which contribute to structuring attitudes, and on which almost everyone has something to say: the Euro, peace or free movement in Europe. In Poland, where the Schengen Area was well identified at the time of the study, the possibility of freely crossing borders is frequently brought up as a justification for positive attitudes towards Europe. In Germany, free movement elicits negative judgements towards workers or 'cheap bad quality products from the East' (M, 40, bike salesman), even if the latter judgement comes more systematically from small businessmen. Conversely, some Polish interviewees associate the free market with a flood of cheap products (because they are 'subsidised') of mediocre quality 'from the West'. The development of low-cost air travel offers a new element of appreciation of Europe for those who have enough purchasing power to experience free movement easily. This is what a 32-year-old German working in the public communication sector conveys: 'Ryan Air or Air Berlin have certainly achieved more for the common construction of Europe than most of the European institutions; because ultimately, we are the first generation who can really experience Europe by travelling cheaply and quickly.'

Everyday or anecdotal experiences are mobilised to support judgements of Europe for those who have few opinions on these matters. Hence, this 24-year-old French nurse working in Versailles:

- In what areas of your everyday life can you see Europe's influence?
- Mmm...I don't know if this is included in your question. But you see, Versailles is really touristy, lots of tourists come to visit the castle and unfortunately there are a lot of them who have heart attacks, it's stupid, huh? So we have a lot of European patients who are hospitalised with us. And then you realise that we don't have the same methods to deal with them, things like that [...] There are lots of countries where, actually, even if the patient has health coverage and they have insurance in their country, they still have to pay all the hospital fees upfront and, then they're reimbursed afterwards. [...] So when they get in, we're careful about them, we don't keep them hospitalised for a long time. There are ways. They get out really early compared to the other patients.

Europe can also be related to family history. To an East German office worker, Europe is a great opportunity to experience otherness. She does so by proxy, through her son's participation in sports competitions throughout Europe, as she already did at the time of the GDR, when her father, a pastor, used to welcome foreign colleagues to their home.

Some interviewees who have run out of arguments to justify their answers may redirect the conversation towards precise aspects around which they build their entire argument. The positive attitude of a 58-year-old French farmer does not concern European integration, but only the Common Agricultural Policy (CAP). Other aspects of the integration process do not elicit a comparable response from him.

- When you think of Europe, would you say, spontaneously, that it is something rather positive or rather negative?
- I see it as rather positive. […] With regard to the markets, on a global level. […] To face the United States, well America, I think that Europe needs to be strong… to stand up to them […] Having said that, not everything is positive. There are good things, but there are also, well…
- Are there things that you…?
- Well on an agricultural level, yes. I'm going to talk to you about agriculture a lot because it's what I know best, it's my field.

There are very disparate visions of Europe: for politicised citizens, the representation of the EU is a political and institutional one. For others, Europe is above all about the Euro, opening the borders, and bringing people and cultures together. For those who are more distanced from European debates, things such as bird flu or the presence of two lines (for EU nationals and non-EU nationals) in airports for immigration checks are 'evidence' of a European reality. An open-ended question on attitudes towards Europe can thus elicit complex answers, relying on different registers. This diversity of arguments encountered in the countries of the study and the low number of elements shared by all social classes within the same country invalidate the culturalist interpretation. This interpretation posits that the attitude of citizens in a given country is structured around the place occupied by that country in the European construction process and the representation of national identity which results from it (Marcussen *et al.* 1999; Diez Medrano 2003; Harmsen 2007; Risse 2004; Schmidt 2007; see also Chapter 6).

Beyond a binary classification: ambivalent attitudes

In order to develop our analysis of the diversity of arguments on Europe, it is important to go beyond the classification of attitudes as pro- and anti-European. Someone who claims to have a globally positive perception of the EU – or has voted 'yes' in the accession referendum in Poland or the ECT referendum in France – can maintain this support on principle, without it being necessarily very structured. Others, who are less convinced, can change their minds, for instance under family pressure. This is the case of this 48-year-old Polish early retiree, who when asked his opinion about the EU, acknowledges that 'for the referendum, under pressure, sort of, from my family, I voted yes, even if I had another opinion. […] I have a slightly less negative attitude now, but nevertheless I am still not the Union's biggest supporter.' For many, Europe can be the object of an unenthusiastic support without explicit 'motives' (Percheron 1991). This result questions the methodology of closed-ended questions, because of the difficulty for some interviewees to clearly position themselves in the pro- or anti-integration debate. In spite of this ambivalence, however, most citizens manage to express their expectations towards Europe or to attribute a number of things to Europe. We now have to find out whether these attitudes are based on patterns identified in the academic literature (utilitarian calculation or values-based judgement).

For or against? The difficulty of replying to a question one has never considered before

Our interviewees – and in particular those from the lower social categories – have trouble justifying their declared support for the EU, not knowing how to answer a question which is visibly too abstract to them. A French plumber wonders: 'what can be good about Europe? It's a good question... [Silence] I say it's positive but I don't really know why'. The manager of a hotel in small town in West Germany states that:

> [Europe] is quite simply important. What is good? Well, ask me questions! For example, is this or that, good or not good... simply... with time...we're no longer alone on Earth. So, ask me your questions so I can give you some answers.

For these categories, the negative opinions expressed in general answers on Europe reveals their feeling of distance from politics (and incompetence) more than a structured opinion on Community policies. A young Polish mother, a victim of domestic violence who resides in a centre for homeless women in a small town, spontaneously responds negatively, before adding 'the Union, the Union, let it exist, but at least there should be solidarity between people, and yet there is no solidarity.' Beyond the idea of an expression of support or refusal, this interviewee, like other working class interviewees, claims that the EU does not have anything to do with her (see Chapter 4). Her call for solidarity reveals less a desire for Europe than a wish related to her own personal situation.

More generally, Europe is almost never unilaterally positively or negatively perceived, including by the most politicised social agents, for instance when going from general topics to more specific ones. The Euro is a good example of the presence of a shift from positive to negative, as this woman working as an executive in the 'Europe' department of a French multinational company says: 'Well as a concept the Euro is positive, but it's negative in our everyday lives because I think that it's resulted in an increase in the cost of living'. A café owner in Germany finds it very good that 'Europe' has allowed the opening of borders and common laws, or has established 'a currency. You don't have to think about that stuff any more.' But in the same breath, she regrets that 'nothing has changed... on the contrary. [...] The currency doesn't belong to us any more. It comes, and it goes... it doesn't have any value any more'. If the Euro is a tangible reality for consumers, it can also be the subject of subjective projections which are very remote from economic reality and the European monetary system: 'In every country the Euro is still not at the same price for everyone [...] for us one Euro is 6.55, for them it might be 5.80, 5.40...' (France, M, 35, blue-collar worker). Yet, the interviewees formulate expectations about Europe. Instead of ascribing 'subjective intentions' to them based on statistical correlations, it is necessary to study the argumentative chains they use in the extent of their diversity.

A Europe of outputs? A vision in practice

In his book, Fritz Scharpf (1999) put forward the idea of an 'output-oriented legitimacy' of the European Union, which completes, or even partly replaces, the insufficient democratic 'input legitimacy'. Indeed, many scholars consider that individuals support the EU or fail to do so based on their practical experience or the anticipation of the costs and benefits of EU public policies that are relevant to them (Binnema and Crum 2007; Gabel and Whitten 1997; Hooghe and Marks 2004), or on the economic transformations which affect them (Christin 2005). While Europe often is credited or blamed for a number of things, we can question the intensity of these ascriptions – according to categories and personal situations – and the link between their occurrence and the legitimisation of the Community edifice.

Initially, it seems possible to make out forms of crediting or blaming Europe which attest to a vague but nevertheless identifiable perception of European policies and regulations. A question on competition policy suggests mostly positive associations in Poland, where it is linked with quality and choice (with an implicit reference to the shortages experienced during the Communist period). This is the case of this 29-year-old salesman, living in a big city, who praises:

> ... the opening of markets to foreign companies, which have been operating for many years, and have higher standards of service than our companies. Other companies get into our markets and take them over, so it's the strength of competition. The cost of living becomes lower, life becomes better; the consumer has more and more rights. This struggle for the customer helps us, it lowers the prices, it helps the customers, the services are better, better and less expensive...

Likewise, the liberalisation of public services is quite widely supported, despite the fears expressed by working class members on the idea of privatising the health sector, envisioned by Donald Tusk's liberal government. This arguably supports the theory which posits that the 'winners' of European economic integration are those who are the most likely to support it (Tucker, Pacek and Berinsky 2002; Jarosz 2005). In our study, some of the most favourable attitudes towards the EU were effectively found in interviewees involved in transnational economic activities. These 'winners' of the common market may reduce the integration process to its mere economic dimension, like this 49-year-old French businessman, who manages a small company specialised in the Indian market. 'Europe' is his 'bread and butter': he has offices in London, Portugal, and Paris. The borders of his activity go beyond France:

> – When you think about Europe, do you see something positive or negative?
> – It's very positive for me [...] Because at a time when with one plane ride you can go as far as 2000 or 3000 miles, and with the train as far as 600

miles, thinking only within the borders of France is very narrow-minded. Also, I really love languages, different cultures. I was a European well before Europe. London for me is just the suburbs of Paris. It's not another country. Spain is our home. [...] Europe is self-evident to me.

Based on these few interviewees expressing favourable attitudes justified by the benefits drawn from European construction, it would be hasty to establish a mechanical link between a high social position and support for the European integration process. Although certain analyses classify them amongst the 'winners' of integration, independent workers and business owners may be rather lukewarm. They mention complex and restricting regulations and standards as well as workforce shortages. This is the case of two German interviewees, the first being the production manager of the second. The first interviewee is very positive about Europe, says he enjoys it during his holidays, but adds: 'to be more specific, I don't really have any precise examples. [...] But it's just a feeling, when you travel abroad, I have this feeling that things grow together'. The second interviewee is also in favour of Europe, especially as he 'benefits' from free movement, living in France and working in Germany. But as soon as the interview begins, he adds:

Right now, too many countries are involved in Europe and each one of them pursues their own financial interests. [...] I see where the problems begin... one of them is simply the problem of taxation. There, you can immediately see that positions diverge greatly.

His opinions on European construction went into great detail and were highly critical during the interview, although he repeatedly pointed out his fundamental Europhilia.

In order to understand these hesitant or ambivalent attitudes of citizens who can objectively be considered as 'winners' of the transformations and EU membership, it is necessary to look at their life paths, their position in the social structure and their perceptions. Polish businessmen, for example, mention competition pressures within the common market. Thus, the 49-year-old owner of a mid-size factory in Lower Silesia has to face, on the one hand, competition from German companies, and on the other, pressure from German customers who expect quality products at low prices from him. Additionally, he is pressured by his employees on wages; they do not hesitate to 'vote with their feet' and are tempted by emigration to the West. Although he used to have one hundred employees, he now only has seventy and relies on non-EU labourers from the Ukraine or Moldavia. His opinion on the EU appears lukewarm at first: 'I used to think it was a positive thing, now I'm not sure'. He develops economic explanations relating to his company's sector of activity:

Western businesses have come in [...], dictating their conditions. [...] We are so often told that in the West – we are of course talking about Western Europe – they don't take bribes, there is no corruption, but all of that isn't true [...]. Let's say that...to get into a retail chain, you have to give someone a provision, a percentage, only just to be able to sell your merchandise there, so there is no difference. At the time of communism... under the commies, it was easier...

This mode of justification is admittedly here based on arguments that might be described as utilitarian ones. However, at the same time this interviewee does not see himself as a 'loser' of integration. He spontaneously mentions that it is more a temporary effect – the increase of the Zloty – that has made exporting difficult, rather than the EU as such. He is part of the wealthiest class, owns several properties and admits to continually investing in his business. He is proud to be able to finance his son's education in an English-speaking international school in Spain. Merely observing his objective interest in the development of economic exchanges is not sufficient to explain his support for integration, even if it is associated with a general view of the social world that is specific to those who hold positions of economic power.

In order to explain the structure of attitudes, other instruments of evaluation must also be taken into account, such as world view and perception of one's own future. This businessman's criticisms are not limited to his personal situation; they are largely based on a vision of the single market where the most powerful economies prevail, even though he admits that the single market is a benefit to him. The interviewee would like to change careers, to become less involved and to move to the countryside. His weariness is less of a direct effect of European construction on his work than that of an increasingly heavy workload in an ever more competitive environment. Here, the critique of economic liberalism is not expressed by a low-income European citizen, with difficulties in accessing the job market and dependence on the State's social expenditure (Gabel 1998a; Gabel and Palmer 1995) but rather by someone, who, in terms of the approaches in terms 'winners' and 'losers' should be an unequivocal Euroenthusiast.

Conversely, interviewees who are 'losers' of the transformations in Poland express hope that community standards and policies will 'bring some order' and make public transportation or the environment 'clean'.

> And the ecology… as far as our country is concerned I think a positive thing is that we are forced to act about the environment. Because we produce too much waste, too many chemicals, those plastic bags.
>
> (Poland, F, 64, home helper)

Although she had practically nothing to say about the EU during the interview, a 60-year-old nurse spontaneously mentions towards the end:

> Maybe this Union is going to teach us how to manage things, order, I mean, it's going to force us to do it. With its laws, it's going to force us to worry about the environment, and bless it for that, caring about order, about cleanliness. It's the only positive thing I can see, really.

The EU sometimes appears as a remedy for the shortcomings of national policies in Poland, which could seemingly confirm the thesis that purports that level of support for the EU is directly linked with the level of dissatisfaction with the national government (Tanasoiu and Colonescu 2008). However, such reasoning prevails among citizens with little political investment and cannot be generalised to the entire sample. Also, the interviewees in question do not elaborate a privative reasoning in terms of immediate benefits – they mention broad values (ecology, order or others).

Other citizens express diverging points of view on European standards and regulations when they discuss the EU. Farmers refer to the Common Agricultural Policy to judge Europe positively, or conversely, to complain about European standards and bureaucracy. Fishermen criticise Europe based on the fishing quotas. Hotel and restaurant owners fault Europe for not lowering the VAT, and the loss of income this entails. To them, Europe is a machine that produces standards that are often perceived as excessive and pernicious, on hygiene, invoicing, hotel ratings, service, etc. The French manager of a mid-size hotel-restaurant thus declares: 'I hate technocrats and bureaucrats because they have the power of life and death over independent workers'. However, only members of a small fraction of the social space directly refer to the costs or the benefits of European standards and regulations to support their judgement on European integration: they are those who directly and regularly have first-hand experience of European standards and regulations. Also, their judgement is not on the EU in general but concentrates itself on their particular sector of activity. They often do not have a lot to say on other European political issues (Common Foreign and Security Policy, the enlargement, the EU's democratic deficit). When they do have an opinion, they tend to dismiss it as unimportant. These results question the potency of the utilitarian hypothesis as an explanatory factor.

Clearly, there is a significant difference between the subjective perception of the consequences of European integration and the direct and objective effects of it. For some, prices have increased with the Euro, but for others, prices have increased for other reasons, whereas for certain people the prices have not increased at all, or they have not paid attention to it. Hence, people with similar levels of education, income or social positions can hold quite varied judgements on causal relationships linked to Europe. They do not all make a connection between the economic situation and the common market. Rather than explaining attitudes in terms of costs and benefits of the consequences of European integration, we need to consider the ways in which certain outcomes are perceived and directly credited to EU public policies or blamed on the EU.

A Europe of values? Beyond Euroscepticism

Some interviewees' judgement of Europe is 'values-based'. They refer to their identification with a community or even religious or political values that they support. Elements of this have already been highlighted in many places (McLaren 2002; Hooghe and Marks 2004; Cautrès and Grunberg 2007). In Poland, young executives in private foreign or multinational companies, living in major cities, experiencing upward social mobility, generally assert their liberal opinions by identifying themselves with the main freedoms of movement of the single market. These interviewees are most often supporters of the Civic Platform (PO), have academic degrees, have travelled abroad and are satisfied with their situation.

However, their ideological point of view often relies on utilitarian arguments, as in the case of this 29-year-old salesman:

> As a consumer, it doesn't matter if I'm going to travel on a Polish or German train. If I'm going to pay less for the ticket than I do now, if I'm going to travel in the best conditions, as a user it doesn't matter whether it's a Polish or a foreign company. If I get a better service, it might as well be a Chinese company, for me there's no difference.

The image of the influence of the EU on civil rights can be observed with this 41-year-old Italian citizen, who manages European projects:

> [Europe is] an opportunity to allow certain countries that might have a less emancipated vision on certain key issues, like gender equality, non-discrimination, certain social rights […]. Europe is […] an opportunity to force certain States whose position is closed on specific subjects to open up if they want to enjoy the economic opportunities.

The power struggle that is visibly brought about by the European Union in the eyes of many citizens can thus be perceived as an opportunity in certain areas. On the other hand, a number of individuals surveyed expressed values thought to be incompatible with the European project, but their discourse makes it difficult to peg them as politically motivated Eurosceptics. They may assert an exclusive national identification, but not necessarily in opposition with the EU, contrary to the claims made in some of the existing literature (De Master and Le Roy 2000; Citrin and Sides 2004). This is the case of a retired Berlin coal merchant, socialised in the GDR, who declares that he lives 'in Europe. It's part of my country, but I am a Berliner or a German. I am not European'. This exclusive feeling of national or local membership does not lead him to support negative positions on the EU, nor does he make any xenophobic comments. 'The most exemplary thing I can think of, the best example I have is the opening of the Polish border, and that we can go there by car and that they can come here'. Some individuals might feel French, German, Polish or Italian because 'Europe' does not mean anything significant to them (Diez Medrano 2010). As a former police officer from the GDR who was forced to retire in 1990 says, 'I feel 100 per cent German. Am I European? I have nothing to do with them. I never go on holiday in other European countries'. His very critical point of view on Europe does not attest to a nationalist point of view, but to the suffering resulting from his social downfall. Nationalism and negative judgement of Europe can be present as arguments among others in the positioning of social agents, but in the latter case, the entire discourse revolves around his perception of German politics since 1990.

Even in the case of individuals identified as close to extreme or radical right-wing parties, their strong feeling of national membership does not necessarily lead them to reject the idea of cooperation between European States. This is expressed by a French butcher and National Front (FN) voter, who voted 'no' in 2005 and who does not feel 'European at all'. Yet, he adds that 'it's a shame because being European, that would be good, it's nice to get together and all that but before we do that everyone should be on the same wavelength, that's all.' Although he has a rather positive point of view on European construction, he rejects the EU as an element of identification and as an institution that produces rigid standards in consumer safety. In Poland, a retired 63-year-old technician, supporter of the League of Polish Families (LPR), reproduces a very radical right-wing discourse with an ethno-centric vision, the glorification of national history, and even conspiracy theories. For him, the rejection of the EU is associated with the fear of German domination and the return to 'totalitarian' structures. His position is constructed around a political nationalism.

> We have fought against each other at the terrible cost of many victims. So this is why we cannot adapt to this creature univocally. And [...] these tendencies of the European Union to unify everything, to create a super-State that we have experimented since '44, from 1945 to the 1990s. We have been through all that, we have behind us this unification and a historical experience is transformed into another with a similar objective and a similar effect.

More generally, according to one of the interpretations put forward in the literature, national identity is linked to xenophobic, authoritarian, rigoristic, anti-universalist, materialistic and pessimistic attitudes, that can be measured on the basis of citizens' opinions on the death penalty or on norms in educating the youth (Cautrès and Denni 2000; Cautrès and Grunberg, 2007). Yet, none of our interviewees directly associates their opposition to European integration with these values. Let us analyse a somewhat telling case; that of a German accountant. His opinions first appear as xenophobic and ethno-centric, in particular when he complains about immigration from Eastern countries, and expresses fears about 'Muslim Turkey' joining the EU. However, he does not criticise European construction, which he is actually inclined to support: 'I would spontaneously say that Europe, in terms of its founding ideas, is a positive thing. [...] The founding ideas of Europe, the common market, common currency, the unified legal system, that was good'. But he claims that 'its evolution, the enlargement, all that has gone too far'. The analysis of his arguments suggests that the effects of European law on his activity as a tax advisor particularly bother him. He does not criticise immigrants in general, but the fact that their presence is, according to him, the result of the liberalisation of the common market. He does not criticise the Euro in general, but the increase in the cost of living. He is in favour of a fiscal harmonisation in the founding countries, as that would facilitate his work. He complains about globalisation increasing competition between European countries, but this is also because of his personal situation and currently decreasing purchasing power. While he uses various arguments, the most frequent ones are not based on xenophobic views, but the concrete consequences of European construction on his personal professional situation:

> It's become impossible to counsel somebody following national law. I am constantly looking at what is happening at the European level. And if I read German law, then I have to look at international law, European rulings. All these elements have to be controlled. It has become impossible to do counselling.

When I tell someone that according to German law their situation is like this, it's possible that according to European law their situation is completely different. And European laws come before our national laws. It has therefore become extremely difficult for me to do my job.

He also says that he talks about Europe with his friends who share this negative image. But he adds: 'with my work, I'm much more aware of what's going on in Europe'. He mentions a litany of professional examples (VAT, paying transporters, the tax system...) where 'two years later, the European court comes and tells us that what we did wasn't right'. This interviewee expresses a cultural pessimism that applies to politics in general, not just to Europe. After having been a Christian Democratic Union (CDU) supporter, he no longer votes because of his 'disgust' with politics. His case is an interesting one, because while it does tend to support his value judgements, his opposition to Europe to a lesser extent also matches the utilitarian theory. His opposition is however not generalised; he also praises certain aspects of European construction, such as the federal system.

This example shows the complexity of the arguments put forward by interviewees. It is very difficult to determine if xenophobia alone determines an attitude. Although the argument is present, it is neither the main one, nor the most developed one. Also, these reactions do not necessarily lead the individuals to identify with a populist or extremist political movement. In other words, their feeling of national membership or their authoritarian attitudes do not necessarily lead them to oppose the EU on a political basis. The arguments are rather cumulative. A judgement in terms of values can acquire greater importance for politicised individuals or activists or sympathisers of a specific political movement or in people who are strongly religious, especially amongst Polish interviewees.

Conclusion

Often complex and ambivalent, attitudes towards Europe are not limited to merely judging the European integration process. We argued that they cannot be reduced to structured political attitudes, whether Eurosceptic or Euroenthusiastic. While these political positions can be found in some interviewees, they are not generalised. Even if the literature puts this categorisation into perspective by distinguishing a 'hard' and a 'soft' Euroscepticism (Taggart 1998; Szczerbiak and Taggart 2008), this notion turns out to be a weakly heuristic in light of our interviews. The idea of cross-analysing the level of support for European integration in general and the opinion on the EU's concrete achievements (Kopecky 2004), even if it was initially meant to apply to political parties, presupposes the existence of a structured relationship between these two political dimensions. However, it is difficult in practice to allot individuals to one category or another. Positive appreciations may be restricted, contingent or hesitant. When negative attitudes are observed, they tend to be the expression of a 'latent or obvious [resistance] towards one (or several) aspect(s) of European integration' (Crespy and Vershueren 2008: 20). In order to understand these attitudes, it is necessary to analyse the arguments put forward by the interviewees as well as to assess the intensity of conviction that they invest in them.

The starting point and the final observation of this contribution is that ordinary attitudes towards Europe are ambivalent and that the arguments used are very diverse. Modest as they might appear, these observations are nonetheless a step forward. They provide us with arguments and elements of demonstration that allows us to dismiss certain preconceptions: the idea that opinions on Europe are necessarily opinions on European integration, that these opinions are politically structured, and that they are based on either 'support' or on 'rejection' of the Community edifice. Once these preconceptions have been left behind, the ambivalence of the attitudes we have observed explains diverse forms of crediting or blaming Europe as well as unequally structured discourses. Thus, the picture of a multiform Europe emerges, with very unequal investments, according to the degree of politicisation and the individuals' personal experience, informed by complex logics of intelligibility, which cannot be reduced to a single explanatory principle.

chapter six | temporality and historical experience in attitudes towards europe: is there a nationality effect?

Dorota Dakowska and Jay Rowell

The date of accession to the EU, and more specifically the distinction between 'new' and 'old' member states is one of the categories often used by experts and ordinary citizens to understand Europe. These evaluative categories are part of a wider series of geographical, historical and cultural divisions used to reflect the diversity and cleavages that run through Europe: 'Northern', 'Southern', 'Eastern' and 'Western' countries; 'big' and 'small' ones; those who have experienced a recent democratic transition as well as older democracies. These frames have provided a set of ready-made explanations available to scholars and ordinary citizens. For the latter, such categories are often used to situate national identities in the time and space of the EU. Scholars mobilise these categories in more or less elaborate forms to explain the dynamics and cleavages within the EU as well as differences in national public opinions with regard to the EU.

The analysis of attitudes and opinions can be broadly divided into two approaches. The first one tends to explain them in terms of sociological variables that link positions, properties and social paths to attitudes, without taking national context into account as a pertinent variable. The second one considers national context to be determinant when it comes to explaining, classifying and comparing attitudes. There is little disagreement that categories associated with the national level – whether through collective historical experience, language, education, or the mobilisation of discourses on the nation in the political or media spaces – have an impact on judgements on Europe. However, the question of the relative importance of the 'national' variable compared to others remains a subject of much debate. In dealing with these aspects, the scientific literature has often focused on the compatibility or the mutual exclusion of European, national or sub-national identities (Schild 2001; Duchesne and Frognier 2002; Bruter 2005; Checkel and Katzenstein 2009). Going little further than statistical correlations, this literature does not satisfactorily explain the way in which individuals mobilise (or not) national categories and references when attempting to give a meaning to an abstract object such as the EU. Others mobilise history or national culture in a selective and *ad hoc* manner to account for differences observed between national samples. They explain such differences by inferring an effect of the number of years of membership in the EU, and by assuming that certain historical experiences or political cultures are more or less compatible with the form and the values of the European project. In this case, history and culture are explanatory variables, mobilised by drawing selectively on a pre-existing stock of characteristics that supposedly contribute to a specific national political culture (for example, the attachment to parliamentarism in Britain, the importance of the idea of the 'greatness' of the French nation, etc.). These approaches, which tend to reify national cultures, often rely on a shaky empirical foundation in the explanation of statistical correlations. They do not tell us why a particular cultural trait or historical event becomes 'active' in structuring opinions and why certain explicative elements are chosen over others within the available stock of cultural or historical characteristics associated with a particular nation.

Our approach does not aim to determine whether the sociological or the national context is more important in structuring attitudes toward Europe. More modestly, we will analyse, on the one hand, how historical references and nationally defined cognitive frames are mobilised in discourses on Europe in various national contexts, and on the other hand, how the mobilisation of these references varies from one social group to another. More precisely, we will examine how collective experiences such as war, communism, democratic and economic transitions – or cognitive categories that are more or less specific to a national context – are reproduced, understood and integrated (or not) in opinions on Europe. With such an inductive and somewhat experimental approach, we cannot address the binary and often simplistic hypotheses that structure many studies of opinions (are identities exclusive or compatible? does the length of EU membership favour a positive assessment of the European project or not? etc.). Instead, based on empirical materials and the comparison of argumentative chains, we will explore how national collective experiences are mobilised, and by whom. Thus, rather than considering national context as a factor that produces uniform effects on all individuals socialised within its framework, we will focus on how the past (European, national or individual) elicits socially differentiated forms of appropriation.

By comparing Poland, a recent member state, and Germany, which is both a founding member of the Community and a newer member – if we take into account the effective accession of the former German Democratic Republic (GDR) in 1990 – we have a sample that is conducive to answering our questions. In Germany, European integration was the object of a large political and elite consensus: the difficulty to express a positive attachment to the nation is presumed to have facilitated identification to a post-national, therefore mainly European substitute identity (Risse 2004). Beyond the case of Germany, the Second World War, an experience shared all over the European continent, was presented both as one of the matrices and one of the main legitimising elements of European construction. Thus, through a German-Polish comparison, we will try to see how this common historical experience is mobilised in discourses on Europe.

Ever since the fall of the Berlin wall and the integration of former countries of the Soviet bloc, communism has no longer been an alternative to market capitalism and European integration. At the same time, as a historical experience, memory and heritage, the forty years of communist rule have had a very strong impact on Poland and on the former GDR. It is more particularly through the comparison between Polish and East German samples as well as the two German samples that we can try to find out what appears specific or common in the way of mobilising references to communism and how these references are combined with other knowledge and experiences.

Beyond the analysis of the effects of 'social frames of memory' (Halbwachs) linked to previous regimes and events, we will also seek to question more recent political, economic and social temporalities present in discourse on Europe. The perception of the EU through the prism of the recent accession process is arguably a specific feature of attitudes of citizens of post-Communist member states in Central and Eastern Europe. In these countries, the perceptions of the accession process and that of the systemic transitions which have taken place since 1989 often converge (Góra 2002; Diez Medrano 2003; Bielasiak 2002). Accordingly, the second part extends the comparison to examine references to systemic reforms in the two countries in the 1990s and how they are linked to EU membership. These reforms took place at the time of accession (in the case of the new Länder) or before the accession to the EU (Poland). Several quantitative studies indicate the existence of a strong correlation between the duration of a country's EU membership and popular support for European integration (Anderson and Kaltenthaler 1996). Survey results are used to defend this observation, whereas deviations from the 'norm' are interpreted using *ad hoc* arguments such as democratic experience or being a net contributor state to the Community budget (Scheuer and Van der Brug 2007).

In addition to the normative dimension of these hypotheses (which amount to claiming 'the more you are exposed to Europe, the more you know it and the more you like it'), the comparison between national contexts shows the fragility of these interpretations. Instead of considering the number of years of membership as a structuring factor in itself, we will study the occurrence and the modalities of the references – direct or indirect – to this temporality. In contexts where EU membership appears as a relatively recent social reality, references to earlier periods and to the immediate consequences of European enlargement allow us to put into perspective, or even question two dominant interpretations of the effects of the length of membership: that the date of adhesion, in other words a 'before' and an 'after' EU membership is important to the evaluation – positive or negative – of EU membership; that the length of membership, often interpreted as a proxy to the length of exposure to – and knowledge of – the EU, plays a significant role in structuring opinions.

Giving meaning to Europe through historical references

The triangular relationship between History, the idea of the Nation and identification to Europe is one of the cornerstones of culturalist explanations of different relationships to the EU (Diez Medrano 2003; Risse 2004; Schmidt 2007; Harmsen 2007). It is commonly assumed that from the German point of view, European construction is a way towards the country's redemption after a troubled past and an alternative to nationalism. In Poland, as in other post-communist countries, the accession to the EU was considered as a return to Europe, as a way of normalising a historical path that was brutally deviated from in 1945. In order to explain the 'Euroscepticism' that is common in new member states, the arguments of recent socialisation to Europe or the persistent predominance of 'socialist values' are often put forward (Rohrschneider and Whitefield 2006).

One of the most stimulating and ambitious attempts to understand the impact of national context on opinions in a comparative framework is Juan Diez Medrano's *Framing Europe* (2003). Starting from relatively simple observations – Europe is discussed in very different ways from one country to the next, language and salient issues vary – the author reconstructs, based on a corpus of interviews, the social frames specific to different countries. These frames are analysed as the expression of shared historical memory. This approach aims to explain differences in attitudes towards European integration which are very imperfectly covered by quantitative methods. While the method used for this study is innovative, it relies on a sample that is essentially composed of highly-educated individuals, respondents who are politicised or who have political responsibilities. In other words this population is professionally and socially predisposed to mobilise historical references in a very well articulated discourse on Europe. These biases lead the author to generalise a specific type of European representation to an entire society, as if, for instance, all German citizens were concerned by intellectual debates on the past such as the *Historikerstreit*. This does not necessarily imply that historical references are not present in other segments of the population, but this is precisely one of the questions we seek to examine more closely. By introducing a historical dimension in the analysis, this tradition of historical culturalism has raised a certain number of key questions concerning the determinants of public opinions which are outside the scope of quantitative research traditions. While they lead to a more complex interpretation of the effects of national contexts on discourse, they tend to treat national populations as an undifferentiated entity and posit the existence of a historical framework producing homogenous effects on the entire population.

We will study below the forms, the intensity and the articulation of two historical moments frequently mobilised by scholars and experts in media and political spaces: the Second World War and Communism. In our corpus, the number of occurrences and the degree of sophistication of these references vary. While there are specific interpretations from one country to another and from one social group to another, the reference to these historical experiences works more as a resource or a repertoire to make sense of an abstract political reality than as a framework linking national and European levels. Moreover, this repertoire is unequally accessible to citizens of different categories.

Talking about war, talking about Europe

Whereas interviewees who are most endowed with academic capital use historical references that go back as far as Antiquity in order to justify the existence of the European continent's cultural foundations, discourses that are more specifically linked to the political project of the EU mostly rely on twentieth century historical references. References to the Second World War are unsurprisingly frequent, since the European Union's pacifying role was one of the cornerstones of its legitimisa-tion. This reference is used differently in Poland than in our samples in France, Italy and Germany, as the end of the war is not associated with reconciliation but rather with the division of the continent. In both Germany and Poland, this resource can take several forms: direct personal experience, reference to family history, or a more academic or intellectual comprehension that reproduces debates on national history and tries to tie these debates into justifications of a positive – or sometimes negative – evaluation of the European project.

While direct or indirect references to the Second World War are present in a majority of interviews from the German corpus, their weight and centrality in evaluations of the EU vary according to the level of political competence. It is indeed amongst interviewees with a synoptic vision or those who are relatively well informed about Europe that the war and the role of the EEC in pacifying the continent are mentioned. For instance, a young German interviewee who holds a university degree in Political Science and works in an association financed by the European Social Fund, expresses a quasi 'official' vision of national history:

> I think it's a good thing that Germany is a member of the European Union. [...] For several reasons; the fact that we are doing our job well [...]. For historical reasons also. [...] It's the history of Germany and the Second World War and the post-Second World War period. That is how Germany [...] was quickly integrated in the Community of Nations. And Germany was one of the founder states. That is a good thing!

While others refer to this past, it is rather as a memory from school lessons that can be significant in very specific contexts. When answering the question on his feelings on being 'German in Europe', this high school student, who shows an un-critical and distant attitude, tells the interviewer about a school trip to Auschwitz – a stark reminder of the shameful national past:

> To be honest, I've always had good experiences. [...] In other countries it happens because of our history... some people can say things. But I can deal with it. Of course I remember when we were at Auschwitz for example... we all felt a bit weird at the time. It was a strange situation. Everybody was looking at us [...]. Well, something happened in the past, and we are living fifty years later. So they can't really say it's our fault... in short, I feel good. I don't have any problem saying, 'I am German'.[1]

In response to the question on positive or negative aspects of Germany's membership in the EU, a 66-year-old retired farmer, who went to university in the United States and who is very interested in politics answers with a reasoning that reflects many official discourses on the importance of binding Germany into Europe and the Western alliance:

---

1. We would like to than Nicolas Hubé for pointing out these interviews.

It is a very good thing... [he laughs]. Because I think that Germans have a tendency to, how can I put this, to solve their problems using violence. It might not be the case today because things are going well and all that, you know, the economy is doing well... but I think if one day things changed, people would be tempted to look for scapegoats. I don't know, maybe the Turks, or others, like the Russian-Germans, all those people who are not very well liked, and then they would abuse them pretty badly. And I think the fact that we are in the EU prevents that.[2]

In Germany, references to the war are often absent from the discourses of people who do not have a high level of political competence, except for those who have experienced it first-hand. 'I think Europe is very important to avoid wars and conflicts and the like. It is really a blessing, isn't it, the fact that we are now so interdependent' (West Germany, M, 85, retired low-level civil servant). But such a direct link between war and the European project is rarely established, even amongst interviewees born before 1935. We find few explicit references to a substitute European identification in lieu of a German identity assumed to be problematic. Even most of the enthusiastic supporters of Europe have little hesitation in declaring that they feel first and foremost German when at home or abroad. Conversely, some well-informed interviewees do not hesitate to criticise the manipulation of the German nation's feeling of guilt by other countries that limits, according to them, the capacity of German authorities to assert legitimate national interests.

- So, if I understand you well, they should have waited a little for the enlargement to the East...
- Yes.
- For how long?
- I can't say, I haven't given that much thought to this question, but we've had negative experiences with the German unification, when they just went 'we are opening the borders and everything will be fine'. This wasn't the way to go about it. And I am afraid we have for some reasons, even for historical reasons, because Merkel made a promise to Kaczynski saying, 'It's okay, you can come in' because of the Second World War taboos, I'm afraid we have shown a lack of objectivity on the issue'.[3]

However, according to some Polish interviewees, when associated with wars, Europe elicits negative reactions. Contrary to the German case, references to wars are not necessarily made by the most educated interviewees, but rather by people with intermediary positions, who in some cases fell on hard times after 1990. In

---

2. Explicit references to the Shoah are rare and often euphemised, like the ones in this extract, except for one, by a Jewish German interviewee who is writing a dissertation on the subject.

3. West Germany, male, 40 years, tax lawyer. Both Chancellor Merkel and President Kaczynski took office after the accession of Poland to the EU.

our sample, these individuals tend to be older and to support views similar to those of conservative or far-right parties, in the discourse of which distrust towards Germany is a key element.[4]

- The word Europe, without anything else?
- Yes, Europe.
- Well, Europe is a continent.
- Do you have rather positive or negative associations?
- Rather negative, if we look at it from a historical point of view.
- And apart from that?
- World wars or other calamities. The French and the October revolutions... You'd have thought Europe was one of the most civilised continents and that these kinds of things wouldn't happen, but they did.
  (Poland, M, 58, municipal employee in a mid-sized town, secondary school educational level, member of the Law and Justice conservative party)

However, such negative references are also made by younger interviewees, such as this 23-year-old shopkeeper, holder of a community college degree. He lives in a village in the Eastern part of the country with his grandfather, who is very critical of the EU and Polish governments.

- Do you have negative associations in relation to the Union?
- In relation to the Union, no. But in relation to Europe, Yes.
- Meaning?
- About Germany.
- What about Germany?
- Hitler started the war and they are richer than us. They should have been poorer since they lost the war.

Though it is not explicitly mentioned, the Second World War sometimes appears to be an implicit justification for interviewees who wish that the EU would have a more active role in settling armed conflicts. The Balkan war and the ethnic cleansing have left permanent marks in discourses of many German interviewees from middle and upper classes. Such marks are much less visible in Poland. These interviewees also mention the Iraq war to show the need for a more affirmed foreign and military policy that could act as a counterweight to the United States.

For example, I'm so afraid of the US, with all their...their power and their... I mean what could happen. When I think of what could happen, I'm afraid, yes... So I think, with all the wars they have experienced, Europeans are more careful, have more restraint, right?
(West Germany, F, 52, university degree holder, housewife)

---

4.   Reconciliation with Germany was central in political discourses in Poland during the 1990s.

All in all, the mobilisation – direct or indirect – of historical references to produce an evaluative discourse on Europe remains mostly limited to the segments of the population that are more politicised or more endowed with cultural capital. Whereas the role of European construction in pacifying the continent is sometimes mentioned, in passing and as something self-evident, interviewees tend to give more in-depth answers related to modern-day threats (wars in Iran and Iraq, cross-border criminality or immigration). In Germany, the current wars, the role of the nation and of the EU are most of the time implicitly linked to the Second World War. In Poland, this reference to the war is overshadowed by references to the Communist past which structures the perception of threats and, in a general manner, judgements made on the country's evolution – or the interviewees' own situation – during the last twenty years.

References to communism: an ever present past?

In an interview chiefly focused on contemporary European questions, in what terms and with which socio-professional categories do references to the period of communism surface, in the Polish and East German cases? For a number of Polish interviewees, the communist past appears between the lines, as a counterpoint to the positive associations linked with accession. The EU is seen as an economically-developed space, full of opportunities (work, travelling) and associated with modern technology. These positive associations are in contradiction with what is said about the former regime, which is considered authoritarian and preventing freedom of movement (all categories mention this) and freedom to conduct a business (this is mentioned by private sector and independent workers). The communist past is associated with food shortages, queues and products of poor quality. The access to consumer goods and their quality during the period of communism are not mentioned in Eastern German interviews, but freedom of travel comes up systematically. On the other hand, mass access to western goods tends to be associated with the German unification and the introduction of the Deutschmark rather than with the simultaneous accession to the EU.

Communism is associated with cumbersome border controls by people who have experienced them or by those who were not able to obtain passports or visas: thus, freedom of movement as a practical experience of Europe is central to positive evaluations of the EU. This is the most frequent argument given by Polish interviewees, regardless of socio-professional category when they discuss their positive associations with Europe. While many interviewees have experience of trips abroad (tourism, trade, seasonal work, buying a used car), others who have never left their country emphasise this point, almost as if they were speaking by proxy ('young people can travel').[5] Mentioning the communist period serves as a

---

5. The high migration flow, increased by the progressive opening up of Western job markets to workers from new Member States, most likely contributes to the salience of this issue. Conversely, some interviewees express reservations on the opening of borders, as skilled workers

counterpoint to talk about these new rights, perceived as a return to 'normalcy'. For instance, a 53-year-old Polish worker in a major steel factory makes numerous critical references to the communist past, with an emphasis on how hard it was to go abroad. He contrasts the past – 'when we were second-class citizens' – to the present: 'we feel like normal Europeans and we want to be treated normally'. Such interviewees want to enjoy the same rights and freedoms as Western citizens, but also often fear that Polish citizens will have an inferior status within the EU.

The question of freedom of movement is indeed also more present in interviews with East Germans than West Germans,[6] except for interviewees who live close to the borders. The separation of the two German states, which tore apart many families, made the strict restrictions on the GDR exit visas a particularly controversial subject.[7] In the interviews, the image of confinement, the feeling of having been imprisoned within the borders of one's own country in the past keeps coming up and freedom of movement, facilitated by the adoption of the Euro, is credited to the EU.

Freedom of movement, which East Germans have enjoyed since 1989, is perceived through personal experience, that is encounters with other individuals and cultures, understood as a form of a 'bottom-up' construction of Europe. But on the question of freedom of movement, seen through the prism of past experience, judgements remain ambivalent. Often, this first positive, and spontaneous, judgement, formulated in reference to periods 'before' and 'after' Unification, is qualified by a more nuanced opinion on the present or potential future impacts of freedom of movement. With this shift in judgement, the argumentative register drastically changes, from personal experiences linked to history to a more abstract and impersonal analysis of economic or security risks associated with immigration, organised crime, business relocations or wage pressure from immigrants, particularly from Eastern Europe.

Polish interviewees refer to the collective experience of communism but also, in a general manner, to a more distant past, and draw parallels between the EU and imperial regimes. Occasionally, this perception of the EU as an empire is not only expressed in critical terms. A retired psychologist, born in 1910, underlines a similarity with the Austro-Hungarian Empire: 'I didn't see any reasons to stay out of the Union. I liked the very idea of the European Union. I knew what the Union was all about, since the Austrian Empire was a similar Union, wasn't it?' A more frequent cognitive shortcut is established between Community constraints and the Soviet rule in Poland (but also in the Czech corpus), built upon the vision of an external power: 'We used to make fun of Communism, of their absurd laws, of their ukases, the injunctions, but with the Union, it's the same thing now' (Poland, M, 48, worker). This parallel is sometimes influenced by anti-accession movements,

---

leave and the risk of illegal trafficking is increased.

6. In the West Germany corpus, the opposition between 'before' and 'after' is used only when talking about the introduction of the Euro, which is said to have facilitated tourism.

7. About two East Germans out of three had relatives in the FRG.

which during the pre-accession period popularised slogans such as: 'Yesterday Moscow, Brussels today'. Declarations from some political leaders have fuelled this type of discourse.[8] The implicit reference to periods of domination by outside powers is recurrent when expressing the fear of seeing Poland exploited ('We're like Cinderella') and of letting powerful European states make decisions for them ('Germany and Britain are making the rules for us'). The parallel with the USSR can also be used to criticise the large-scale pro-European campaigns that preceded the accession referendum in 2003, which was perceived as an operation of propaganda, producing a '*déjà vu*' effect:

> Sometimes I think this is all a bit too much, because back when I had just started working, everything revolved around the Soviet Union, and now it's the European Union, so, going from one to another is a bit too much.

> (Poland, F, 58, retired schoolteacher from a village in Lower Silesia)

This shortcut is necessary for understanding recurrent eschatological declarations made by some Polish and Czech interviewees,[9] according to whom the EU 'is going to break up' and cease to exist in the medium term, just as other empires have fallen.

This parallel drawn between the EU and an Empire – Soviet or any other – is completely absent in the East German corpus.[10] Rather than the Soviet rule, the economic and symbolic domination of the Federal Republic of Germany (FRG) during and after the fall of the Wall is taken into account to explain the political form of the EU and its articulation with national sovereignty. In order to assess the importance of the experience of the German unification in structuring attitudes, we need to study how the change of regime and its consequences are put into words and related to European integration in interviews.

Socialisation to Europe: understanding the effects of 'European seniority'

The difficulty in establishing convincing causal relationships through statistical correlations is particularly evident in the study of post-communist countries. While some authors consider trust in government at national level an important factor of support to European integration (Anderson 1998), other studies on new Member states develop the opposite argument (Tanasoiu and Colonescu, 2008). A similar correlation of survey results suggests a somewhat paradoxical argument, according to which the worse the economic situation of a candidate or recent member, the more support there is for European integration (Christin 2005; Sánchez-Cuenca

---

8. We thank Ondřej Novotný for this comment on the Czech case.

9. While Russia is more often identified as a major international power by East Germans than by West Germans, it is essentially the asymmetrical relationship between the old and new Länder that structures East German discourses.

10. We would like to thank Katarzyna Jaszczyk for pointing this out.

2000). This argument contradicts the interpretations usually made about the indicators of support observed in older member states.

Beyond these results, which show the reversibility of statistical correlations with general interpretative pretensions, we would like to analyse the effects of the number of years of Community membership, focusing on two main questions. First of all, we will study the uses of the recent collective experience of systemic transformations in the early 1990s in Poland and in the new Länder in the formulation of opinions on Europe. In a general manner, the word 'Europe' refers to heterogeneous spatial, geographical or political representations. Does national context and the length of socialisation to Europe have effects? These questions must be answered in an indirect manner, through the spontaneous associations provoked by the wording of the questions.

To what extent are systemic transitions structuring experiences?

Among the distinctive collective experiences, we would like to find out whether, and in what way, systemic transformations structure individual discourses. Because of specificities in the way past regimes ended and in the terms of accession to the EU, the visibility of European matters in public discourses was very unequal.

Several studies posit a strong connection between the individual or collective experience of systemic transformations and the perception of changes induced by the accession to the EU (Bielasiak 2002; Jasiecki 2005; Mach and Niedźwiedzki 2002; Tucker, Pacek and Berinsky 2002). However, in our empirical material, the frequency of references to the period of transformations varies in intensity and importance according to the contexts and the social categories. A major difference between the West German and the East German corpus lies in the mobilisation of the German unification process as a cognitive prism to understand the EU enlargement to the East. This parallel tends to be drawn by the interviewees who are better informed and most interested in politics in West Germany. Although it is not systematically mentioned in East-German interviews, unification is frequently mobilised by interviewees, even the least politicised, in order to give meaning to a number of questions discussed in the interview: the effects of the Euro (a parallel with the 1990 monetary unification), the Eastern enlargement, the differences in living standards and the presumed effects of European funding policies.

- Yes, the money flew in, but where did it go? Straight to the pockets of some Wessis (West Germans), who were quick to bring it all back home. The companies that constructed here were all from the West. And where did all the money go? Back to the West. [...]
- So, what do you think about, for instance, the accession of Poland, and now Romania, Bulgaria ... the Baltic states to the EU. Do you have an opinion on that?
- Yes, they have always been a part of Europe. [...] Now they are in the EU. All that is wonderful. But they are going to do exactly what they did here

in the East. They are going to pull the same stunt. Several thousand people from here are going to make millions on their backs.

(East Germany, M, 46, 8 years of education)

Many interviewees who have little information to build a coherent discourse on the EU mobilise a discourse 'available' in the new Länder to save face during the interviews. In the extract above, the East-West problematique is revisited in terms of rich and poor, exploiters and exploited. Other interviewees, for whom it is difficult to mobilise the binary East-West opposition, only rely on the opposition between the relatively unspecified 'fat cats' and 'the small guy', identifying themselves with the latter.

For people who have spent part of their adult life in the GDR and are struggling to find points of entry to comment on Europe issues, the interview is structured by their personal experiences. Judgements on the unification and economic transformations are then more or less directly projected onto European themes. If the cognitive assimilation between the unification and the EU is more often found amongst 'losers' of the transition, 'winners' can also refer to it as a cognitive framework of a more abstract discourse:

People had a whole lot of dreams, hopes and so on and so forth after the change [of 1989], and they were greatly disappointed, because, because... I think it was also because the EU was probably counting too much on economic integration. Same thing as in the GDR, yes: 'Now everyone will have the Deutschmark, and everything will be alright for you', right? And now look at East Germany today, and we also know about Slovakia and the rest, on a greater scale... No, so what I'm saying is that the power relations between FRG and GDR, in fact it's Western Europe, Eastern Europe, it's the same thing. Of course, I find this totally problematic. [...] Actually, what I don't like at all about the EU is this, this well, this current neo-liberal evolution.

(East Germany, M, 29, engineer)

Whereas in Poland, the accession to the EU gives some interviewees hope for improvement in public intervention on poverty, in the new Länder, the consequences of the East German economic meltdown in the early 1990s were counterbalanced by the welfare state, which is itself today thought to be threatened by the pressure from the economic competition of Eastern countries. In Poland, the interviewees make direct or indirect references to the transition period, but not systematically and in different ways. The period of transformations is mentioned through fragments of life stories without necessarily being associated with an opinion constructed in relation to the EU. Thus, the experience of unemployment leaves a permanent mark on the lives of people interviewed. A technician, laid-off from a big public company just before her retirement appears to be very affected; however, she does not relate this to her perception of the EU. In her non-negative distanced evaluation, she claims to be favourable to the EU and confirms she doesn't 'see the reason why [she] should be against it'. Interviewees who are critical of their living conditions may occasionally follow such observations by a favourable appreciation of the EU, as is the case of this former management assistant of a major public company, holder of a Matura in Economics, and who has been unemployed since 1990 (Poland, F, 52, unemployed). She keeps her distance from politics, and develops a critique of social policies in Poland that is informed by her own experience. What she apparently expects from the EU is a positive evolution for people living in poverty.

– During communism, I was leading a better life. And today I can't even find a job; I have become a victim of unemployment. I am homeless [...]

– Has Poland's accession to the EU had an impact on your situation or on your general perceptions?

– You know, I'm no politician, I've never done politics, but in Poland, everyone can comment on this subject, and today, we can even say a lot of things. This accession, well yes, I think it has done a lot of good for our country; that is to say, various funds for development... of towns. For example, in my town there is a bridge now, there were no access roads and they constructed them; this is also thanks to European Union funds. And here for example, this shelter [for the homeless], we are given food [...]. And these goods come from the EU, it says so on the package. Pasta and buckwheat... So, our accession to Europe is a good thing [...] since there's been some progress on social issues, for the unemployed and the homeless. Everyone receives something.

Some interviewees justify their decision to emigrate by the fact that their difficult social situation has been worsened by the liberal reforms of the 1990s. This is the case for this daughter of a couple of farmers, who now lives in Brussels. She mentions economic difficulties in her region of origin to justify leaving ('Life is hard back home in Poland'), but she also refers to her image as a poor immigrant ('They treated us like Africans', 'they didn't know that we also had cars') (Poland, F, 36, cleaner). To this politically disinvested interviewee, the EU is where her employers work: buildings she has never been to even though she lives nearby. Thus, even when people lacking political competence can experience the EU on a day-to-day basis as expatriates, European institutions remain invisible to them.

To the Polish interviewees who evoke a negative experience of the transformations or have felt a decline in their career perspectives, the 'transition' appears to be confused with the changes related to the accession to the EU. This is the case for several interviewees who are above sixty years old. For this generation, it is thus the year 1989 and not 2004 that constitutes a biographical break point. This does not prevent these people from interpreting political, social and economic reforms as responses to the European Community's demands.[11] The opposite is observed for people whose experience of the common market is based on commercial exchanges and on the regulations to which they are subjected, such as

---

11. We thank Katarzyna Jaszczyk for bringing this point to our attention.

businessmen. They seldom mention the period of transformation except to say, 'Communism was overthrown'. They make references to concrete implications of the 'acquis communautaire', by insisting on the anticipation effect at the time of the accession.

> We were no longer a communist country before our accession to the EU; there was a free exchange market and everything already worked like in the West. It is just that we had not yet officially signed up as members of the EU. But we had adapted all the principles and norms to the Union in such a way that even before accessing the Union, in principle, everything worked the same way as in the Union.

> (Poland, M, 36, owner of a small delivery business)

The subjective temporalities of systemic transformations and of accession differ according to the individuals' social positions. The upper socio-professional categories, that is to say those who participate in economic exchanges within the single market or those who have a high level of education, perceive the EU as a tangible reality which had in fact penetrated Poland long before 2004. For lower categories or for people who have experienced a decline in social or professional status, the EU remains a distant and abstract horizon. It is sometimes perceived as a dangerous external force that penalises the losers or on the contrary, as a welcomed constraint to overcome the failings of the Polish state. In this case its effects only became visible after the accession through tangible achievements or the ability to find work in Western Europe.

Our study confirms the hypothesis that the *de facto* accession of the five new Länder to the EU has pushed aside specifically European issues. As the accession to the EU was a side effect of the unification, without any public debate, it was mainly on the basis of an opposition between new/and old Länder that various criticisms were attributed to the transition period rather than EU membership as such. In Poland, a closer link between systemic transformations and the accession to the EU can be observed, reflecting the importance of a series of different reforms without all the interviewees considering accession as fundamental. Interviewees belonging to lower socio-professional categories, who have a hard time expressing opinions about the EU, can without going very deep into the subject ('what I would say is that it is a good thing'), use the question of accession as a springboard to refer to the economic situation in the country, which they consider bad ('if only things could change a little in our country'). Generally speaking, the cognitive assimilation between transformations and accession to the EU does not hold the same meaning for those who suffer from these processes and for those who seize the opportunities they offer.

The effects of accession on representations of Europe

Our results show that it is simplistic to reduce support to the EU to a conception of temporality limited to the number of years of Community membership. Beyond possible ambivalences, the word 'Europe' leads to interpretations that vary from one context to another. In France, political and scholarly discourses have imposed a synecdoche to consider a part (the EU) as the whole (Europe). In new member states, this superposition of Europe as a cultural or geographical space with the European Union is not self-evident. In political discourses, being a part of Europe in the broad sense of the term was a legitimising element to justify the accession to the EU. This is useful to explain why many German and Polish interviewees belonging to upper or intermediary social categories ask the question: 'Do you mean Europe or the European Union?'. When talking about the EU, Polish interviewees – including nurses, blue-collar workers or homeless people – generally use the term 'Union'. This consideration of the different meanings of 'Europe' informs the representations of Europe in the discourses. In Germany, most of the interviewees consider Europe above all as a positively connoted geographical, historical and cultural space ('cultural, historical roots', 'Mitteleuropa', 'art'). They differentiate it clearly from the European Union, a vague political object which often elicits spontaneously negative associations in all categories of the population, although it is described with variable registers and themes. In Poland, the term 'Europe' triggers geographical (continent) and historical associations, with frequent references to educational experiences ('cradle of democracy', 'Greek goddess') or emotional experiences ('one big family').

Amongst the interviewees who have less cultural capital, it is more especially visits abroad, which have become easier thanks to freedom of movement and the Euro, that constitute a thread of a vision of Europe as a space of exchanges. They allow interviewees to associate Europe to the EU and point out its specificity.

> What I find very positive is, hum, multiculturalism; we have many, many countries with many different cultures, hum, which is not the case in the United States or Australia, or in Asia. The history of Europe is more interesting, I think, than that of any other continent. And personally, I think the density of Europe is more interesting compared to other continents for example, the fact that from Germany it takes an hour to get to Denmark or two hours to get to Poland.
>
> (East Germany, M, 28, cook, travels a lot in his free time)

Freedom of movement and discovering European nations and cultures are particularly present in discourses of interviewees socialised in the GDR, as well as in Poland, and often mentioned early in the interview. If these elements are not absent in West Germany interviews, for many East Germans this is a true divide in their biographical experiences.[12]

---

12. This generally positive association with travel in the EU can be a negative one for economically-marginalised citizens, who do not have enough resources to enjoy freedom of movement.

In addition to these generally positive references to Europe by Polish interviewees, references to the division of the continent during the Cold War are occasionally made. They emphasise the geopolitical situation of their country in the Soviet sphere of influence. The western part of the continent, or even sometimes the European Community, is therefore associated with democracy and economic progress. The position of exteriority in relation to the EEC is interpreted negatively as a factor of marginality and backwardness.

— Europe is above all a land, that's what I think, a territory; positive or negative, I can't say. It can be both. Do I take Europe as a whole or do I divide it into Eastern, Central and Western Europe, that is to say, we can explain it like this: the East makes me think about rather negative things; the reasons are obvious; I'm a middle-aged person, so, I remember very well the way things were before in our country and this does not evoke positive associations to us. But if I take Central and Western Europe, of course the associations are positive…

— You mentioned memories, memories of the past in relation to Eastern Europe, what were you referring to?

— I was thinking about the former system of this country, communism. It was based on tons of restrictions with total absence of democracy and always, always older people who were better informed about what was happening in the world at the time, huh, who were against this system and were always saying, we always heard them say that the system in Western Europe was far better and more democratic.

(Poland, M, 40, former PE teacher, now an entrepreneur)

Reference to the division of the continent is not limited to people who have a lot of cultural capital; it can be expressed with less self-confidence.

Geographically we are European, right? […] But when it comes to commercial objectives, we didn't belong to Europe, we belonged to the Eastern part, right?

(Poland, M, 56, farmer)

The East-West distinction, which explains some of the positive connotations associated with the EU in Poland, is present in interviews conducted in both parts of Germany but takes on different meanings. For many West German interviewees, in all sectors of society, it is strictly economic. Whereas most interviewees consider the accession of new member states to be a good, or inevitable thing, the economic lag of the East is perceived as a threat. In this case the enlargement is associated with the relocation of German businesses looking for cheap labour and lower taxes (the case of Nokia, which relocated a factory after having benefited from German state grants was mentioned by several interviewees from all social categories but the most underprivileged) or with the cost it represents to the German taxpayer.

East Germans have a more ambivalent view than the Polish and the West German interviewees on the distinction between the East and the West. The more undetermined geopolitical 'Other' is expressed in two main ways. The first one emphasises the differences in living conditions and wages that are immediately visible when crossing the German-Polish border: themes developed by West German interviewees reappear, sustained by personal anecdotes and experiences. In the second case, the West German person or system is often considered as the 'Other', which reveals an interpretation that is more focused on a social divide between the powerful and the weak than on a geopolitical one. In Poland, many interviewees from different categories describe the 'Union' as a dominant Other who 'commands' and 'imposes' its preferences.

Conclusion

The comparative analysis carried out in Poland and Germany shows that temporality and collective experiences are important differentiating factors. While historical references are not structured in the same way in each national situation, these mentions of the past are rather articulated in an allusive manner, *a contrario*, or by referring to personal experience. Hence, we cannot look back to the historical past and memory and find an overarching frame weighing equally on the citizens of each country. Rather, there is a repertoire of available references; these references can be used in different ways according to the degree of politicisation, the level of education, family context or individual experience.

The comparison allows us to point out similarities between the two cases studied, although they are very different: general references of Europe through categories reflecting what was learned in school, the appreciation of freedom of movement by those who were once deprived of it, the feeling that the EU re-establishes pre-existing power relations expressed by those who are 'dominated'. However, these power relations are perceived and expressed differently: for example, the relationship between the East and the West specific to unified Germany on the one hand; the political and economic domination of larger 'old Europe' countries, feared by Polish interviewees, on the other. Differences are also observed in historical accounts: in the two countries, Europe can be associated – although not by the same categories -with the pacification of the European continent, or on the contrary, with past conflicts and the division of the Cold War. The study allows us to question certain preconceived ideas. In Germany, the consensual character of political discourses on Europe does not prevent people from holding critical opinions and the intellectualist discourse on the national past and identity dominant in the political and media spheres finds little echo in the middle and lower regions of the social space. In Poland, commenting on 'Europe' temporarily allows certain categories of the population to break their usual silence and give limited but clear opinions on the perceived effects of accession. The subjective construction of temporalities reveals assimilations (transition/accession, enlargement/German unification) and connections (Second World War/Iraq war, EU/empire), in which the reference that is the most heavily invested by the interviewee eventually prevails. These asynchronous figures, related to diverging discourses on the nation and/or Europe (is European construction a pacifying or divisive element?), confirm the value of a comparison focused on the notion of temporality.

chapter seven | talking about europe: techniques and resources in the formulation of opinions on the eu

Philippe Aldrin and Marine De Lassalle

Most of the academic literature on the 'European citizen' or the 'European voter' investigates correlations between socio-demographic properties or nationality and support for the EU. As they rely on Eurobarometer data, studies on relationships of ordinary citizens to Europe traditionally tend to emphasise the correspondence between 'Europhilia' or 'Europhobia' and a series of social characteristics. Thus, level of education, income, occupation and age have emerged as the main variables discriminating attitudes towards political Europe (Cautrès 2001). The almost systematically observable link between level of education and 'Europhilia' has led certain scholars to interpret this correlation as causality; these variables are thought to exert a mechanical effect on the relationship to Europe. The causal link between variables is expressed in the claim that only the most educated citizens can accomplish the cognitive effort required to understand European issues – defined as remote, complex and technical (Inglehart and Rabier 1979). This theory of 'cognitive mobilisation' is coherent with other theses that also combine the same discriminating variables. Hence, individuals who feel physically, economically and professionally safe are supposed to be more able to face the challenges of European integration and subscribe to the 'post-materialist values' it embodies (Inglehart 1990).

Regardless of the explanatory model deployed,[1] all these studies are ultimately based on two postulates: the Europeanising, even Europhilogenic effect of a small set of socio-demographic variables (mainly, level of education); the individuals' psycho-cognitive ability to evaluate and judge Europe and to take a personal stance on the opportunities or risks it represents. These postulates are the main theoretical foundation of the systemic prism through which 'European public opinion' is usually studied, which holds that the European political space is both the matrix and the product of citizens' European attitudes.[2]

---

1. Three main models explaining European attitudes can be distinguished: the utilitarian (or economic) model, wherein citizens assess the cost/benefit ratio of European integration; the ethical-identity (or psychological) model, which investigates the values and identities through which citizens experience Europe; the configurational (or political) model, focusing on the effect of political factors, especially national ones, on the formation of European opinions. On these three traditions, with a different terminology and a different analysis but using a rather similar categorisation, see Hooghe and Marks 2005.

2. Since the beginning, the theoretical production on European public opinion has been largely inspired by the 'Eastonian analysis' (Bélot and Cautrès 2008) and has therefore explained the

In this chapter, elements from individual and collective interviews are highlighted that corroborate or reveal limitations of the main theses developed in the specialised literature. By focusing on the different ways an interviewee produces a point of view on political Europe, we are not trying to establish direct links between social properties and the contents of opinions on Europe; rather, we aim to study the resources and techniques used, depending on their social environment, to respond to a solicitation to produce a discourse on Europe. Based on a predominantly qualitative material, we will observe the types of social knowledge and techniques mobilised by interviewees to talk about Europe, and we investigate correlations between the way they talk about Europe and their social position and environment (level of education, profession, job experiences and prospects, living standard, way of life).

Talking about an often unfamiliar object

Solicited opinions as a sociological object of enquiry

When invited to answer questions in the form of an interview on European matters, interviewees react to the successive solicitations and express a point of view on Europe. The form of the exchange – semi-structured individual or collective interviews (see Chapter 3) – puts interviewees in a situation which allows them to verbalise opinions on Europe, a reputedly technical and difficult topic. Unlike surveys that rely on closed-ended questions, this method reveals a great variety of expressions and arguments; individuals elaborate on their own frames of understanding and judgement, as if the exchange was based on the following implicit demand: 'What stance can you take in public on political Europe?' If this type of solicitation – especially when addressed to people who have some degree of familiarity with the interviewer – has some similarity to ordinary conversations on political issues, the inscription of the verbal exchange in a survey produces effects on what is said, as the discourse is recorded and is thereby transformed into 'data' with sociological properties. The reliance on an interview template (which sets a theme, a vocabulary, a certain way of asking questions, and a specific order), the configuration of the exchange (assigning specific roles to the participants of the verbal exchange), the presence of a recording device, the reference to the university that commissioned the survey: all these elements contribute to making the interviewees' answers more formal and to lead them to try to be more coherent than they would be in an everyday conversation.

The survey method tends to produce individualising effects in the sense that it creates a context which implicitly rests on a socially defined framework – through socialisation and citizen status – favouring a formal expression of a personal point of view on political questions. In this regard, the semi-structured interviews conducted during our research can be explored in terms of how the interviewees inter-

---

relationship to political Europe first through inputs (the 'permissive consensus' acting as diffuse systemic support), then through outputs (perceptions of the efficiency and benefits of EU policies).

pret the solicitation, assert a posture and finally mobilise various resources in order to express a personal opinion on Europe.[3] From this point of view, it appears that the interview set-up does not exert the same degree of constraint for all interviewees. According to their occupation or social circles, some interviewees possess 'markets' where they can regularly exchange ideas on Europe and are accustomed to expressing their opinions (Bourdieu 1999). Others, on the contrary, seem to be ill at ease in an unfamiliar situation and sometimes even express embarrassment or their feeling of incompetence when faced with certain questions. Also, the difficulty, the discomfort or, on the contrary, the ease in responding to certain questions depends on the forms of public debates on Europe in each country and on the varying levels of interest and involvement in European issues of different social segments. The social factors which determine the interviewee's attitude towards the interview set-up – and therefore their aptitude –are a very important element of our research on opinions on Europe. By mainly focusing our attention on this attitude, we hope to denaturalise these opinions in order to analyse them not as an expression of a pre-existing individual judgement (determined by socio-demographics and cognitive abilities) but as the operationalisation of the disposition to formalise a judgement in a given interaction (based on an experience of the social world and a socialisation to political exchanges).[4]

The constraints of producing an opinion in public

In following this logic, the ways of expressing political opinions on Europe will be analysed by comparing the argumentative and explicative material mobilised by the interviewees to the general posture they adopt. Attitudes do not only result from the interviewees' 'personality'. They also depend on social factors: being familiar with this type of social situation, feeling competent on the subject of the interview, the social distance with the interviewer. Furthermore, as the interview situation makes it nearly impossible to 'opt out', the interviewee is left with no outside resources, they have to make do with what they are and with what they know. On this point, qualitative studies emphasise the composite character of the techniques and the instruments used by interviewees in formulating their answers or in expressing their relationship to politics (Lane 1967; Eliasoph 1990; Gamson 1992; Bourdieu and Wacquant 2005). This literature highlights different effects, which vary according to the interviewees' profiles and the techniques used (speaking in public, debating with other individuals or expressing one's opinion

---

3. In Goffmanian terms, we can define this type of interview as a 'transformed frame', which refers to a subversion of the social frame of conversation in a face to face or in a small group configuration. The codes of expression are only at face value identical to those of a 'normal' social framework. The presentation of self, the 'face work' is related to the mediate or immediate evaluation of the specialised interviewer (whose job often precisely consists in evaluating people). See Goffman 1974.

4. Pierre Bourdieu suggests that we should treat opinions 'not as things liable to being mechanically and passively added up, but as *signs that can be changed by exchange*, by discussion and confrontation' (Bourdieu and Wacquant 2005).

at length to an interviewer) on the expression of a personal opinion. These effects are mainly due to three constraints imposed by this type of interaction: the necessity of justifying an opinion (based on a knowledge assumed to be subjective or rooted in a subjective, but incontestable experience); taking other opinions into account (as expressed by the interviewees or implicitly as part of the interviewer's questions); and maintaining a social face (every answer or every non-answer is explained so as not to lose face, or be perceived as a violation of the 'interaction order' and thereby preventing its 'felicity').[5] This configuration of constraint therefore acts as a conformation of the individuals to an unwritten social norm for exchanging opinions. This compliance can be observed in the way interviewees attempt to render their ideas and arguments coherent and in the manner in which they interpret the solicitation and assess their ability to answer (Eliasoph 1990). In this perspective, our analysis of opinions collected for the Concorde programme focuses on the process in which the interviewees attempt to lend coherence to their position on Europe, both seeking to categorise the interviewees' postures (based on the resources mobilised) and linking these postures to their objective and subjective position in the social and political space. The indicators of this position are the social and economic situation, educational qualifications, occupation, the social environment, way of life and nationality. These indicators will be taken initially as localising operators, which the interviewees universalise to various extents (Boltanski *et al.* 1984), and then as signs of a socialisation to Europe *lato sensu* (as a geographical continent, cultural space or institutional edifice) or to the 'realities' through which the interviewees encounter Europe.

Postures and resources of opinions on Europe: three modes

Establishing the interviewee's posture allows us to describe and explain the way in which they hold (or do not hold) an opinion on Europe. To avoid reducing this question of posture to a purely psychological problem, we have tried to isolate distinct forms of social identification in the interviewees' discourse. In the expression and justification of their personal position on Europe, they are more or less likely to use 'I' or 'we'. And yet, the use of personal or collective pronouns is linked to social dispositions and not randomly distributed sociologically (Bernstein 2003). It proceeds from a practical sense of classification which allows interviewees to see and position themselves in a structured and hierarchical social space in which they can also perceive and locate others. This dimension, linked to social position (objectively assigned and subjectively occupied), is associated here to the perception of the position they occupy as more or less structured by Europe. Beyond the use of 'I' or of 'we' – which can both refer to one or several collective memberships (occupation, nationality, generation, etc.) – the register of identification favoured by the interviewee indicates several elements of their posture in relation

---

5. Maintaining the 'social face' involves a mutual work aimed at avoiding 'offences' (with regard to the frame of exchange and other partners) and 'stigma' (Goffman 1983).

to Europe. Through the registers of identification they use, interviewees always connect the self to a social locus (geographical origins, family structure, professional background, age group, way of life, etc.) that may (or may not) link them to Europe. Therefore, beyond the use of 'I' (which can be personalising or universalising) or the use of 'we' (which can refer to highly structured or loose group memberships), the register of identification refers to repeated indicators by which the interviewees express from where (reference to a social, geographical or cultural locus) as who (reference to biographical individual properties) or as what (reference to social, professional, geographical or cultural groups) they express their judgement on Europe.

The posture is therefore not randomly chosen or distributed; it is determined by what every interviewee chooses – and can afford – to hold in public as a personal opinion on Europe given the objective and subjective constraints of the situation. Again, social standing, occupation, educational and cultural capital act as operators of connection, even as operators of the appropriation of European issues which partly differ from the usual forms of the relationship to politics and where belonging to a national space produces significant effects (in terms of political context, reference to a cultural frame or collective identity). For instance, Europe represents a possibility for change, a new horizon in new Member States; personal interest in European issues extends beyond socially 'homologous' categories of interviewees in founding countries. But, generally, the resources which the interviewees are capable of mobilising to help them express an opinion on Europe are the ones that condition the posture they adopt. We have observed that these resources vary. Answers combine elements of knowledge from school or university lessons, media discourse, anecdotes, etc. In order to classify these multiple resources, we have used the source of mobilised knowledge as the discriminating criterion. This allows us to distinguish between, on the other hand, impersonal knowledge based mainly on 'school' knowledge (including general technical knowledge such as the democratic principles, the history or institutional organisation of Europe) and on media discourse, and on the other hand, personal knowledge based on practical experience or anecdotes that the interviewees have retained.

Based on this double premise (register of social identification, source of mobilised resources), our analysis of the different ways to hold a solicited opinion on Europe aims at producing a sociological and typological interpretation of the qualitative material characterised by countless combinations of affects relating to personal experiences or to collective or universal values; apparently unrelated references to events or debates; various acquired dispositions (diversely acquired according to the interviewees' life experiences or to the effects of the national context) to think and talk in public about political topics. A close examination of the available interviews allowed us to identify three main modes of production of opinions on Europe:[6]

---

6. For a schematised representation of these modes, see Table 7.1 at the end of this chapter.

1) The first mode is that of the 'decentred' point of view, mainly characterised by the interviewee's tendency to place their comments on Europe on a general socio-political plane – therefore beyond the self – and to mobilise other points of view in and on Europe. This category of interviewees generally shows awareness of political games and issues through references to the mediatised, and therefore impersonal, frames of public debates on Europe as well as through a more or less ostentatious familiarity with the vocabulary and the concepts of these debates. The model of a singular concern for Europe (which can lean towards Europhilia or Europhobia, or generally more composite perceptions) may stem from an activist engagement, or, more often, through certain types of university courses and/or professional activities where political Europe (as an object) makes sense. If the arguments put forward by these interviewees aim to universalise their point of view on Europe, they also aim to singularise it, i.e. to turn into a personal production.

2) This tendency to integrate otherness to one's own thoughts and rhetorical structures – in other words, to dialogism – is clearly less present in the second mode. The latter is characterised by the interviewees' more systematic reliance on their own personal experience: their point of view on Europe is inspired mainly by experience (specialised technical knowledge, travel or cultural exchanges, professional or family life). The point of view on European institutions and questions is based on a self that has an identified and identifiable location in the social space in reference to Europe. But talking about real life experience, their environment, and their reality allows the interviewees to refer to a social locus or to a 'we' from which they tend to generalise towards Europe. Although related to personal knowledge, the preferred register of identification tends to indicate an intention of embedding opinion on Europe in a collective situation (social, professional, geographic, political or cultural) rather than focusing on a personal dimension, where holding an original, independent viewpoint is an expression of social worth of well educated interviewees,[7] which leads us to refer to this mode as socio-centred point of view.

3) A significant number of interviewees do not succeed in embedding themselves and their opinions in the context of Europe. These interviewees present an external point of view to the interviewers in the sense that European affairs seem to remain a foreign entity. The interviewees show little inclination to mobilise knowledge (personal or impersonal) or to utilise a register of social identification allowing them to connect to Europe. The lack of opinion on the questions asked and the incomplete answers can also be explained by audience effects, which make it all the more difficult to

---

7. Using a collective identity as a support which is more or less objective or substantialised indicates that we are dealing with the production of a *sameness* identity rather than a *selfhood* identity (more observable in the first mode), to summarise the distinction proposed by Ricoeur (1995).

express an opinion. Furthermore, the lack of an objective and/or subjective attachment to a social locus connected to Europe leads the interviewees to express, with more or less clarity, a feeling of foreignness in relation to the institutions or issues of Europe. Symptomatically, Europe is described in terms that attest to the abstract, or even fictional character it assumes in their eyes. In contrast to the first two modes, these interviewees cannot or do not try to establish a general, coherent opinion on Europe, and they tend to deal with every question or subject from the interview template separately.

These three modes of holding an opinion on Europe can be perceived with varying degrees of clarity in all interviews. However they are shown here as tendencies – to decentre, socio-centre or externalise – insofar as, with the exception of a few interviews closely matching the archetypal form of one of these three modes, most of the interviews are somewhere between two modes, which will lead us to introduce interstitial modes.

The decentred point of view or Europe beyond the self

In an interview situation, decentred interviewees are characterised by three principal traits: a sustained interest in politics in general, from which a certain closeness to European questions ensues (high level of politicisation); a tendency to structure the point of view outside the self and therefore to universalise one's point of view on Europe (tendency to decentre); the assertion of their ability to express an autonomous opinion, by using political and media discourses but by opposing and criticising particular points of view to present personal opinion (singularisation of the point of view).

An affinity to politics…and to political Europe

Decentred interviewees strive to give a purely political opinion; this is the main element that sets them apart from the interviewees in the other two groups. Their investment in European issues comes out as a 'natural' extension of their open affinity with political questions, and reduces or cancels the inhibitory effects of the interview set-up. The interviewees respond with a certain dexterity, try to make their answers coherent, often anticipate the questions and subjects included in the interview template. Despite its relative artificiality, they interpret the interview situation as an invitation to give their personal point of view on Europe. Another distinctive feature in their posture consists in taking into consideration a variety of positions and arguments defended in the public debate on Europe on the subject discussed. In the process, not only do they show their knowledge of the debates, of the oppositions that structure them and the main actors involved, but they also reveal their ability to specify their personal point of view.

I know the arguments Europe's detractors use, I know it upsets people that they feel they are no longer masters in their own home […]. Obviously, there are more of us now, so more people are involved in decision-making. You have to admit that sometimes you need to make an effort to accept the majority's opinion, that's what democracy is. And as a rule, I always stand behind European decisions, even if people might wrongly think they're going against the national interest.

(FR, M, 47, engineer)

The tendency to decentre the point of view – in relation to the national prism in this extract – stems from the interviewees' habit of exchanging points of view on political questions in the course of private, activist or professional activities. Participating in such markets of political conversations allows them to share information, to compare arguments on Europe, and to have a more or less precise overview of the available positions on the subject. The interview is seen as a continuation of previous conversations on European issues (decision-making process in the EU, problems of constitutionalising treaties, new Member States joining, etc.), which are less abstract to these interviewees than they are to others. By referring to their own opinions, they demonstrate to the interviewer both the anteriority and the consistency of their opinions.

I had a good friend who was against Maastricht, I was for it and there was a debate on the subject […]. [At the time of the 2005 referendum campaign] I wanted to vote yes. And then I told myself it wasn't possible (because it was Maastricht all over again)… So I had arguments with all my friends who voted yes. And then I talked to a friend who's writing a PhD thesis on Community law and who is actually really clued-in on these subjects and he gave me a few ideas.

(FR, M, 32, lawyer)

The regular confrontation of ideas on Europe mostly occurs with politicised interviewees, either through activist involvement and/or familiarity with activists, or through social relationships with others sharing a high level of education. Following a common sociological pattern, the members of upper categories, due to their social and professional position, are generally informed and interested by public political debates. These distinctive positions and dispositions give them access to debates on Europe, and also force them conform to the social norms of their milieu to be interested and to have something to say about political subjects. These interviewees have mostly graduated from university or elite schools, are mostly men with liberal (lawyers, doctors, consultants) or intellectual occupations (teachers, journalists) or more generally men who have executive or management positions; they assert an autonomous political point of view, simultaneously singular and universal.

Posture and resources of a singular point of view on Europe

The specific social and cultural capital of these interviewees gives them a certain legitimacy (objectively defined and subjectively accepted) to discuss and judge politics in general and Europe in particular.[8] With a systematic use of 'I', this legitimacy to give political opinions is linked to a process of singularisation of their point of view. They make an effort to mention the more or less diverging opinions of those close to them or of groups who are socially, ideologically and geographically further away, in order to differentiate or qualify their own position, thereby showing how easy it is for them to navigate Europe's political territory. Although singular, their point of view claims to be objective, in that it involves references to universal categories. References to personal situations are only made to illustrate a more general point that often relies on concepts, key figures or events of the public debate on Europe. Yet, they make a point to avoid identifying themselves with particular analytical frames used by the media and political professionals on Europe. Likewise, when they refer to certain concrete subjects which encapsulate recurring debates on Europe (social Europe, political Europe, Europe of liberalism, Europe of regions, Europe of Nations, North/South relations, financial Europe and Europe of employers, of bureaucrats, etc.), they do so in order to emphasise their personal position. By establishing themselves on an equal cultural and cognitive footing with the professional producers of political positions, they display their self-confidence as a way to face the effects of the presence of an audience. Generally speaking, the manipulation and especially the mastery of diversified impersonal knowledge confers to their answers the efficiency of dominant discourses and works as a legitimate resource to guarantee that their point of view is well-founded and objective.

> [On the constitutional treaty] I voted yes and I was sure about it. What I found interesting was the campaign for the 'no', with opposition blocs which, to me, seemed extremely different, or even divergent. There was a bloc of, let's say, anti-liberal thought: 'We don't want liberal Europe'. To that I'd say they should have realised that earlier, because it's not exactly breaking news, that Europe is a group of countries that are part of a liberal economy. I think it's pretty striking that the socialist party is this strongly at odds with the other European socialist parties. There was this feeling that 'we want to go on doing what we like in this country', what you call the Europe of nations, national sovereignty.
>
> (FR, M, 60, retired researcher)

The strong denotation of the discourse, achieved thanks to the precision of the information mobilised, generally ensures its greater transparency.[9] Often, in-

---

8. This legitimacy implicitly refers to the dominant frames and the social principles of classification of public political stances, which value the use of a specific vocabulary and knowledge (see Bourdieu 1984).

9. In the sense that the speaker disappears from the discourse. Jean Dubois (1969) defines the degree

terviewees shift from the theme initially discussed to a related theme, or redefine the question asked, in order to link their answers and give a general coherence to their point of view. They free themselves from the wording of the question or even impose other concepts and ideas to be able to produce coherent conclusions, and sometimes adopt an authoritative tone. This posture sometimes involves mentioning key actors (founding fathers such as Konrad Adenauer, Jean Monnet, Alcide de Gasperi, Helmut Kohl or Jacques Delors) and more often key episodes of European history (the major 'crises' of the European project, the Single Market, Maastricht, the fall of the Berlin Wall and the enlargement in Eastern Europe, the constitutional treaty). This way of holding a decentred opinion on Europe through this relatively sophisticated use of European and national history legitimates (or attempts at legitimating) generalisations on European questions and conveys the sense that these interviewees have a command of the 'big picture'.

> This is a recurrent problem in the EU, we've seen it in an extreme form with the Kaczyńskis. Tusk smoothes out the edges, to take the Polish example, but ultimately his approach is still in the same direction, only more nuanced and a little bit more forward-thinking, but he says so very clearly. Poland wouldn't have made it alone, but then again, above all, he says the Poles should learn to become Polish again, not too nationalist, but as Polish as the French are French [laughs]. Well, I say French, but you could say Germans. But we don't really assert our national identity that much anymore, we stick to the EU level, and it's fine that way. And, of course, Poland has to go through that process extremely quickly. And within that context, I would have waited before the accession to the EU. Leave them alone first, support them and all that, obviously, but still, leave them alone a bit. I think it worked out well, anyway, and they're still better than the Italians, from that point of view, right?
>
> (FR, M, 60, retired researcher)

Decentring, which consists in expressing a point of view beyond the self, entails having the socially recognised resources to back up this claim for objectivity. Paradoxically, then, the highest social positions with the highest amount of cultural capital, singular life experiences (especially professional or activist ones), and socialisation to legitimate knowledge determine the disposition towards decentring. It is very much the position and the social trajectory that condition these interviewees' postures and resources on Europe. In this sense, this is more precisely a socially embedded point of view, but one that is expressed in a decentred form. For this reason, among interviewees who share the general characteristics of the decentred point of view (pre-eminence of impersonal knowledge, sensitivity to political questions, decentring and autonomy of the point of view), we observe significant variations in the posture according to the ethos, social origin, occupation, and nationality of the interviewees.

---

of transparency of the enunciation as the social latitude of understanding the discourse, from the speaker to the entire society.

From an empathetic 'I' to a detached 'I' (interstitial postures of the decentred mode)

As far as political ideas are concerned, claiming to see the 'big picture' implies a form of selflessness, which these interviewees generally express by distancing themselves from expressing direct or and personal interests and valuing the common good. They also have a tendency to set their own situation aside and take into consideration the viewpoints of those who are less privileged than they are. The construction of the decentred point of view is not aimed at objectivity based on knowledge of historical facts, but rather at objectivity through empathy, by displaying virtues such as compassion or indignation in the face of social and economic injustice. While they produce a singular judgement, some postures betray a socially determined disposition towards moral altruism.[10]

> [Asked about the Euro] I travel around a lot, and I can say it's a good thing, overall. I think economically it was a very bad thing [...] retailers didn't play the game, prices really increased quite a lot. [...] And then there's a problem with all the people of a certain age. They don't realise that ten cents of Euro amount to sixty cents, almost seventy cents [in Francs]. But in terms of moving easily in Europe, it is really quite practical.
>
> (FR, M, 50, university professor)

This posture of the empathetic 'I' presupposes particular social properties, in the sense that it is based on a knowledge of diverse and sometimes contradictory consequences of Europe (in this instance the Euro). This posture can be rooted in a socialisation to other life experiences, as for interviewees with modest social backgrounds who have experienced various forms of upward social mobility or social workers who have regular contact with people who are affected by unemployment and economic problems. These individuals are often prone to moral activism (Agrikoliansky 2001) and assert their closeness (at least ideologically) with the man in the street. This posture can sometimes be expressed through the use of 'we', even if it is never completely subsumed by the group,[11] in which case it is closer to the socio-centred mode.

> The problem with Europe is that it's made for those who defend a certain level of wealth. We work in the social sector, our job is to support people, help them be less alone and suffer less. When your father and your mother are unemployed, or when your mother's husband has left her, or you've got kids, you've got three or four you have to look out for, etc. I'm sorry, but these people are not allowed to talk about Europe, they don't give a damn about

---

10. Similar to the gestures required by the imperative of 'noblesse oblige' (Elias 2006), this mode of expression contradicts the utilitarian hypotheses developed in some studies of European attitudes (Gabel 1998b).

11. The posture of representation allows both social proximity and social distance. See Bernard Pudal's analysis of French communist party leaders (1988).

Europe. [Louder] As long as there's so much unemployment, precarity, as long as people have no access to housing, you can't talk about Europe. [...] I'm interested, I get paid at the end of the month [...]. I'm doing fine so I can talk about it. If tomorrow, I'm unemployed, you can talk to me about Europe and I'll say 'Sorry, I've got no time for this, Europe is too far for me'.

(FR, M, 40, community centre manager)

Conversely, other interviewees who seem to have the necessary resources to produce a decentred political opinion are less comfortable with European questions. These interviewees claim to care about Europe, but do not manage to singularise their point of view. Their authority in expressing an opinion is undermined by a feeling of incompetence on Europe in comparison to other political topics. This is the case for some students, executives whose sectors are not very 'Europeanised'; women from wealthy and educated social backgrounds who do not work, or no longer do. In spite of their command of 'legitimate' knowledge on Europe, they turn out to be more sensitive to the presence of an audience than other decentred interviewees. They delegate their opinions more often,[12] express their points of view with less self-confidence, have a tendency to admit incompetence on certain questions: this leads them to adopt a more distant posture when faced with the interviewer's solicitations, a sort of detached 'I' which brings them closer to the third mode (or excentered point of view).

[About information on Europe] We're not very well informed. I watch the news on TV, I listen to the radio, I listen to foreign stations too. [...] Given our social, educational and cultural level, I should know much more about how Europe works than I do. But I don't really try to. Normally it should be floating around and I should have absorbed it. [...] After all, we do know how the French system works, by and large [...]. I don't know if it's more complicated [for Europe], but I know less about it.

(FR, F, 69, housewife)

12. The delegation of opinion, or *fides implicita* (implicit faith), to people or groups who are considered more apt at judging politics is most often observed in the more socially dominated categories (young people, women, poorly educated, the poor), and therefore those who possess the least authority to publicly express political considerations (Bourdieu 1993).

The socio-centred point of view or Europe viewed from the self

In contrast to the objectivity put forward by decentred interviewees, many interviewees mainly rely on their personal experiences or conversations to formalise
and to hold a coherent opinion on Europe.[13] The interviewees who produce this socio-centred discourse are characterised by three principal traits: an interest limited
to certain political questions, occasionally connected to Europe (a politicisation on
specific issues or sectors); a tendency to construct their point of view on Europe
based on their own social experience (tendency to socio-centre); the justification
of an opinion referred to an often collectively experienced 'reality'– using 'we' –
often used to stigmatise the lack of realism or the absurdity of political and media
discourses (particularisation of the point of view).

A sectoral relationship to politics…and to Europe

The structure and the coherence of socio-centred interviews are built upon experience. Personal knowledge plays an important role, as a main source of arguments,
as a principle of justification of a posture, and as evidence drawn from observation or from practical experience to support a point of view. These interviewees
show and sometimes even admit that their interest in politics in general, and in
Europe in particular, is limited to specific themes or moments of the public debate
or to sectors of public intervention (fight against unemployment, rising prices, tax
policy or crime). This differential interest in the subjects of the interview is demonstrated by a selective involvement in the questions asked by the interviewer.
Lacking the 'statutory' political competence based on academic, media and purely
political knowledge on Europe, they nevertheless have enough social self-confidence to produce, structure and defend a point of view on the subject. This self-
confidence can derive from their professional situation, their life experiences or
specific forms of social integration. It is therefore through the prism of profoundly
personal knowledge that they succeed in coping with the constraints of an interview situation.

This socio-centred discourse consists in holding a shareable point of view on
Europe based on personal or vicarious observations drawn from practical experience of the social world (social networks, professional circles), of the economy
(consumption, wages) and cultural activities (hobbies, travelling, consuming cultural goods) which can be linked to Europe. Some of these interviewees may have
professions for which EU laws and policies particularly matter, but others have
'inherited' dispositions to European citizenship from an unusual family history
(children born to bi-national couples, descendants of concentration camp prisoners, experiences in other member states). For this reason, they are prone to use

---

13. By 'coherent', we are not referring to ideological or intellectual coherence of political opinions, in
the sense that they might be structured by objective knowledge and rational aims. Here, we refer
to the process of attempting to formulate correspondences that are logical for the interviewee and
for the interviewer, which does not preclude contradictions and dissonances.

'we', often referring to a community whose relationship to Europe is socially and culturally defined, and sometimes to a more uncertain group – facing an uncertain Europe – then mentioned with vague designations, like 'them' and 'they' generally referring to political elites or to European civil servants without naming them. Sometimes this 'we' is more structured, even defensive when it is rooted in a geographical territory (in the case of regionalist or nationalist discourses) or in a given economic sector described as affected or threatened by Europe, and conscious of its interests.[14]

> With the laws they gave us, in January, right, we had new laws on trawl net mesh sizes. They never go out to sea, they come up with laws that are, eh… […] Europe, no! Yeah, it's quite negative for us. Higher prices. […] They increase really, really fast. Gas… everything's increased. […] We went on strike two or three times but it didn't really have any effect. They promise us a lot of things and in the end we get nothing. […] Let them stop coming up with completely useless laws when they don't know anything about fishing.

> (FR, F, hairdresser, married to a fisherman)

The process of giving coherence to the successive answers aims – just as much as it does in the decentred mode – at proving the validity of the posture. In this instance, however, this process consists in listing motives of grievance or satisfaction towards Europe. Interviews are more fragmented, alternating between moments when a question elicits very long answers and others when the interviewer goes through the questions from the interview template without getting much reaction. This is due both to the varying levels of interest in the specific European issue discussed and to the fluctuations in feeling entitled to express an opinion on a given topic. While they are prone to discuss questions which make sense to them, because they echo their own life experiences as taxpayers, voters, fishermen, farmers, gays, truck drivers or hunters, they become more withdrawn, less talkative as soon as the questions concern more distant technical or institutional domains.

Posture and resources of a particularist point of view on Europe

While decentred interviewees try to assert the singularity of their point of view, the socio-centred interviewees try to particularise a collective point of view in opposition to what they perceive to be dominant discourses. In both cases, the goal is to autonomise positions in relation to the media or political frames on Europe to which they have access; the first to assess their own position, the latter to mark their distance. Postures also differ. While decentred interviewees strive for universalism, socio-centred interviewees seek to share an opinion expressed from a specific locus in the social world and in Europe. When references to personal

---

14. In the sense of the group 'for the self' (Marx), or of class as effectively mobilised following Bourdieu (1985).

experience lead them to use 'I', it is linked to a position as a member of a professional or cultural group (e.g., farmers, young graduates, Italian citizens).

> I'm an administrator. I represent breeders at the [French] cattle breeding federation and so, precisely regarding the whole evolution of the common agricultural policy and all that, we went to meet the European commissioners to try to give them our point of view from the field. Because those people, they're completely disconnected from that.

> (FR, M, 50, cattle breeder)

Insofar as answers are mainly determined by personal knowledge, it is not always easy to articulate them with Europe. Yet, they often skilfully exploit this personal prism to shift towards political Europe, either by metaphor or by analogy, judgements based on less directly political dimensions of Europe by mobilising based on a linguistic, geographical, cultural or professional register. One of the interviewees extends the metaphor of industrial cooperation throughout the interview, based on his professional experience, which also conditions his concrete experiences of Europe. The failure of the Airbus project allows this interviewee to evoke 'national selfishness' based on his professional experience.

> Let me give you an example. What was originally going on with Airbus [several countries were involved in a common project] was a good thing. And once again, you can see Europe's limitations. Everyone tried to profit from the situation as much as they could. Maybe there are not enough exchanges, and in the end, you see that Airbus, even though it's a great project, is now struggling. Everybody wants to defend their own prerogatives. Once again, Europe is a good thing, there's still an awful lot of stuff to do, but I think there are also limitations that you can clearly see.

> (FR, M, 30, industrial executive)

Sharing socio-economic or professional features, however, does not equally determine the ability to generalise personal experience towards Europe, as the case of two small businessmen in north-eastern France shows. These two Alsatians of rural origin speak the Alsatian dialect, studied at the same engineering school and both manage a small family business. Both reformulate the questions to suit their status as businessmen and the specific problems of their sector in a borderland. Whereas one maintains the socio-professional prism throughout the interview in order to respond on practical or general European problems ('The enlargement is like a business: when you grow, at some point you have to absorb the growth'), his counterpart does not manage to mobilise this experience which would have allowed him to grasp of the political aspects of Europe. He repeatedly admits his lack of knowledge on the institutions, and reacts to many questions as if he were being questioned by a severe schoolteacher ('Actually, I can see that I don't know anything'). The territories of the self, of experience, the 'field', 'reality' do not always allow the interviewee to deal with the interviewers' solicitations.

Attempting to link the social world experienced to Europe, the socio-centred discourse offers more diverse points of view than the decentred mode, where arguments more systematically refer to the political discourses and to the themes of the public debate. One interviewee, who often travels with her family in Europe in a camping car, evaluates Europe and the economic situation of the Member States in the light of the countries she visits. Other interviewees, of Algerian or Tunisian origin, mention discrimination as a reason to doubt 'Europe's bright promises'. Another interviewee forms analogies between the Europe of exchanges and the numerous bi-national marriages in her family. Less equipped with socially legitimate knowledge on political problems, these interviewees have more original opinions on the definition and the representations of Europe. The very characteristics of the socio-centred point of view (pre-eminence of experience, interest limited to specific political questions, particularisation of the point of view) make it easy to recognise it in interviewees despite their very diverse sociological profiles. Although these interviewees share a core of common features in the way they deal with the survey situation, the register of social identification allows us to identify two distinct variants.

From the globalised 'I' to the egocentric 'we' (interstitial postures of the socio-centred mode)

Depending on the interviewees' material and symbolic properties, their social identification can either tend to a universalising or a personalising point of view. In the first case, the interviewees, while relying on experience, adopt a posture close to the decentred mode (see above). Here, the territory of the self includes a sufficient quantity of social supports, economic, cultural and symbolic resources to allow them to take other points of view into account. The possession of educational and linguistic capital, of experiences of travelling and meeting people in Europe allow the formulation of a singular point of view (register of the 'I'), which nonetheless remains mainly based on experience.

> I was a European long before Europe. To me, London is just a Parisian suburb. It's not another country. Spain is home. [...] And to me, Europe is self-evident. On Monday I'm not here, because I'm going to London. I don't say 'I'm going to England', I say 'I'm going to London', as if I was saying 'I'm going to Lyon'. [...] When my children go to London, it feels like home to them. [Asked about European information] Well, on Europe, personally, I get my information mostly from people I work with, since I work with several European countries. So earlier I was on the phone with a Spaniard; as soon as we're done with the interview, I'll phone my English accountant.

> (FR, M, 49, CEO of a small business)

While this interviewee has the resources to universalise his opinion, the discourse is less transparent compared to the interviewees of the decentred mode insofar as it is never constructed outside of his own situation and his experience of the Common Market. Conversely, some interviewees attempt to produce a socio-centred discourse, but seem to lack the forms of experience and mechanisms of social identification necessary to make their point of view universal and share-able. While they manage, throughout the interview, to articulate a point of view on Europe based on their own experience, the lack of obvious or visible links to Europe forces them to hold a very personalised vision, one which cannot easily be generalised. While this ego-centering brings them closer to the interviews of the external mode, these interviewees, who distinguish themselves through their abili-ty to overcome, rise to the challenges of the presence of an audience (including the necessity of justifying the opinion) and are capable of holding a particular opinion on Europe. This is clearly shown by the case of a worker in a meatpacking plant, who builds his entire point of view on his experience of the Euro, to which he relates all the questions, including those that have nothing to do with the subject.

The external discourse or Europe outside the self

This last category includes interviewees who are incapable of sustaining a point of view when interviewed. The reasons for their inability to respond politically to questions on political Europe are diverse, but mainly manifest themselves through a lack of school and media knowledge on the subject, coupled with the impos-sibility of interpreting personal experience and knowledge in relation to Europe. The self and the personal territories of these interviewees seem to be confined to the periphery of Europe, or even outside Europe, its issues and its problems. The effects of the presence of an audience, including maintaining social face, are also experienced as unusual constraints, which are hard to overcome. As a result, their discourse remains external, insofar as the fragments of opinion they provide remain outside the realm of Europe. Three principal traits characterise these in-terviewees: a material and symbolic sense of remoteness from politics and even more so with European questions (political distance); a tendency to define Europe outside the self, as a fiction (tendency to externalise); the absence of an affirmation of a personal and general opinion on the subject (deprivation of the point of view).

A remote, invisible Europe

The interviewees of the excentred mode are, or feel, powerless in the interview situation. Even beyond the theme on which their opinion is solicited, the idea of giving political judgements in public makes them uncomfortable. Talking politics is not something self-evident to them, especially on a distant and technical subject such as Europe, on which they have no opinion prior to the interview. Seeing as they have to face the solicitation of the interviewer, they attempt to explain why the questions are beyond them. Because the subject has no political or practical significations for most of them, they are simultaneously forced to deal with (the interview situation, Europe) and to deal without (a point of view, knowledge, and experience of Europe). They try to piece together answers with snippets of every-day experience and generalities without ever really succeeding in linking them to Europe. Such argumentative improvisation, which is incidental in the sense that it is imposed by the interaction between the interviewer and the interviewee, does not produce a solid point of view on Europe.

Europe really doesn't affect me. Well, except for the Euro. Of course! But otherwise, no, not at all. I don't really feel concerned. I told you, I don't feel European because Europe doesn't affect me.

(FR, M, 27, unemployed cook)

The interview feels like a trial to them, and they ostensibly show their surprise and disarray when the questions are formulated. The interviewee's wait-and-see attitude and discomfort, contrasting with the interviewer's supposed authority, implicitly transform the interview into a school test, i.e., an evaluative and asymmetric interaction, far from ordinary political conversation.[15] This shift from the original framework of the interaction can be observed in the long silences following the questions or between bits of answers, as well as the many apparent contradictions[16] expressed in the interviews.

[Europe?] It's something positive. Well, because it's nice to be more... hmm... amongst the big ones. Because there are many big ones, and they're going to swallow the small ones, so we need to... [later] After everything I told you, I think I probably don't have much of an opinion. Because I'm not interested... hmm... the word 'interest' isn't... maybe I'm uninterested...

(FR, F, 70, former housewife)

Thus, interviewees give judgements which neither claim to the objectivity of dialogism (decentred mode) nor to the irrefutable character of concrete experience (socio-centred mode).

Expressions of an opinion without a point of view

These modes of reaction do not have the properties of a founded point of view on Europe. They appear fragile, fragmented, artificial, and are often ridiculed by their own authors. These 'opinions by eclipse' (Gaxie 1990) are indeed expressed with little self-assurance. This can be interpreted as a way of showing just how little they value what they say and of pointing out the fact that the interviewer's questions are not suited to their competences. If they conform to the interaction unfolding before them, they only do so on a superficial level and because they feel they are forced to. Often, these interviewees show goodwill when the interview begins. Progressively, the feeling of foreignness and abstraction they claim to have in relation to Europe affects their willingness to play the game of questions and an-

15. In collective interviews, this dimension is less present because of the social proximity of the respondents and the less central role played by the interviewer/evaluator. While most participants experience the same difficulties in replying to questions from the interview template, they manage to feel entitled to give their opinion by collectively shifting the frame and the vocabulary of the interview.

16. Contradictory only in relation to the dominant definition of opinion, i.e. the expression of a consistent attitude based on specific reasons.

swers. Some retreat and only reply to admit their incompetence, which they laugh off with a sometimes bitter self-mockery. The absence of a point of view on the subject forces them to give snippets of opinions throughout the interview without any overall coherence. Relying on ethical principles ('It is better to not go to war') and common sense assertions ('United we stand, divided we fall'), they stick to rather vague general statements, which ultimately do not allow them to sustain a point of view throughout the duration of the interview: little European countries united against the superpowers of the world or the noble original European idea.

So, to me, Europe, in order to be able to counter the US or the other superpowers, like China, we need to be able to get together to be stronger, to me unity is strength.

(FR, F, 30, accountant)

The idea was to find a way to unite countries to prevent them from attacking each other. That was it, that's how Europe was born. And then there are details I don't know about.

(FR, F, 25, teacher)

When they are expressed, positions are most often based on domestic experiences. The critique of the Euro, and specifically of its consequences such as the decline in purchasing power is thus mentioned in many interviews. However, this 'experience' is not always linked to European institutions; it is associated with a vague 'Europe'.

[When among friends, would you say you discuss European issues often, occasionally or never?] Very rarely. There were some opportunities for discussion at the time when the media were talking about the introduction of the Euro [...]. But it was about the Euro's effects; I can't say it was a discussion on Europe.

(IT, M, 38, steelworker)

Some French interviewees refer to the constitutional text that they received in the post at the time of the referendum. But this experience also serves as an illustration of their distance from Europe: they did not read the voluminous, incomprehensible text and ultimately came to see it as a wasteful extravagance, a symbol of how out of touch with reality 'Brussels' is. And once the illustrative virtues of this failed encounter with Europe have been exhausted, the interviewees tend to switch off during the interview, and fall into laconism or even silence, which protects them from the symbolic violence of the interview. In addition to knowledge and experience of Europe, these interviewees also lack registers of social identification. The 'I' does not allow any singular point of view to be structured, the 'we', which generally refers to politically and socially inconsistent and moving categories (peers, colleagues, friends or family members), does not seem to be embedded in any community of condition linked to any concrete situation and is only defined implicitly, as opposed to undetermined 'they' and 'them'.

The Euro, all that stuff, well, I don't really care... I can't say whether I'm for or against it... [...] Europe? We [me and my friends] we don't care about Europe, so... I never talk about it. The older people, though, they say 'Yeah, the Euro pisses us off' and all that.

(FR, F, 27, unskilled worker)

While their embedded allegiances allow other interviewees to position themselves in relation to Europe, here, the interviewees' social worlds are completely separate from European problems. They generally belong to the most fragile and dominated sectors of society: unemployed, under-qualified workers, blue-collar workers, housewives, etc. Nevertheless, some of them are not totally deprived of all forms of educational, economic and social resources (graduates, teachers or executives). While they tend to have a distant relationship with politics, they are occasionally able to say something about national politics, and sometimes be interested in it. Yet, they suffer from the absence of material and/or symbolic links to Europe.

'Couldn't care less', guilty indifference and fragmented critique (interstitial postures of the external mode)

Some of the extracts quoted above express indifference towards Europe and a claim that it is not a personal concern. The feeling of exclusion thus leads to a 'couldn't care less' attitude, which characterises a certain popular outlook towards the serious, esoteric world of politics (Hoggart 1969; Eliasoph 1990). This attitude is mainly observed with blue-collar workers, employees, unemployed persons or those who have relatively little education – interviewees who are deprived of social, economic and cultural forms of capital allowing them to conceive Europe as a space of economic and cultural exchanges. As they lack the resources to travel (money, free time, command of a foreign language), Europe remains abstract to them, and its opportunities are seen as benefiting others ('bosses' or 'politicians'). Their exclusion from Europe should be first understood as a consequence of their economic, cultural and political marginalisation. Like many interviewees of the socio-centred mode, they belong to the middle and lower social segments, but do not identify themselves to a class, insofar as their position in the social space is not politically structured. The numerous young workers in industry or services in this category of interviewees have little politicisation.[17] They also tend to have irregular professional trajectories, marked by mobility and alternating periods of unemployment and employment, which prevents their genuine socialisation to the wage-earner's condition. Just as they are isolated in the face of precariousness and of their own aspirations (Schwartz 1990), they seem to have no ports of call on the territory of politics, let alone European affairs.

At odds with this 'couldn't care less' posture, lack of knowledge of Europe can also be experienced through a feeling of guilt. Other interviewees, who are objectively better equipped in terms of education and professional socialisation,

---

17. This is obviously a consequence of the declining culture of collective and political action in working-class environments (Beaud and Pialoux 1999).

perceive Europe as a political object, something they think deserves attention based on the prevailing social norms, which they are socially not likely to question. This posture is often adopted by women, who experience their lack of interest in Europe as an issue of citizenship ('I'm not a good citizen') and as a result of their personal laziness, which causes guilt ('I feel like it's not right when I say I'm excluded and I'm not informed, when I myself don't really seek out the information'). Beyond the gender-based interpretation – the theme of the interview activates a more deferential feminine relationship to politics (Achin *et al.* 2007) – for these interviewees, the impossibility of producing a point of view results more generally from the impossibility of identifying themselves with social groups that are mobilised or politically structured by Europe. Many interviewees attest to the key role of family and friends in the definition of the self, arguably due to the failure or the disenchantment of more socially integrative forms of identification (the Nation, the profession, the generation).

Lastly, unlike the indifferent interviewees who either 'couldn't care less' or feel guilty, some interviewees who do not have any actual point of view on Europe appear, however, to care about it. While they only sporadically trace back certain actions to Europe, they manage to say something about it by applying opinions they have developed on other subjects. Focused on the problem of unemployment, a young female employee in the hotel and restaurant sector relates all the questions to this issue:

> [Asked about the enlargement] I know that in terms of agriculture, we're going to have the first Polish farmers coming into France. [On public services] Precisely, there's going to be even more unemployment in France if we bring in foreign companies. [On business relocations] They have the right to relocate; supposedly it doesn't create unemployment in France but when you see all the factories closing, all the people who are unemployed... [On the VAT] So, with a 19.5 per cent VAT, there are no new jobs. If we weren't in Europe, France wouldn't need the others' opinion and would just do what it feels like.

(FR, F, 24, receptionist in a hotel-restaurant)

In this type of posture, judgements are scattered throughout the interview without any attempt at coherence. Their reliance on partly politicised elements of identification brings these interviewees closer to the socio-centred mode, although their prevalent feeling remains that of being external to Europe.

Conclusion

When we set out to study the ways of talking about Europe, we focused on the existence of practical knowledge and non-specialised, everyday methods used to deal with political Europe. Rather than highlighting political opinions and attitudes, we wanted to investigate the process of articulating a point of view and its conditions of possibility, in a situation where respondents disposed of diverse (and often missing) resources. In this research perspective, two elements of conclusion should be underscored.

Table 7.1: Talking about Europe: Tendential and interstitial modes of solicited opinions on political Europe

		Decentred mode	Socio-centred mode	External mode
Registers of social identification	Posture towards Europe	Closeness to political Europe	Sectoral relationship to political Europe	Distant relationship to political Europe
		Consistent interest in political Europe	Intermittent interest in political Europe	Distance towards political Europe
		Involvement	Sectorised involvement	Detachment
	Uses of the self	Universalised 'I'	Personalised and socially embedded 'we'	Politically undetermined 'I-we'
	Type of support on the political 'territory'	Appropriation and ability to circulate on the political territory	Limitation or delineation of specific political territory	Lack of determination of a specific/political territory
Resources used to produce a point of view	Type of knowledge mobilised on Europe	Impersonal knowledge (Main sources: media, public debates, educational and academic knowledge)	Personal knowledge (Main sources: social experiences, the 'field', everyday life)	Knowledge and experience not relatable to Europe
		Mastery of different elements of the public debate (legitimisation)	Reference to some issues of public debate (justification)	Ignorance of European issues (distancing)
		Personal experience as illustration	Personal experience as evidence	Personal experience as anecdotes

(Contd.)

Table 7.1: (Contd.)

		Decentred mode	Socio-centred mode	External mode
Resources used to produce a point of view	Producing an opinion on Europe	Prone to hold a singularised point of view (decentring, dialogism) (tend towards) Objectivity Making opinions coherent with public debate (transparency) Generalisation	Prone to hold a particular point of view (socio-centring) (assert) Subjectivity Effort to justify with actual experience (personalisation) Relative generalisation from experience	Prone to hold opinions without specific point of view (externalising) (admit feeling of) Confusion Fragmentation of the opinions (opacity) Generalities
	Interstitial modalities	European 'I' Empathetic 'I' Locution with argumentative function/ production of a logic effect	Egocentric 'we' Fragmentary judgment Metaphors and analogies / production of a justification	'Couldn't care less' Detached 'I' or guilty indifference Digression/laconism
	Expectation towards Europe	Demand of clarity	Demand of materiality	Absent or confused demand

First, we have seen that unlike national politics, which produces a tangible world of administrations, systems, personalities and opposing programmes, Europe is often perceived by interviewees as a complex, invisible and elusive organisation. Hence, by imposing the theme of Europe and the problems related to it to solicit opinions, the interview template heightens the individuals' unequal dispositions to respond politically to political questions. The major inequalities we have observed in the ability to deal with audience effects and the symbolic violence of the interview show that the legitimacy in giving opinions on political Europe hinges on social factors, just as much as the legitimacy in giving opinions on national politics, but in a different way. Indeed, discussing and evaluating European problems entails having encountered them through access to legitimate knowledge (secondary and university education, information in media, activism) or through practical experiences (professional activities, trips, etc.). These possibilities of encountering Europe, however, are, on the one hand, reserved to certain social profiles, and on the other hand, limited by the relative invisibility of the interventions of the European institutions themselves. For this reason, the threshold of access to Europe generally seems very high, including for individuals who are well endowed with economic or cultural resources that usually help them to 'talk politics' more easily. This relativisation of the effect of assigning status partly contradicts the classic studies that link level of education, level of income and support for the EU.

Then, we have laid particular emphasis on the interviewees' identification with a number of social worlds and categories. By studying them as resources used to support, justify or withdraw a self defined in relation to Europe, we have shown how these worlds are likely to converge with Europe or not. Europe remains a vague political object, with few identifiable symbols, and there are therefore many available angles to formulate a point of view: the founding philosophical principles, economic imperatives, distributive policies (Common Agricultural Policy, ERDF), normative action, the cultural or geographical space, competition between social systems, economies, companies and workers... By observing the types of knowledge and personal experience used to discuss and judge Europe, we can see that it 'comes' to interviewees in various ways, and does not always have meaning in relation to their horizon of existence, even if they are educated and qualified. But while the ability to express a political judgement on Europe is less widespread than for other now routine national political objects, the ability to judge political Europe upon request is also more diversified than studies on the sociology of political opinion have claimed so far. The differences in exposure to Europe and its identification with various social universes are probably too often neglected in studies based on the secondary interpretation of Eurobarometer data. Aside from the violence inflicted on raw data, the mechanics of big numbers tends to reduce the social contingency of people's lives to a small handful of variables. Yet, in practice, opinions remain to a large extent impermeable to statistical reasoning.

chapter eight | producing opinions on european questions: a specific competence?

Patrick Lehingue

It is widely acknowledged and deplored that the European citizens' information level on different aspects of European construction is low. But symptomatically, this problem is often neglected or downplayed in *ad hoc* surveys which often reflect expert preoccupations much more successfully than those of citizens. Thus, out of the nearly 150 questions (or sub-questions) in the 2007 Eurobarometer survey wave, only twenty attempted to investigate the interviewees' level of information. Furthermore, out of these twenty questions, seventeen focused on subjective feelings of being well informed, and only three closed-ended questions can be considered as partial measurements of the interviewees' cognitive resources. No cross tabulation allowed for an understanding of the rather uneven social breakdown of these elements of knowledge. Thus, it is implicitly assumed that one can understand what 29,222 Europeans think of Europe (2007 sample) regardless of what they actually know and regardless of who they are socially. With a focus on acquired and required information, this chapter will investigate the European specificity on the now classic issue of competence in producing opinions.

For some fifty years, the most in-depth political sociology studies have converged, despite a few terminological differences, on several empirically confirmed observations:

– The political competence[1] of citizens is generally limited, as is their knowledge and comprehension of phenomena usually labelled as political.
– This competence is very unequally distributed in society, and remains generally linked to the logics of domination that define, structure and organise the social space.
– This level and this social distribution inform relationships to politics both in terms of general interest in political issues (and the possibility to recognise them and give a detailed personal judgement on them) and in terms of specific electoral behaviours (unequal probability of being registered on voting lists, voting regularly, and producing votes with stable patterns).

Based on repeated semi-directed interviews over a period of two years carried out with a contrasting (if not representative) sample of twenty-two people who

---

1.   Here, as it will allow us to discuss the distinction between technical competence and statutory competence (or self-empowerment), thereby distinguishing a 'cognitive' dimension (accumulated knowledge liable to be mobilised) from a 'juridical' dimension, we borrow the French terminology used especially by P. Bourdieu and D. Gaxie.

were already acquainted with the interviewers,[2] we argue the following: As expected, the interviewees' amount of information on European institutional issues is related to their general political competence (in this case, tested with questions concerning France) and to their positions in the social space. However, their linkage suggests a much higher threshold of accessibility to European problems than to 'national' issues, or, in other words, reveal the necessity of possessing a 'specific technical competence' when producing an opinion on Europe. To some extent, this elevation of the level required in order to express a sufficiently well-argued, articulated and informed judgement on 'Europe' is a result of the lack of opportunities for interviewees to make up an argument based on cognitive shortcuts and other auxiliary resources that many analysts offer citizens (for example in closed questions), thereby (sometimes quite generously) granting them the status of judges, enlightened enough to make conscious choices. However, in an apparent paradox, and in certain specific circumstances (an electoral mobilisation such as the French referendum on the ratification of the European constitutional treaty in 2005), and for some social agents (mainly young and less informed), the lack of technical competence –when it is too openly stressed – can sometimes trigger a burgeoning statutory competence allowing the less competent to express themselves on (and in general, against) texts that are clearly presented as too complicated for them.

Three tests of technical competence

Methodological notice

Our idea was, during one of the interview waves (the second), to construct, on a strictly and voluntarily cognitive base, several scales of political competence, objectified through (evidently arbitrary) 'scoring' (distributing points for each answer to the three types of questions asked). The determination of average scores was meant to 'rank' the interviewees, and especially – and this is indeed where the potential interest of the system lies – to compare these 'rankings' (are they congruent?), to match them with the interviewees' social characteristics, and with broader discourses in response to more open questions on Europe asked during previous interviews (opinions on the accession of Turkey) or subsequent interviews (on the referendum on the European constitutional treaty).

The first competence test ('the portraits test') consisted in showing seven photos of political figures (M.-G. Buffet, T. Blair, A. Juppé, Marine Le Pen, L. Parisot...[3]) to the interviewees and asking them to tell their names, the organisa-

---

2.   Quotations are drawn from a corpus of interviews conducted between 2005 and 2007 at the CURAPP research institute of Amiens by a group of researchers (F. Buton, D. Delacourt, F. Krawczyk, C. Marchand, P. Lehingue, N. Mariot, S. Rozier and A. Vauchez) working on the social embeddedness of political preferences. I thank them all for giving me the opportunity to present these initial and partial results, whose interpretation here should be considered as mine only.

3.   Marie-George Buffet is the first secretary of the French communist party since 2001; Alain Juppé is a former Prime Minister and current mayor of Bordeaux; Marine Le Pen is Jean-Marie Le Pen's

tion to which they belong, to say which mandates they have held and which functions they have exercised, and to formulate a judgement on each of them.

The second test ('the drawings test') consisted in submitting six photos (a young girl of North-African origin wearing a tricoloured flag as a headscarf during a march, a picture from a campaign of the Ministry of Social Affairs on 'the elderly and solitude') or humoristic sketches (a drawing from *Le Monde* cartoonist Plantu depicting a couple; the husband shouting to his wife: 'You, in politics? You don't even know how to fake an invoice'...). The goal was to assess the interviewees' capacity to explain the situations using terms of the established political debate.

The last test ('Europe') consisted very classically in a series of open questions to which the interviewees were free to answer in more or less detail and with more or less words.[4]

All these questions were then coded ('graded') according to the scope of the answers provided; with scales from 0 to 20 on each of these cognitive tests for comparison purposes.

Even though it is based on a small sample (n=22 individuals subjected to about thirty questions), and the statistical treatment (even reduced to the calculation of an average, standard deviations, and pair correlations) presupposes the comparability of individuals (in this case, of the interview situations) and the commensurability of the three tests carried out, this experiment, which would need to be reproduced on a larger scale, can be represented using the table below:[5]

---

daughter and a prominent member of the FN; Laurence Parisot has been the head of the MEDEF employers' union since 2005.

4. *What does the Maastricht Treaty evoke for you? Do you remember the names of the founding countries of the European common market? What does the acronym CAP mean to you? In 2005 there was a lot of discussion about the Bolkestein Directive; do you remember what that is? Approximately, what was the percentage of 'no' votes in the 2005 referendum on Europe?* In case the interviewee was unable to reply, which happened frequently, the interviewers provided some cues (for instance, CAP = Common Agricultural Policy) in order to continue the interview.

5. The comparability of these interviews is an issue, and scoring and standardising answers only superficially solves the problem. The comparison must indeed take into account the following: the types of interactions between interviewers and interviewees and their degree of familiarity; the stakes of the interview (not losing face, not making the other lose face); the way each interviewer deals with the interview template; their desire to 'come to the rescue' of struggling interviewees by making suggestions in order to prevent the interaction from deteriorating; lastly, our somewhat naive announcement that these tests would be like 'games', as we assumed that this experiment would soften the symbolic violence which inevitably comes with such 'questioning' on what people know and what they can tell from it. The degree of comparability of the tests, which, although they are all cognitive, sometimes require different skills (the ability to take a cartoon seriously and to decode it, for instance) is also problematic in many respects.

	Harmonised Average /20	Standard deviation	Correlation coefficients		
			Average 3 tests	Portraits test	Drawings test
Avg. 3 tests	8.7	3.8	1		
Portraits test	10.1	4.1	0.73	1	
Drawings test	8.5	4.4	0.80	0.55	1
Europe test	7.5	5.4	0.88	0.68	0.7

The purely quantitative study of the results of these three political competence tests, which for many interviewees were a trial (*'Boy! I'm useless!'*), allows us to draw three conclusions:

1) As the correlation coefficients suggest, the cognitive competences tested for each interviewee in three contrasting manners and on three different dimensions, are inter-correlated, with the 'Europe test' being the one that is statistically the most associated to the others, and, supposing that this indicator makes sense, the most correlated to 'average' political competence. In other words, the competence on producing an opinion on European problems probably follows the same patterns observed for 'ordinary' political competence (i.e. linked to 'national' problems, issues, institutions or political figures). This ability is even probably more dependent on the general political competence here than it would be for other subjects.

2) Information literacy is generally weaker on European issues, with lower average 'scores'; for half of the interviewees, cognitive performance proved to be lower on these subjects. The European competence seems to be more selective, and confessions of ignorance are more frequent and more likely, which previous comparable tests have already suggested.[6]

3) Similarly, standard deviations are higher on Europe-related questions, with a wider range of 'scores'.[7] This might confirm the necessity to be endowed with a specific technical competence in order to formulate judgements on Europe.

Although the size of the sample prevents us from over-generalising, the inequalities in cognitive competence observed confirm recurrent observations on gender (lower response rates for women and/or more frequent spontaneous confessions of ignorance), age (generally lower scores for the youngest) and socio-professional status (when interviewees come from the same social class, relative

6. See for instance Favre and Offerlé 2007– especially the passage on 'the capacity of questions to test cognitive differences between social groups'.

7. A similar observation can be made for the aforementioned study on cognitive performances of French students: apart from the question on the writings of Tocqueville, it is the question on EU Member States which produced the highest relative standard deviations between students based on both their parents' professions.

differences in numbers of years of formal education seem to account for discrepancies in information levels). As our sample does not include individuals who are political activists or have a practical relationship with Europe (e.g. farmers, fishermen, truck drivers or people living in border areas), it is here impossible to assess the weight and the impact of these compensatory attributes. Tourist experiences abroad however undoubtedly increase the dispositions to respond, regardless of social status.

At this point the question still stands: Can we argue that there is a globally weak and unequal competence, which is even weaker and more unequally distributed when it comes to European questions, based only on such uncertain and rough indicators?[8] Several elements derived from our sample suggest that this is possible.

First, European questions appear to most interviewees as esoteric and byzantine, unreal and distant, strange and foreign hardly a year after the 2005 referendum, in which all interviewees claim to have participated. When asked which issues they would like to see discussed during the forthcoming presidential campaign, the most pressing matters that, according to them, need to be resolved in France and the decisions that they themselves would take if by any chance they were to be elected President of the Republic, their answers did not include any mention of a Europe-related measure, issue, or action. When asked again, a month before the presidential election on 27th April 2007, which issues that they wish the candidates would address, the interviewees (including the those who had previously declared themselves openly and unconditionally pro-European) failed to mention the European level.

The objection concerning the artefactual character of such tests needs to be examined.[9] An interviewee (a 22-year-old student in art history, with a working class background, and earning her living from part-time jobs) explains that the reasons for her opposition to the European Constitutional Treaty (ECT) are due to the fear of business relocation or social dumping, and when interviewed some time later on a closely related topic – 'the Bolkestein Directive' – says that this does not ring a bell. Such an example appears to invalidate the evidential strength of cognitive indicators; even when one is completely unaware of an issue's official political labelling, one can still provide arguments on that issue. However, upon closer examination, it reveals, to some extent, the disinvested, uncertain, vague, unstable character and the lack of coherence of the opinions uttered by the interviewee throughout the interviews[10] and the misunderstandings to which she is exposing

---

8. This legitimate interrogation echoes the objections formulated since the publication of Converse's typologies in 1964 about studies focusing on the question of political competence (or political 'sophistication'), which sometimes derive from a will to deny the scientific (and political) value of this problem.

9. In short, as they are produced by academics for academics, these indicators are accused of showing nothing but the ethnocentrism of their authors.

10. Originally a fervent S. Royal supporter, and hostile to F. Bayrou six months before the presidential

herself and the interviewers in their interpretations.

- Did you vote in the European Constitution referendum?
- Yes!
- Do you remember how you voted?
- 'No', I voted 'No'.
- Could you remind me why?
- What made me think twice was the decentralisation [sic] of companies, factories, especially French ones to Poland or to Eastern countries.
- Right, you did tell me that before. Do you know when you decided to vote that way, was it a last minute thing or…?
- Not long before going to vote, I was undecided on this subject. There are positive points but it is this particular one that made me vote 'no'.
- Which argument convinced you the most?
- This one, the one I just told you about.

Twenty minutes later:

- What about the Bolkestein Directive?
- Oh, I have no idea.
- Does it ring a bell, or not at all?
- No, what is it?
- It is the name of a guy, a European commissioner. He was mentioned a lot during the European Constitution referendum campaign, you see?
- No, what did he have to do with that?
- Well, in short, it's a matter of liberalisation of labour in the EU…
- Free movement of workers…?
- Yes, that's it, free movement of workers and the liberalisation of labour in the EU…
- Not bad!
- Yeah, but at the same time it was the labour laws of the workers' country of origin that was to be applied. So, for example, there was always this dumb example of a Polish plumber coming to work in France, and you could make him work as much as you please, and pay him Polish wages, etc.
- Ah, okay so he wasn't defending European labour laws. Wasn't this problem raised?

---

elections, she later claimed that she had hesitated up to the end between Bayrou and Besancenot, even though nothing from her past or present perceptions of the campaign allows us to explain her 'volatility', apart from the social networks she was successively involved in (in France, then in Portugal when she stayed as part of the Erasmus exchange programme), and how distanced from the political universe she is.

- No.
- Yeah, it's always the same people who take advantage of things.

As questionable as they are, cognitive questions are often sufficient to assess the capacity of individuals to interpret political discourses, to size them up and to spot, even crudely, the expression of the interests that they want to defend and or oppose.[11] Though they may be overly blunt indicators, they reveal other more qualitative and more subtle dimensions of political competence such as 'the capacity to associate the different points mentioned, to produce a coherent viewpoint, to systematise' or 'the capacity to have in-depth discussions on a point mentioned', to make spontaneous (and politically relevant) digressions; the capacity to de-centre, to distance oneself (adopting several viewpoints) and more generally, the capacity to put oneself in others' shoes (empathising, taking into consideration a logic that is unfamiliar or different from one's own logic, a capacity that is socially more developed in women); the capacity to vary the methods of reasoning used: logical (for instance, deductive), through associations ('this reminds me of…'), or using metonymy; the level of commitment or personal involvement in the production of a viewpoint ('Personally, I think that…'), or even the capacity to challenge the interviewer's questions or to prevent or anticipate the purposes of interaction.[12]

Based on their answers to questions on the accession of Turkey to the EU during our first wave of interviews, the interviewees, regardless of their positions (favourable, against, self-confident, perplexed or uncertain) on the substance of the issue, can be classified according to these criteria which have proven to be often congruent, and apart from one case,[13] generally coherent with their 'cognitive performances'. But we have observed more especially that these different capacities to defend and to argue a viewpoint are more frequently and more easily activated or mobilised when it comes to producing an opinion on 'internal' issues rather than European ones (besides, almost always, the relationship with Europe – when there is one – is always considered from a strictly French perspective[14]).

Producing an opinion on Europe: the case of the European Constitutional Treaty

When discussing the institutional futures of Europe, some of the older interviewees tend to respond in very confident ways, activating a particular 'class habitus',

---

11. For a confirmation based on questionnaires, which in France would, however, be considered as constitutional law multiple-choice tests, see Delli Carpini and Keeter (1996).

12. I owe these criteria to the critical observations made by Sabine Rozier, whose terminology I borrow here.

13. A liberal surgeon, about 40 years old, with little interest in politics, is yet eloquent on the subject of Turkey, about which he alternates perspectives, but at the same time he refuses to take the game of cognitive questions seriously and answers evasively or ironically.

14. I borrow this synthetic observation from C. Marchand.

a perception of the world based on binary oppositions between big/small or boss/worker. Daniel, 63 years old, who holds a CAP[15] in mechanics, retired after having spent all his professional life in the same company (from skilled worker to staff manager before being laid off for economic reasons). He lives alone in a small village in the Northern region of Picardie, voted for Jospin in the first round and for Chirac in the second round of the 2002 presidential elections:

- – Have you followed the campaign closely?
- – Yeah! Of course I followed a bit. What Bayrou said… he also said 'no' I think? Same for De Villiers. To me, this Europe they are constructing is for the rich and the capitalists. We don't want anything to do with it. Too much capitalism. And too much capitalism means more poor people…If you give the current government a chance, they will end up taking away half of your salary. At X [the name of the company where he was working], they took away 2000 francs from the equipment supervisor. He was earning 11 or 12,000 francs and they took 2000 away. They told him 'you earn too much for what you do' even though he had that job all his life. You think that's fair? There are workers who work for peanuts already, and if we continue to vote this way, we'll end up getting less and less. When you're a worker, you have to think 'social' rather than capitalism, industry, etc.
- – I understand, but there are not only workers in France…
- – No, but there are more of them
- – Hmm, I don't know… the 'workers' category as in…
- – I don't know them all, the categories, really but maybe, maybe… those who are right wing supporters, some people, they wanted this law to pass…
- – They voted 'yes'…
- – There is another category… more humane, from the middle class, who perhaps thought, yes, this all sounds good, but maybe we have to think about those who've got less… not those who are very rich. The rich do not give a damn about the poor.

Supposing we identify them, the positions of national-level politicians might act as 'cues', information signals, or as compasses of sorts, allowing voters to find their way and make up for the aforementioned cognitive deficiencies. Although the referendum campaign on the ratification of the ECT was, according to the observers, remarkably lively and stirred heated debates within primary groups (family, neighbourhood, friends and colleagues…),[16] its impact was probably more superficial than has been claimed, feared or hoped. A year after the consultation,

---

15. Certificat d'aptitude professionnelle: certificate earned following vocational classes and work internship.

16. In stating that they did not discuss this with anyone, a third of our interviewees contradict the ideal picture of a generalised deliberative arena.

three of our interviewees find it difficult to remember how they voted, and do not try to hide it; one of them mistakes the issue for that of the accession of Turkey. Even amongst those who hesitated a great deal, no one says that they would vote differently if they were to vote again now, and close to half of the interviewees do not remember the main argument that influenced their vote that day ('it was a long time ago ...')[17] or only remember it vaguely.

- Did you vote?
- Anne (58, holder of a BA in Humanities, retired teacher, voted for Chirac in 2002 in both rounds): – Yes.
- How did you vote?
- I voted 'yes'.
- Why?
- Because I find the idea of a European union to face other great nations interesting... China amongst others...
- And do you remember the moment when you actually decided to vote 'yes' or...?
- [long silence] The moment?
- Yeah, yeah, what were the reasons?
- Yes, Yes, but I forgot all that since, I forgot all that, you know, water under the bridge... No, I don't remember anything, we were...when I was into it, you see, at the time, since there were all these ... debates, at the time, I would have been able to explain to you, but since then I ...
- You followed quite a bit then...
- Yeah, exactly and ...
- And your opinion changed in the course of the campaign or...?
- Oh, no! I was always for it.
- And you never doubted?
- No!
- And were there arguments that reinforced your choice of voting 'yes' or...?
- Oh, yes! There has to...there must have been some but, I told you, I don't remember anything
- And if you had to give one argument?
- Yeah, I would say, the power of... of this union of countries against others.
- There was also talk about a social treaty too, the lack of a social aspect. I don't know, all these issues, didn't they...
- Oh no! I really don't remember a thing, not a single thing. When was it again?

---

17. Needless to say, all these interviewees have the poorest cognitive performances in our sample.

- A year ago.
- Really?! What were the social ideas?
- To the Treaty's opponents, it was that Europe was going to be all about competition and that indeed there was no...
- I see! With the Polish or the ...
- That they would threaten public services for instance...
- Hmm... hmm, I'm sorry... I... I don't follow enough anymore to...

Hence, it is worth questioning the status and the degree of reality of these 'shortcuts' – national campaign arguments on European issues – especially since they have so little impact once the election is over.[18]

If we leave out periods of mobilisation, such as referendum or election campaigns, the double hypothesis supposing there was a reliable inventory of these 'cognitive shortcuts',[19] the aforementioned hypothesis of a specific technical competence, or, in terms of giving opinions on European issues, the hypothesis of a higher threshold of accessibility – could be backed-up by the scarcity of information signals from European institutions (see Chapter 10). The absence of a precise location (Brussels, Strasbourg, The Hague, Frankfurt), the impossibility to personalise debates and as a result to perceive them in terms of political allegiances, physical appearance, nationality or social characteristics of a policy-maker, the baroque and changing institutional architecture, the decision-making process considered as meandering and anonymous, the difficulty of identifying (positively or negatively) the source of Community policies, the complexity or elasticity of the fields of competence: most interviewees mention these characteristic features of a vague set of institutions that they have trouble characterising quickly and typifying roughly, regardless of their vote in the 2005 referendum.[20]

Answering the question 'What made you decide on the treaty?', Amélie (59, a retired nurse, left-leaning tendencies, voted 'yes' to the ECT) says: 'I suppose I thought it's better to try to improve things... because, well, you believe what you're told, because in a way you don't have enough knowledge to know if you're being told the truth, for instead in EDF-GDF I don't know who's telling

18. For a critique of this alternative paradigm (in a few words, although voters know little and their degree of information is very unequal, this cognitive paucity in no way invalidates the principle of equality of citizens insofar as 'shortcuts' allow the less interested citizens to produce a judgement), see Gaxie 2007.

19. While they cannot be faulted for their lexical imagination ('rules of thumb', 'accessibility bias', 'judgemental heuristics', 'cues', 'low information signals' and/or 'shortcuts'), the advocates of this 'new orthodoxy' have yet to clarify the distinction between these concepts by providing a working definition that would allow one to differentiate between them, and that would elaborate on the conditions of the appropriation and use of these cognitive shortcuts by 'ordinary' citizens.

20. In this universe where there are few practical points of entry, the establishment of a single currency is the only exception, albeit often used to crystallise criticisms (high cost of living and insidious decrease of purchasing power).

the truth, so I can't give an opinion on Europe. I think they told us that the Nice treaty was less good than the one they were suggesting to work with twenty-five states, and what I thought was that the most important thing was to try and have the twenty-five countries work together even if it didn't work that well yet. And to say 'no' because it's not going to work well enough, I find that ridiculous because that means there's a standstill… and to stand still is to move back. But those technicians, they still aggravate us with their recommendations, the texts and all that, because they cannot stop working, them.

– Which technicians?

– Well, all the European administration, they still churn out all these directives…so I voted 'yes' anyway because…though I actually knew that it was not very social and all that.

The structure of Amélie's tentative argument (a critique of technocracy counterbalanced by the phrase 'To stand still is to move back') is symptomatically the same as that of two vehement 'No' voters (who share her dislike of a technocratic approach deemed as not 'social' enough) except that here Max transforms the saying: to go forward too much (when forced to) – is to risk moving back:

Also, they didn't explain it enough, they didn't discuss it enough in the media and on television. They introduced it like a fly in the soup; well, I don't know what you think about it but I think that we were not brought up to speed on the matter in time, there really weren't enough details. (…) The French are not more stupid than the other Europeans. And what pisses me off about all that they are trying to push through is that they do not say things clearly. It's like when you buy something and they give you the general conditions and then you have a tiny asterisk at the bottom with the special conditions and since it's too small you don't read it and if you don't read it you get screwed. And that's what politics are all about. The treaty did not pass. But if it had, who knows what we would have had to deal with! We could have been skinned alive. I think sometimes it's better to take a step back in order to be able to progress better.

(Max, 34, holder of a professional baccalauréat in electronics, came to Paris after passing an exam to work as a technician at France Telecom. He regrets the commercial orientation of his company and plans to change professions and work in the socio-cultural sector)

Technical incompetence and statutory competence: How a 'voice' emerges

In all of these excerpts, a pattern emerges – lack of information – and between the lines, there is an acknowledgement: the interviewees' incompetence. Many responses spontaneously discuss the issue of the knowledge required in order to allow themselves to produce an opinion on European issues. In itself, despite the elitist connotations and the professorial postures such an approach conjures up, this fact argues for raising the issue in cognitive terms, since social agents themselves often spontaneously put the question in those terms.

In sociological research on political competence, technical competence (i.e. cognitive) is closely linked to statutory competence, which allows – and in some situations, forces – individuals to formulate judgements. This self-empowerment, both socially conditioned and required, in return feeds a process of accumulation of informational resources ('noblesse oblige').

Here we can formulate the hypothesis that the lack of technical competence, when it appears as too openly asserted by those who are supposed to be universally capable of producing an opinion, paradoxically generates minimal forms of statutory competence, and thus frees and disinhibits expression. In very different ways, several interviewees attest to this and clearly invalidate the equation: '(technical) ignorance' = '(citizen) incompetence'.

- How do you explain the fact that the 'no' won? ... In this referendum...
- Jacques (CAP craftsman in metallurgy, SNCF employee, FN voter): The 'no', well, it means that the French are not that stupid.
- And could you see other arguments?
- Daniel (63, former specialised worker in early retirement, already cited): I can't remember. I had, I have the book here [he casts a searching glance towards the kitchen windowsill]... You see that: they're having a laugh, aren't they? Can you see the book we have to read?
- Oh, the treaty?
- Yes; I must have thrown it into the garbage bin... [he laughs] Did you see what we had to read? Did you see how small the font is? My...
- You opened it but you never read it?
- Of course not; I'm not gonna read all that. I don't have any time to waste on this bullshit. Did you see the treaty they came up with? They should have made a small manual with an outline of the key points. This was much too complicated.
- It was legal...
- We didn't need any of that. We just needed all the key points, all the basics...I don't know, 200 headers, or something like that, right? ... a book like that...And did you see the price?
- How do you explain the fact that the 'no' won?
- Well, people are not as stupid as, hum... the right-wing. Today everyone is educated. It's either you are not interested and you don't do anything about it, or you are interested and ... But everyone is educated. So, everyone can...
- Some have said that such a vote was short-sighted and narrow-minded, what do you think about that [laughs]?

– They think people are idiots. Those who say that really think people are idiots. There are no idiots. Even the least educated are not stupid, right? They know a lot of things. If you explain to them, they know. They're not dumb, they act. Only the crazies, what do you call them…the mentally ill can't react. The guy who said that, he thinks he's above everyone else. He thinks he's God Almighty, that guy. He's got work to do.

This feeling of wounded dignity, which feeds more or less pronounced forms of 'voice' is particularly found in younger people, who are still experiencing academic evaluation, and have a very hard time dealing with a personal incompetence that they attribute to the disastrous pedagogy of politicians. The type of 'considerations' (Zaller 1992) mobilised or 'popular wisdom' (Gamson 1992[21]) in this case would be 'when in doubt – about purposely hermetic formulations – do not abstain!'

– Did you vote?
– Manon (22, student in Art History, in an unstable situation, has received a left-wing family socialisation but has no asserted political convictions, reveres her father, whose opinion she often adopts on political issues): Yeah, I think I voted. I voted 'no'.
– Do you remember why?
– Oh because I think there was… No, I know! Because I didn't understand a thing! [laughs] It was pure madness! I tried to read it, and I listened to some things, but I didn't understand a thing. Nothing was clear. So, at the same time they said that it was a good thing because… I don't really remember why… and I told myself that it wasn't a good thing because this or that country would be able to access the European Union and I didn't agree. At the same time, they were telling me that it had nothing to do with that, that it didn't necessarily mean that these countries would be in, that these were two different things; in short, I had doubts, so I voted 'no'! There you have it! I had doubts, so I voted 'no' after all. I couldn't understand a thing anyway. I thought, 'on the day it becomes clear, I'll vote 'yes', but this'll teach them to do their job well'. Maybe if my father had told me to vote 'yes', I might have voted 'yes'. Just because he is my father and I feel like he knows everything, but otherwise… there's nothing else…
– And your father, do you remember why he voted 'no'?
– I think it's just that we all didn't understand! We didn't understand and we didn't see the use. We didn't understand the… and we were afraid of change. That's how I felt about it at the time, anyway. I don't want things

---

21. In his research on focus groups, Gamson (1992) distinguishes three types of 'material' allowing 'working people' to express themselves on subjects known to be very complex: media discourse, experiential knowledge, and more diffusely, forms of common sense or popular wisdom, which might be expressed in sayings and proverbs.

to get worse, and I liked Europe how it was just fine. I prefer if things stay the way they are and don't get worse. So in doubt…

– And how do you explain the fact that the 'no' won?

– Well, because in France, word really didn't get around. I voted 'no' myself, but maybe half of the population just didn't understand, like me. You don't understand a thing, so you vote 'no' because you're afraid of screwing up.

– And if you had to do it all over again, would you still do the same thing?

– If I still didn't understand, yes, I would vote 'no'!'

Elyséa (student, 18th arrondissement (Paris), father holder of a CAP in tool making, contract worker in the entertainment sector; mother employee then middle manager in the insurance sector, very sporadic interest in politics):

They give you a constitution that's impossible to read, really difficult to decode, then you feel dumb, and well, it pisses you off.

The hypothesis that the lack of technical competence observed paves the way for the emergence of a statutory competence is appealing because of how unexpected it initially seems and how clearly it is formulated in some interviews. But it cannot be generalised easily.

Indeed, its domain of validity appears significantly limited by the conditions in which we have collected and recorded discourses on Europe (a year after the ECT referendum) and, even more so, by the circumstances in which a judgement on Europe was officially requested (referendum with universal suffrage). Perhaps the uncomfortable distance between the principle of equality of citizens and the widespread perception of informational resources as very limited and unequal partly feeds this paradoxical mechanism. The paucity of expression inherent to electoral procedures (in this case, a binary choice) also reinforces this feeling of indignity: facing such a simple and cut-and-dry alternative, how can one produce an opinion with so little information, without the possibility of ticking one of the 'refuge' boxes in survey questions such as 'yes, rather'/ or 'no, rather not')? Our hypothesis was also validated by the fact that there was the widespread idea (an actual shortcut) that by sending a text which everyone knew (and had personally experienced as) utterly unreadable, 'they' were openly showing 'us' 'their' superiority and thus 'our' ignorance.

Our paradoxical hypothesis quickly finds a limitation in the fact that all the interviewees voted, or at least declared they had voted. What is left to find out, then, is whether below a certain threshold of competence, of understanding or minimal interest in a game perceived as utterly foreign to the problems faced by interviewees on a daily basis, 'exit' might prevail over 'voice'.[22]

---

22. In contradiction with a number of comments enthusiastically praising 'the extraordinary reaction of the people against the elites' that the victory of the 'no' supposedly represented, the in-depth ecological analysis of abstention rates shows that substantial gaps (about 1/3) remained between residential areas and housing estates. It seems that in 2005, these gaps have even become wider since the first European referendum (1992). See Lehingue (2007a) for additional precisions.

chapter nine | the european puzzle: gathering, sorting and assembling piecemeal information

Giuliano Bobba, Katarzyna Jaszczyk and Muriel Rambour

Citizens generally have a very patchy knowledge of Europe. To some extent, this observation applies to all the categories of interviewees, regardless of their age, gender and level of education. This situation is also perceptible in self-assessments of the level of knowledge of institutions and EU policies. According to Eurobarometer 68 (2007), the majority of Europeans still think they lack information on European political issues. Even though the EU claims the development of an efficient information policy is one of its priorities (European Commission 2006), only 18 per cent of Europeans saw themselves as 'very well' or 'fairly well' informed on European issues in 2007.[1] Likewise, in 2008, 47 per cent of respondents disagreed with the assertion that they understand how the EU works. In the media, national daily newspapers cover Europe more often than television news where European issues are marginal (Garcia and Le Torrec 2003; Cepernich 2005; Baisnée 2006). For instance, in Italy, only 5.5 per cent of the entire broadcasting time was devoted to Europe (Osservatorio di Pavia 2009). In France, in 2007, only 2.2 per cent of the subjects treated by television news teams dealt with European affairs (Ina'Stat 2008), less than half the coverage allotted during the referendum on the constitutional treaty in 2005.

European construction frequently appears as a remote preoccupation, with a high level of abstraction and complexity, requiring significant 'cognitive mobilisation' (Inglehart and Rabier 1979). Yet, it is not only mere exposure to European information that determines the level of knowledge on the subject, but also the ability to piece together these dispersed bits of data (Gaxie 2007), to give them meaning according to one's dispositions, knowledge, convictions and pre-existing representations (Neuman *et al.* 1992; Gerstlé 2001). European construction was introduced into the lives of Europeans by successive developments, whose stakes were not always clearly identifiable to citizens unequally prepared to follow the EU's political evolution. This complexity has, for a long time now, contributed to reinforcing the widespread image of an anonymous and 'faceless' Europe. It is therefore particularly tricky to evaluate what citizens 'know' about Europe, especially when mobilising information gathered through in-depth interviews rather than by administering a questionnaire aimed at assessing the knowledge of a given European institution or decision. In this chapter the intention is to study how, in

---

1. In countries studied in this chapter, the proportion of respondents claiming to be 'very well' or 'fairly well' informed was 17 per cent in France, 18 per cent in Italy and 21 per cent in Poland.

a public space where coverage of European topics are diffuse and diverse, individuals manage with the information they receive on European affairs. The focus will be on individuals in France, Italy and Poland. How can ordinary citizens find their way to make sense of a very weakly personalised European political field? Which of the sources do each type of public rely on for its information on Europe? Is information on Europe perceived differently according to the individuals' social properties? Does the level of competence in European affairs vary between citizens from older and newer Member States? The interviews we have conducted were not simple question and answer sessions seeking to ascertain the level of information or the subjective interpretation of being well informed or not. We have let the interviewees develop their thoughts, in order to collect the elements of information they mobilise to discuss Europe, to identify variances in the way a question is understood, and more generally, to highlight the elements of support, practical knowledge and stratagems used to piece together an opinion in an interview situation.

Sources and means of information on Europe

In all countries considered, interviewees identify the media as the main vehicles of European information. Unsurprisingly, only a small number of individuals, mostly belonging to the upper and/or politicised categories, adopt an active attitude towards information, characterised by frequently consulting a relatively wide range of sources (the press, TV and radio, Internet). As Daniel Gaxie has pointed out on political competence, 'it is the best informed who are most likely to seek out information and thus gather even more information' (Gaxie 2007: 750).

The media participate in shaping the citizens' ordinary knowledge on European affairs by imposing certain themes: hence, 'the strong media visibility of a theme influences the public and induces a hierarchisation of priorities' (Gerstlé 1996: 739), even if 'this apparent power of the media, however, depends on [the] person's properties and dispositions' (Gaxie 2003: 335).

The way in which interviewees acquire and perceive information on European issues is mainly determined by their cultural resources, interpretative competences, and their level of interest in politics. In most cases, information produced by media discourses or everyday conversations are the main 'shortcuts' used to formulate a judgement on Europe (Popkin 1991; Gaxie 2007: 740–1). The experience of certain dimensions of European construction, for instance in the context of a professional activity, can also work as a means of information and orient stances. Those who work in the sector of agriculture, who have an intense, yet sectorally limited involvement in European construction, essentially perceive Europe through the regulations it issues. To a 40-year-old French landowner specialised in cattle breeding:

> Seen from the agricultural world, it's an opportunity to market the product... even though behind that there are constraints, of course [...] But then, the negative thing, still as far as my line of work's concerned, is all the legal

aspects imposed by Europe, that would certainly have come a lot later if we were only French...

Through an informational shortcut, the EU is reduced to the standards it enforces. In these sectors, information on Europe mostly comes from professional organisations which provide guidance to help its members navigate a reputedly complex European legislative sea. Asked about his sources of information, a cereal farmer says that he is 'very well informed', without 'any problems', by the 'technical magazines' he claims to read on a regular basis and 'by the union', where, according to him, Europe is 'all they talk about'. He jokingly observes that in his sector, 'people are very well informed, almost too much'.

These categories of the public, who are very competent within the context of their professional preoccupations, and who are sometimes assiduous readers of specialised publications, are at the same time generally helpless when faced with general questions on the EU's functioning or recent developments. Being engaged in a profession which might be assumed to be particularly concerned by a specific European legislation is not a guarantee of broad knowledge on the subject. Asked about the Bolkestein directive, a French plumber says he has 'heard about it' but tells us he is unable to give an informed opinion on the content of the text. When the interviewer reminds him of the directive's theme, he recalls the subject being mentioned during the constitutional treaty campaign: 'Oh, so that's it! The infamous Polish plumber! I keep hearing about it but I don't understand why people talk about the Polish plumber and not about the Polish mason or whatever else'.

In Italy, some interviewees have contacts with various EU organisations for professional reasons and this makes European institutions more visible to them. Such is the case of a young consultant on European projects, who votes for Rifondazione Comunista and has a master's degree. The second thing that occurs to her upon hearing the word 'Europe' is:

> ... the supranational political system that organises Europe. I'm thinking about the European Commission... The Directorates-General that make up the Commission, the other institutions like the Parliament, the Committee of the Regions... I think about them because that's my work.

For more politicised interviewees, information on how Europe works can also be related to the exercise of a political mandate. Such is the case of a French real estate agent, member of a regionalist party and former regional councillor. His interest in politics leads him to seek out information from several sources (regional, national press and Internet), which allows him to have knowledge on themes he says are unfamiliar to the majority of the population: 'There are things that should be simplified for a wider audience, it just so happens that I understand them because I'm interested in them'. A similar discourse can be observed in the Italian case. A high-ranking public manager from Turin expresses doubts that an ordinary citizen who has not studied law or political science might be able to understand the way EU institutions work: 'it's hard to give a positive idea of Europe, because you can clearly see that the citizens, most citizens [...] don't like it, don't understand it'.

When the interviewee is a student or has attended university, information on Europe can be directly related to this academic experience. The degree of precision in the answer, however, is related to the type of coursework. A French student, who is training to become a senior civil servant, hesitantly formulates an answer on the interest in European questions:

I remember when I studied at the IEP [Institute of Political Studies], I was under the impression that Europe was something a bit vague. [...] I didn't read the press all that much at the time... And... I don't know; it didn't really speak to me.

A magistrate in his thirties, who went to the same school, has a more assertive attitude on European subjects, because he had practical experience during an internship, which allowed him to develop a precise and critical outlook on EU enlargement. These two cases show that perceptions of Europe are not only influenced by exposure to information, but also by the experience of Europe.

Also remarkable is the gap between what the interviewees learned at university and their life experiences. A literature student at the University of Turin, also holder of a master's in tourism economics, displays an above average knowledge of EU institutions. But her information on Europe's role in her everyday life as a student remains limited: 'I think somehow Europe has consequences [on my life as a student], but I'm not entirely sure on what exactly, I don't have enough information'.

Direct experience plays a key role for the familiarisation to the EU of many interviewees, especially from the lower and middle categories of society. Their vision of Europe is shaped by their daily contact with a number of realities experienced as interventions of the EU in their familiar world. Knowledge of Europe is in those cases limited to the individual's everyday life. This is demonstrated by the example of an interviewee who owns a house in the south of France, and who associates Europe with the distribution of mail in her village, even though she claims not to have any particular knowledge of the directives on public sectors like the postal service and electricity:

I'm in favour of public services, because they guarantee a measure of equality for the distribution of electricity, of mail. Profits shouldn't be the main priority. But now I fear it could be like in other countries, just to make money. If only for the mail; in the small village I was talking about earlier, three years ago, they took away our post box.

In Poland, for some interviewees, who are often otherwise poorly informed on abstract European issues, concrete personal experience favours a particular approach of Europe, following a synecdochical logic somewhat similar, under certain aspects, to the farmers' perceptions mentioned earlier. A homeless and unemployed woman who has never left Poland builds a reflection on Europe's influence on her life based on the observation of the EU's concrete and perceptible presence in her immediate environment. For her, the changes she detects in the familiar space of her town and of the shelter where she resides become an incarnation of

Europe. Interestingly, this interviewee emphasises the legitimacy of the average citizen, who like her does not have any specific political competence, to express himself or herself on European questions, precisely on the basis of their ordinary experience of Europe in everyday practice, a legitimacy which she contrasts with the statutory legitimacy of politicians:

> I'm not a politician, but right now, here, anybody can say something [about the EU] Even here at the shelter... They give us food: cheese, jam. [...] And precisely, these products come from the European Union, it even says so on the labels. So I think it's a good decision, this accession to the Union.

Among interviewees with little cultural capital, information often spreads via interpersonal relationships, notably in families. A 56-year-old Polish meat-processing worker, whose daughters have often travelled in Europe and have pro-fessional contacts with European organisations, explains that his children, who have university degrees, are the ones who taught him the basics of Europe and opened him up to the world: 'I was ignorant on all these [European] questions because I grew up in another era and it's only my daughters who simply told me about all that and prepared me'.

Other interviewees lacking reliable touchstones on European questions refer to certain opinion leaders. A retired farmer, trained as an electrician and a practising Catholic, remembers her parish priests' words of reassurance in the days that fol-lowed Poland's accession to the EU:

> When people didn't know how to apply for these direct subsidies yet, the priests would encourage them [...] they explained to these poor, hard-working people that they shouldn't be scared, they should measure their fields and all that, go to the municipality to ask for information... What I heard them say was quite positive, at least in my parish: they told them to apply and not to be scared.

The village priest also encouraged her to take part in the referendum on her country's accession to the EU, emphasising the civic duty to vote.

Apart from the generalist audio-visual media, which, as we have seen, devote little time to Europe, well educated and politicised individuals generally seem to favour written sources or to resort to their academic knowledge, whereas inter-viewees who have little cultural capital tend to rely on their concrete experience of Europe or on conversations heard or shared in their social circles (see Chapter 12). Generally, the posture of 'oblique attention for public matters', which is frequently adopted by those 'who might feel attracted to public intrigue when major events such as a war or a scandal occur [...] but usually go about their business with-out trying to influence the course of public affairs' (Cefaï and Pasquier 2003: 49) seems to be particularly present when it comes to European matters. Interviewees thus use readily available instruments to get information on European issues: aca-demic and media references, general or activist for those with a synoptic attitude, and professional activity for those who perceive Europe essentially through the prism of their experience limited to certain concrete manifestations of European construction.

The feeling of being informed on Europe

The state of an individual's knowledge does not only depend on exposure to European information; it mainly hinges on their ability to decode the message conveyed. For most citizens, the EU is thought to have a threshold of cognitive accessibility that is much higher than for national politics. Hence, a shoe salesman on a Polish market sarcastically claims that in Europe 'there's nothing complicated. Everything is just easy as pie… Well, only half of the population doesn't know what a treaty or what the Union is'. A young woman, with a five year university degree, who manages European structural funds observes that:

> Bureaucracy is complicated: in order to do something [in the Union], it's such a winding path that it's hard for an ordinary person to find their way. The Parliament, the Commission… They vote over here, it gets passed on over there… It's witchcraft.

Self-assessments of knowledge need to be analysed with a great deal of caution. Measuring the effective level of competence on European questions from subjective statements on the feeling of being well-informed as is often done can lead to a series of misunderstandings. Interviewees have very diverging representations of what 'being (well) informed' actually means. There is also an interactional effect that sometimes prevents certain actors who are aware of the stakes of the interview situation and eager to 'save face' from admitting their lack of knowledge; answering 'I'm not (well) informed' allows interviewees to avoid having to say 'I don't understand', which can be interpreted as an admission of intellectual weakness.

Despite these limits, the most widespread idea is that there is a deficit of European information, in terms of perceived everyday realities and professional life, as well as the interdependencies between national socio-political life events and the EU. The owner of a French transport business admits that it is hard for him to know who to talk to when he has a specific question regarding his company:

> At this point, I can't see what kind of assistance, what kind of facilitation of my day-to-day management Europe can bring me. We have very little information on Europe. […] We're not informed, we don't know what Europe has brought us. It's a problem.

Interviewees who only have a limited perception of European construction often relate their lack of information to their occupation. A fisherman's wife, who helps with selling the fish and manages the accounts, complains about having only heard about new standards on fishing net size from her colleagues.

In Poland, some interviewees, who generally lack political touchstones, express hesitations on European construction's concrete usefulness. They regret their ignorance of potential EU-related opportunities and threats for their country, as well as of the benefits they could draw from it themselves. Many feel that the political decisions they perceive as EU-related are made 'in their backs', as European political life is not mediatised enough. Similarly, a 64-year-old Italian interviewee, a hospital employee considers that her generation:

... obviously hasn't been informed on Europe in school, in terms of economic and political union. [...] There's no real information from politicians, they should make an effort to inform their voters who are a little bit less... aware [...] You learn stuff by listening to the news on TV, but not that much.

When asked about their level of information on European questions, the middle-class categories of the French sample even express a feeling of strong unease. Their reactions often silently reveal a form of symbolic violence, as the case of this interviewer in her seventies, a former teacher and thereafter a housewife, who expresses a form of political incompetence and is unable to position herself on the political map: '[Long silence] Oh well [laughs], it's enough for me! [She bursts out laughing]. You know, you're interviewing a really simple person right now!'

Many Polish interviewees, endowed with little cultural capital, express confusion in the face of the media information that is available to them. They do not feel able to decode it or to assess its political dimension. Such is the case of a young man, living in a small town, who holds a three year university degree in tourism and has recently founded a small business. Unable to distinguish between political parties in Poland, he claims to know 'what you need to know' on Europe. When asked how he intends to vote in the case of a referendum on the Lisbon treaty, he expresses his feeling of incomprehension on the information he gets from the media to the interviewer:

On TV there are a lot of 'truths', in the news they say there's a scandal... but they don't explain how it began, why that is. [...] The problem remains and they talk about it over and over, but actually we don't know what it's about. Ordinary people have no clue what it's about. It's the same thing for this referendum... Who really knows what's in there? What are the benefits, what are the results?

The self-assessment of the level of information depends on the social definition of 'what you should know' which varies greatly from one social segment to another. This calls into question the entire methodology of the Eurobarometers. European information, seen as more complex than information on national political questions, is indeed often perceived by members of the lower categories as not meant for them, by definition, due to their low social status and their lack of educational capital. Two Polish pensioners, with a primary school level of education, initially confidently claim that they are well informed on Europe: 'Of course, yes. There's TV, there are... several news shows... so many sources. We watch the news on TV and all the information shows'. They claim that they get enough information on how the EU works from the media. Yet, they are embarrassed when the interviewer asks them a specific question on the institutions. One of them explains that she does not go 'in-depth' into these questions, and the other spontaneously associates the question asked to remote, school-related competences. A Polish worker mobilises the same type of reasoning; he considers that he has the basic knowledge that suits his social status. While certain European problems are unknown or unclear to him, he ultimately believes that he is not meant to understand them, that he is not the intended recipient:

The essential things that I want to know, I know them. But, say, the Constitution... Not everyone has read it among those who are higher up the ladder than I am. [...] I can understand all that I need... And what I can't understand... Well, apparently [it's] for those who... have to... who work in that kind of field... As far as I'm concerned... everything is... clear... I think.

Such an attitude consisting in valuing useful knowledge is also related to the internalisation of a statutory incompetence created by the impression of the EU as an unintelligible polity. To a 45-year-old French baker, in order to read the European Constitution, 'you need to have an education that I don't have. I don't have what it takes to read it'. According to people who have little cultural capital, one of the main obstacles to understanding European information is the use of sophisticated vocabulary. A couple of French pensioners consider information on Europe 'complex' because 'they use scholarly words'. A manager in a brewery says that 'if you didn't go to the ENA [French National Administration School], you can't understand the words they use' in media reports on Europe.

Though the idea of a deficit of information on Europe is widespread in lower categories, this is less the case in intermediary and upper categories, whose members are likely to produce a more synoptic discourse. These interviewees maintain that there is too much information on Europe, and that as a result it is hard to sort it out and understand what is important. The director of a French bank branch – whose positive judgement on Europe is both global and related to his occupation – claims that citizens are 'overwhelmed with information' and that 'over-information, when you lack training, leads to under-information'. Similarly, a 69-year-old Polish engineer, the co-owner of an architecture firm and a EU supporter, defines the European information in the media as 'informational chatter'. In Poland, several interviewees refer to the major communication campaign that preceded the country's accession to the EU as 'propaganda' to refer to the European information provided during that period. A retired schoolteacher even draws a link between her perception of a recent omnipresence of European matters in schoolbooks and the former abundance of ideological elements related to Soviet domination. In the Polish context, that of recent integration in the EU, many interviewees from intermediary and higher categories – even those who have limited European knowledge – feel relatively well informed. Including those who are unsure about their knowledge, many claim that European information is accessible and understandable to them. Several interviewees acknowledge their share of responsibility for their lack of information. When asked about her feeling of being informed on Europe, another retired schoolteacher, with secondary school level education and who supports the EU, confidently answers:

I'm very well [informed]. You just have to want to be; personally, I can use the Internet, there's the press. If somebody's interested, he's informed. [...] Like I said, all the information is accessible, if I want to know something, I can look for it.

The sample's lower and intermediary categories thus include citizens whose self-limitations can be understood mainly in two ways: either they limit their efforts to seek out information in general insofar as they do not feel competent enough to develop opinions on European issues on the basis of the information they receive, or they limit the information they seek out to useful knowledge, to themes which resonate in their personal lives. On the other hand, interviewees who have a synoptic point of view on Europe (or at least some of them) feel that they are well informed, either globally or in terms of a more limited interest in specific aspects of European construction. But they also emphasise the wealth of information on Europe, the lack of clarity and how difficult it is to understand, including for themselves.

Complexity and confusion

European institutions are the source of much confusion, and the subject is often perceived as embodying the complexity of the European architecture. On the one hand, citizens have patchy knowledge on the subject, and on the other, many are bewildered by certain characteristics of how Europe works: '[In Europe] power is scattered between authorities that are no longer hierarchised, spread into the EU's institutional space. It is somehow "delocalised", in the etymological sense of the term, i.e. it no longer has a definite and stable location' (Magnette 2000: 204). Moreover, the division of power, which differs from the traditional tripartite structure, without any clear separation of competences between the executive, legislative and judicial branches, does not facilitate the understanding of the Community institutions' respective roles.

Despite this difficulty in identifying the complex mechanics of the working of the institutions, respondents to Eurobarometer questions proclaim a surprisingly high level of trust in institutions. Thus, according to EB 69, 50 per cent of respondents trust the EU. In Spring 2008, 52 per cent of individuals trusted the European Parliament (EP), 47 per cent trusted the European Commission, and 43 per cent trusted the European Council. However, spontaneous opinions recorded in semi-directive interviews highlight the limitations of these closed questions on trust in European institutions. The case of an unemployed French woman in her forties is a typical illustration of this. Asked about the extent to which she trusts European institutions, she assertively replies: 'I trust the institutions', but she is much more unsure about the institutions' actual roles: '[On the role of the EP] No, I'm really ignorant... [On the European Commission] I don't know either. The Commission proposes and the Parliament decides?' In Poland, the interviewees' responses are similarly significant. The uncertain answers of an administrative employee, with a secondary education, show the discursive efforts made by an ordinary citizen asked to take a stance on questions she has never considered and on which she does not have sufficient information:

- [The European Parliament] makes me think about a gathering of many people from different countries so...
- But do you trust it?

- I think so... I think they have specific people in specific positions over there.
- And the European Commission?
- I suppose it also has a certain function... so I think, too...
- And the EU Council?
- I think so.

Memorising names and places plays a significant role for interviewees who are more inclined to trust institutions because they have heard their names mentioned in the media. Yet, the media's specific event-based logic does not favour the pedagogic dimension of presenting the institutions and the way the EU works. Rather, infotainment news programmes determine which Member of the European Parliament's (MEP) name is the most widely known, especially by audience members with the lowest levels of cultural capital. Admittedly, on the other hand, the routine European political debate, free of major ideological cleavages, is not well suited to attracting a wide audience, as many viewers are often attracted by conflict in politics.

The EU's institutional workings appear complex both to interviewees from lower categories, with a distant relationship towards Europe, and to many persons from upper social categories who might be assumed to have a better command of these questions. The comparison of two interviewees conducted in France coming from radically opposed social environments attests to this, showing close similarities in the reactions on a question on knowledge of the institutions. The discomfort created in the interview situation recalls the embarrassment that questions on the feeling of being informed on European issues elicit. A 26-year-old cleaner, who does not have a diploma, is placed in an uncomfortable situation by her lack of knowledge of the institutions. During the interview, the interviewer has to prompt and tries in vain to put the interviewee on the right track:

> Are you familiar with the European Parliament? [She shakes her head sheepishly] Not at all [...] The European Commission? [She looks similarly embarrassed] You don't know... the Council... of the European Union, you don't know that, it's okay...
>
> - See, if you explain it to me, then I would know, but...

The same list of questions, asked to a bank executive with a left-wing politicisation elicits the same incompetence, yet expressed with a more self-deprecating tone, in explaining the role of the institutions:

> - The European Parliament, does that ring a bell to you?
> - No, I told you, I suck. [...] No, I know... don't the deputies sit in the Parliament? [...] But I don't know what they do. Then again, even in France, I don't know what they do. They make laws, right? What do deputies do? I don't know... I sucked at civics.

Polish interviewees sometimes have trouble grasping the nature of European construction as such. Hence, a young accountant, who graduated from university, admits to the interviewee that at the time of Poland's accession to the EU, he gave a lot of thought to how it is possible to 'manage such as a big State and so many human resources from a single point, a single location', whereas a 31-year-old sales clerk, who is relatively informed on Europe, builds his conception of the European structure around a familiar analogy with Polish realities: to him, the EU is, in reference to the national administrative division, a 'big State with twenty-five voivodeships'.

Often, the interviewees' representations of how EU institutions work are based on approximations. For a Franco-German interviewee who perceives the impact of European construction through her personal situation, the European Parliament 'manages Europe', even if she does not know exactly how. Asked about the role of the EP, a Polish priest does not feel any more competent to answer: 'I know it exists... they meet, they debate things, but what, how, why, where...'. As far as the Commission is concerned, a French student sees it as a specific organisation made up of experts: 'A European Commission is sort of like opinions of the expert commission, something like that'.

As knowledge of how EU institutions work tends to be very rudimentary regardless of the interviewees' level of education and occupation, the main difference between the upper and lower categories often resides in the way they admit their own incompetence (or not). Unsurprisingly, interviewees who have little cultural capital are more direct, as the case of a Polish cleaner who lives in Brussels illustrates. Perplexed by the question on trust in the institutions, she claims: 'I've never needed something like this'. Conversely, more educated individuals tend to piece together an answer from their available supply of general and political knowledge.

Claiming to be well informed on European institutions is not a guarantee of effective knowledge, regardless of the type of public. When asked how he is informed on Europe, a 47-year-old French car mechanic – who 'listens' to politicians but does not trust them – says he is 'well informed' by television and newspapers. On European issues, 'on the news, there's no hypocrisy, scandals burst, we're well informed'. Immediately, however, there is a noticeable gap between this general level of information and his individual understanding of European institutional organisation: 'No, all that goes on in Brussels is too dull. There are too many parliamentarians... I don't even know how many there are, 500?' When the interviewer replies that there are more than 700 MEPs, the interviewee expresses surprise and shifts the discussion towards financial aspects: '700? That's an awful lot... With all the costs it must entail. Do we need that many people? Especially since you can't see the decisions right away'.

The case of a French teacher shows even more precisely that claiming to be informed on a regular basis, including on Europe, does not amount to accurately understanding European mechanisms. This interviewee discusses politics and Europe with her friends and colleagues, and defines herself as a curious person who makes the effort to seek out information daily: 'Yeah, but that's because I make the effort. [...] Everyday I go and have a look'. Yet, her knowledge of Europe remains vague. She thinks that Wagner wrote the European hymn and that the Bolkestein directive has something to do with the accession of Turkey. When the interviewer mentions the 'Polish plumber' controversy, she claims to be unable to remember what it was about, saying that she was too busy with work at the time to keep up on the debate. She trusts European institutions but cannot precisely define each institution's role:

So, the European Parliament, to me, is... everything that takes care of... constitutions. [...] The Commission, that's... To me it's sort of like the antechamber [...] in which there's, well... all the pending problems. [...] What it does exactly, precisely, I don't know. [...] The members of the Commission? No. I wouldn't know who they are [...] It's never been explained, actually.

In Italy, a trade union representative, who votes for the Rifondazione Comunista party, has direct but limited and incomplete knowledge of Europe. He expresses a critical point of view on Europe's institutional functioning:

It's a far too obscure mechanism! There's not a lot of openness, but maybe that's because it's the way this parliament works. There's a lot of distance between this parliament and the conditions of those who live here on an everyday basis.

According to an army general, a centre-right voter, 'I feel that Europe is still rather remote [...] so it's hard for me to understand it'. For a unionised mechanic, a centre-left voter: 'I don't like how distant I feel from the European institutions themselves at all'.

The complexity of the European institutions causes much confusion. For interviewees who have no university education and little politicisation, the first obstacle in an interview situation consists in the presence of complex words from the political vocabulary used in the media. Many interviewees are embarrassed and confused by terms such as liberalisation, European integration or the democratic deficit, such as this retired Polish cartographer:

– What do you think about the idea of European integration?
– Well... I think... I'm in favour of it. [...] Integration is integration. Meetings, that kind of thing. [...] So that they get to know each other better, politicians... right? These integration meetings... I don't know, we'll see what comes out of it, if it materialises.

The EU's institutional functioning thus appears as the subject that triggers the most hesitation from interviewees, regardless of their background. In Italy, the discourse on European institutions is very similar to the one observed in France in most respects. The knowledge of the Schengen Area makes it possible to distinguish interviewees who have no interest in politics from those who have no direct experience of Europe and others. Most members of the Italian sample, indeed, have some knowledge on the subject. Yet, levels of information remain varied among interviewees. Only individuals who have a direct relationship to Europe and its institutions and/or a synoptic vision of the subject have a sufficient informational baggage to understand the question, or even spontaneously discuss it. Conversely, people who only have a limited involvement in European issues, or who do not seek out information on a regular basis, and have little cultural capital, are confused by the topic. Their answers only consist in mentioning short-cuts – in reference to borders, customs – without any references to the Schengen Agreement, of which they are not aware, requiring explanations from the interviewer. Such is the case of a florist, with a secondary level of education and who shows a lack of interest in politics: 'Oh yeah, I know… It's the customs' speech'.

In Italy, the Bolkestein directive is perceived as a very technical subject, on which there were no public debates. Only those who have a professional experience of the EU are aware of it. The level of information on this directive clearly shows that, failing a political and/or media debate popularising the most complex questions, only elites who work with European institutions are aware of certain issues.

In Poland, mentions of the directive, on which there were similarly no public debates, find no echo in interviewees, even those who are very competent on European matters. Likewise, the presumed 'democratic deficit', an issue of which some French interviewees are particularly aware, has no meaning for many interviewees; for others, its interpretation undoubtedly hinges on the national context and on the Polish citizens' specific perception of their position within the EU, where fear of domination by the bigger countries is very present. Nevertheless, while Polish interviewees are ignorant on these issues, most of them have, as in the Italian case, heard about the Schengen Area and opportunities of free movement. Many of them are also aware of the debate on the possible inclusion of the Invocatio Dei in the European Constitution, which was particularly heated and publicised in Poland.

The comparison of these countries shows that 'European' competences are related to the national media's hierarchisation of the issues. This condition appears as necessary for the production of opinions on Europe: themes discussed on the news are mentioned to support developed arguments, which differ from one country and from one period to the next. It is not sufficient, however, since interviewees appropriate this available information in complex ways.

Information proxies

In order to cope with the complexity of information on Europe, interviewees develop substitute arguments. To answer questions, they rely on whatever short-cuts come to mind (Zaller 1992; Sniderman 2000), even though these elements do not necessary have informational value or reflect a well thought-out argument or full understanding by the interviewee. If they do not have in-depth knowledge of European matters, ordinary citizens memorise snippets of information collected here and there, which they later piece together. In order to find their way in a non-personalised European world, they rely – in France, Italy and Poland – on forms of anecdotal memorisation which give them the feeling of being able to say 'something' on a subject they only approximately know. A French rail company executive hence refers to his memory of multiple meetings and translations into all the EU languages: 'I think the way it works, Europe, right, it entails a lot. [...] They have meetings in Luxembourg, in Brussels, in Strasbourg. They translate all that into God knows how many languages'. According to a member of a regionalist party, EU institutions produce many texts: 'There's so much stuff, so many treaties'. Individuals whose relationship towards Europe is remote construct a form of reflection on how EU institutions work on the basis of reminiscences from distant information. To a former hospital human resources manager in her eighties, the European Parliament 'takes care of a bit of everything, it takes care of budgets, of the length of daisy stems, it takes care of a whole bunch of things nobody really knows about'.

In Poland, a pensioner who claims to be well informed because she 'watches the news all the time' collects whatever media snippets and hearsay she catches to support her argument on European institutions:

- Do you trust the European Parliament?
- If it inspires trust... They take different decisions, but... For instance regarding those clauses... The Parliament also adopts them, I think...
- Which clauses?
- The clauses on the [Christian] roots [of Europe]... that too, I think... Because if they're in favour of that, I'm going to support them, otherwise, no. [...]
- What about the European Commission, do you trust it?
- The Commission... who knows... the Commission... There are fewer Poles there I think... compared to the others... Other countries have more... they can adopt things with a majority, I think, different...

In Italy, interviewees generally only have precise knowledge on the European standards that have direct impact on their professional life. Yet, they sometimes manage to express opinions on regulations that they do not know, but from which they have retained selective elements of information, which they then combine with their everyday experience to draw conclusions on Europe. Indeed, after having discussed how the implementation of the Single Market and the VAT affects her, a clothing store saleswoman extends her argument to the field of food quality, even though she has no direct experience of it: 'There's been a drop in the quality of our products. I remember that the quality of olive oil was supposed to be excellent. Accession to Europe has made the quality drop. Even though I'm not expert in the field.'

Among other information substitutes mobilised to identify the European Parliament's role, the argument of the geographical location of Community buildings is often used in France. A group of French students remember the existence of the European Parliament in Strasbourg because they 'rode [their] bikes past the building'. Such awareness of Europe is based on utterly anecdotal elements.

Cities that host European institutions then become reference points of sorts in the European space. A young member of a regionalist party remembers that there is 'also something, in Brussels', but since she lacks interest in the question, she admits she no longer knows 'what it's called'. A retired teacher acknowledges that to her, European institutions are 'rather vague', she ventures that the Parliament is based 'in Brussels' but then quickly adds 'I just said something totally wrong, though'. Such reactions are expressions of the embarrassment elicited by questions on European institutions, when interviewees who have no particular relationship to Europe are faced with their inability to express an opinion on such remote objects. In Italy, 'Strasbourg' is hardly ever mentioned; interviewees talk about 'Brussels' when they discuss Europe.

Anecdotal memorisations sometimes cause interviewees to make mistakes. The French teacher who claims to be regularly informed on Europe but shows her lack of knowledge on European institutions mixes up the European Court of Justice and the International Criminal Court in The Hague. The group of students who recognise the EP from riding their bikes past the building fail to explain the attributions and the localisation of the institutions: 'There's the European Court of Justice in The Hague, but I don't remember where that is, in Holland or Belgium'.

In the case of a 50-year-old Polish unionised interviewee, who works as a foreman on the Gdańsk Shipyard, the confusion between the institutions (the Commission and the EP) appears all the more surprising as he refers to a personal experience of travelling to Brussels, in the context of a protest. Asked about his trust in the European Parliament, he spontaneously answers:

> Twice we went in front of the Parliament [actually he was at the Commission headquarters] [...] We always want to defend the shipyard [...] so actually we had to deal with this European Parliament... and over there... I can tell you that that they received us properly.

In France, political figures can also work as reference points to produce an opinion on Europe. The lack of precise knowledge on how EU institutions work does not prevent some interviewees from generally trusting them, thanks to the presence of well-known political actors, who serve as landmarks in a political landscape where popular figures are scarce. For instance, an employee in a car rental company, who has a remote evaluation of European construction, admits that he 'tend[s] to trust' MEPs, because 'they are representatives of each country'. He identifies 'famous people', elected in different periods, who became more familiar at some point through media coverage, such as Simone Veil, the first president of the EP, or 'Vatanen, a former rally driver, a Swede, I think' [actually Finnish]. This example shows how the media emphasise certain actors and participate in limited memorisation processes which, however limited they may be, structure perceptions. A retired postal worker, who admits her limited knowledge of MEPs, is nevertheless able to mention a few names: 'You have Delors, you have Roselyne... [She pauses] Roselyne Bachelot, that's it! She has a seat too... Well, hey, I don't know that many'. A nurse in her forties recalls famous MEPs:

You hear about certain European deputies quite a bit, Daniel Cohn-Bendit for instance, Martine Aubry's father as well [referring to former European Commission President Jacques Delors, a sign that she merges the national and European political spheres], I don't remember his name, you hear about him quite a bit too.

In Poland, many mention Bronisław Geremek.

While political figures are used to support the construction of arguments on Europe, they are not always clearly identified. Based on vague memories of the European Convention, a couple of French pensioners claim they have heard of Valéry Giscard d'Estaing but do not know to which European institution they should link him: 'Isn't it Giscard who... is in charge of... the Parliament? Or the Commission?' In the Italian sample, there is virtually no personalisation of European politics: there are only a few references to the Prodi Commission, a derogatory comment on a Northern League MEP and one mention of Jean-Claude Trichet, the president of the European Central Bank.

In addition to geographical approximations and more or less uncertain references to national political figures, the interviewees' relationship to European institutions sometimes also takes the form of an analogy with the national institutional functioning. In both contexts, the interviewees often have trouble identifying the institutions' roles. A 36-year-old French marketing employee points out the complexity of the institutional game at national level to explain that, according to her, understanding the European institutional space is even more difficult: 'The European institutions, yeah... I struggle even with the French institutions sometimes'.

To make up for their lack of knowledge of how European institutions work, interviewees express opinions based on snippets of information they have gleaned on the way national political systems work. A fashion saleswoman, who does not have a diploma, perceives the role of the EP through an analogy with the national parliament. Asked about the EP's role, she initially remains silent for a long time. When she eventually ventures an answer, she first seems embarrassed, not sure what words to use: 'To me, the role of the European parliament is precisely [...] to review all these laws a bit. Well, when I say laws... treaties. And to be very careful about what gets voted eventually'. This extract shows the distance from the official vocabulary; the interviewee mixes up laws and treaties, her choice of words remains uncertain, even if she perceives the institution's role as important.

In Italy, confusion in the identification of the EU institutions' duties is also widespread. The analogy between national and European institutions is the most widely used shortcut to attempt answering the questions asked. To a bank employee, 'the European Parliament... is the same thing as our Parliament, it's about trying to take into account all the countries' problems and deal with them on a European level'. This device does not work systematically for people who do not trust the European institutional architecture at all. The question on the role of the European Central Bank shows how merely relating national and European dimension can cause a strong distortion effect. Such is the case of a florist, who, when comparing the ECB to his own experience of banks, expresses a strongly negative judgement, even though he has failed to grasp the very object of the question: 'The bank never gives you anything… Whether they're European or Italian, if you have guarantees, it's all right… If you have money, they'll give you money. But if you're poor, you stay poor.'

Such erroneous interpretations are not only made by individuals with a low level of education. They are also found in individuals with more cultural capital, but who are not at all interested in European issues or politics in general. An Italian interviewee, for instance, who works as an assistant researcher in engineering, discusses the ECB as if it were merely a big bank:

I tend to like banks more when they're smaller… When they were more local realities, you could see small banks investing in small territories... Not like [this European bank], where you have a big concentration of people who manage everyone's money. It scares me, because if a bank becomes the only bank around, then if it decides to finance or build weapons to support a country, it becomes too strong economically.

Ultimately, answering information questions on Europe is difficult for most interviewees, whether they feel that they are not informed on the subject or, conversely, overwhelmed by information. Facing complex European themes, interviewees mobilise three main resources: information snippets, personal experience or 'common sense' or 'popular wisdom' (Gamson 1992). They build arguments that are often quite far from classical political logics, attempting to appropriate part of this abstract, intangible Europe by using, as a strategy, as an expedient or as a reflex, the categories of everyday life.

chapter ten | european worlds
Marine de Lassalle

Differential appropriations of a remote institutionalisation process

The European Parliament, the Euro, 'Brussels' directives, European commissioners, Schengen, Bolkestein, the common agricultural policy, the enlargements, the services directive, the European constitutional treaty, etc.: all these 'things', these achievements of EU institutions contribute to defining the world of the European Union (on the concept of 'world', see Becker 1982), particularly for Community professionals, media analysts and European studies scholars. The Concorde interview template was partly built around these 'objects', insofar as we aimed at describing, understanding and explaining how ordinary citizens perceive these objectified forms of the EU (see Chapter 3) by linking their discourse to their life experiences. Yet, when citizens are asked about their perceptions of this world, it quickly appears that its existence is vague and confused, except, and only to some extent, for a minority of citizens who have the required political capital and experience. All the authors in this volume have observed the difficulty in acquiring knowledge on unfamiliar institutions and the resulting distance from Europe, regardless of the angle used.

Materialised through high abstention rates, indifference towards election campaigns and numerous criticisms, this distance from EU institutions has been analysed in the field of European studies as the manifestation of a 'democratic deficit'. Several hypotheses have been formulated on this deficit: for instance the lack of a European *demos* (Strudel 2008), the inexistence of a European 'political market', the analysis of a complex institutional machinery (Bélot, Magnette and Saurruger 2008) and the role it plays in Europe's 'unreadability' (Rozenberg 2009). Focused on institutional Europe, these studies present a relatively unified conception of the EU, its institutions and actors, and they make the assumption that the EU has a direct impact on the citizens' perceptions. This in turn implies that all citizens have a perception, however vague, of EU institutions, and that the latter are their main 'gateways' to the EU. Lastly, this perspective implies that reducing the democratic deficit and the distance of ordinary citizens towards the EU merely entails improving political communication and making an effort of pedagogy (Inglehart 1970; Inglehart and Rabier 1979). Yet, many citizens do not only perceive Europe through its institutions.[1] Indeed, when citizens talk about the EU,

---

1. While national political capital, measured on the basis of the highest position held before being appointed as Commissioner, has increased as European construction developed (Döring 2007), the emergence of a specialised 'class' of European Commissioners has not been observed, unlike the Directors-General and their careers in the Commission (Georgakakis 2009).

we have observed that while, following the 'paradigm of minimalism' (Converse 1964; Sniderman 1998), the Schengen Area or the European Parliament only make sense to a minority, other spontaneous representations emerge. The '79/409' directive, the SPS, 'paperwork', 'fishing net mesh sizes', 'forward motion', the 'Europe of exchanges', 'coastal shipping', 'Mozart' also embody Europe for certain categories of the population. Indeed, when a solicitation on Europe produces such a variety of references based on such specific experiences and spheres of social life, the idea of a single European world centred on political institutions makes little sense: there are several European worlds, and several relationships to Europe and ways of talking about Europe.

In this chapter there are two main objectives. First, I will discuss the process of institutionalisation of Europe, its objects, its institutions, and the actors who embody them. I will however relate it to the worlds in which these processes are likely to acquire meaning, in order to shed light on different forms of appropriating Europe, the product of the convergence between the forms of a social agent's experience and the institutional manifestations of Europe in specific sectors. Then, I will analyse the reasons for which this institutionalisation process produces distance, and the specific forms in which this distance is expressed, including among categories of the population which European studies have brought us to expect to be very close or highly exposed to EU institutions.

To that end, in the first part of this chapter the Europe of institutions will be confronted with the population that is the least distant from it, that is the minority of citizens who have the social or political capital necessary to access it. Developing as a 'world apart', whose activity finds little echo in national societies, this Europe of institutions fails to take on a recognisable shape for politicised citizens in Member States. In the second part the focus will be on the worlds in which the Europe of institutions is less tangible, even though the institutionalisation of Europe has effects on them, by studying two 'groups' expected to be directly concerned. First, I will address those who are affected by the Europe of public policies, through the example of farmers and fishermen; then, I will direct my attention to the Europe of economy and business by analysing the discourse of business owners.

A Europe of institutions for competent citizens?

Several decades of European construction have contributed to shaping a political centre (Bartolini 2005; Beck and Grande 2007), both distinct from – and interdependent with – the national spaces in terms of institutionalisation. This process of construction has generated specific rules and issues and contributed to the selection and socialisation of agents endowed with singular features, constituting a specific social world. The lack of embedding in national contexts results in the difficulty of personifying Europe for politicised citizens.

A world apart from national contexts

Many studies have analysed professionals of European politics as producers of the institutionalisation of the EU's political centre. Be they European civil servants (Georgakakis 2008, 2009; Georgakakis and de Lassalle 2007a), MEPs (Marrel and Payre 2006; Beauvallet and Michon 2010) or Commissioners (Joana and Smith 2002), and regardless of their varying degrees of 'permanence',[2] these actors play a key role in forging the Europe of institutions. Studies of these actors emphasise the transformation of their social properties, with the growing importance of a specific European institutional capital. Also involved in this process are intermediaries between EU institutions and the populations affected by EU public policies: lobbies, interest groups, workers' or employers' representatives, members of non-governmental organisations (NGOs), legal firms, advisers, offices of national or regional representations, etc. These intermediaries have increased in number, especially in the context of the negotiations on the Single Act (Greenwood 1997). Among these makers of Europe, we can also mention national civil servants, seconded experts or members of committees (de Maillard and Robert 2008) whose careers bring them to the Schuman Roundabout on a temporary or more long-term basis. The conditions of their access to these institutions are linked to specific resources and properties: frequent experience of European institutions, multipositionality, international careers (Cohen and Weisbein 2005; Lequesne and Rivaud 2001; Robert 2004). All these actors involved in the making of the Europe of institutions are thus endowed with singular properties, dispositions, resources and forms of capital adjusted to the rules of the space they invest. They are materialised in specific forms of a professional ethos, whose structuring contributes to the autonomisation of the space, and they constitute groups that are distinct from their national counterparts.

One of the main structuring features of this institutionalisation process lies in the fact that these actors distance themselves from everything that might have a national connotation. In the college of commissioners, for instance, and in the more informal group of the Commission's Directors-General, national properties (starting with nationality and language) are those that elicit the most self-censorship and denial (Georgakakis and de Lassalle 2007a). More generally, the construction of a group of European civil servants involves forms of 'stylisation of life' whereby a set of multinational values breaking from state bureaucracies is valued (Georgakakis 2009). In the Parliament, the plurinational dimension of the issues defended, multilingualism, and the distancing from postures overly related to national contexts are among the legitimate requirements to ensure access to the institution's rewards, and the MEPs' ability to be convincing depends on their ability to mobilise denationalised and depoliticised arguments (Beauvallet and Michon 2010).

Such distanciation from national ties is indeed related to a form of depoliticisa-

2. In the sense that the political options of the policies conducted are not considered as relevant information for the readers or viewers.

tion that constitutes the second feature of the process. It is both produced by the distance shown towards national categories and labels and by the 'consensual' character derived from the interdependencies of the institutional game. This depoliticisation contributes to shaping the European civil servants' ethos and working practices (Robert 2007), as well as those of the MEPs (Costa 2009). Similar patterns of mutual trust, cooperation and reciprocity as well as reflexes of coordination and conflict prevention (Juncos and Pomorka 2006) can also be observed in the Council (Lewis 2003) or the Commission's working groups (Dehousse 2003).

In order to succeed in these both consensual and denial-filled modes of 'doing politics' (Robert 2007), expertise becomes the legitimate mode of action: this is the third structuring feature of this game. The figure of the 'technocrat', constructed in opposition to the Member States, goes hand in hand with the high value granted to expert and intellectual capital (Georgakakis 1999). In the EP, the technicisation of practices, the specialisation of actors, the emphasis on technical competence and expertise are structuring features (Beauvallet and Michon 2010). The importance of the culture of consensus and scientifically based legitimacy, together with the idea of sharing a scientific or professional culture beyond national interests, similarly characterises the committees (Bergstrom 2005). Studies stress the role of expertise and of rational arguments, including in venues of political negotiation (Hauray 2006).

These practices are therefore distinct from those found in political configurations more familiar to politicised citizens. If there is a 'European political agenda' (Muller 1995), it is never the object of an activity of political brokerage aimed at or mobilising citizens, making it necessary to publicise, spread, explain or justify these practices. The only significant opportunities for encounters between actors of this European political field and ordinary citizens are European elections, often thought of as 'second order' elections, and which only serve to elect a fraction of Community actors following a process of list constitution in which national party leaders play a significant role (Lefèbvre and Marrel 2009; Rozenberg 2009).

Thus, political brokerage aimed at citizens is not seen as a necessity in this institutional world. Nevertheless, the latter structures the identity and professional roles of go-betweens. Journalists specialised in Europe have a hard time defining and covering a game 'whose political personnel is unknown, with an absence of political symbolic value, relying on mechanisms that are relatively original in comparison to the division of power at the national level, and whose debates and issues are thought to be esoteric' (Guiraudon 2000). This difficulty can also be attributed to the fact that those who take on this role of broker between national and European level are close to the European political centre and share many of the defining sociological features of the European institutional world.

The media coverage of EU activities has given rise to an institutional journalism and the progressive emergence of a role of expert, technical, depoliticised[3]

---

3. These practical skills include writing position papers, monitoring legislation, discussing texts in working group meetings, negotiating, etc.

journalism, more preoccupied by Community policies than Community politics. They are described in the academic literature as part of a tight-knit Brussels group, representing those who are 'included', confronted with the lack of awareness and the provincialism of those who have remained 'desperately national', and struggling to translate European political games in vernacular frames and terminologies which they no longer command (Baisnée 2007).

Also belonging to this group are those who claim to embody European 'civil society', and who partly base their legitimacy on the representation of ordinary citizens. These Brussels representatives, however, act more as gatekeepers and sources of information of the Commission than as mediators. Their legitimacy depends on their status as recognised interlocutors of EU institutions (Guiraudon 2000) more than on their relationships with national societies. As Hélène Michel shows, this specific mode of interest representation is earned through a form of permanence, learning the consultation practices favoured by the Commission, and mastering technical skills, which prevail over numbers-based representative legitimacy (Michel 2007b). Lastly, euphemisation (moderation) and neutralisation of political discourses, as well as the centrality of expertise and compromise in European arenas, shape the role of spokespersons of national organisations representing working class interests at this level (Wagner 2005).

This does not mean that European citizens are absent from the European institutions' preoccupations. Since the early stages of European construction, the question of popular support has been raised in the EU (Aldrin and Utard 2008), contributing to the production of instruments of measurement and forms of objectification, starting with the Eurobarometer (see Chapter 2). The initial communication strategy deployed from the 1950s to the 1980s, based on informing pre-determined audiences (farmers, academics, journalists), was progressively replaced by a communication strategy aimed at a wider audience, in line with developments such as the direct election of MEPs in 1979 and the accentuation of the 'democratic deficit' theme. This transformation in the target audiences has not changed the forms of this communication, which aims at increasing the popularity of institutional Europe by informing people on its history and its action. The failures of the national referenda during the 1990s, and the criticisms formulated by opponents to the EU in public arenas that began to emerge after Maastricht, transformed the Commission's institutional communication strategy. This strategy now focuses on putting on display the EU's proximity to citizens and relies on improved access to European information, notably on the Internet, and on exhibiting a Europe that 'listens to citizens'. This shift goes hand in hand with the promotion of the 'new European governance' (Georgakakis and de Lassalle 2007b), meant to be based on a civil society conceived as substitute for more traditional forms of political representation (Michel 2007a, 2007b; Weisbein and Mischi 2007).

The paradoxical distance of politicised citizens from the Europe of institutions

This communication policy implies a figure of the 'European citizen' who is almost as educated as an expert, liable to understand a Community interest (i.e. with little or no overtly national or political preferences), post-materialistic, with strong dispositions for consensus, reasonable, even rational: in other words dispositions which are similar to those required to act in a relevant manner in the Community polity. This figure of the 'ideal citizen' can be observed in the methods used to evaluate the demands of target audiences (the use of polls and surveys by questionnaire has been generalised), in campaigns (copies of the European constitutional treaty during the 2005 referendum campaign were sent to French voters), in the production of the 'scholarly commentaries' that have preceded or followed referendum campaigns (Lehingue 2007a), and in the questions asked by Eurobarometers to European citizens on their trust in EU institutions (on the incongruity of such questions, see Chapters 2 and 9). Resulting from the cynicism or the sociological illiteracy of elites eager to indulge in passive and distant support, this figure, however, raises the issue of the feeling of 'wounded pride' (to use Patrick Lehingue's phrase) we have observed during interviews, especially in judgements on this incomprehensible communicational content giving many interviewees, including some politicised citizens, the impression that they were taken for 'idiots'.

> Well, they gave us that document, right... it was too long really [...] I think nobody read that thing, you know... I'd have wanted something clearer honestly... I'd have read it, I think [...] They don't explain anything to us... we are told that it will be better for us but we are not told how and why it will better for us, or when it will be better for us in truth you know... they just tell us it will be better for you, so you sign! Well I just don't agree you know [...] that's why I didn't vote, know what I mean? They were messing with us! [...] I'm not going to vote for something I don't understand anything about, you know... all I knew is apparently if we voted 'no', well, we'd be screwed... and so you had to vote 'yes'... well... sounded like bullshit, right!
>
> (FR, M, 24, unemployed)

> I voted 'no'. I hesitated a lot, but... Precisely... because at some point, they almost got me with their blackmail, I suppose... hmm... [Impersonating a stern tone] 'So watch out, right, if you vote 'no', that's not good at all. You're not a nice, good European.' I said no... [...] No! Because of how dishonest the approach was, I think... [...] They tried to force that stuff on us as if it were all part of a package, right? As if some peddler was selling us... hmm... his cheese grater... [...] So you have the cheese grater, and then you have the vegetable peeler... and then... and then in the package you also have a corkscrew! Europe, European construction, it's... it's not supposed to be the work of peddlers!
>
> (FR, F, 50, youth worker)

These examples – and I could list many more – raise the more general question of the reception and perception by politicised individuals of this Europe of institutions, embedded in spaces they have no access to, and which is not visible or translated into national contexts.

Some of the interviewees, whose representations have been collected, can be referred to as politicised citizens, insofar as they feel entitled to give a political opinion. While the heterogeneity of their social characteristics makes it impossible to say that they share a similar world, they share a similar relationship to politics, the command of specialised vocabulary and references, similar ways of getting information (eclectic practices, recourse to various media supports including the 'quality press'), and are used to talking politics (see Chapters 4 and 7). These citizens, while they may not invest in European issues *per se*, at least do so insofar as they are an extension of ordinary political issues. They are often considered as important and as generating profits of distinction, because they know that few people are interested and that they are currently less demonetised than national political issues.

Yet, even within this minority of citizens who are particularly interested in politics, few are those who actually perceive the specificity of European politics. This obscurity entails that, aside from political competence, additional first-hand experience of the institutions is required. This experience may be an intellectual one, linked to a professional and/or political activity of 'representation' in a party, a union, a professional organisation, but it draws its efficiency from giving access to a world that remains imperceptible in ordinary contexts.

Such is for instance the case of a young graduate, who is familiar with the EU through her academic experience: she has studied abroad with the Erasmus programme, followed classes on Europe, made trips to see the institutions (in Luxembourg, Brussels and Strasbourg) and written a master's thesis on 'the EU and the environment'. This familiarity with the Europe of institutions is reactivated by family relations (some members of her family work in European institutions) and reinforced by her political activity (she is a member of the Green party, and represented them in the Nantes youth regional council).

> It can also be a new way of making democracy: when you have lobbies in the EU, in Brussels – lobbies for big companies, etc. But there are also many lobbies for environmental organisations – people who are in Brussels, and who are there to do lobbying, to try to influence the directives issued... to me, that's also another form of democracy, and maybe it's working well... [...] Federations are associations of citizens – so that's also another way to have your say. The power struggle is the same, in this kind of negotiation or this kind of lobbying, as it actually is... it happens on another level, that's all.

Such is also the case of an academic, who has an executive position in the political bureau of the Syndicat National des Enseignements de Second Degré (SNES, the main French union in the sector of education), and who has developed a specific knowledge of the institutions, having had the opportunity to oppose the Commission's 'policies' within the framework of his union activity.

It's always been a bunch of technocrats from the European Commission who decide, and that's it. The European Parliament was a small step forward. But it has so little power, even though it should be in charge. It should be. I'd say it's a completely feudal system, where you have a few lords from the European Commission as leaders, and nobody controls them. Nobody, because the European Parliament's control is nothing.

(FR, M, 50, fine arts professor)

I can also mention the case of this European project manager from Italy who, based on his professional experience, criticises institutional bureaucracy, or that of an agricultural federation representative who opposes the 'Danish agricultural model' embodied by commissioner Mariann Fischer Boel. These interviewees all share a personal experience of European institutions. As a result the Europe of institutions is a tangible reality to them, even though, as the young Green party member who compares the European level to what 'actually' happens implies, this experience is always a bit less real than that of national or local institutions. When they lack such experience, even the most attentive ordinary citizens are deprived of the routine salient points that usually give access to politics. The neutralisation of the messages (Guiraudon 2000) emanating from European institutions contributes to their unintelligibility for citizens socialised in national spaces and acculturated to their more cleaved forms of debate. These have historically involved, and still do, political organisations that offer world views, leaders who embody them and occasionally reassert them, opportunities for debates and confrontations, etc. This is not the case here. The Europe of institutions is still perceived by interested citizens as relatively abstract. It is represented more in terms of symbols (the flag) or material objects (buildings, rooms) than by identified political figures, or even institutions that would 'speak to them':

Well, it's silly... The first word [that comes to mind] when you say Europe, is the flag... It's the symbols. But I mean, huh... Brussels, huh... The Commission, the institutions, the European quarter, hmm... Yeah, all these big institutions... All these nationalities crossing paths... Well, I can picture the rooms [...] I don't know the Parliament. I'm thinking about the Commission's rooms.

(FR, F, 33, engineer, works as a project manager
in the Ministry of Agriculture)

[Brussels] doesn't mean anything to people [...] on a daily basis, you don't follow the life of... of that dimension of Europe... In France, you hear about the Council of Ministers. [...] Some minister presented something to the Council of Ministers or... [...] that they debated some issue... For Europe, I don't think they tell us about that.

(FR, F, 50, youth worker)

You always see that exclusively from the French point of view, right? Even in the press there's no support for Europe... they're always going on about France in Europe and how European decisions negatively affect France. And

I think it's the press's fault but it's also Europe's fault because Europe... for most people, myself partly included, it lacks definition.

(FR, H, 24, studying to become a senior official)

Many citizens thus denounce the invisibility of the European political personnel and institutions, in contrast with the materiality of their national counterparts, who can be named, classified, known and recognised and who serve as practical and ordinary touchstones in the world of politicised citizens.

You know, when you told me you wanted to do this interview, I thought I should at least know the name of the president of the European Parliament... Guess what, at work, nobody did! Nobody was able to tell me, the psychiatrists, the doctors or the gardener... people have no idea and they don't care.

(FR, F, 47, special needs worker)

They don't meet enough, they should be like the deputies, the senators: you can see them.

(FR, M, 87, retired schoolteacher)

We have a European government, we don't know them [...] We know the French government, the Minister of Health, we know what his name is, we know what he does, more or less. There's a European Commission; we don't know it, we don't know who's in charge of it.

(FR, M, 45, baker, socialised to politics in his family)

Unlike most, these interviewees do not presuppose a higher level of complexity of the Europe of institutions. Their degree of political competence entitles them to think that they are able to understand it. They are aware that institutions exist, and that they should know them in the same ordinary manner that they know politics in general. Hence, they may regret that these institutions do not 'come' to them:

With our social, educational and cultural level, I should know how Europe works a lot better than I do [...] We should know about these things. At least we know how the French system works, more or less. What the role of the Senate is, what the role of the Parliament is, stuff like that. I don't know if it's more complicated [for Europe] but I know less about it. Information does not come the same way. Information does not come just like that.

(FR, F, 69, executive, Harvard graduate)

For attentive citizens, the distance from the Europe of institutions is especially strong as the lack of embedding in national public spaces is added to the lack of personification and embodiment by its promoters.

Research on political parties has shown that no governing party – at least in founding Member States – could afford to risk its political credit by overtly endorsing a posture likely to be interpreted as Euro-critical (Fertikh, Hû and Juhem 2007). Hence, criticisms of Europe are formulated by more marginal political organisations. Similarly, a number of authors have emphasised the national elites' alternative strategies of 'blame-shifting' and 'credit-taking' for EU policies (Schmidt 2007), even if these actors seek to benefit from European funds. The fact that involvement in European political games entails no national or local recognition of Europe does not work in favour of its promotion in ordinary political contexts. This is also reinforced by the characteristics of European movements, which reproduce those of the central Community space (elitism, exclusivity, etc.) and do not contribute to encouraging encounters between Brussels and the local societies of which these movements are part (Weisbein and Mischi 2004, 2006; Sawicki 1997).

Eliciting no strong political investments within governing parties, Europe does not polarise citizens much. This lack of salience in the political field does not encourage journalists to cover Europe (Juhem 2001) and reinforces its invisibility in the media (Garcia and Le Torrec 2003). More generally, the lack of European political 'news' (Hubé 2008) and of a recurrent European political agenda hinders any form of 'continuous socialisation' to Europe. When interviewees mention mobilising junctures – such as Maastricht, the constitutional treaty, the accession campaigns in new Member States – they also frequently emphasise their very sporadic character. As the young Green party member mentioned earlier regrets, 'There was real momentum [...] now there's nothing left'. A senior civil servant also laments the fact that 'there's virtually no mention of the European Union [in the presidential and legislative 2007 campaigns]... Two years ago, on the other hand, people were passionate about it'. The absence of Europe prevents the acquisition of specific skills on European issues, regularly sustained by rites and events:

> I don't know, I can't remember... I can't remember at all, it really didn't leave a mark on me. At the time I read the treaty, I looked for information, we made reports. [...] And I thought that was really good. But I don't remember anything. I don't remember anything, I'm realising that right now with you. It's a bit scary.
>
> (FR, F, 25, civil servant working in the senate)

Constructed far from ordinary citizens and politics, the European political and institutional games are thus nearly imperceptible, including by the most competent citizens, unless they have a quasi 'professional' experience of the Europe of institutions. Consequently, citizens who do not possess the codes required to access 'legitimate' politics are even more distant from the Europe of institutions. Yet, the prism of cognitive competence is too limiting and does not fully reflect the diversity of the relationships to the res publica. In order not to hastily conclude that there is a form of political illiteracy measured by the yardstick of the legitimist and intellectual relationship to politics, we need to focus on other effects of the institutionalisation of Europe. By producing objects other than political institutions and categories, such as regulations, standards, a currency, funds, etc., Community institutionalisation indeed favours other forms of exposure and other forms of appropriating Europe.

The worlds of Europe beyond the institutional world

After focusing on the institutionalisation of a European polity, this section will focus on the existence of other forms of Europe and relationships to institutional Europe than those implicitly described in the literature on European attitudes, generally based on data from polls. The Concorde material allows us to perceive a diffraction of Europe and to study the multiplicity of the meanings that can be assigned to it, provided that we are attentive to the worlds in which objectifications of Europe can develop and take on meaning. Focusing on the Europe of public policies, by briefly studying the examples of farmers and fishermen concerned by structural policies, and the Europe of business in the world of business owners, I will elaborate on the analysis of the forms of distance inherent to the processes of institutionalisation of Europe, and on the specific ways in which this distance manifests and expresses itself.

Europe as an administration and the effects of 'multi-levels'

One of the forms institutional Europe takes is the Europe of public policies. In a concrete and visible manner, it is embodied by 'outputs' produced by Europe (Scharpf 1999). Many citizens 'perceive' something from it, even though this vague and remote perception varies depending on national contexts. For instance, the existence of funds granted in the framework of the Common Agricultural Policy (CAP) is not only known by farmers; in Central Europe, many know about the new roads funded by European structural funds. However, the Europe of outputs is still far from being known by all, in the sense that its tangibility is related to experiences that are specific to certain professional groups (farmers, fishermen, independent workers, etc.). Even if it is connected with ordinary worlds, does Europe become ordinary in such worlds? Many authors see the Europe of outputs as a solution to the EU's crisis of legitimacy. The Europe of regions has thus been considered in EU and academic circles (Hooghe and Marks 1996) as one of the methods to reduce the democratic deficit. In relation to the weakness of the EU administrations and budgets, this has led to the adoption of 'shared policies' (Smith 2008), whose definition and implementation involve concerted procedures linking several government levels (regional policies, common agricultural policy, etc.). However, the autonomisation of EU political and administrative sectors eager to produce specific styles of regulation distinct from Member States and their traditional methods has led to reinforcing Community procedures governing at a distance (Verger 2008). These sectors have institutionalised standards and principles, defined objectives, and set up procedures on which the distribution and control of funding depends. Unable to fully control implementation, they have delegated the task to national or regional authorities. This has led to increasing the size of specialised services in national, local and decentralised administrations, but also contributed to making their relationships more bureaucratic and increasing the administrative complexity of applications for European funds. It is uncertain whether this has favoured the diffusion of a positive image of Europe in local spaces. Local specialists of Europe go to Brussels only rarely, and their existence allows their counterparts in Brussels regional offices to remain distant from these local spaces. At the interface of Europe and the local level, these specialists are also prone to making Europe more complex in order to justify their role as simplifiers (de Lassalle 2010). Ultimately, the creation of specialised services at all administrative levels tends to contribute to dividing up the EU at the local level, spreading the idea of a technical and complex Europe, rather than promoting the Europe of proximity to the target populations.

– Do you feel that you are well informed on the decisions taken at EU level?

– Not really; just now they came up with this regulation on fishing gear, including trawls. This regulation was voted by the EC in 1998, and we were informed in 2006. […] I don't know if you realise, but that's six… seven… eight years later! […] We weren't even informed by Maritime Affairs, by the authorities! We were informed by… companies that sell fishing gear! It was a measure on trawl mesh sizes, on the size of the nets, to put it simply. […] And they're taking me to court precisely for that. […] That's where the contradiction is, because Europe has allowed us to only have 70–79 ft. trawl nets […] since 1998 and we didn't know, whereas France allowed 80 […] [But to get information] we don't know who to talk to! Maritime Affairs, they're supposed to be our administration, since we depend on them, that's where we pay our contributions, and when we go to see them […] either they can't see us, or they don't know […] Even they haven't got a clue because… I see now, they're taking us to court even though the European law allows us to do what I was doing […] Even they don't seem to know what they're doing. Seems crazy but that's the way it is. […] Well, we're a bit lost with all that…

(FR, M, fisherman)

In order to show these effects of 'multi-level' governance in more detail, the example of farmers and the CAP is telling. There is no overall homogeneity in the discourses of the farmers we interviewed on Europe. The local representative of the French cattle breeders' federation, an organic apple juice manufacturer, or the farm owner who is proud of his management software: these members of the agricultural sector are very different in many respects. They are also not always directly concerned by the CAP; the apple juice manufacturer does not benefit from any European funding, and he interprets a question on the effects of Europe on his professional life in terms of his potential contacts with other Europeans:

Europe doesn't mean all that much to me, because it's, you know… I don't work with Europeans directly… but it happens once in a while. Sometimes there are Italians who come and buy some apple juice, Germans, Belgians, English people.

(FR, M, apple grower and apple juice producer)

These farmers, however, share a number of references that distinguish them from other citizens. Their 'ordinary world' – the world in which they work every day, the people they meet, the objects that have meaning in it, the activities they have – is more or less strongly affected by the CAP. They are the typical example of a group whose social destiny is *de facto* linked to Europe, and it is not absurd to think that their concrete and everyday life integrates a part of Europe. Most farmers know what the CAP is and have an opinion on its effects on their existence. They mention it as soon as Europe is discussed, and link it with their revenues and/ or the fact that they have to comply with standards related to 'European directives'.

> For a farm like ours, the CAP amounts to 80 per cent of our income […] part of it's French but there's a lot of Europe. […] For instance, we have to comply with specifications on storing plant protection products for wheat processing. Now we are forced to have a locked storage place with a sign that reads 'Caution – dangerous substances', with these European directives…
>
> (FR, M, 41, farm owner)

Those who are the most supportive of the EU are those whose income depends on the CAP. Yet, this support is often forced and sometimes expressed with regret, far from the general and Euro-enthusiastic support often assigned to the 'utilitarians' of the Common Market.

> I don't want any subsidies myself, I want my product to sell at a fair price; this way, we no longer need subsidies, we no longer depend from them… We can get rid of Brussels' constraints… [But] you have to understand that without subsidies, there would be no farmers left in France… Farmers can't live without the subsidies, that's the problem…
>
> (FR, M, 48, cereal farmer)

These interviewees, often speak in terms of constraint and obligation:

> We're forced to keep up with Europe, we're forced to keep up a bit… We're forced to comply with the standards for certain things, right. […]There are things we are forced to do […] We were forced to use a new kind of gas [for the cold storage room], a European one, for the environment or whatever. […] There are many things we have to do because of Europe…
>
> (FR, M, 58, farmer)

Many complain that their work does not have the same meaning any more, and say that they would rather make a living from their production than from subsidies, even though the youngest and more educated, and those who manage the largest farms, may value the 'management' dimension of their activity.

Familiar as the CAP may be, it does not make Europe a much more concrete reality. For all the administrative procedures they are subjected to, farmers have to deal with the same people that usually embody national administrations and, more generally, the state. Getting information, subsidies, managing CAP applications, implementing the standards: the same ordinary administrative mediators – in national or local administrations – embody Europe on a concrete level.

If we receive information or new European texts, the French Ministry of Agriculture sends them out, so France informs us, not Europe...

(FR, M, 24, farmer)

In terms of breeding, we have a premium per cow... we fill out a yearly statement and we have a quota... which is set by the departmental direction for agriculture... they have a quota for each department.

(FR, M, 41, farmer)

We have a CAP application; we have to fill it out [...] before May 1, we have to forward it to the DDA...

(FR, M, 58, farmer)

Since there are no physical EU agencies to receive applicants (Dubois 2010), there are no concrete and everyday relationships with Europe; ordinary relationships with agents in administrative offices are largely constitutive of the representations of the institutions and of the relationships to them in these categories of the public (Bourdieu 2002; Siblot 2005).

– With the farm, you must be getting quite a bit of contact with Europe?
– Well, hmm, personally I don't [...] individually, no, people like us, we don't have any... as a simple farmer you don't get to have any contact with them.

(FR, F, 62, farmer)

Ultimately, to these interviewees, Europe is one more administrative layer for them to deal with. It is difficult for them to distinguish it from the French administration, and it appears even more remote and dematerialised, even blamed for the increase in red tape: 'There's loads of paperwork... The paperwork, I can tell you... We're knee-deep in paperwork!' (FR, M, 58, farmer). These fractions of the public describe a Europe made of acronyms (CAP, SPE), letters, administrative delays, directive numbers:

If I'm not mistaken, it's directive 79/409 [...] on migratory birds. The thing is you can't shoot them when they're nesting. [...] In Haute-Vienne, this year, we were no longer allowed to shoot pigeons... blah... well, starting from February 10, well as game. Then you can shoot them as harmful birds, until March 31. In England, they can hunt them until late June. [...] On the one hand, they shorten the periods because supposedly we're reaching nesting periods, and on the other hand, it's no longer hunting, it's destruction. It really doesn't make sense. That's what 79/409's about.

(FR, M, 44, farmer)

Such relationships are obviously not likely to shape a general relationship to the EU and the institutional construction process by capillarity. These farmers' relationship to the EU remains essentially limited to the CAP and to daily realities such as the Euro or administrative hassles.

> Europe is not something we really talk about... But it's true, when you talk about Europe, sometimes, you stop for two seconds, and think, and you realise you don't really know what it is... that's right [...] We know what it is, professionally, we know what Europe brings us, but apart from that we don't know what it's doing.

> (FR, M, 24, farmer)

> We're not concerned by Europe, you know. Except for the Euro and the CAP, you know, the rest... It sort of goes over our heads...

> (FR, M, 44, farmer)

> Apart from that, apart from the Euro and the paperwork...

> (FR, F, 49, farmer)

More generally, these interviewees do not express their relationship to the Europe of institutions in the same way as politicised citizens. They do not express the need to know what EU institutions do. However, their ordinary relationship to politics is based on interactions with familiar politicians and civil servants (Briquet 2003); these relationships favour the recognition and the legitimacy of political activity. There are no such relationships with the EU: these citizens do not know the EU and the EU does not know them, which they perceive as a problem.

> On the municipal level, it's closer. When we have meetings, when we want to say something... [...] on the cantonal level, I know the departmental council, I know them well [...] Even a deputy, if necessary... I can contact him whenever I have a project... But beyond that, Europe, it's more distant... It's far, right?

> (FR, M, 58, farmer)

Despite the claims made in utilitarian theories, these farmers' support is not particularly enthusiastic; nor does it entail a wider support for the European construction process or a connection with the Europe of institutions based on a singular experience. They have a significant experience of the EU, but not one that corresponds to what is reflected in polls, communication policies or European studies. This experience forms the basis of a relationship to Europe that is distant, and to some extent one that is not without puzzlement or frustration.

Conversely, an entirely different reality of Europe emerges in the last European world I will analyse now, that of the common market.

The Europe of the Single Market

Our research has been conducted in the context of the consolidation, since the 1990s, of a Europe often described as 'neo-liberal' (Jobert 1994; Denord and Schwartz 2009). Several hypotheses, not necessarily exclusive, are directly rooted in the institutionalisation process, and either emphasise the key role of the promoters of neo-liberalism in this institutionalisation (Denord and Schwartz 2009) or the low level of institutionalisation of a transnational 'Euro-Atlantic' space where state power is 'demonopolised' (Cohen, Dezalay and Marchetti 2007). A number of secondary processes are linked to this, such as the rise of economists in a European Commission that has long been an institutional haven for jurists (Vauchez 2007; Georgakakis and de Lassalle 2009) or, for the promoters of a European social model, the internalisation of their inferior position, preventing them from making 'political' initiatives (Robert 2007). Several studies on the Member States' conversion to neo-liberalism (Jobert 1994) confirm that this neo-liberal inclination is also the product of certain 'uses of Europe' in national struggles, even though a 'liberal' strategy might not be primarily or deliberately pursued (Garcia 2007). These studies do not claim that the Commission and EU institutions in general have monolithically forced neo-liberalism on Member States (Robert 2007), but in our research project, we have observed that Europe is primarily perceived by ordinary citizens in economic terms, if only because most interviewees are able to talk about Europe starting from the subject of the Euro. Some citizens have a favourable outlook on this economic union, because they believe the EU should first and foremost be about a process of economic integration allowing to significantly bolster the national position, or because they think that nations should remain the essential players in European politics. Others are reserved because they would like Europe to be an essentially social or cultural entity. The most frequent perceptions, however, revolve around 'freedom of movement' and the Single Market, which suggest different representations depending on the individuals. While some are unhappy with this freedom, others like entrepreneurs or industrials embrace it (see Chapter 5).

Among the latter category, we have interviewed diverse individuals; the owners of small or medium-sized companies, with various levels of international activity, they also vary in terms of level of education (from being self-taught to graduates of major engineering or business schools) or social origins (self-made men or heirs). Yet, they share common interpretations and evaluations of the Europe of business, of the Single Market.

> The European market is becoming a market of its own, it's one of the most important markets! So... hmm... being against Europe today doesn't make a lot of sense to me.
>
> (FR, M, engineer in the construction sector)

While in the first two cases analysed, Europe was characterised by its lack of materiality, these entrepreneurs describe a very concrete Europe; it is a physical territory that they travel across easily and often, both in a professional and personal capacity:

The European Union makes transactions easier, and it's very easy to go to Germany; I do my shopping in Germany. It's not an issue for me. Since we have a single, shared currency, I go to Italy, I've just come back from Spain, that's good.

(FR, M, 40, owner of a small company)

The simplifications induced by the EU have reinforced their dispositions to mobility. They are endowed with linguistic capital, which they got from school or on the job, and which makes their circulation in Europe easier, as well as their ability to establish contacts.

I'm bilingual in English. I learn German and took it in all my exams […] I also speak Spanish and Portuguese, and French obviously.

(FR, M, 47, owner of a small consulting business)

Europe has thus become a 'second nature', the territory on which they raise their children and plan their strategies of social reproduction (Wagner 1988)

Our four kids […] they have all lived… in Europe, yeah! You see, the youngest, Guillaume, he's living in England now, he's going to spend three or four years in England so… to learn stuff… he's going to finish school in England. Nicolas spent three years in Germany, Valérie spent three years in England, Charles spent three years in the US, but Europe, for them… they have friends, one of them is married to a Dutchman, another is married to a German guy, so it's not a problem for them, even much less than it is for me.

(FR, M, owner of a company with 1,000 employees)

As this excerpt implicitly reveals, these entrepreneurs do not distinguish between Europe – limited to a group of Member States – and the international or transnational level. Essentially, they see Europe as an extension of the financial markets in which they can 'do business'. Therefore, they do not need any explanations when the interviewer mentions the Schengen Area ('Schengen! It might be the best thing about Europe, it's made exchanging goods easier and brought free movement') or the Bolkestein directive, because these EU achievements have a very concrete relevance to their lives on a professional and personal level.

I can tell you that my business is completely different now. My merchandise used to be stuck for days on end, and now I can have my merchandise circulate everywhere in Europe. I make a better living too, so honestly, I'm not going to complain about the situation.

(FR, M, 40, owner of a small business)

Several other EU achievements are also assessed in terms of business opportunities and the economic climate. On the Euro, unlike the other citizens, these interviewees very rarely broach the issue of purchasing power; they focus on monetary policy, or more simply on the simplification of doing business.

The Euro is mostly a good thing. For the countries, to negotiate and compare prices, the Euro is a good thing indeed […] but now there's a danger – that's the value of the Euro against the dollar. […] But it's a truly positive thing, having a single currency with countries we're directly doing business with.

(FR, M, 45, owner of a company with forty-five employees)

There are pros and cons to the Euro, but it's a currency that exists now and for us as exporters… we all have the same currency. So there are more fluctuations. We don't all speak the same language but we speak the same currency. […] For us, the Euro parity is […] net industrial profit.

(FR, M, owner of a company with 1,000 employees)

The issue of the accession of Turkey is similarly discussed from a business angle, when other citizens generally put forth cultural or religious arguments:

Turkey? We don't see business the same way.

(FR, F, 59, owner of a hotel in Paris)

The accession of Turkey can happen because economically, they're a bit stronger than other countries that have already accessed the EU.

(FR, H, 40, owner of a small company)

I don't have any… I work with them, I have personal relationships just as I do with, say… Poles or Spaniards or whatever, it doesn't make a difference… So it's not a problem for me.

(FR, M, owner of a company with 1,000 employees)

To them, more than the EU institutions or the actors who embody them, Europe is a group of Member States. Each of these states is an economic partner or competitor, and they are assessed and hierarchised on the basis of their performance.

Europe will always be centred on the blue banana – we're stuck on the banana, but it's a driving force… The rest is people who… they will always remain peripheral zones.

(FR, M, 38, engineer in the construction sector)

Madrid is starting to be a bit excentred, and until now, even if it's changing, it still isn't a very significant country, in terms of GDP.

(FR, M, 47, owner of a small consulting business)

These interviewees judge the Europe of institutions from their position as entrepreneurs. Generally claiming to be 'liberal', they remain distant from the political world, in a perspective of division of social work where they are in charge of production, which they deem to be important.

I believe that economic power is greater than political power... maybe it's ambitious to say that! But I believe that politicians wouldn't be there if businesses didn't run well. And if businesses didn't create jobs, social responsibility, wealth for the country, the politicians wouldn't exist without us. So... I believe I have a lot to do.

(FR, M, owner of a company with 1,000 employees)

Their information on Europe depends on their professional activity:

I get a lot of information about laws on labour and movement of goods.

(FR, M, 40, owner of a small company)

I get my information mostly from people I work with, since I work with several European countries. So earlier I was on the phone with a Spaniard; as soon as we're done with the interview, I'll phone my English accountant.

(FR, M, 49, owner of a small consulting business)

While they generally claim to be quite badly informed, the information they lack is not – as in the case of politicised citizens – about EU institutions, in which they have little interest, but rather about the practical aspects of the Europe of business and finance.

On banks, all that stuff. Being informed... [about] investments, for instance on the European market, on the advantages to... I don't know... Say I want to buy a flat in Barcelona, for instance, I'd like to know more about the law, the legislation, and on the movement of capital. Individually, we don't have that information. [...] Likewise, it's also complicated for an international investor, not for multinational companies, but for a small business, it's still very complicated. You should be able to buy something in Bratislava without having problems with national legislations.

(FR, F, 59, owner of a hotel in Paris)

Effectively, their judgement on EU institutions is not based on the way they work, on the policy process, on their democratic or invisible character – it is perceived in terms of economic efficiency. This is shown by the recurrent criticisms formulated on the waste of money inherent to the dispersion of the institutional sites, or on their location and their place in the 'international economy':

To me, choosing Brussels was a huge mistake to begin with. Go and explain to a Korean that Europe's headquarters are in Brussels. Where's Belgium? What's Belgium? To me [it should have been] London. [...] My Japanese customers, or the Korean ones, when they say 'I'm going to Europe', first they land in London, and then they see, they go to the provinces, to Berlin, to Madrid...

(FR, M, 47, owner of a small consulting business)

The issues raised are related to the institutional deficit, but are actually centred on the harmonisation of the conditions of economic competition between Member States.

> On the other hand, some things will certainly have to change in Europe... Europe cannot only be a word... and... whether in terms of taxation, or in terms of a number of things [...] As far as standards go, as far as... things being different from one country to another... so, well, it's far from being unified yet, right. Between consumer standards in France, Spain, Germany, you can't compare, there's an ocean between them!

> (FR, M, 41, owner of a company with 1,000 employees)

Unlike the other categories studied in this chapter, whose political distance to Europe is often not of their own choice, these entrepreneurs thus stay deliberately far from the Europe of institutions. The latter's invisibility is neither specific nor seen as problematic. This is also because while these entrepreneurs support the EU for reasons close to those described by utilitarian theorists (Gabel and Palmer 1995), they do not support the Europe of institutions but rather a large economic market extending beyond the borders of Europe.

Conclusion

Before I conclude more generally, let me point out that the examples analysed here obviously do not exhaustively account for all the possible relationships to Europe observed in the interviews conducted during this research. Focusing on other ordinary words, I could have investigated the Europe of standards, the Europe of peace, or the Europe of cultural exchanges – other objective forms through which other citizens interpret and appropriate other manifestations of institutional Europe. Nevertheless, one of this chapter's contributions lies in jointly studying processes of European institutionalisation and the worlds in which they unfold and take root, thereby reintroducing the 'effects of Europe' into the overall research perspective presented in this book.

More generally, in this chapter a more focused and sociological approach of populations in studies on European public opinion is pleaded for, showing how appropriations of Europe depend both on the way Europe is experienced in specific social worlds, and on how it may make sense in them according to diverse living conditions and life experiences. As far as the theory of cognitive mobilisation goes, given what we have shown on the distance of politicised citizens to EU institutions, it appears difficult to go on thinking that merely improving institutional communication or transforming the institutional process (for instance, from a working to a talking parliament) will change things significantly. My demonstration ultimately confirms the importance of political brokerage in the process of constructing citizenship and identification with political institutions (Garrigou 2002; Briquet 1997, 2003). At the same time it demonstrates the weaknesses of the thesis of cognitive mobilisation around a Europe of institutions, based on a diffusionist perspective. Politicised, educated and supposedly more Europhile citizens promote and impose social norms of being a good European citizen; i.e. being interested, informed, concerned and participating in the process of European construction. Lacking the concrete access points to get more familiarised with European politics, politicised citizens are not able to play the role of opinion leaders that the scholarly literature and communication policies are so quick to assume. Lastly, on utilitarianism, this chapter shows very contrasting forms of support of realities that, while sharing a common label, such as Europe or utilitarianism, actually refer to entirely different interpretations, realities and experiences when contextualised in different social settings. All these arguments suggest that we should continue to engage in more qualitative research in the sociology of European opinion, a field all too marked by sweeping generalisations that fail to adequately reflect a diversity of meanings and representations.

chapter | europe in the popular milieus:
eleven | what 'silent citizens' perceive of
| europe

Christèle Marchand and Pierre Edouard Weill

> Polls and surveys give a voice to the 'silent citizens' – the people who do not vote, do not take active part in political life, do not channel their opinions through groups of interests or citizens organisations.

> Margot Wallström, Vice President of the European Commission, Institutional Relations and Communication Strategy. Opening speech at the stakeholders conference on 'Understanding public opinion', 27th October 2006.

One of the objectives of the Concorde project consisted in interviewing 'silent citizens'. This category of the population, the most distant from politics and political mobilisation, are thought to express themselves through polls. However, as Daniel Gaxie and Jay Rowell pointed out in their chapter on research methodology, it is precisely this category that is under-represented in public opinion polls. Do they show any interest in an abstract entity such as the European Union and if so, on what basis are opinions formed? Studying this (occasional) interest, which is largely dependent on a more general interest in current affairs and politics, entails raising the following question: what do we effectively measure when we try to understand the ordinary conceptions of Europe? We have deliberately chosen the vague term of 'popular milieus' to designate the individuals we are talking about, but this choice requires a terminological clarification. On this point, we share the reluctance expressed by Samia Moucharik (2008) regarding the use of the expression 'classes populaires' when considering the diversity in relationships – and non-relationships – to politics. In addition, terminology based on social classes (working class, underclass, blue-collar workers) is both normatively laden and reduces social stratification to the social division of labour. However, many of the most 'silent citizens' neither have a class conscience, nor are they members of professions associated with the working class; in fact many are on the margins of the labour market. Sociologically defining 'popular milieus' requires considering the lower regions in the social space – citizens who have little cultural capital and little economic capital. Today however popular milieus are not only defined by belonging to a specific socio-professional category, such as workers (Leonardi 2008), they may overlap with other professional groups whose boundaries have become porous (Mayer 2002: 509), and have become marked by increasingly precarious job situations and a succession of periods of inactivity or short-term contracts, for instance in the service sector. All of these attributes help to define individuals who could assigned to the 'popular milieus', under the condition that the individuals share 'a condition in which they follow orders, are dominated at work and are socially and economically vulnerable' (Schwartz 2002: 10).

The properties of CONCORDE interviewees who can be considered as coming from a popular milieu

This study relies exclusively on first-hand qualitative data. We have not used data from Eurobarometers, as they do not enable a precise investigation of this particular category. Our chapter is based on seventy-two of the 333 interviews conducted for the Concorde survey in France. This sub-sample includes eight individuals without any degree, two BEPC holders,[1] three Certificat d'Etudes holders,[2] eleven CAP[3] holders, fourteen BEP[4] holders. For nineteen of the interviewees, the level of qualification is not known but we can assume, given their professions, that it is not very high. Two interviewees hold a general Baccalauréat and five hold a professional Baccalauréat. Finally, five BTS holders[5] and three interviewees who possess only a short or interrupted university course were included in the sample, because they came from a working-class family background, are unemployed or have menial jobs. Although they are considered as belonging to 'popular milieus' for the purposes of this study, these eight interviewees are borderline cases, distinguished by a greater amount of cultural capital, which enables us to specify the plurality of this category. Concerning the profession of the sample, forty-one interviewees are classified as rank and file 'employees' but the boundary with some more intermediate professions (six in our sample) is sometimes difficult to establish. The sample also includes nineteen blue-collar workers, an independent worker (home hairdresser), and a student who works as a waitress. With four interviewees unemployed, one receiving minimum benefit payment, twenty-four in unstable jobs (temporary, part-time, or fixed-term contracts), nine who have retired and one on invalidity benefits, more than half of the interviewees in our sample are in a relatively difficult financial situation. Also, twenty-two interviewees have an immigration background (mostly of North African and Turkish origin). Among the forty-two men and thirty women, all the age brackets are represented. The geographical distribution is rather diverse. We have given little emphasis to the urban or rural environment of the interviewees, as this is perceived as an unreliable indicator to precisely evaluate the social environment of the interviewees. Many interviews were carried out in small or mid-sized provincial towns.

When do interviewees from popular milieus talk about Europe and with whom? When and how do they encounter Europe and take the time to think about it? As it turns out, many never do outside the exceptional context of the interview. For many, discussing Europe remains reserved to an elite and requires a certain legiti-

---

1.   The Brevet d'Etudes du Premier Cycle du second degré, now called Brevet, corresponds to a ninth grade education.

2.   The Certificat d'Etudes which no longer exists, certified the completion of primary school.

3.   The Certificat d'Etudes Professionnelles is a certificate earned through vocational classes and an apprenticeship.

4.   The Brevet d'Etudes Professionnelles is a vocational high school diploma.

5.   The Brevet de Technicien Supérieur is a two-year post-secondary vocational diploma.

macy (Bélot 2002). This distance from Europe shows in the following remark of a warehouse worker: 'Well, if you ask me, like that… I think you're the first guy that has ever asked me that, stuff about Europe' (FR, M, 26, born in Morocco, holder of a BEP). In analysing the discourse of individuals whose knowledge of Europe is often very limited, we should not assume the existence of politically structured attitudes, regardless of the varieties of 'Euroscepticism' or 'Euro-optimism' discussed in the field of European studies. Individuals from popular milieus often seem openly unconcerned by European political affairs. The subject is far from their everyday preoccupations, too complex, and they are generally not ashamed to admit that they know nothing about it. Unlike that which is observed on national political issues, the interviewees almost never seem to feel exposed as inadequate citizens when admitting ignorance on European issues. They feel as if they are not the only ones who do not understand anything about Europe and to a large extent they are at ease about this. Among citizens who are not aware of the EU's political organisation, the EU can appear as an object of indifference (Duchesne and Van Ingelgom 2008), but the real or imagined consequences of European construction on their everyday lives may provoke feelings of worry, hope, satisfaction or dismay. Focusing on ordinary conceptions of Europe means focusing on the interest in Europe shown by ordinary individuals. How are popular milieus interested in Europe? In other words, what is at stake in this relationship for each interviewee? What does a positive or negative judgement on Europe involve for them? How do they find the means to become concretely interested in Europe? How do they find the resources to talk about it and to feel entitled to do so? Which social experiences do they succeed in mobilising to construct a relatively coherent discourse on Europe? In their discourse, members of popular milieus mostly express ambivalent feelings, in the sense that they have two sides (positive/negative for instance) that are not necessarily opposed or ambiguous (Percheron 1991): Europe is alternatively positively and negatively appreciated. It can be assumed that for some respondents, saying that 'there is good and bad in Europe' is a way of not taking a clear stance – like placing oneself at the centre on a left-right political scale.

When a strong interest in Europe is observed, whether this is positive or negative, the interviewees' profiles tend to be atypical compared to those that prevail in popular milieus. For example, they are strongly politicised through trade union or party membership; open to other European countries through the existence of social contacts with Europeans; are involved in Europe-related associations; have professions which are directly linked to Europe or influenced by it. In order to define the interests of those who have specific reasons to be interested in Europe, it is essential to consider associative interests, activism – Front National voters for instance –, professional interests – professions more or less directly 'threatened' by European-driven liberalisation such as truck drivers – or identity interests – European citizenship can be a positive identity 'refuge' for certain people with an immigration background. Occasionally these diverse interests and experiences can factor into the expression of relationships to Europe. In other words, this interest in some aspects of Europe of those who do not have the cultural capital required for a 'disinterested' interest in Europe, is perhaps, compared to other social milieus (see other contributions in this volume), expressed through the interviewees' practical experiences of Europe,[6] insofar as they do not have a cultural baggage that would enable them to talk about Europe in another way. Because of the structuring of social contacts, interviewees from popular milieus are less likely than those from other social classes to know people whose professions are directly linked to Europe. These two reasons explain why popular milieus are particularly distant from institutional Europe; but nevertheless they do not allow us to claim that their relationship to Europe is profoundly different from most other social milieus where this distance is also the norm. In fact, it seems that they share a relationship characterised by the 'intertwining' of more or less well-argued 'favourable and critical judgements' with the majority of citizens well documented for other categories in this volume. To be able to speak about the European Union, since this is what we ask them to do, the interviewees handle their 'lack of information'[7] by mobilising three discursive forms: for those who are most familiar with Europe, activist experiences are mobilised; those with no direct relationship to European institutional realities but possessing some social resources and networks make the most of personal experiences linked to Europe to generate a discourse; and finally for those who are most ignorant of European realities and without direct or indirect experience through travel or acquaintances, the focus is on concrete and personal concerns to make sense of Europe.

Most interviewees within this category nonetheless share a 'remote evaluation' of European realities, and are vaguely positive and/or generally negative. This type of relationship can however coexist in some individuals with a 'limited involvement' pertaining to issues or experiences linked to their profession – truck drivers for example. Furthermore, a minority of interviewees possess substitute forms of cultural capital, often accumulated through participation in political, union or voluntary organisations. These elements allow us to distinguish between those who possess some political or social capital and have a politicised perception of some European debates, the majority of individuals in this category who are more 'remote' from European construction, and those who are complete 'strangers to Europe' and are the most ignorant of its institutional realities.

The 'politicised': hostility towards liberalism as a vector of familiarisation with the European Union

This first group is made up of individuals with very different, or even opposing political preferences: from retired National Front activists to young immigrants from southern countries, or activists or sympathisers of left-wing associations or unions. The anti-liberal point of view in this subgroup is pronounced and European enlargement is often seen as a threat. Both anti-globalisation and nationalist or

---

6. These experiences may be similar to the 'experiences, not necessarily intellectually constructed, which are related to the social space of everyday relationships' (Blondel and Lacroix 1996).

7. Echoing the 'lack of political information of ordinary citizens' discussed by Sniderman (1993).

even xenophobic discourses are expressed. Nevertheless, the arguments mobilised in order to evaluate the EU are often related to day-to-day concerns and cover a more limited number of issues compared to interviewees in the middle and upper segments of society. The interviewees of this first group thus oscillate between the ideal types of 'general' and 'limited' involvement. Accounts of their situations and personal experiences are interwoven with references to party slogans and elements from the discourses of anti-liberal political figures. However, a strictly political analysis of relationships to Europe limited to a minority of politically competent interviewees, in opposition to a more social analysis of the rest of the sample, would not do justice to the complexities of the discourses.[8] The existence of partially structured relationships to Europe based on a form of politicisation contradicts the miserabilist conception of a generalised dispossession of popular milieus with regard to European political questions. These interviewees frequently express support for a 'social' Europe – this social dimension is perceived to be insufficient or non-existent – against a 'liberal' Europe and its consequences on the job market and purchasing power. Their electoral participation in national and European polls is relatively high. The 'dilution of the electoral norm' specific to popular milieus in France is not observed in the case of these interviewees (Braconnier and Dormagen 2007). The presence of politicised discourses and electoral participation is strongly linked to the intensity of primary or secondary political socialisation.

Although this element distinguishes these individuals from other interviewees in our sample, further distinctions need to be made within this group. The fact that they all originate from popular milieus is not sufficient to understand the multi-dimensional character of their hostility to a 'liberal' Europe. The study of the political socialisation process further shows that there is a link between the perception of the consequences of European construction, and the existence and the nature of a politically structured vision of the social world. Living in a quiet residential area or in an 'at-risk' neighbourhood, belonging to the population of non-European immigrants or not are variables which can contribute to explaining the nature of a politically hostile perception of the Union. Some interviewees from the first group have experienced a primary political socialisation with activists in their family circles. These individuals, who have reached baccalauréat level or even spent a short time in university, did not benefit from their studies as they had expected, and were unemployed or had unstable jobs at the time of the interview. Other interviewees accumulated a cultural capital of substitution during their secondary socialisation in a professional or activist context. Qualified workers or low-level employees, BEP or Certificat d'Etudes holders, they are less qualified but often have relatively stable and well-paid jobs.

One of our interviewees (FR, M, 32, BEP holder), a specialised worker in the automobile industry, lives in a block of council flats in the suburbs of Strasbourg. His relationship with Europe combines a negative evaluation, justified by his situation and personal experience, with certain characteristics of a limited general

---

8.   On the traditional opposition between these two types of interpretations, see Lehingue 2007c: 18.

involvement: he makes vague references to European institutions. Based on the consequences of the Euro on the decline of his own purchasing power, he attempts to denounce the bias in the calculation of the 'European Central Bank price index', but tends to confuse it with the one used by the French national statistics institute (INSEE): 'They calculate the consumer price index with the wrong products... You have to take everyday products like bread, fruit and vegetables into account... But they take cars even though you only buy one every five years...' An active member of the local branch of the Confédération Générale du Travail (CGT) union, he refers directly to specific socialising experiences to justify his knowledge on some of the issues of the process of European economic integration:

> Bolkestein... yeah, I know about that...the protests against the neo-liberal directive thing! (...) So like, they bring a Polish guy to France and pay him with a Polish salary, right? Well of course, when you live in France, you don't really agree with that... Finding a French person to work on a Polish salary, that's not damn easy ...there's a union strike actually which was against the project of...anyway, it was aborted, right?

While individuals who have little educational capital tend to refrain from generalising, this interviewee has acquired a substitute cultural capital that allows him to do so: 'The freedom to be able to work anywhere in Europe...not a bad thing for everyone... at least as I was saying for Bolkestein, for the people who are from the smaller countries, they can be lucky...'. For these fractions of the public, the party or union slogans are wielded in different ways and are related to different themes. Elements from an available 'anti-liberal' discourse are therefore used selectively, depending on personal situation and experiences. We can, in fact, observe that some issues are more or less salient and conducive to the production of a political argumentation according to the position in the division of labour. Thus, for the above cited automobile worker, the CAP is a difficult subject to politicise in this way: 'agricultural directives, the Common Agricultural Policy... I don't give a shit'. Despite some mobilisable cognitive shortcuts, these interviewees remained ill at ease or indifferent in discussing most topics related to EU institutions. In spite of the long-standing friendly relationship between the interviewer and the interviewee quoted above, the symbolic violence of the situation tends to reactivate a certain social distance between them. Less eager to assert a personal opinion than members of the upper categories of the social space, they tend to follow the union or party line. For example, a railway worker at the SNCF, a member of the National Front, followed party instructions in the 2005 referendum: 'I voted in all honesty. I voted 'no' and followed the ideas of the Front National as usual...' (FR, M, 47). For a young unemployed salesman, holder of a BTS, hostility towards 'liberalism' is a very strong ideological principle inherited from his Algerian parents, former Communist Party members. This primary political socialisation structures his vision of the social world and explains his rejection of the functioning of the European institutions, resulting in a politically motivated negative vote in the constitutional referendum:

- Competition creates inequalities... also, the economic system as it is today is not working for me... [...] Well it's the less well-off who are going to accept the lowest salaries, so yeah there you go... and that is really going to leave them in deep shit, and in the rich countries like us, well that's going to create unemployment that's all... economic growth at any price, law of supply and demand... you see... it's kinda shit... it screws us and it screws everything else as well... the Constitution that was proposed to us was a neo-liberal thing, and I didn't like it'
- What did your parents say about that?
- They said: 'It's bad my son!' (FR, M, 25).

All the interviewees in this group are hostile to privatising public companies – privatisation is spontaneously linked to European construction, but often from an ethical point of view: 'It's larshouma [a disgrace]! Even in the health sector it's all about making dough'. This critical representation of privatisation is strongly influenced by morals bordering between Islam and Marxism, which have been inculcated ever since infancy. For the auto worker, this representation comes from personal experience, which turned into political conviction: his union socialisation contributed to his hostility towards the idea of competition and his attachment to public services: 'Competition...in general I'm against it. Anyway, the cash belongs to the State... the problem is that afterwards, when you have problems, are they there to intervene or not? ... If it's privatised, I don't trust it...' (FR, M, 32). Some interviewees, like the young unemployed salesman, are also more willing than others to convert practical issues linked to the introduction of a single currency into a more specific political issue: 'We don't benefit from it. The little man pays the price, you know... we buy our sandwich for four Euros even though it used to be twelve francs...' (FR, M, 25). A modest pensioner from the South of France, who is a National Front voter, denounces the economic 'elites', those in power in opposition to 'the people': 'The Euro killed us... Me, I always think about the salamis I buy, I used to get them for twenty-four francs and now they cost more than thirty, my salamis. I'm talking in francs on purpose.' (FR, M, 72). Whether their choice of sandwich is salami-pickles or tuna-harissa, these interviews mobilise everyday experience in the same way to make arguments against the Union's monetary policies. Opposing political orientations may even converge, as in the case of the SNCF employee: 'I agree with... This might shock you, as a former Front National supporter, but I agree with Olivier Besancenot[9] on social issues...' (FR, M, 47).

However, these occasional convergences should be put into perspective. There are major disagreements as to the measures that should be taken in relation to the delegation of sovereignty or to the enlargement of the Union towards Eastern European countries or Turkey. Hence, several tendencies should be distinguished within this first group. Concerning enlargement, National Front activists express

---

9. Far-left (Trotskyite) leader of the New Anti-capitalist Party (NPA).

fear that France might have less international influence, that opening borders could lead to an uncontrollable rise of immigration and unemployment, and see the integration of Muslims, who 'should be dropped from their charter flights into the Mediterranean' (FR, M, 72), as impossible in a Christian Europe. However, National Front voters or activists do not have a monopoly on hostility towards the new or potential member states. A Franco-Portuguese employee, who claims to be 'nationalist like all Portuguese', insists on the negative aspects of the Eastern enlargement for France, before claiming that 'enlargement was a good thing at the beginning, like in '86 when Portugal joined...' (FR, M, 32). Enlargement is commonly perceived as a threat for salaries and jobs. However some interviewees, such as a waitress in a fast-food restaurant, who is an activist in an organisation associated with the Kurdistan Labour Party, or a youth worker in a state subsidised job, emphasise the benefits enjoyed by citizens of new member states. They express their solidarity with the poorest countries and support the distribution of European funds to promote their development. According to them, the EU should not be dominated by the founding countries, while unionised workers do not question the dominant position of 'big' countries in the Union. Thus within the 'anti-liberal' group of the sample, we observe disagreements which are related to the nature of the 'national' or 'international' prism through which the consequences of European construction are evaluated. Qualified workers, whether they are CGT union members or activists or National Front voters, tailor their discourse around specifically national frames (Déloye 2007). Contrary to these 'sovereignist' stances, some interviewees see liberal European construction, globalisation and financial capitalism as the same thing, in opposition to what 'social Europe' should be. The fast-food waitress even refers to the advent of a 'global Europe' as a hypothetical model of political regulation. Borrowing several elements from 'anti-globalisation' discourses, these individuals share some characteristic features with the ideal type of limited general involvement. Yet, their discourse often relies on moral values and considerations.

But unlike other members of our sample, these politicised interviewees hold some precise knowledge on the functioning of the Community on several subjects. They regularly follow political shows on TV, and read the local press or even party-related publications.[10] Noticeably, the interviewees from popular milieus who have the most informational resources are also the ones who claim to be the most 'ill-informed' or distrustful towards the information they receive. Thus, it is not necessarily the people who experience the most objective consequences of the construction of the Union who are the most openly hostile, but rather those for whom Europe is visible in the media and who use elements of their primary or secondary political socialisation to make sense of this information. Although they have more capital than other interviewees from popular milieus, they are not more satisfied with their living conditions. On the contrary, they know that they

---

10. *Minute* for National Front activists, *La Forge*, a weekly paper linked to the far-left *Parti des Travailleurs*, or the Communist daily newspaper *L'Humanité*.

have something to lose and worry about the security of their professional situation and the possibility of social decline; all the more so as they demonstrate a greater ability to anticipate the future than other segments of the popular milieus who we will now analyse.

'Another' Europe: the ambivalence of a 'remote' relationship to Europe

The second sub-group of interviewees includes individuals who have a relationship to Europe, fluctuating between relative satisfaction and disappointment, depending on the issues brought up during the interviews. These individuals are particularly remote and wary of politics. They often blame politics or politicians, albeit in a vague and general manner, for certain consequences of European construction on their everyday lives. They nevertheless share an overall positive outlook on the European project, based on 'post-materialist' conceptions usually considered in the literature as specific to more educated fractions of the population (Inglehart 1971). These conceptions are expressed in the mobilisation of social experiences that are mostly perceived in terms of affects. We will subsequently seek to grasp the cognitive instruments used to evaluate European construction.

As the imposed theme of Europe is largely unfamiliar to them, interviewees in this group, the largest of our three subgroups, are often exposed to questions and themes which they have never heard of or thought about and improvise answers to 'save face'. Less politically competent than members of the group studied in the first section, they nevertheless feel entitled to express themselves on Europe, but often in ways that differ from politically structured opinions or attitudes, on condition that the interviewer puts them at ease and provides them with a 'sense of social ease, favourable to plain speaking, provided by various kinds of secondary solidarity liable to offer indisputable guarantees of sympathetic comprehension' (Bourdieu *et al.* 1999: 612). Age and place of residence do not differentiate these individuals from the rest of the sample. However, the proportion of women in this sub-group is much greater and the interviewees come from particularly modest backgrounds. Most interviewees did not have a high school diploma and most followed short vocational courses after middle school and are either unemployed or working in part-time jobs. Very few have secure contracts which are not fixed term. These interviewees are not members of a political party or a trade union. They have not been exposed to socialisation processes,whether in their family, or in their occupational or leisure activities, although some have been marked by religious values in their youth. With little political competence, they are close to the ideal types of positive and negative remote evaluation defined by Daniel Gaxie.

The construction of the European Union appears as an object which is far from the ordinary preoccupations of the interviewees, for whom politics remains a rare topic of conversation, both with friends or with colleagues: 'To be honest when I'm on the job, with my colleagues it's more like: "Yo! You watched the game last night?"' (FR, M, 26, ambulance driver). Respondents don't demonstrate a particular inferiority complex or sense of guilt when admitting that they have little political information and demonstrate little interest:

I don't think that I'm particularly ill-informed but let's say that I don't take the time to get information. If there was more free time maybe, but in my free time I have other things to do than get information on Europe'

(FR, F, 22, waitress)

An ambulance driver working for Europ Assistance and the eldest son of a large family of migrants from Mali, while discussing his informational practices, opposes a 'popular' daily newspaper to publications which he knows have more legitimacy: 'I'm not gonna read, hmm, what are they called... *Libération*, *Le Monde* etc...! No, no, I like to read the *Parisien*! The newspaper for people in the inner city!' (FR, M, 26). His discourse on political professionals evokes the 'cynical chic' type mentioned by Nina Eliasoph when referring to the 'irreverent' style of those who evoke their ignorance or their lack of interest (Eliasoph, 1990: 193): 'National or European [politicians], they're the same, right... we don't really know what they do, politicians... they are like the Mafia! Some of the people in prison are crooks, but those guys, they are the real crooks!' The expression of this distance to politics, referring both to the European and national level, cannot be necessarily considered as apolitical (Gaxie 2001). A slaughterhouse worker, who says he is completely disgusted by politics and knows 'zilch' about it, claims that 'the world is messed up' and 'anyway, it's all Maastricht's fault' (FR, M, 53, worker). Those who have a hard time making ends meet even though they have a job are amongst the most virulent, but do not show political, statutory or objective competence. A janitor with civil servant status claims that 'France is one of the European countries that have the lowest wages' (FR, M, 38). A bachelor, he is not satisfied with his life in a tiny studio apartment and links his disinterest in Europe to his social situation: 'What I see about Europe is my own personal case: my money and my lifestyle. If the European Parliament raises my salary, then yes, I'd like to know more about it.'

The remote critical relationship to politics leads interviewees to negative perceptions of the EU. The same kind of attitude can be observed in the discourse of a seasonal worker in the hotel and food industry when he discusses his lack of motivation to vote:

> On a political level, citizens or whatever, they don't explain anything to us... we are told that it will be better for us but we are not told how and why it will be better for us, or when it will be better for us in truth you know... they just tell us it will be better for you, so you sign! Well I just don't agree you know...I don't listen to people like that... for the European Constitution...Giscard d'Estaing, he did his thing, he was like, alright... there you go... that's why I didn't vote, know what I mean? They were messing with us! It goes over people's heads... right, we don't understand anything but I don't think I'm the only one, actually! Anyway, maybe politicians are more qualified to talk about European problems but anyway, in France they don't represent us so at the European level forget it... It's beyond hopeless.

(FR, M, 27, unemployed)

This justification of abstention in the 2005 referendum, which includes a critique of the representative link and a mention of the President of the Convention on the future of Europe, shows how some interviewees tend to exaggerate their ignorance, their lack of attention to politics. In fact they display an episodic politicisation in the context of certain events such as Presidential elections or the 2005 referendum which triggered an 'increase in the social fluidity of political attention' (Aldrin 2003: 189) in social groups ordinarily distant from politics. The young ambulance driver partly justifies his negative vote by referring to what he perceived to be the majority opinion in his neighbourhood: 'People went "no, no!" We talked about it in the neighbourhood...people were against it...' (FR, M, 26).

This fraction of the population rarely refers to TV, radio or newspapers to support their judgements and relies on personal experience (Gaxie 2003). Beyond the socialising role of some events, some forms of informal politicisation on issues which directly affect the interviewees or their social circle can be observed, which nonetheless doesn't modify their structural distance from the political field. It is first and foremost the everyday use of the Euro which determine negative evaluations of the EU. Perceptions are oriented by a relative weakness of economic resources, especially for those whose political socialisation is limited. As they link the advent of the single currency to the decline in their purchasing power, the generally shared support or benevolent neutrality for the idea of European construction can hardly be explained in terms of expected or perceived economic benefits for them or for their country.

'The Euro is great, we're gonna screw the dollar [they said], but man, we got so hammered': between enchantment and disenchantment, the ambulance driver's exclamation shows the ambivalence of his relationship to Europe, combining a negative remote evaluation of political representatives, who are held responsible for the decline in purchasing power, with a positive evaluation of his own European encounters or contacts, during his professional trips:

> Well yeah I find that when I'm abroad, people have more respect for ambulance drivers... we're are bit like the SAMU [French emergency medical service] over there...but here, forget it, they don't give a damn, brother, oh yeah! In other countries you get respect...they give you the right of way even when you don't have it...

> (FR, M, 27)

These individuals, who very rarely travel abroad for leisure or for work, offer a representation of these experiences that are all the more enchanted as they are relatively few and far between. The 'Europe of cultures', in the words of a builder of Romanian origin (FR, M, 53), is initially conceived as an achievement embodying values of openness towards the others, exchange, and dialogue between populations. This discourse can also be observed very clearly in the words of a secretary in continuing education working in a travel agency, married to a blue-collar worker, who shows openness to European languages and cultures, by combining practical and ethical relationships to Europe. The identification with Europe can also be based on a community of social experiences shared by ordinary citizens, related to certain forms of cultural practices: for instance football, as a player, spectator and/or fan. To a large extent depending on the interviewees' social characteristics, the cultural exchanges between Europeans mentioned in the interviews are related to 'popular culture'. A temporary worker in a car rental agency emphasises his personal experience of national particularisms linked to football and highlights the feeling of cultural enrichment that he got from it:

> I even met young English people who came to France. We played football and it wasn't the same way of playing, it was really interesting... the qualities of the game and all that, it's different...meeting another culture is good, especially as for the English, football is pretty much a religion!

Talking about football does not exclude, far from it, the possibility of moving on to broader subjects as the conversation develops: 'What's important is to understand that Europe is not the destruction of national cultures, that things which are specific to each country of origin are not abandoned' (FR, M, 28). As with other male interviewees from popular milieus, the values displayed in football competitions often appear as more 'noble' than the values of political competition. We were thus able to observe representations that are quite far from traditional European political issues, but which are linked to European construction through the affirmation of a number of core humanist values of mutual recognition, respect for other cultures and tolerance. Without even thinking about it reflexively, these individuals may express ethical relationships to Europe. An 82-year-old former postal worker, who experienced World War II, makes numerous positive historical references to peace between Member States. A soldier (FR, M, 26) places 'human rights' at the centre of representations of a 'European model of defence' in reference to his missions abroad. This ethical relationship is partly built on an opposition to a system of values often referred to as 'American' and considered as a nationalist retreat and the rejection of others. Phrases such as 'United we stand against the United States' are recurrent in the interviews, and re-interpretations of the European founding myth are formulated: 'In the beginning, Europe, it was against the United States right?' (FR, M, 27, unemployed). We could make the hypothesis that such a value-based relationship is linked to the fact that many individuals in this group are practising Catholics or Muslims. The enlargement of the EU to Turkey is generally perceived as impossible for religious reasons and some of the interviewees (mainly the practising Muslims) consider their own beliefs as 'blacklisted' because of their supposed incompatibility with dominant values. Belonging to the Muslim community generates disappointments towards Europe, but also sometimes gives rise to certain prejudices against gypsies structured around perceived disparities between the 'old' European countries and the new Member States, in contrast with the idyllic representations of a 'Europe of football and human rights'. The waitress talks about the 'Europe of the Middle Ages' (FR, F, 22) to refer to Eastern European countries, while the ambulance driver, who lives near the largest Roma camp in France claims that they 'are always smashing the parking ticket machines'; the rental car employee says that 'Eastern Europeans, they don't know how to work. If I was a construction boss, I'd rather hire Portuguese, at least they know how to work!' (FR, M, 27). To a certain extent, these interviewees, who often have a migrant background, assert their 'European identity' in contrast to an even more stigmatised group, considered to be even less 'integrated' than they are. Following the intuitions of Georg Simmel, we can argue that conflict may be a source of regulation which structures collective relationships and strengthens, or even creates, the social identity of individuals in search of 'attention' and 'protection', in a political space whose Europeanisation is perceived as inevitable.

This idea is expressed by a cleaning lady of Portuguese origin, for whom going beyond the national framework is perceived as an obligation, something self-evident, given the evolution of the world:

> Normally, we have a government, they govern us, but we have to ask the Council of Europe and they deprive us of this, or we can't do that... for everything... Now we depend on those people, from all those countries, right...'

(FR, F, 42)

But the interviewees of the second group are a lot more resigned than the more politicised group studied in the first section, because they give less credit to political representatives, and expect less from them. They are generally satisfied with their social situation and confident in its evolution, in spite of the fact that they are objectively more often confronted with a more precarious economic situation. If they express few fears about the future, it is also because they are less prone to anticipating it. In spite of these limitations, members of this second group express themselves with relative ease, as most of them work in the service sector, and are therefore often in contact with clients. This element can help explain why they are more talkative during interviews, and tend to improvise answers based on limited institutional knowledge. In William Gamson's words, the 'conversational techniques and resources' of these rank-and-file workers make them collectively feel more competent than other fractions of popular milieus (Gamson 1992: 20).

Strangers to Europe: those who talk about other things when talking about Europe

We refer to a third group of interviewees as 'strangers to Europe' because they know nothing or little on the subject, but do not necessarily refrain from discussing it, even if they may end up talking about something completely different. They are literally 'ignorant' of European realities. This group thus includes those who do not know how to talk about Europe, an entity which for them only exists in name. Their discourse is built around general claims for equality (between countries, wages...). They do not have the ability to anticipate their future social situation or tend to be resigned. They have a low level of statutory competence and have not experienced a significant primary or secondary political socialisation. They do not read the press or follow political shows on TV and they generally don't vote. Without significant professional qualifications, they most often hold menial, part-time, low-paying jobs. Interviews with these 'strangers to Europe' are often very short. When they are longer, they are not about Europe, but are centred on often painful personal experiences. Indeed, whenever they have a hard time expressing themselves because they do not have much of an opinion on the subject discussed, the first reflex is to talk about who they are. Europe may then be blamed for almost anything: swine flu, the social security deficit, the 9/11 attacks, or stress-related disorders for instance.

These interviewees see Europe as politics at their most complex and incomprehensible. For example, a divorced part-time cashier with no diploma, who does undeclared housework to make ends meet, states: 'I don't even know what Europe means... what the point is [...] unless someone can explain it to me right, so that I can understand, in French...' (FR, F, 50). These fractions of the public never discuss Europe spontaneously, say that they do not understand it and do not feel concerned. They are also those who are the least familiar with political issues in general. They are not activists or union members and often claim that politics disgusts them. A waitress, who left school at sixteen and does not vote, expresses this remoteness from political and European issues – on the TCE referendum: 'I find it important to vote but not when we don't understand what it is. I don't think my vote would have been useful. Better let people who understand vote' (FR, F, 23). Europe seems to justify her self-exclusion from the political system because of its dizzying complexity. To many interviewees, understanding Europe requires an education that they lack:

I don't think about it, actually [...] I've never been interested... I... and even as far as school is concerned and all that, I've never... you know, I've never listened, actually... I've never been interested, I listen to the news and all that, and it just goes over my head... Because I've never started... the beginning...'

(FR, F, 26)

This cleaner, in secure employment but with no professional qualifications, emphasises in this extract how foreign the EU is to her. There is a feeling that education is an unattainable prerequisite to be able to understand and be entitled to express a viewpoint. For this interviewee, there is too much catching up to do, to be able to get involved in the subject. The fact that she says 'I don't think about it, actually' also illustrates this distance to Europe in her daily life. Beyond this educational competence, speaking about Europe also requires a linguistic competence that appears insurmountable to some interviewees.

They already have their own language, it's not something that everybody understands...It's their own language...and their own jokes, they're the only ones who laugh...they go 'socialist', yeah! They laugh. Yeah ok but, for everybody, what does 'socialist' mean?' You know, not everybody knows...

(FR, M, 26, born in Morocco, holder of a BEP)

He does not vote and has never understood the difference between the right and the left: 'It's hard to understand, right, you really have to understand things before you can really give your opinion…The vocabulary that they use…not everybody can understand it […] Everything is complicated since I understand nothing'. These respondents are either totally indifferent or ignorant towards Europe, which is inevitable insofar as they associate Europe to politics, and are distant from politics in general. At best, they claim political preferences that they have trouble justifying, but most no longer vote or are registered on voting lists and claim that voting would not change anything anyway.

They are completely indifferent towards the subject of the interview but are nevertheless relatively satisfied with their lot in life. They do not know Europe but they do not condemn it either. As the following excerpt from a retired truck driver shows, these respondents are not even in a position to realise their lack of knowledge:

- Are there things that you like about Europe?
- Well… I like it; it's my work, that's all.
- When you hear the word Europe, what do you think about first?
- Not at all…
- Doesn't it make you think about anything?
- I don't think about anything… My boss, my pay check [laughs], that's all.

(FR, M, 67)

This interviewee is a typical case of a non-answer on Europe. The interview takes place in an office of the company owned by his former employer, who still has him come in to work without declaring him. The interviewee is present at the start of an interview conducted with another truck driver and finds himself sitting in front of us after a joke made by one of his colleagues, who suggests that he should do an interview as well. He does not know what we are going to talk about but accepts in order 'to be like the others'. He is the archetype of an interviewee it is almost impossible to meet, who sociologically has no chance of responding to a telephone survey and who never gives his opinion, as he is not registered to vote and is not involved with a union or any volunteer organisation. A French citizen of Algerian origin, he has been living in France for nearly forty years. He never went to school and has always worked in transportation. His job is at the heart of his existence, socially as well as financially. He has trouble understanding French: questions have to be reformulated and simplified. He often replies with 'it's good' or 'it's not good'; he has no idea of the potential consequences of European construction on his life. He expresses a positive vision of his own existence and says he is satisfied. He claims to understand nothing about Europe and seems to expect nothing from it. In spite of his lack of resources, he does not seem uncomfortable in the interview situation. This is an unusual situation from him, but he is not ill at ease, contrary to a construction worker who states: 'I don't know… your questions are tough, I don't know anything about Europe' (FR, M, 27). In his case, although he is as distant to Europe as the truck driver, the interview becomes a pretext for him to expound with bitterness on his standard of living. The interviewees in this

third group are all in objectively destitute situations, but there is a division between those who are satisfied or even very satisfied with their lives and those who
are in situations of social, economic or emotional distress. While some of these
'strangers to Europe' can mobilise a feeling of private emotional security deriving
from their family to compensate for their professional and economic difficulties,
others talk about hard or even traumatising periods of loneliness and isolation. The
interview, which expresses a non-relationship towards Europe, is also for them an
opportunity – albeit an unusual one – to express their hardships.

The persons, whose reactions we have just analysed, are for the most part representatives of the most silent citizens who were often found by luck or chance.
These unlikely encounters were made possible by mobilising the social network
of the interviewers, but often through chance encounters, misunderstandings, or
progressively building trust. They were possible only because some of the interviewers have social relations within the lower marginalised social spheres. These
relationships require time, investment and interpretation. The reception of the
questions and the difficulty in exploiting the answers make their analysis very
complex. Still, the distance that separates Europe and, by extension, politics from
these individuals is evident. By studying the interviews and the way they unfold
step-by-step, revealing the social properties between the lines of the verbal exchange, we have sought to understand those who have no opinion and the reasons
for this lack of interest (Lehingue 2007a: 5).

Conclusion

The originality of the results presented here lies in the fact that we have studied what ordinary citizens do not know about Europe as thoroughly as what they
know. We have opened lines of enquiry that may help us understand the negative
reactions to European construction among those who still vote, and still accept to
give voice to their dissatisfaction, possibly before they in turn become discour-
aged and ultimately indifferent:

> In France, in wealthy neighbourhoods as in other regions of the current
> segregated social space, the popular classes have become largely 'invisible'.
> Since we never see them in the public space, we come to talk about them
> without knowing them, identifying them through social prejudice – in short,
> we risk reverting to 'class racism' (Beaud and Pialoux 2006)

Our analysis is an attempt to talk about popular milieus by talking with them
and exploring representations and relationships to abstract entities such as Europe
by understanding patterns of socialisation and their social context. Members of
popular milieus do not necessarily have nothing to say on Europe, but they often
express what they do have to say in a socially illegitimate language. They may
focus on one aspect and neglect others. We are interested in seeing how they manage to express themselves and what resources, often extra-political ones, they can
mobilise in the process:

– When you hear the word Europe, what do you think about first?
– Damn, this is hard, I have no idea... oh yeah, the Champions League! No, I don't know... to be honest, Europe doesn't make me think about anything... except football [laughs]'

(FR, M, 26, ambulance driver)

In order to be able to grasp this complexity, we kept in mind Jean-Claude Passeron's methodological advice: he wrote that it is necessary to refrain from 'treating as shortcomings non-responses, non-practices, low levels of competence and interest, what interviewees from popular classes may oppose to questions elaborated on the basis of the leading classes' modal practices' (Grignon and Passeron 1989). We have therefore attempted to account for this 'intelligence of the social at work in the individual's narrative productions' (Dubar 2003) in order to analyse what allows them to say what they say, and especially what explains what they do not say. Based on interviews conducted in France, but following the terms of a comparative research agenda, our attempt to reconstitute the modes of production of the popular milieus' relationships to Europe emphasises the key role of the individuals' socialisation processes as well as context-related effects. Regardless of the interviewee's country of origin, a number of significant variables appear to inform ordinary conceptions of Europe. In a comparative perspective, further research needs to assess the role of national historical events considered as salient by ordinary citizens as well as their perceptions of the transformations of public action linked to Europe.

chapter twelve | when europe mobilises...

Nicolas Hubé, Jean-Matthieu Méon and Sébastien Michon

Europe is rarely the object of political mobilisations. European elections are marked by relatively low voter turnout and are considered in the academic literature as 'second-order elections' (Reif and Schmitt 1980) and it is often stated that Europe is not a mobilising political subject (Cautrès 2001, 2003; Bélot and Greffet 2005; Schmitt and Binder 2006). Accordingly, as other chapters in this volume demonstrate, Europe tends to be far from many citizens' central preoccupations. When they are made visible, attitudes towards European construction are generally solicited by the interviewer in semi-directive interviews, or in opinion surveys such as Eurobarometers, in which interviewers conduct a questionnaire face-to-face. They are thus the product of partially artefactual situations in the presence of an interviewer (Labov 1972). What can be said about the expression of attitudes which are not directly produced by the techniques of social science enquiry? One way of observing such attitudes in a more spontaneous form consists in studying letters addressed to the editors of regional daily newspapers and magazines, as well as responses to an online survey on Europe.

This contribution aims at grasping the arguments of mobilised citizens and some of their social characteristics. We have observed attitudes towards Europe in the specific context of the referendum on the Treaty establishing a constitution for Europe (TCE), which was held in France on 29 May 2005. This political event elicited a specific mobilisation, especially from the time when the 'no' vote began to lead in the polls (Gerstlé and Piar 2005; Gombin and Hubé 2009). The analysis of letters sent to the press and responses to an online survey have given us the opportunity to collect and characterise an active discourse on Europe. This chapter is focused on the French case. During the study, it was the only country out of the five included in our programme where such a European political mobilisation occurred. A similar approach would probably have been possible in Poland and the Czech Republic at the time of the accession referendums in 2003, but we were unable to access that material.

We collected letters addressed at the time of the TCE referendum to two regional, i.e. Alsatian, newspapers (*Les Dernières Nouvelles d'Alsace* and *L'Alsace*), regardless of their object. This material allows us to observe if and when Europe becomes an object of attention for letter writers. The two other types of empirical material are more specific to Europe itself. First, they are letters addressed to the weekly cultural magazine *Télérama*, which during the debate hosted an 'open forum' in its pages: 'It's your turn to speak'.[1] Secondly, they are answers to the online survey 'L'Europe et vous' ('Europe and you'), set up by an official institution after the referendum with the aim of re-creating the link between the citizens

---

1. Jézégabel Marc, "Europe. Oui ou non ?", *Télérama*, 13 April 2005, p.7.

and Europe from the French website on the EU: *Toute l'Europe.fr* (see details in Box 12.1).[2]

This rich material consists of 1660 letters to the regional press, 1399 letters to *Télérama*, and 1298 responses to the online survey. This corpus gives us the opportunity to observe opinions more than attitudes, strictly speaking. Letters to the editor are indeed a specific form of expression. In the Alsatian newspapers, for instance, the inclusion of the phrase prière d'insérer ('please publish') in a fourth of the letters shows that these are opinion letters with a purpose of public expression. Even though these expressed opinions are amongst the closest to political debates, their authors present their own interpretations of the central issues of 'Europe'. This material illustrates in another way the ambivalence of attitudes observed during the interviews. The Europe that makes people react is not necessarily, or not only that of the European integration process. Non-responses to the online survey allow us to stress the extent to which the complexity of the 'Europe' object is insurmountable for many citizens, including particularly concerned and dedicated citizens who took the time to freely answer questions of an online survey. Letters to the editor are of course not a completely 'ordinary' discourse: to be published, they must comply with discursive standards (Boltanski, Darré and Schiltz 1984). They deal with a political theme and are aimed at a specific public. As we know, when media appeal to readers, they make hypotheses on the social characteristics and expectations of their public. They are enterprises in political representations: by their choice of subjects, by the language used, they are 'bound up with a whole life-style', with a 'relation to the world' (Bourdieu, 1984: 462). On the side of the recipients of media, the strong link between politicisation and attention to the media (Gaxie 2003; Charpentier 2004; Pierru 2004), between attention to the media and political competence (Gaxie 1978) can also be observed in letters addressed to the press.

Letters to the editor or responses to a survey open to all Internet users allow us to reconsider the idea of 'citizen participation' in the political debate on European issues. This chapter also allows us to elaborate on questions which traverse this entire volume: participation and political competence; the absence of interest in Europe of a large fraction of the public; the extreme ambivalence of attitudes towards Europe; the effects of political and social competence on positions on Europe. However, contrary to the empirical material used in other chapters, the analysis of letters focuses our attention on citizens who feel particularly legitimate and entitled to express opinions about such a 'complex' issue as Europe in the form of a letter which could be published. These hurdles imply that many members of the public are *de facto* excluded. Broadly speaking, the positions expressed follow the register of the restricted general involvement ideal type (see Chapter 4) in regional newspapers, which may be classified as an 'intermediary' media, and

---

2.   We would like to thank Guy Marchal of *Les Dernières Nouvelles d'Alsace*, Francis Claudel and Francis Laffon of *L'Alsace*, Marie-Francoise Cholot, Régis Confavreux and Jean-Claude Loiseau of *Télérama*, Mathieu Lerondeau and Benoit Thieulin of the *Centre d'Information sur l'Europe* for making this material available to us. We also thank Anaïs Hamelin for her help in processing the database of answers to the Toute l'Europe surveys and Paris 1 students for their input on the coding system.

are more synoptic in the national media. However, as we will show, the mobilisation of these opinions is sometimes related to the media debate itself more than to the European integration process as such.

Box 12.1: General properties of the public and characteristics of the material collected

The aim of this summary is to outline properties of the public and of the media studied, and the characteristics of the material collected, including its heuristic limitations.

Two regional newspapers: L'Alsace and Les Dernières Nouvelles d'Alsace

The first part of the data is comprised of letters received by two daily Alsatian newspapers: *Les Dernières Nouvelles d'Alsace* (available in the entire Alsace region, particularly present in the northern department, the Bas-Rhin) and *L'Alsace* (available in the entire Alsace region and part of the Belfort Territory, particularly present in the southern part of the Region, the Haut-Rhin department). The first had a circulation of 191,743 copies in 2005 and the second of 111,204.[3] 49 per cent of the readership is female and 51 per cent male, aged predominantly between 25 and 59 (53 per cent against 37 per cent over 60).[4] In 2007, 49 per cent of the readership did not work (including 32 per cent of pensioners); 43.5 per cent were workers and employees (active or not), 19 per cent were in intermediate professions, and 18.5 per cent were craftsmen, CEOs, executives and liberal professions.[5] These papers target an audience that roughly matches the social distribution of the population (with a slight over-representation of working-class members).

Overall, 1660 letters (mailed, emailed or faxed) were analysed. They were received by *L'Alsace* between January and December 2005 (n=1272) and by the *Dernières Nouvelles d'Alsace* between December 2005 and May 2006 (n=388).[6] We had access to the original letters. There were some uncertainties regarding the material. It is unclear how the stock of letters we received was constituted; the material includes letters which were subsequently published, others which were rejected, and yet others whose status is unknown. We ended up using all letters mentioning Europe, European countries, the EU and/or its institutions, or European or European Community events (referendum, demon-

---

3. Source: OJD, 2005 (www.ojd.fr).

4. Source: EPIQ survey on reading habits, July 2005-June 2006 data on the Alsace region.

5. Source: TNS SOFRES EPIQ survey on reading habits, July 2007-July 2008 data. PQR 66 – UDA6 – East survey on the readers of the regional press in Alsace, Lorraine and Franche-Comté.

6. Even though we have not distinguished the two corpuses, the difference in the period when the letters were received by *L'Alsace* and the *DNA* has certain consequences. The proportion of letters mainly dealing with Europe or the TCE is higher in the *L'Alsace* corpus (44 per cent) than in the *DNA* corpus (18.5 per cent). Letters addressed to the *DNA* mention, for instance, the "no" vote in the TCE referendum to support other comments on events such as the demonstrations against the first employment contract (CPE) in the spring of 2006.

strations, etc.) The results presented here are based on this corpus (n= 182 letters, 11 per cent of the material). Occasionally, a distinction was made between
letters dealing directly and indirectly with Europe. The analysis of this corpus,
like that of the *Télérama* corpus, takes into account the available socio-graphic
elements on the readers, the object of the letter, the mode of enunciation, the
presence of standardised phrases, and especially the themes discussed (national
or European ones).

A weekly magazine: Télérama

Founded in 1947, Télérama is a left leaning cultural weekly providing both in-
depth articles on news events, and reviews of weekly cultural and media events
(television, cinema, book reviews, theatre and arts). We analysed the mail received and retained by the magazine during a period of three months preceding the 29 May 2005 TCE referendum as well as the two issues following the
referendum. A corpus of 1,399 letters was analysed, based on the archives of
Télérama's mail service. As in the case of the Alsatian press, there is no certainty that all the mail received by the magazine was archived. It is possible
that letters about the referendum were received before March 20 and after June
8. Letters received between May 19 and 25 are missing from the archives. All
letters were analysed based on the same criteria as the corpus from the regional
newspapers.

   Télérama's readership is concentrated in the higher spheres of the social
space. In 2004–2005, 69 per cent of the readers had a university degree (including 48 per cent holding a Bachelor's or more). In terms of occupation, the
readership is mostly found in three major socio-professional categories: 25 per
cent of 'executives and higher intellectual professions'; 20 per cent in 'intermediate professions' and 38 per cent are non-working (including 16 per cent of
pensioners). 54 per cent of the readership is female.[7]

   The analysis of the letters addressed to *Télérama* is also specific because,
for the editor in charge of reader mail, the TCE referendum was a 'landmark'.[8]
At that time, the editorial staff observed a high level of involvement from the
readers and an exceptional increase in the numbers of letters and posts made
on the message board.[9] These reactions followed a strong, unmitigated call for
the 'yes' vote by the chief editor. In the April 13, 2005 issue, Marc Jézégabel
announced that 'to me, all things considered, the 'yes' wins, clearly.'[10] This
editorial was published after the March polls announced a 'reversal' in voting
intentions with the 'no' narrowly leading since mid-March (Gerstlé and Piar
2005). Due to the number of letters received, *Télérama* doubled the space de-

---

7.   Source: AEPM survey on reading habits, July 2003-June 2004 data.

8.   Interview with the chief editor of *Télérama* in charge of reader mail (May 2006), conducted with
     Fanny Fromental.

9.   For a study of the message board, see Mange and Marchand 2007; for a study of the letters
     published in three magazines, see Hubé 2008.

10. Marc Jézégabel, "Europe. Oui ou non ?", *art. cit.*

voted to reader mail. The cover of the May 4 issue even read: 'YES/NO to the European Constitution. Our readers speak out.'

The online survey 'L'Europe et vous', on the Sources d'Europe/Toute l'Europe.fr website

The third type of data collected consists of the responses to a survey on Europe available on the *Sources d'Europe* website between 9 May and 1 September 2006. Now called *Toute l'Europe.fr*, the *Sources d'Europe* page is the website of the 'Centre d'information sur l'Europe', an 'economic interest group found-ed in 1992 by the French government and the European Commission', whose mission is to 'inform French citizens on the EU, its policies and achievements'. Different types of questions are asked in the survey about European identity, the Euro and enlargements: open-ended and closed-ended questions; simple choice; multiple choices (between three statements). While anonymity was guaranteed, the survey did not allow several registrations from the same IP ad-dress, which limited the possibility that the same person might respond several times. The database includes a total of 1298 individuals; effectively between 600 and 800 people responded to more than a dozen questions. The gaps can be explained by the wording of the questions – sometimes very technical – and by the nature of the tool – the online tool makes it easier for respondents to stop an-swering questions than a face-to-face or telephone survey where an interviewer can prompt respondents. In addition, open questions require a greater level of implication than closed-ended questions, thereby lowering response rates.

Three main limits related to the method and the data need to be addressed. First, this survey was published on the *Sources d'Europe* website by its sponsor. Not all citizens have access to Internet connection or spontaneously visit this page or answer the questions, producing an important sample bias. However, this bias is actually productive for the purposes of our study as it gives us an opportunity to observe a population which spontaneously expresses opinions. Secondly, much like the Eurobarometer methodology (see Chapter 2), this data raises a number of questions in terms of the imposition of issues. Yet, the fact that the public is particularly invested in these issues reduces this imposition effect, as does the fact that interviewees can choose to ignore questions without having to deal with prompting or deploying face-saving strategies in surveys administered by an interviewer. Thirdly, the construction of several of the ques-tions is problematic, notably because of the normative orientation of the ques-tions: for instance, on the introduction of the Euro, three negative modalities, five positive ones and an 'other' modality are suggested to the respondents.

Nevertheless, aside from collecting opinions on Europe of people who are invested in the subject, the major interest of this survey lies in the presence of questions related to the respondents' socio-demographic characteristics (gen-der, age, level of education, socio-professional category, place of residence), which gives us a rare opportunity for analysing data on the social profiles of those who spontaneously express their opinions on European issues.

Mobilising on Europe? A rare option for a politicised public

Generally rare, public stances on Europe become more frequent when European issues are on the agenda, as was the case during the referendum campaign on the TCE.

Following the media's agenda

The letters addressed to *L'Alsace* and to *Les Dernières Nouvelles d'Alsace* (*DNA*) show that Europe is generally infrequently discussed: barely 3 per cent of our corpus of letters focuses on the EU (n=45); 11 per cent mention 'Europe' or a European country. The expression of European themes appears dependant on the political and media agenda. Only when citizens were called to vote in the 29 May 2005 referendum on the TCE did some readers write to offer their input. More than a third of the letters received by regional newspapers that mention Europe refer to the referendum (36 per cent of the corpus, sixty-six letters).

In the letters analysed, Europe features in the background, as an element among other subjects used to comment on national situations and issues. A European theme may be discussed without actually talking about Europe. A significant example is that of the referendum on the TCE. Half of the letters mentioning the referendum are not mainly focused on European integration, and two thirds deal with national issues. The dock workers' demonstration against the EU project of liberalising port services, which took place in Strasbourg in January 2006, was the subject of five letters, three of which did not make any reference to the directive in question or to social Europe (see Box 12.2). Similarly, MEPs are only mentioned twice, in letters on the excessive and expensive number of administrative levels in France. 'Europe' is only a preoccupation of the readership when there is a Europe-related event covered in the media. In such cases, it is rarely if ever related to the European integration process.

Box 12.2: Comments on a demonstration of dock workers against a European Directive

---

Letter to the *DNA*, January 2006: a personal denunciation of the event's violence

'Object: following the incidents resulting from the dock workers' demonstration in Strasbourg.

I've always respected freedom of expression; the freedom of speaking out, of defending your livelihood but Enough is Enough. I'm the father of a 16-year-old girl who, coming home from her day of work (trainee) found herself in the middle of the demonstration. Surrounded by marchers and policemen in the middle of tear gas, she experienced pure violence. Scared and lost, she was somehow able to make it back home, but she had lost the illusion I had been trying to keep alive since her adolescence. [...] What kind of world are we leaving our children?'

Letter to the *DNA*, 17 January 2006: an ethical indictment of political irresponsibility.

'I was hardly surprised when I saw how virulent the dockers were. [...] I was able to observe that we could indeed have avoided this kind of outburst, especially as this text had been defeated in 2003. I wonder if every morning someone has a crazy idea about destroying certain things that were set up, fully knowing that the project wouldn't come to fruition and because of this we have the provocations and all kinds of outbursts that occurred on 16 January 2006. Why destroy goods, wait until there are injured people on both sides to finally get to the point that the text has no chance of going through. Everyone will have to pay the price. Gentlemen in Parliament, think about the dramatic consequences this might have and of course check how certain countries are run.' (*in extenso*)

Letter to the *DNA*, 18 January 2006: the resurgence of old national political cleavages

'Object: dock workers
During the Indochina war, the injured soldiers who were coming back from the battlefields on stretchers were 'welcomed' in Marseilles with bolts and screws etc. by the dockers! All the papers reported it at the time, and published photos. "The apple never falls far from the tree". Something to think about!' (*in extenso*)

Letter to the *DNA*, 23 January 2006: a critique of the European government's 'irresponsible and incompetent' 'mollycoddling'

'Commissioner Barrot regrets... [...] after the serious incidents and the enormous costs caused by the European miners [*sic*]. What is this out-of-touch mollycoddling. Did he think that the tough guys from the harbours were coming to kiss him on the forehead? [...] It seems to me that this useless provocation only amounts to waving an exasperating red rag. Tell me, gentlemen: is this Europe? Well, what a fine government we have here! So, tax payers, pull out your wallets, the irresponsible and the incompetent are having fun! When we send them into orbit, they won't ever stop spinning...'

Letter to the *DNA*, 10 April 2006: a localist view on the event and on European waste

'Object: Strasbourg and the European institutions
It is very good to gather in Brussels what was with such a great cost (our tax money!) shared between Brussels and Strasbourg. This will not take anything away from our city's European identity, forever inscribed in its history, in its monuments, its inhabitants. [...] In the future, will this gathering of 'power' in Brussels spare us from seeing demonstrators-rioters rush into Strasbourg if they have to protest measures taken by this 'power'?'

Many *Télérama* readers wrote on the theme of Europe, but the trigger was not so much the Treaty itself – rather, it was the fact that the magazine took a stance on the subject (see Figure 12.1). Readers wrote mostly after Marc Jézégabel's editorial. While during the three previous weeks, the magazine only received thirty-five letters on Europe, in the week after the editorial was published (11 to 17 April 2005), 197 letters on the theme of the TCE were received. Readers reacted even more strongly to the special issue of May 4 'YES/NO to the European Constitution. Our readers speak out'. During that week and the following, 536 letters were received (more than a third of the letters received). This mobilisation seemed to ebb a few days before the vote.[11] The event-based mobilisation pattern observed in the regional press was confirmed after the voting results. The day after the referendum, *Télérama* received 151 more letters (126 more in the following three days and twenty-five on the following eight days). On this point, the agenda of the citizens' preoccupations follows that of political professionals and editors of the national daily press (Gombin and Hubé 2009).

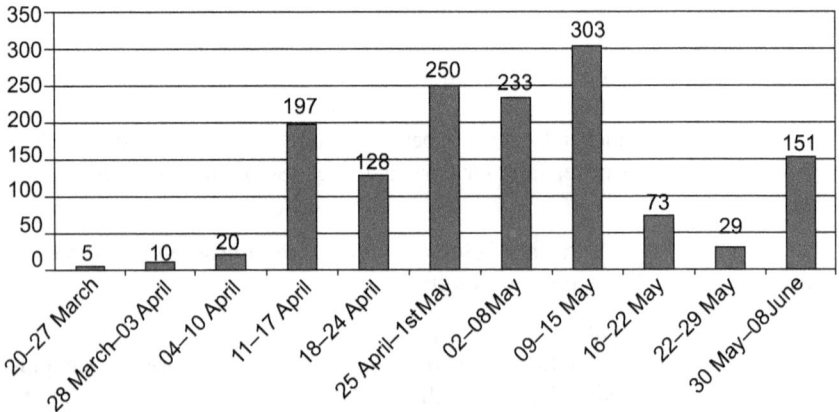

Figure 12.1: Number of letters received by Télérama

For the daily press as well as the cultural weekly press, the citizens' mobilisations are thus related to contextual elements. Europe is not a routine preoccupation for ordinary citizens.

---

11. Between May 16 and 29, only 102 letters can be found – much fewer than in the preceding six weeks, even though letters received between May 19 and 25 were not available to us. On the decrease in the number of letters between April 18 and 24, two hypotheses can be made. The first is that Pope John Paul II's death and the conclave electing Benedict XVI might have diverted the readers' attention. The second is that of a mobilisation related to the magazine itself: as *Télérama* no longer spoke out in favour of the TCE after the first editorial, once the first reaction passed, the readers were less stimulated to react.

Political opinions on display

The 'letters to the editor' section organises a space for discussion within the readers' political community (Ebel and Fiala 1981; Pounds 2006).[12] In the referendum period, when the debate cleaved political positions, many factors contributed to making the readers take sides. The development of such a space of discussion was all the more robust as editors publicly spoke out in favour of the 'yes' vote. Few published letters are clearly in favour of abstention (sixteen letters in total) or fail to mention voting intentions or the debate (thirty-four letters). The discourse of citizens mobilised in this debate comes from politicised readers, who react to the prescriptive and official stance of their weekly in favour of the 'yes' vote. Readers who speak out in favour of the 'no' amount to nearly half of the letters received (46 per cent, 646 letters), whereas there were 28 per cent 'yes' supporters (391 letters);[13] a quarter of the letters do not express a stance on the vote, but comment on the way the debate is unfolding.

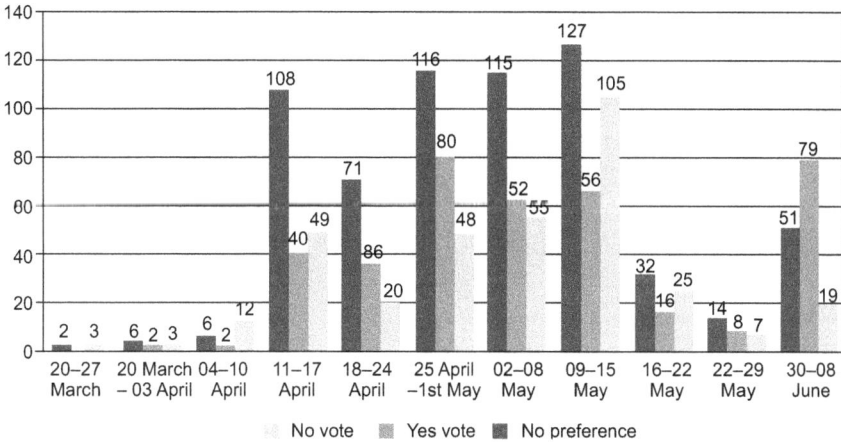

Figure 12.2: Number of letters received by Télérama arranged according to voter's preferences for the referendum

Adopting a diachronic perspective (Figure 12.2), we can observe that 'no' supporters reacted very strongly to the editorial and the issues published before the vote, whereas 'yes' supporters mobilised after the vote to denounce the choice made by voters in the referendum.[14] This propensity to assert a political choice em-

<hr>

12. According to *Télérama*'s chief editor, the magazine lost 0.5 per cent of its subscribers because of its stance on the European referendum. Interview with the chief editor of *Télérama* in charge of reader mail (23 May 2006).

13. In an effort to comply with the rule of journalistic objectivity, *Télérama* published 48 per cent of letters in favour of the 'no', and 39 per cent in favour of the 'yes' (Hubé 2008).

14. This surge of 'yes' supporters in editorialists and political professionals can be observed in national daily papers (Gombin and Hubé 2009).

phasises the fact that political opinions are mobilised by a Europe-related event, but that they are not necessarily triggered by issues related to European integration.

Table 12.1: Rate of response to the fourteen most answered questions of the online survey on the website Sources d'Europe

	Sample	% of responses	% of non-responses	Total
Do you feel: French and not really European, both French and European, European or not really French, neither French nor European? (1 response)	719	55.4%	44.6%	100%
Which conclusions do you draw from the introduction of the Euro? (max. 3 responses)	700	53.9%	46.1%	100%
What defines European identity the best according to you? (max. 3 responses)	665	51.2%	48.8%	100%
What should be Europe's main missions? (max. 3 responses)	654	50.4%	49.6%	100%
According to you, who has benefited from Europe in France? (1 response)	653	50.3%	49.7%	100%
According to you, in which geographical direction should Europe be enlarged first? (1 response)	653	50.3%	49.7%	100%
What are Europe's main benefits for France? (max. 3 responses)	633	48.8%	51.2%	100%
According to you, what should Europe ultimately become? (max. 3 responses)	632	48.7%	51.3%	100%
Which conclusions do you draw from the enlargement? (max. 3 responses) ?	621	47.8%	52.2%	100%
According to you, what was the main effect of the 'no' vote in the referendum? (1 response)	613	47.2%	52.8%	100%
What are Europe's most negative effects on France? (max. 3 responses)	604	46.5%	53.5%	100%
What do you think should be done regarding the European constitution project? (1 response)	596	45.9%	54.1%	100%
Does the single market make worker mobility easier? (1 response)	391	30.1%	69.9%	100%

Europe remains remote: respondents to the online survey

Even when a population that is potentially receptive to European issues is concerned – such as people who visit websites dedicated to supporting the project of European construction – the questions asked are not always self-evident. Non-responses to questions of the online survey are relatively numerous: between 44 per cent and 79 per cent (see Table 12.1). These non-responses are not distributed uniformly. They are fewer for questions on the introduction of the Euro (46 per cent), a topic that affects the entire population, or the enlargement (50 per cent and 52 per cent for both questions on the topic), an object that is perhaps easier to grasp. There are more non-responses to 'technical' questions, for instance on the single market (70 per cent).

Response rates are distributed unevenly according to the respondents' social characteristics (Gaxie 1978). The older, less educated respondents, often housewives, jobseekers or pensioners, have the lowest response rates.

- On who has benefited from Europe in France: more than 60 per cent of non-responses for respondents aged over sixty, against less than 50 per cent for those aged below forty; 75 per cent for jobseekers, 62 per cent for non-working respondents, and 53 per cent for executives and students.
- On the main effect of the 'no' vote in the referendum: 63 per cent of non-responses for those who are below baccaularéat level, against 55 per cent for those who have completed four years of university-level education or more; 72 per cent for jobseekers, 62 per cent for non-working respondents, 57 per cent for executives, 56 per cent for students.
- 'What do you think should be done regarding the European constitution project?': 63 per cent of non-responses for those below baccaularéat level, 59 per cent for those with four years of university-level education or more; 69 per cent for jobseekers, 68 per cent for non-working respondents, 60 per cent for executives, 50 per cent for students.

Box 12.3: A critical assessment of Eurobarometers

Distance towards Europe, the high rates of non-responses to questions on Europe and their uneven distribution between respondents highlight the obvious limits of the Eurobarometer surveys' protocol and of their results studied by Philippe Aldrin in this volume. Eurobarometers demonstrate that there are almost no non-responses. While it is possible to answer 'don't know' to each of the questions – the closest to a non-response – this choice is not made very often: only 12 per cent of the respondents of the 2006 EB65 and 2008 EB69 surveys made use of this option. This entails that a public assumed to be representative of the population responds more easily to questions on Europe than a mobilised public, who make the effort to freely participate in an online survey, and who, as we will see, are more highly educated than average. Such differences lead us to question the conduct of Eurobarometer surveys.

Hence, responses to an online survey on Europe are distributed in a manner that is quite close to those of other opinion surveys: non-responses, which are particularly numerous, are distributed unevenly according to the respondents' social characteristics. However, the gaps observed remain relatively small compared to other surveys on political objects. This can be attributed to an effect of over-selection in terms of social status or closeness to Europe (see above) of those who decide to respond to such a survey.

Defining the social features of a mobilised public

The mobilisation of these three materials shows the exceptional character of these positions on Europe, especially related to their presence on the media agenda and its politicisation. Europe is only rarely the object of specific attention, and when it is the case, it often expresses a remote relationship to European issues and institutions. The analysis of our data also informs us about the atypical character of the mobilised public. The propensity to speak out on this political subject is related to the feeling of being 'entitled to express an opinion' (Bourdieu 1984: 411). It also seems to be conditioned by a form of political 'goodwill'. While it is difficult to obtain precise data on the subject,[15] we have been able to observe that these opinions are most frequently expressed by highly educated men.

A male discourse

58 per cent of respondents to the online survey, 83 per cent of those who wrote to the regional press and 72 per cent of those who wrote to *Télérama* were male.

The conditions of expressing opinions on Europe do not differ greatly from those observed for other political objects (Achin *et al.* 2007: 111–15). While 49 per cent of readers of the regional press are women, women represent only 9 per cent of the letter writers. *Télérama* has 54 per cent of female readers; 22 per cent of the letter writers are women. The online survey yields more balanced results: 41 per cent of respondents whose gender was identified[16] are women – this is most likely related to that specific public's level of education and occupation.

An educated public

The social agents mobilised indeed belong to the best-educated categories of the social space. In the case of the online survey, the most discerning variable is the level of education: among the 773 respondents who have mentioned their level of education, 86 per cent hold a baccalauréat or a higher-level degree (against 33

---

15. These characteristics are often not presented, because by disregarding them, the paper can create a 'community of readers' (Arban 2003).

16. Only 55 per cent of the people who have responded to at least one question in the survey have mentioned their gender.

Table 12.2: Gender of the respondents to the online survey, of readers who wrote to the editor, and of the entire readership

	Télérama			Regional press			Sources d'Europe	
	Number of letter writers	% of the letter writers	% of the readership	Number of letter writers	% of letter writers	% of the readership	Number of respondents	% of the respondents
Women	308	22%	53.9%	17	9.3%	49%	297	23%
Couple	5	0.35%	–	–	–	–		
Men	1000	71.5%	46.1%	151	83%	51%	421	32%
N/A	86	6.15%	–	14	7.7%	–	580	45%
Total	1399	100%	100%	182	100%	100%	1298	100%

Sources: for the weekly press, AEPM survey on reading habits, July 2003 – June 2004; for the Alsatian press, EPIQ survey on reading habits, July 2005 – June 2006.

per cent for the entire French population in 2007[17]), 53 per cent have completed at least four years of university education, i.e. five times more than the entire French population. Another variable that indicates a certain specificity of the participants is occupation. Executives (a third of the 784 respondents to this question) and students prevail (a fourth, compared to 11 per cent of the French population above fifteen pursuing education), whereas workers and employees are under-represented (respectively 1.5 per cent and 15 per cent, even though they represent respectively 23 per cent and 30 per cent of the active French population).[18] Other categories also have a noticeably high level of education: 53 per cent of unemployed respondents have completed at least four years of university education; 46 per cent of students; 43 per cent of independent workers; 42 per cent of 'other socio-professional categories', 36 per cent of pensioners and 26 per cent of employees.

In addition to social dispositions to enunciate an opinion on a political subject, these mobilised populations often have concrete international or European experiences: 23 per cent of 391 respondents in the online survey's question on the single market making worker mobility easier stated that they have already worked in another EU country. This social selection of the public concerned by European issues is confirmed by the letters sent to *Télérama* where the writer's occupation is known (ninety-one letters). Nearly two out of three are in the intellectual spheres of the social space: twenty-five are classified by the National Institute of Statistics and Economic Studies (INSEE, French national institute of statistics) as holders of 'upper intellectual professions' (university lecturers and professors), sixteen are teachers, thirteen are students (including PhD holders and PhD students in law and political science). Other letter writers also have specific profiles: professionals of European institutions ('Honorary Director-General at the European Commission', 'President of the European Parliament's Committee on Economic and Monetary Affairs'), members of major public institutes ('Engineer at the Ecole des Ponts'), professionals of law ('lawyer at the Paris Court of Appeals').

A majority of respondents from the Paris region

These intellectual profiles are combined with an over-representation of inhabitants of the Ile-de-France region (Paris metropolitan area): 33 per cent of respondents to the online survey and 35 per cent of those who wrote to *Télérama* (compared to 18 per cent of the entire population), including 14 per cent from the city of Paris itself for both data sets (3.5 per cent of the French population).

Readers from the Paris region and from major cities (see Table 12.3) tend to be 'yes' supporters, whereas those who live in small towns tend to be more hostile towards the TCE. Readers from the Paris suburbs express much less support for the TCE than those from Paris itself – a result which is undoubtedly related to social differences between Paris and its suburbs.

---

17. Source: INSEE's 2007 employment survey.

18. Source: *ibid.*

Table 12.3: Place of residence and voting intentions of letter writers to Télérama

Place of residence	Number of letter writers	% when cities mentioned	Voting intentions (in %)				
			No	Yes	Abs.	Don't know	N/A
Paris	124	13.98%	34.68%	41.94%	2.42%	1.61%	19.35%
Ile de France (outside of Paris)	187	21.08%	48.66%	26.20%	0.53%	2.14%	22.46%
City with more than 100 000 inhabitants	198	22.32%	42.93%	37.88%	2.53%	1.01%	15.66%
City from 20 000 to 100 000 inhabitants	110	12.40%	51.82%	20.91%	0.91%	1.82%	24.55%
City with less than 20 000 inhabitants	155	17.47%	55.48%	20.65%	-	1.94%	21.94%
Rural towns	110	12.40%	57.27%	23.64%	-	2.73%	16.36%
EU foreigner	3	0.34%	-	66.67%	-	-	33.33%
N/A	512	-	43.16%	25.78%	1.17%	4.1%	25.78%
Overall	1399	≈100%	46.18%	27.95%	1.14%	2.64%	22.09%

A readership of activists?

While we can assume that the letter writers of *Télérama* tend to be left-leaning intellectuals, the data makes it difficult to specify this assumption. Only thirty -seven writers to *Télérama* state their political preferences, including two who insist that they are not members of an activist group. Among the few who assert their political engagement, seven mention their professional status, including a retired member of the 'section of interned prisoners and families of missing persons' who, by calling attention to this, aims at pointing out one of the principles that founded European construction: peace. Most of those who mention a collective activity are members of an association: nine are members of the 'Mouvement pour l'initiative citoyenne' (Movement for citizen initiative), four of action groups of 'no' supporters, and others are members of NGOs (Fondation Abbé Pierre or the French League of Women's Rights). A few are members of left-wing parties (socialist, communist or green party) or unions (CGT, Sud). It is possible that letter writers anticipated that asserting these features would make it more difficult to get published.

Ultimately, being a man, educated, in the intellectual spheres of the social space, with a certain degree of politicisation and international experience, favours giving opinions on issues related to European construction and influences the way they are discussed.

Which Europe? Studying attitudes

Which Europe do these writers refer to? What are they saying about it? Most letters sent to papers refer to a Europe whose limits are vague, discussed from the point of view of national political activity and economy. The political nature of the subject encourages generalisation and privative discourses are generally excluded (Boltanski, Darré and Schiltz 1984). The modalities of expression of these opinions vary according to the type of media to which letters are sent: an intermediary type of attitude can be observed in the case of intermediary media (the regional daily press), while a synoptic one is observed in the cases of the cultural weekly magazine and the website on European issues (see Chapter 1).

Writers to the regional press: restricted general involvement

In their use of the term 'Europe', and their evocation of themes which may be linked to European integration, letters addressed to the regional press show the diversity of the elements used to relate to Europe as well as their dispersion (which confirms observations made in Chapter 5). 'European' issues are perceived primarily in economic and national terms – which is supported by a feeling of national decline – and are hence not directly linked with the issue of European construction.

Letters sent to the regional press, indeed, show the extreme plasticity of the term 'Europe'. Nearly two thirds of the letters refer to a European entity (geographical, political, economic...) (n=109) or use the term 'Europe' with no further precisions (n=67). Around a quarter of these letters use the more precise 'European Union'. Others (11 per cent) rely on metonymy (Brussels), specialisation ('Eurozone') and outdated expressions (European Community) or approximations (Council of Europe of Brussels).

Nearly a third of the corpus (31 per cent) contains an economic dimension, through wide-ranging themes such as competition, the market, liberalism or realities that are more immediate for letter writers such as wages, prices or production. Employment alone is mentioned in 6 per cent of the corpus. Taxes are mentioned in 4 per cent of the letters, linked to Europe in an indictment of 'squandering'. However, few letters discuss the Euro (three letters, i.e. 1.5 per cent of the corpus). One specifically deals with the Eurozone and another 'warn[s]' readers against an illegal invasion' of Chilean pesos because of their similarity with Euro coins. Agriculture is the subject of only one letter, which criticises the non-observance of European standards by farmers. Overall, letters express everyday preoccupations, told in an intermediary register where the general (the project of constructing an economic space) mixes with the specific (wages and prices) or even the anecdotal (fraud due to the similarities between coins).

Beyond the economy, other themes are also present. The most frequent is that of EU enlargement (9 per cent of the corpus), mainly focusing on the hostility towards the accession of Turkey (nearly two thirds of these letters, n=11), perceived as a cultural and economic threat for Europe. Immigration (notably related to Turkey) preoccupies more than 5 per cent of letter writers. The issue of enlargement exposes a certain anxiety towards the foreign in contrast with very general values ('civilisation', 'culture'). 'Peace' (5 per cent of the letters) is mentioned in this register, with a reference to the Alsatian past – a recurrent theme in the material analysed – marked by the wars between French and Germany between 1870 and 1945 which European construction brought to an end. One letter supports 'May 8' as a day of 'celebration of Europe'. Here again, the discussion of European political issues (enlargement or European construction) is related to intermediary preoccupations (the effects of immigration or European construction on the borders of the region in which the letter writers live).

This reduction of the issues of Europe can be observed in the fact that 56 per cent of the corpus includes a national dimension and is related to national issues, with considerations on the national economy, the national political game, living standards, the state of France, etc. Similarly, the importance of the national prism can also be observed in the comparisons made by writers to the regional press (40 per cent of letters rely on national comparison as an argumentative form), since most of them are made with specific countries (twenty-three European countries are mentioned in the corpus, but comparisons are mostly focused on four countries – primarily, Germany, which shares a border with Alsace (42 per cent of the comparisons, n=30) and more rarely, Great Britain (19 per cent, n=13), Italy (11 per cent) and Spain (8 per cent)). European issues exist only insofar as they are linked to a national framework of reference.

It is probably in these 'national-oriented' letters that the 'culturalist' dimension of the relation to European integration as it is often presented in the literature can be best observed. Indeed, a theme runs through all these letters: the decline of France and the inefficiency of the country's elites. 10 per cent of the letters claim that France holds 'the last place in Europe', is 'Europe's laughing stock', or the country where 'everything goes wrong'. Nearly 15 per cent involve a direct indictment of political leaders and representatives, the government, or President Chirac himself (one of the few names that are regularly mentioned). Incompetence, inefficiency, greed and thirst for power are some of the main criticisms levelled against these elites. These themes are generally expressed following a pattern of 'us' vs 'them', 'small' vs 'big' where downward social mobility appears to be an important factor. In these letters, Europe is revelatory of decline (through comparison), a symptom (of the surrender of national responsibility) and a cause (squandering of taxpayer money, etc.). Indeed, more than half of the letters that include a national dimension mention the referendum (52 per cent of these letters, or 29 per cent of the entire corpus). The links between Europe and national framework work in two ways: European issues are assessed in the light of national (or even regional) issues and Europe is mobilised as a criterion (among others) to evaluate national politics. Accordingly, a letter addressed to *L'Alsace* compares the merits of presidents De Gaulle's and Mitterrand's periods in office mentioning their roles in European integration, whereas another turns the 'no' to the TCE into the expression of a 'localist' critique of Jacques Chirac:

> Oh, so, President Jacques Chirac is not coming to unveil the Alsace-Moselle Memorial? Well, so be it: if this is how we are being abandoned once again, I cannot see why I, who was formerly conscripted into the German army, would go and please our President by voting for this constitution that he likes so much!

The letters addressed to these intermediary media display the features of the restricted general involvement ideal type. Judgements rely on practical and instrumental considerations as well as on general but rather vague arguments, often different from those formulated in political debates. This can be observed in letters that lament the decline of France and the incompetence of French elites by mobilising 'common sense' and ethical judgements. In a minority of letters, this intermediary posture is however closer to a synoptic attitude (i.e. more like the letters addressed to *Télérama* – see below), with political generalisations and more informed discussions of the issues mixing together. This is essentially the case of letters that mainly deal with Europe, and especially the TCE (a dozen letters). Their authors specifically discuss European issues, mobilising precise elements (social Europe based on articles of the Treaty, comments on the decision-making procedure used for VAT-related decisions, quotations from a European commissioner) while still displaying a number of 'intermediary' characteristics, such as a hesitant or confused argumentation (which sometimes complicates coding) or a personalised and particularising writing style (using the first-person singular and referencing one's personal situation). Given the lack of information on the letter writers' social characteristics, it is difficult to say anything beyond the fact that these types of letters exist and that they represent a minority of letters. Yet, we can remark that several of these letters are atypical in more than one respect: they come from associations (two letters), extra-regional writers (an email from Lyon) or anonymous authors (two letters). This minority of letters validates our observations further. To the readership of the daily regional press, Europe 'in itself' is a rare theme, discussed by readers whose ways of expressing themselves and social characteristics are also atypical, and/or in contexts where the agenda favours generalisation.

The specific posture of synoptic writers to Télérama

The analysis of the letters sent to *Télérama* reveals many more synoptic expressions of opinion. This can arguably be explained by the composition of the weekly magazine's readership and of the mobilised fraction thereof, whose motivations appear as much more political, in the context of a reaction to the electoral endorsement of the director of the publication.

However, they react with their own preoccupations and cognitive frames which diverge somewhat from the dominant arguments found in the political debate or among political pundits and editorialists (Lehingue 2007a; Gombin and Hubé 2009). The opinions of mobilised individuals expressed in our corpus hardly match the categories of Eurosceptics, xenophobes, authoritarian or utilitarian citizens outlined by many observers (Eurobarometer 2005).[19] The letters received (n=1399) only rarely mention Turkey (ten letters), enlargement, the loss of national sovereignty, the Bolkestein directive (around 1 per cent) and European integration (4.5 per cent) (see Table 12.4), which differentiates them from their counterparts of the regional press. The utilitarian dimension is more present, although not prevalent since the economy (14 per cent) and social questions (13.3 per cent) represent only little more than a quarter of the letters.[20] French politics are mentioned in one fourth of the letters; letter writers preoccupied by economic or social issues tend to be 'no' supporters (respectively 125 letters out of 196 and 124 out of 186). The motivation of the TCE's opponents is linked to the economy, but not to their personal situation. On the contrary, it is linked to a general discussion on the Treaty, liberalism, and the process of European construction. This is expressed by a woman who wrote the following on March 26: 'If I say "Yes", am I saying yes to a doctrine or to a Constitution? If I say "No" am I hindering European construction? Do we want a free Europe or a liberal Europe?'.

---

19. Similarly, a poll published by the weekly news magazine *Marianne* (26 March – 1 April 2005, pp. 20–21) indicates that 31 per cent of 'no' supporters are against Turkey's accession; 29 per cent think that voting 'no' will lead to a new social orientation of European policies and 20 per cent express their dissatisfaction with the Raffarin government. On the other hand, 46 per cent of 'yes' supporters claim to support Europe and 33 per cent think that having a constitution for Europe is important.

20. Letters discussing liberalism, competition or economic policies were coded under 'economy' whereas letters on labour laws or pensions were coded under 'social'.

Letter writers follow and criticise the framing of their media but express a personal viewpoint. The social profile of informed and educated writers probably explains their propensity to write in the first person. A typical letter first discusses the Treaty as a whole (38 per cent of the letters), presenting various arguments, sometimes supported by quotations from the text itself. Among them, sixty-six directly quote and discuss one or several articles of the Treaty to support their argument. This is the case of a pensioner who, in a May 4 letter, blames *Télérama* for 'so many beautiful, great, generous ideas and not a quote from a single article'. She claims that the weekly magazine distorts the debate by passing off letters from 'no' supporters as 'rants' even though they are supported by precise examples drawn from the text. She uses articles III–122, I–41.2, I–41.7 to support her own arguments. Conversely, a honorary European Commission official harshly criticises the chief editor: 'No, Mr Jézégabel, the treaty isn't unreadable'. He points out that a 'recent poll has revealed that the French people's attachment to public services does not prevent them from wishing the Treaty would be voted'. Another reader, writing on April 29, thinks that 'we shouldn't fight the wrong battle', because by refusing the TCE, 'we'd favour Maastricht and Nice to the [TCE's] improvements: new fundamental and social rights' – he makes references to articles II–87, II–91, II–75, II–94, III–233, III–235, III–278, II–96, III–122, III–167, III–180, III–184, I–11 and III–259.

Table 12.4: Topics addressed in letters to Télérama

Topics addressed	N =	%	Topics addressed	N =	%
TCE in general	531	38%	Environment	21	1.5%
French politics	360	25.7%	Bolkestein directive	16	1.1%
Economy	196	14%	European citizenship	16	1.1%
Social	186	13.3%	Loss of sovereignty	14	1%
Political Europe	167	11.9%	Police and security	13	0.9%
European integration	63	4.5%	Enlargement	11	0.8%
Peace	56	4%	Turkey	10	0.7%
Referendum	55	3.9%	CFSP	8	0.6%
Institutions	44	3.2%	Poland	4	0.3%
International politics	35	2.5%	Agriculture	3	0.2%
Secular principle/religion	24	1.70%	Other	406	29%

The most sectoral elements of European policies (CFSP, secular principle or Bolkestein directive) are also used to support arguments. This point of view results from a generalisation from the Treaty or national politics. Far from constituting a public forum (Pounds 2006), the letters rarely react to other letters (only 59 letters react to a published letter) – letter writers rather adopt a position of editorialists, expressing a political point of view. The published readers tackle the same subjects, but do not answer each other directly.

This generalising posture can also be found in the justifications for the act of writing (Boltanski, Darré and Schiltz 1984). Some aim at expressing a general point of view on the Treaty and restoring the 'truth' on the text itself (38 per cent). Others act as observers of the political game, reacting to a debate presented in the wrong terms 'by the media' (7 per cent) or by the actors of the political game (19 per cent). A high school student, who wishes she had the right to vote, writes to remind Laurent Fabius that article 210 of the TCE is the same as article 137 of the Nice Treaty.

The discourse mobilised is thus the expression of a synoptic point of view, politically engaged and documented. The opinions contribute to the general political debate. The tone used is often a professorial one (17 per cent), as in the case of this reader, who has been a subscriber for twenty-five years. On May 2, he writes 'Dear *Télérama*, any honest and not overly ignorant soul' should refuse to 'stupidly say yes to a fraudulent operation'. An architect states that:

Box 12.4: Multiple correspondence analysis

This statistical technique consists in drawing correspondences between a number of variables. By studying proximities and distinctions between variables and groups, we can describe the structuring of the space of responses to the online survey according to social characteristics (socio-professional category and level of education), distributing the main links on axes. The analysis proposed here involves all respondents (n=1298) and twelve active variables (twenty-five associated modalities), constructed on the basis of the responses to the most answered questions on attitudes towards Europe:

 - Having chosen (or not) the answers proposed on European identity defined as: a shared history; democracy and human rights; a shared culture and heritage.

 - Judging (or not) that: one of Europe's main missions is contributing to peace and democracy; that France has not profited from Europe in any way; that worsening unemployment is one of the negative effects of Europe on France; that Europe has not had any negative effect on France; (on the Euro) that the Euro has made prices increase; that the Euro makes us stronger against the dollar; (on enlargement) that some countries should not have entered the EU; that enlargement offers new opportunities for businesses.

 - Lastly, the answer to the question on who benefited from Europe in France.

Levels of education and socio-professional category have been set as illustrative variables. They are therefore not taken into account in the construction of the axes. However, their modalities can be projected next to the modalities of active variables. The analysis thus allows us to observe their distribution in comparison to responses to questions on Europe.

The 'no' here is the other name of a project that remains to be formulated, Europe, and which should itself possess the ability to surpass itself, to go beyond the constitution – the foundations for this being, if I may borrow Emmanuel Lévinas's concept, is peace and proximity.

Conversely, few adopt a privative posture to discuss their personal situation (3 per cent). Few people also present themselves as 'victims of the system', as a woman does, by describing herself as a representative of 'the middle class struggling more and more to make ends meet', and who, in an April 26 letter, as she does not feel concerned by these 'European' preoccupations (her emphasis), calls for abstention. Few (6 per cent) reject politics or explain that 'millions of French people who were rather in favour of the YES, will probably vote NO, or not vote at all' because they will vote against Chirac, against the 'scheming' of the last right-wing governments, accused of being 'crooks' (undated letter, received between May 9 and 15). These types of letters clearly have specific characteristics: their spelling and syntax are more hesitant than those of other writers. Their profile can also be very specific, as in the case an 'undecided' voter, who thinks that voting 'no' cannot make Europe any worse, as he has personally already hit rock bottom: 'I am young, educated, I speak several languages, but I am poor, up to my neck in debt, looking for a job and currently homeless' (May 8 letter).

Culturally cleaved representations

The online survey provides us with additional elements, insofar as it gives us the possibility to link opinions with the social characteristics of those who formulate them.

Thanks to a multiple correspondence analysis (see Figure 12.3) based on responses to the online survey, we can picture the space of responses to questions on Europe and observe the distribution of social characteristics. This analysis shows an opposition between two types of stances on Europe, more or less characteristic of two ideal-types described above, notably on the first axis, the most explanatory one.

On the left side of the first axis (20.09 per cent of overall inertia; see Figure 12.3), we find those who are critical, think that France has not benefited from Europe in any way, that European identity does not exist, that nobody has reaped any benefits from Europe – or at least only a few categories of the French population –, that certain countries should not have accessed the EU, and that worsening unemployment is one of the negative effects of Europe on France. They are only a minority of the respondents to the survey – hence, the asymmetry of this axis. They are opposed to those who consider that European identity is defined by a shared history, culture and heritage, by democracy and human rights, that Europe's mission is to contribute to peace and democracy, that the entire French population has benefited from Europe, that the enlargement offers new opportunities for business, and that the Euro makes us stronger against the dollar (right side of Figure 12.3). In short, they match the ideal-type of positive synoptic involvement.

These two poles are not only linked with different opinions about Europe; they

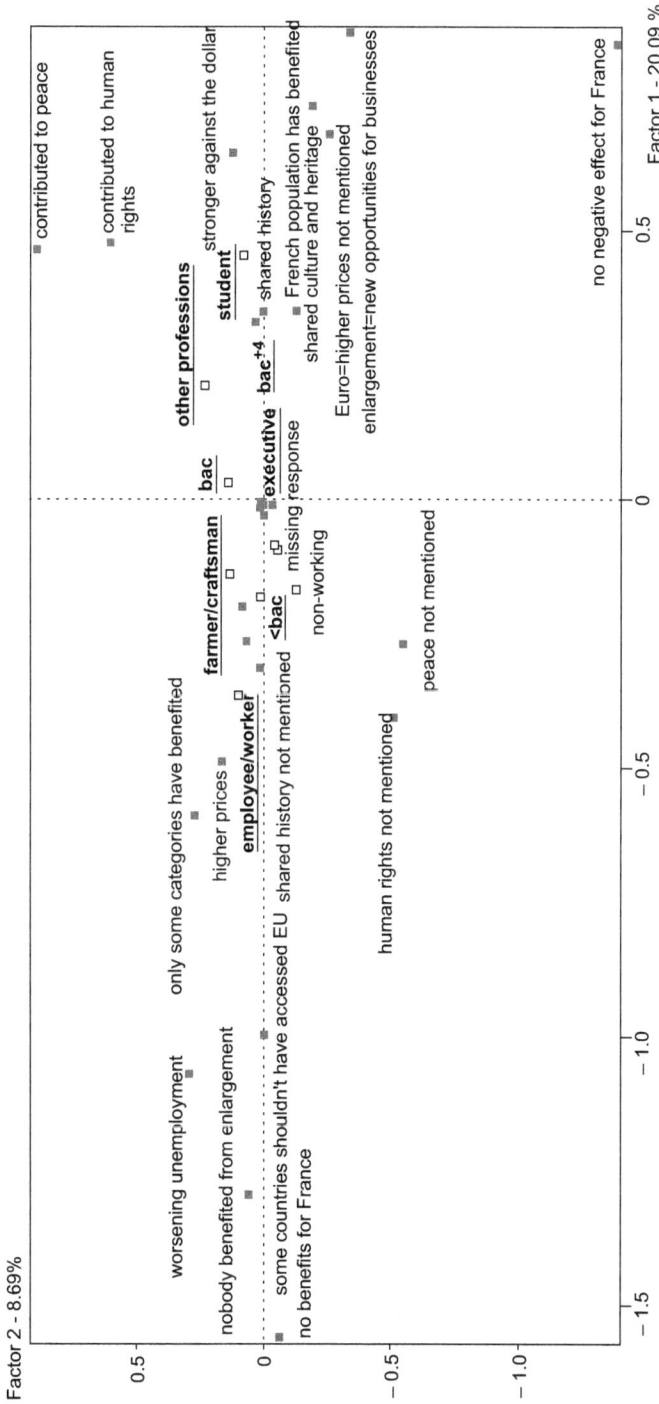

Figure 12.3: *Multiple correspondence analysis representing the distribution of responses to the main questions of the Sources d'Europe survey with projection of occupation and level of education (n=1298) (projection of axes 1 and 2)*

are also related to different positions in the social space. Indeed, the projection of level of education and socio-professional category allows for a better characterisation of the critical respondents. They are more frequently employees, workers, farmers, craftsmen or non-working, with low levels of education; respondents who have a positive synoptic involvement appear to have high education levels (at least four years of university education), and to be students or executives. In this sense, critical respondents are close to 'interstitial' ones (see Chapter 7): they are politicised and sociologically close to people for whom European issues are remote.

Negative evaluation is more characteristic of those with lower levels of education. Their representations of Europe are more related to their everyday preoccupations, such as employment. More of them consider that one of Europe's missions is to fight against unemployment (59 per cent of those below baccalauréat level, against 40 per cent for those with at least two years of university education). While they express more critical viewpoints, for instance when they say that there is no European identity (29 per cent below baccalauréat level, 15 per cent with baccalauréat level/+2 years, 10 per cent with at least four years of university education), that Europe has not benefited France in any way (a quarter of employees and workers against 1 per cent of students), that is also because it is easier to be optimistic when one is in a secure or positively orientated social position. Positive synoptic involvement is, on the other hand, characteristic of the most educated, culturally and socially endowed respondents. They distinguish themselves by structured opinions on Europe, materialised by a low rate of non-responses. More of them express a general outlook on European issues and think that the French population as a whole (general viewpoint) has benefited from the EU. 44 per cent of those with at least four years of university education say that what defines European identity best is a shared culture and heritage (39 per cent with two years of university, 32 per cent with baccalauréat level, 14 per cent below baccalauréat level).

The second axis (8.69 per cent of the inertia) differentiates answers that are positive towards Europe along two registers: the first (top left quadrant) is a moral, altruistic, universal and intellectual one (Europe has contributed to peace and democracy; Europe represents democracy and human rights); the second (bottom left) is a more economic or even utilitarian one (enlargement offers new opportunities for business, the Euro has not led to higher prices; the French population has benefited from Europe; there has been no negative effect on France). These two registers could be representative of an immaterial/material divide of Europe (Hooghe and Marks 2009), itself representative of a left/right political debate and of differences in the 'structure of the capitals held' in the sense of Bourdieu (1984) – the first being rather from the cultural-intellectual spheres of the upper categories of the social space, the second from the economic sphere. More precise data is however necessary to further test these hypotheses.

The mobilisation of 'spontaneous' original data provides some insights on certain types of attitudes towards Europe. Despite its limits, it confirms observations made on the basis of interviews. Because this data implies the intention of writing, a specific political object (the constitutional treaty) and active attitudes of which this object is the product, it only concerns specific citizens: laymen with postures of experts. While polls or interviews may concern the entire population, we can see that the public mobilised by these questions is much more limited, and that it is mobilised because of the contents of the media agenda: opinions on Europe are rarely expressed overall, but they appear more often on the few occasions when Europe is at the centre of the media's agenda. Without the specific context of the possible negative vote in the TCE referendum and its consequences for political institutions (*Sources d'Europe* being an institutional media) or the press (the surge of mail received by *Télérama*), it would not have existed. This study has also allowed us to characterise those who spontaneously express their opinion on Europe: they are more frequently male, with a particularly high level of educational attainment. There are few differences between 'yes' and 'no' supporters here; participation in the debate is above all explained by social properties. Lastly, our research shows how Europe is discussed by these publics. They often have a political point of view on Europe, but also on national politics, the economy and the organisation of the political debate. The positions expressed are only rarely privative. The choice of the letter's recipient is linked with two types of attitudes: intermediary in the case of the daily regional press, synoptic in the case of the weekly magazine and the website on European issues. Consequently, these results attest to the heuristic character of the mobilisation of approaches that provide an alternative to responses to closed-ended questions in order to study the diversity and the ambivalence of relationships towards Europe.

conclusion

Daniel Gaxie

This book seeks to specify citizen attitudes towards European construction. This question has been widely debated in the media, in political discourse and in a prolific and ever growing body of scientific literature. The original contribution of this volume to this important debate resides in several elements: we built our research hypotheses around the idea of the diversity of attitudes which appears more realistic than the rather vain search for a single explanatory factor or variable; we have implemented a research methodology allowing us to observe this diversity; reactions from all categories of the public have been observed, including those who are the least concerned by European issues and debates; qualitative comparative methodologies have been used – mostly in-depth interviews with open-ended questions.

This approach has yielded a number of results. We have described subjective perceptions among various categories in the public in detail, including segments of the population which are generally ignored because they rarely respond to solicitations to participate in quantitative surveys and because their attitudes are at odds with several widespread assumptions of the mainstream literature. We have highlighted unequal information levels and the overall lack of familiarity with European issues. We have shown the diversity in the ways of expressing viewpoints on Europe; the diversity of attitudes towards European construction; the unequally structured character of these attitudes and the diversity and the complexity of the factors orienting perceptions of Europe. We have analysed the impact and the limits of the specificity of national experiences of European integration.

These results suggest that such a qualitative sociological approach should be used and developed further. This is evidently not the only possible approach. Research methods should be combined. Surveys should take into account the respondents' actual degree of familiarity with the questions asked. It is also necessary to observe whether and how questions are understood, as well as the degree of conviction and the modalities of the answers. Using more open-ended questions would be a way to reach these goals. This volume also shows that it is necessary to use very subtle indicators in order to measure the 'effects' of socio-demographic characteristics on attitudes towards Europe.

One of the lessons that can be drawn from the research presented in this book is that citizens' dispositions towards Europe are complex. Europe is not perceived by all citizens in the same way and the EU is not clearly identified in all segments of the public. Insofar as 'European' attitudes exist, they are not always clearly oriented. Not everyone is 'for' or 'against' Europe; some do not know whether they support or oppose it. Many reactions cannot be classified, or are contradictory or composite. On the other hand, some attitudes are stable, but despite what is frequently assumed, they are not all structured by preoccupations related to the political issues of European construction as they are framed and debated by politicians, journalists or commentators.

The in-depth interviews conducted within the framework of this research show that only limited segments of the public have a grasp of the debates on European construction. Insofar as structured attitudes exist, they rely on considerations whose status varies. Attitudes towards Europe are notably affected by the unequally distributed feeling of being (or not being) entitled and informed enough to speak on questions perceived as complex and disconcerting. Interviews on such subjects suggest reactions that are more or less self-assured, and therefore unequally significant. Viewpoints expressed during an interview do not always have a political signification or potential for political mobilisation.

Some of the results of this volume echo often-formulated hypotheses in European studies, but they also emphasise their over-simplification. For instance, we have shown that while certain European attitudes are linked to political preferences, the nature of this link varies according to cultural capital and the level of politicisation. Some categories of the public place their trust in a party or its leaders, which leads them to endorse their general views on European issues without themselves having a grasp on specifics. In other cases, ideological preferences lead interviewees to support both a 'personal' vision of European integration and an organisation or a political leader that shares them, albeit in a relatively disjointed manner. In intermediary cases, support for a party or a leader comes with a more or less uncertain endorsement of their stances on European issues. In some cases, apparently 'anti-European' attitudes do not result from 'European' considerations, but rather from a general mistrust of politics or a general scepticism based on various personal hardships.

The explanations put forward in the academic literature often generalise their claims – whether 'national' dispositions or the interests of 'winners' or 'losers' of market integration – to an entire public. Conversely, this book shows that different interpretations should apply to different segments of the public. Hence, the validity of some current explanations is conditional rather than general. For instance, the version of the utilitarian hypothesis according to which individuals judge Europe according to the benefits they think they get out of it is confirmed by our own observations, but only for the fractions of intermediary populations that are directly affected by EU public policies. Once a determinant of European attitudes has been identified, it is necessary to observe for which segments of the public and in which circumstances it is likely to matter. In this sense, this book confirms that a number of attitudes towards Europe are based on economic rationales that some refer to as 'utilitarian'. But these rationales are very diverse. In the educated, informed and politicised fractions, 'macro-economic' arguments tend to prevail. In intermediary publics exposed to the policies of EU institutions, attitudes result from direct exposure to EU directives and regulations. In some working-class populations, on the other hand, an often indistinct 'Europe' is blamed for many everyday problems. Only certain segments of the public explicitly justify their viewpoint based on their personal economic interests and perceptions. Such opinions are not projected onto the EU as a whole, but are limited to some of its actions considered as salient.

By contrast, higher social categories appear particularly reluctant to stress their personal interests when asked to speak about Europe. They justify their support or opposition to European construction through general appreciation in economic, political, ideological or international terms. Hence, when a businessman says he is happy that Europe favours exchanges and development, he is not referring to his personal economic situation, but it is obvious that his specific personal position also informs his point of view.

Authors have debated whether the economic basis of judgements on European integration really are 'objective' or 'subjective', 'individual' or 'collective', 'economic' or 'political' considerations. Qualitative studies suggest that it is sometimes impossible to choose one single option. Some individuals mobilise both economic and political arguments. Certain political or ideological viewpoints may be based on indistinct collective and individual economic preoccupations. Similarly, evidence of an independent effect of national experience or history may be observed in many interviews but they are also explicitly linked to collective and individual economic considerations.

Thus, it is necessary to untangle all these motives and reasons in order to make some progress in explaining the reactions of ordinary citizens to Europe. In this field as in others, this implies an in-depth understanding of individual subjective perceptions and appreciations. Without the means necessary to investigate the ways in which questions are understood and to understand motives behind the answers, secondary analyses of opinion surveys only provide limited information on the interviewees' subjective representations. Dealing with answers to closed-ended questions can even lead to a distorted view of what citizens think about Europe. Adding together formally identical answers to closed-ended questions artificially homogenise opinions and attitudes of respondents who are unequally familiar with – or interested in – European issues. This contributes to the intellectual ethnocentrism which prevails in many interpretations of mass attitudes: it is assumed that all categories of the population have access to debates, even though numerous qualitative studies show that these debates are actually completely foreign to them.

Issues discussed in restricted political, media and intellectual circles are often assumed by scholars to preoccupy the entire population. Consequently, the ability of political parties to impose their analyses on the general public or even their voters is overestimated. Observation shows that only the educated and/or politically mobilised fractions of the population are able to appropriate or spontaneously express arguments that resemble those of parties or political leaders. Many citizens are too distant from debates on European issues to be influenced. In intermediary populations, only snippets or slogans from party discourses leave a discernible trace. Many ordinary citizens rely on their personal experience and express viewpoints independently from the parties. Thus, critical positions on Europe were observed in countries such as Germany, where political elites massively support European integration. Our research confirms that there are distinct national experiences of European integration, but they are not necessarily shared by the entire population or interpreted in the same way.

For the same reasons, the issue of identity tends to feature only in the background of our own observations, whereas it is very much in the foreground in much of the literature. We have only observed a few rare cases of interviewees spontaneously asserting a European identity. National identity is more frequently asserted, generally in relation to critical views. But these references have varying statuses. In circles that are close to right-wing 'sovereigntist' movements, they are an element of a more or less systematic ideological vision. Reference to nationality is also mobilised in categories of the public that are not concerned by political controversies on these subjects. In doing so, they express their attachment to various aspects of a familiar environment – for instance social protection systems – and defiance towards evolutions that may threaten them. For instance, some interviewees blame 'Europe' for allowing foreigners to profit from various social benefits that they feel entitled to themselves without necessarily supporting a nationalistic or xenophobic ideology. Invoking national identity is a means for them to claim their priority – albeit not exclusive – in their access to welfare. Similarly, many working-class interviewees consider that the introduction of the Euro has led to increasingly high prices and some state that they miss the former national currency, but none mention that they are attached to the political system of the Nation-State.

This research sought to provide a more detailed description of attitudes of various categories of the population towards European construction. In an academic and political landscape seeking simple explanations (and solutions), our contribution goes against the tide. However, we have provided a more complex, and therefore a more realistic set of explanations, which reflects the national and sociological diversity of the 500 million European citizens.

| bibliography

Achin, C. (ed.) (2007) *Sexes, genre et politique*, Paris: Economica.

Adam, F. (2008) 'Mapping social capital across Europe: findings, trends and methodological shortcomings of cross-national surveys', *Social Science Information*, 47: 159–86.

Agrikoliansky, E. (2001) 'Carrières militantes et vocation à la morale: les militants de la Ligue des droits de l'homme dans les années 1980', *Revue française de science politique*, 51(1): 27–46.

Aldrin, P. (2003) 'S'accommoder du politique. Economie et pratiques de l'information politique', *Politix*, 16(64): 177–203.

— (2010) 'L'intervention de l'opinion publique européenne, Genèse intellectuelle et politique de l'Eurobaromètre (1950–1973)', *Politix*, 23(89): 79–101.

Aldrin, P. and Utard, J.-M. (2008) 'The Ambivalent Politicisation of European Communication', GSPE Working Papers, http://prisme.u-strasbg.fr/workingpapers/WPAldrinUtard.pdf Accessed on 14th May 2010.

Anderson, C. J. (1998) 'When in doubt, use proxies: attitudes toward domestic politics and support for European Integration', *Comparative Political Studies*, 31(5): 569–601.

Anderson, C. J. and Kaltenthaler, K. C. (1996) 'The dynamics of public opinion toward European Integration 1973–93', *European Journal of International Relations*, 2(2): 175–99.

Arban, G. (2003) 'Des lecteurs aux publics: Les communautés de lecteurs et l'espace public de *Télérama*', in C. Barril, M. Carrel, J.-C. Guerrero, and A. Marquez, (eds), *Le public en action: Usages et limites de la notion d'espace public en sciences sociales*, Paris: L'Harmattan.

Aspinwall, M. (2002) 'Preferring Europe: ideology and national preferences on European Integration', *European Union Politics*, 3(1): 81–111.

Baisnée, O. (2006) 'Les médias et l'Union européenne: un espace public encore introuvable', in C. Bélot and B. Cautrès (eds) *La vie démocratique de l'Union européenne*, Paris: La Documentation française.

— (2007) 'En être ou pas, les logiques de l'entre soi à Bruxelles', *Actes de la Recherche en sciences sociales*, 166–7: 111–22.

Bartolini, S. (2005) *Restructuring Europe: Centre Formation, System Building and Political Structuring Between the Nation State and the EU*, Oxford: Oxford University Press.

Beaud, S. and Pialoux M. (1999) *Retour sur la condition ouvrière: Enquête aux usines Peugeot de Sochaux-Montbéliard*, Paris: Fayard.

— (2006) 'Racisme ouvrier ou mépris de classe? Retour sur une enquête de terrain' in D. Fassin and E. Fassin, *De la question sociale à la question raciale?* Paris: La Découverte.

Beauvallet, W. and Michon, S. (2010) 'Members of the European Parliament: the professionalization and socialization of MEPs', *French Politics*, 8(2).

Beck, U. and Grande, E. (2007) *Cosmopolitan Europe*, Cambridge: Polity Press.

Becker, H. (1982) *Art Worlds,* Berkeley: University of California Press.

Bélot, C. (2000) *L'Europe en citoyenneté: Jeunes Français et Britanniques dans le processus de légitimation de l'Union Européenne*, PhD thesis in political science, Grenoble: Université Pierre Mendes France.

— (2002) 'Les logiques sociologiques de soutien au processus d'intégration européenne: éléments d'interprétation', *Revue Internationale de Politique Comparée,* 9(1):11–29.

Bélot, C. and Cautrès, B. (2008) 'Opinion publique', in C. Bélot, P. Magnette and S. Saurruger (eds) *Science politique de l'Union européenne*, Paris: Economica.

Bélot, C. and Greffet, F. (2005) 'Une Europe en quête d'électeurs: Retour sur différentes lectures de l'abstention aux élections européennes à l'occasion du scrutin de juin 2004', in P. Delwitt and P. Poirier (eds), *Parlement puissant, électeurs absents? Les élections européennes de juin 2004*, Bruxelles: Editions de l'Université de Bruxelles.

Bélot, C., Magnette, P. and Saurruger, S. (2008) *Science politique de l'Union européenne*, Paris: Economica.

Bélot, C. and Pina, C. (2009) 'Des campagnes européennes non disputées et sous contraintes', *Revue politique et parlementaire*, 1052: 62–72.

Bennett, S. E. (1988) '"Know-Nothing revisited": the implications of political ignorance today', *Social Science Quarterly*, 69: 476–90.

Berelson, B. R., Lazarsfeld, P. F. and MacPhee, W. N. (1954) *Voting. A Study of Opinion Formation in a Presidential Campaign*, Chicago: The University of Chicago Press.

Bergstrom, C. F. (2005) *Comitology: Delegation of Powers in the EU and the Committee System,* Oxford: Oxford University Press.

Bernstein, B. (2003) *Class, Codes and Control*, London: Routledge.

Bielasiak, J. (2002) 'Determinants of public opinion differences on EU accession in Poland', *Europe-Asia Studies*, 54(8): 1241–66.

Binnema, H. and Crum, B. (2007) 'Resistance to Europe as a carrier of mass-elite incongruence: The case of the Netherlands', in J. Lacroix and R. Coman (eds) *Les résistances à l'Europe: Cultures nationales, idéologies et stratégies d'acteurs*, Bruxelles: Editions de l'Université de Bruxelles.

Blondel, J. and Lacroix, B. (1996) 'Pourquoi votent-ils FN?' in N. Mayer and P. Perrineau (eds) *Le Front national à découvert*, Paris: Presses de Science Po.

Blondiaux, L. (1994) 'Le chiffre et la croyance: L'importation des sondages d'opinion en France ou les infortunes d'une opinion sans publics', *Politix* , 7(25): 117–52.

Boltanski, L., Darré, Y. and Schiltz, M-A. (1984) 'La dénonciation', *Actes de la recherche en sciences sociales*, 5: 3–40.

Bon, F. (1991) *Les discours de la politique* (Textes réunis et présentés par Y. Schemeil), Paris: Economica.

Bourdieu, P. (1984) *Distinction: A Social Critique of the Judgement of Taste*, London: Routledge.

— (1985) 'The social space and the genesis of groups', *Theory and Society*, 723–44.

— (1993) 'Public opinion does not exist', *Sociology in Question*, London: Sage.

— (ed) (1999) *The Weight of the World*, Palo Alto: Stanford University Press.

— (2002) *Le bal des célibataires : Crise de la société paysanne en Béarn*, Paris: Seuil.

— (2008) *The Bachelor's Ball: The Crisis of Peasant Society In Béarn*, Oxford: Polity.

Bourdieu, P. and Wacquant, L. (ed.) (2005) 'The Mystery of Ministry: From Particular Wills to the General Will' in *Pierre Bourdieu and Democratic Politics*. Cambridge, UK: Polity Press, 55–63.

Braconnier, C. and Dormagen, J.-Y. (2007) *La démocratie de l'abstention*, Paris: le Seuil.

Bréchon, P. (2002) 'Les grandes enquêtes internationales (Eurobaromètres, Valeurs, ISSP): apports et limites', *L'Année sociologique,* 52(1): 105–30.

Bréchon, P. and Cautrès, B. (eds) (1998) *Les enquêtes Eurobaromètres: analyse comparée des données sociopolitiques*, Paris: L'Harmattan.

Briquet, J.-L. (1997) *La tradition en mouvement: Clientélisme et politique en Corse*, Paris: Belin.

— (2003) 'La politique au village: Vote et mobilisation électorale dans la Corse rurale', in J. Lagroye (ed.), *La politisation*, Paris: Belin.

Bruter, M. (2005) *Citizens of Europe: the Emergence of a Mass European Identity*, Houndmills/New York: Palgrave Macmillan.

Bryant, C. G. A. (1985) *Positivism in Social Theory and Research*, New York: Palgrave Macmillan.

Campbell, A., Converse, P. E., Miller, W. E. and Stokes, D. E. (1980) *The American Voter*, Chicago: The University of Chicago Press.

Carruba, C. J. (2001) 'The Electoral Connection in European Union Politics', *The Journal of Politics*, 63(1): 141–58.

Cautrès, B. (2001) 'L'électeur européen: une émergence difficile ou improbable?', *Politique européenne*, 4: 47–72.

— (2003) 'La participation aux élections européennes comme problème de représentation politique' in S. Saurugger (ed.) *Les modes de représentation dans l'Union Européenne*, Paris: L'Harmattan.

Cautrès, B. and Denni, B. (2000) 'Les attitudes des Français à l'égard de l'Union Européenne: les logiques du refus', in P. Bréchon, A. Laurent and P. Perrineau (eds), *Les cultures politiques des français*, Paris: Presses de Sciences Po.

Cautrès, B. and Grunberg, G. (2007) 'Position sociale, identité nationale et attitudes à l'égard de l'Europe: La construction européenne souffre-t-elle d'un biais élitiste?', in O. Costa and P. Magnette (eds) *Une Europe des élites? Réflexions sur la fracture démocratique de l'Union Européenne,* Bruxelles: Editions de l'Université de Bruxelles.

Cayrol, R. (2000) *Sondages, mode d'emploi,* Paris: Presses de Sciences Po.

Cefaï, D. and Pasquier, D. (eds) 2003, *Le sens du public,* Paris: PUF.

Cepernich, C. (2005) 'La notiziabilità dell'Europa: Attori, eventi e temi nella copertura della stampa', in C. Marletti and J. Mouchon (eds) *La costruzione mediatica dell'Europa,* Milano: FrancoAngeli.

Champagne, P. (1990) *Faire l'opinion: Le nouveau jeu politique,* Paris: Editions de Minuit.

Charpentier, I. (2004) 'Une pratique rare et sélective: la lecture de la presse d'information générale et politique', in J.-B. Legavre (ed.) *La presse écrite: objets délaissés,* Paris: L'Harmattan.

Checkel, J. T. and Katzenstein, P. J. (eds) (2009) *European Identity,* Cambridge: Cambridge University Press.

Cheveigné, S. (2004) 'L'opinion publique européenne et les biotechnologies', in M. Aligisakis (ed.) *L'Europe et les biotechnologies: Urgences et impasses d'un débat démocratique,* Genève: Publication de l'Institut Européen de l'Université de Genève.

Christin, T. (2005) 'Economic and Political Basis of Attitudes towards the EU in Central and East European Countries in the 1990s', *European Union Politics,* 6(1): 29–57.

Citrin, J. and Sides, J. (2004) 'More than Nationals: How Identity Choice Matters in the New Europe', in R. K. Herrmann, T. Risse and M. B. Brewer (eds) *Transnational Identities: Becoming European in the EU,* Lanham: Rowman and Littlefield.

Cohen, A., Dezalay, Y., and Marchetti, D. (2007) 'Esprits d'Etats, entrepreneurs d'Europe', *Actes de la recherche en sciences sociales,* 166–7: 7–13.

Cohen, A., and Weisbein, J. (2005), 'Laboratoires du constitutionnalisme européen: Expertises académiques et mobilisations politiques dans la promotion d'une constitution européenne', *Droit et Sociétés,* 60: 353–69.

Coman, R. and Lacroix, J. (2007) 'Présentation', in J. Lacroix and R. Coman (eds) *Les résistances à l'Europe: Cultures nationales, idéologies et stratégies d'acteurs,* Bruxelles: Editions de l'Université de Bruxelles.

Conti, N. (2007) 'Domestic parties and European integration: the problem of party attitudes to the EU, and the Europeanisation of parties', *European Political Science,* 6: 192–207.

Converse, P. (1964) 'The Nature of Belief Systems in Mass Publics', in D. E. Apter (ed.) *Ideology and Discontent,* New York: The Free Press.

Costa, O. (2009) 'Le parlement européen dans le système décisionnel de l'Union européenne: la puissance au prix de l'illisibilité', *Politique européenne,* 28: 129–55.

Crespy, A. and Verschueren, N. (2008) 'De l'euroscepticisme aux résistances: contribution au débat sur la théorisation des conflits sur l'intégration européenne', *Cahiers du CEVIPOL,* 5.

Crespy, A. and Verschueren N. (2009) 'From Euroscepticism to resistance to

European integration: an interdisciplinary perspective', *Perspectives on European Politics and Society*, 10(3): 377–93.

CVVM (2005) Enquête, *Naše společnost 2004* [Our society], 4–9.

Dakhlia, J. (1995) 'La question des lieux communs: Des modèles de souveraineté dans l'Islam méditerranéen', in B. Lepetit (ed.) *Les formes de l'expérience*, Paris: Albin Michel.

de Lassalle, M. (2010) *Multilevel Governance in Practice: Actors and Institutional Competitions of the Regional Policy of the EU in France*, forthcoming.

de Maillard, J. and Robert, C. (2008) 'Gouvernement par comités' in *Science politique de l'Europe*, Paris: Economica.

De Master, S. and Le Roy, M. K. (2000) 'Xenophobia and the European Union', *Comparative Politics*, 32(4): 419–36.

Deflem, M. and Pampel, F. C. (1996) 'The myth of postnational identity: popular support for European unification', *Social Forces*, 75(1): 119–43.

Dehousse, R. (2003) 'Comitology: who watches the watchmen?', *Journal of European Public Policy*, 10(5): 798–813.

Dell'olio, F. (2005) *The Europeanization of Citizenship: Between the Ideology of Nationality, Immigration and European Identity*, Aldershot: Ashgate.

Della Porta, D. and Caiani, M. (2007) 'Addressing Europe: How domestic actors perceive European Institutions and how they try to influence them: The Italian Case in comparative perspective' in J. Lacroix and R. Coman (eds) *Les résistances à l'Europe: Cultures nationales, idéologies et stratégies d'acteurs*, Bruxelles: Editions de l'Université de Bruxelles.

Delli Carpini, M. X. and Keeter, S. S. (1996) *What Americans Know about Politics and Why it Matters*, New Haven: Yale University Press.

Delli Carpini, M. X. and Williams, B. A. (1994) 'The method is the message: focus groups as a method of social, psychological, and political inquiry', *Research in Micropolitics*, 4: 57–85.

Delmotte, F. (2007) 'Les résistances à l'Europe au prisme de la sociologie historique de Norbert Elias', in J. Lacroix and R. Coman (eds) *Les résistances à l'Europe: Cultures nationales, idéologies et stratégies d'acteurs*, Bruxelles: Editions de l'Université de Bruxelles.

Déloye, Y. (2007) 'Le vote européen entre implication et réaction', *Revue française de science politique*, 57(2): 266–7.é

Denord, F. and Schwartz, A. (2009) *L'Europe sociale n'aura pas lieu*, Bellecombe-en-Bauges: Raisons d'agir.

Desrosières, A. (1993) *La politique des grands nombres: Histoire de la raison statistique*, Paris: La Découverte.

Diez Medrano, J. (2003) *Framing Europe: Attitudes to European Integration in Germany, Spain, and the United Kingdom*, Princeton/Oxford: Princeton University Press.

— (2008) 'Europeanization and the Emergence of a European Society', *IBEI* Working Papers, 12.

— (2010) 'Unpacking European identity', *Politique Européenne*, 30(1), 45–66.

Döring, H. (2007) 'The Composition of the College of Commissioners: Patterns of Delegation', *European Union Politics*, 8(2): 207–28.

Dubar, C. (2003) 'Entretien de recherche en sociologie et relation analytique: des fécondations possibles', Paper presented at the annual conference of the European Psychoanalysis Federation, Sorrento.

Dubois, J. (1969) 'Enoncé et énonciation', *Langages,* 13: 100–10.

Dubois, V. (2010) *The Bureaucrat and the Poor: Encounters in Welfare Offices,* Aldershot: Ashgate.

Duchesne, S. and Frognier P.-A. (2002) 'Sur les dynamiques sociologiques et politiques de l'identification à l'Europe', *Revue française de science politique,* 52(4): 355–74.

Duchesne, S. and Van Ingelgom, V. (2008) 'L'indifférence des Français et des Belges (francophones) pour leurs voisins Européens: une pièce de plus au dossier de l'absence de communauté politique européenne?', *Politique Européenne,* 26: 143–64.

Dumoulin, M. (ed.) (2007) *La Commission européenne, 1958□1972: Histoire et mémoires d'une institution,* Luxembourg: OPOCE.

Ebel, M. and Fiala, P. (1981) 'La situation d'énonciation dans les pratiques argumentatives', *Langue française,* 50(1): 53–74.

Eichenberg, R. C. and Dalton, R. J. (1993) 'Europeans and the European Community: The Dynamics of Public Support for European Integration', *International Organization,* 47(4): 507–34.

Elias, N. (2006) *The Court Society,* Dublin: University College Dublin Press.

Eliasoph, N. (1990) 'Political culture and the presentation of self: a study of the public sphere in the spirit of Erving Goffman', *Theory and Society,* 19(4): 465–94.

European Commission (2006) *White Paper on a European Communication Policy,* COM (2006) 35 final.

Favre, P. and Offerlé, M. (2007) 'Connaissances politiques, compétence politique?', *Revue française de science politique,* 2(3): 201–32.

Ferry, J.-M. (2006) 'The New European Question: The Problem of Post-National Integration', in A. Dieckhoff and C. Jaffrelot (eds) *Revisiting Nationalism: Theories and Processes,* London: Hurst and Company.

Fertikh, K., Hû, G. and Juhem, P. (2007) 'L'expression des résistances à l'Europe dans les partis socialistes et sociaux-démocrates en France et en Allemagne', Paper presented at the AFSP conference in Toulouse.

Franklin, M., Marsh, M. and McLaren, L. (1994) 'Uncorking the bottle: popular opposition to European Unification in the wake of Maastricht', *Journal of Common Market Studies,* 32(4): 455–72.

Fuchs, D., Magni-Berton, R. and Roger A. (2009) *Euroscepticism: Images of Europe among mass publics and political elites,* Opladen and Farmington Hills: Barbara Budrich Publishers.

Gabel, M. (1998a) 'Economic Integration and mass politics: market liberalization and public attitudes in the European Union', *American Journal of Political Science,* 42(3): 936–53.

— (1998b) 'Public support for European Integration: an empirical test of five theories', *The Journal of Politics*, 60(2): 333–54.

Gabel, M. and Palmer, H. (1995) 'Understanding variation in public support for European Integration', *European Journal of Political Research*, 27: 3–19.

Gabel, M. and Whitten, G. D. (1997) 'Economic conditions, economic perceptions, and public support for European Integration', *Political Behavior*, 19(1): 81–96.

Gamson, W. A. (1992) *Talking Politics*, Cambridge: Cambridge University Press.

Garcia, G. and Le Torrec, V. (eds) (2003) *L'Union européenne et les médias: regards croisés sur l'information européenne*, Paris: L'Harmattan.

Garcia, S. (2007) 'L'Europe du savoir contre l'Europe des banques? La construction de l'espace européen de l'enseignement supérieur', *Actes de la recherche en sciences sociales*, 166–7: 80–93.

Garrigou, A. (2002) *Histoire sociale du suffrage universel*, Paris: Le Seuil.

— (2006) *L'ivresse des sondages*, Paris: La Découverte.

Gautier, O. (2007) '"L'Autre Europe" du Mouvement pour la France (MPF) et l'européanisation du souverainisme', in O. Baisnée and R. Pasquier (eds) *L'Europe telle qu'elle se fait: Européanisation et sociétés politiques nationales*, Paris: CNRS Editions.

Gaxie, D. (1978) *Le cens caché*, Paris: Seuil.

— (1990) 'Au-delà des apparences…: Sur quelques problèmes de mesure des opinions', *Actes de la recherche en sciences sociales*, 81–2: 97–112.

— (2001) 'Les critiques profanes de la politique: Enchantements, désenchantements, réenchantements in J.-L. Briquet and P. Garraud (eds) *Juger la politique: Entreprise et entrepreneur critiques de la politique*, Rennes: Presses Universitaires de Rennes,.

— (2003) 'Une construction médiatique du spectacle politique? Réalité et limites de la contribution des médias au développement des perceptions négatives du politique', in J. Lagroye (ed.) *La politisation*, Paris: Belin.

— (2007) 'Cognitions, auto-habilitation et pouvoirs des "citoyens"', *Revue française de science politique*, 57(6): 737–57.

Georgakakis, D. (1999) 'Les réalités d'un mythe: figure de l'eurocrate et institutionnalisation de l'Europe politique', in D. Dulong and V. Dubois (eds) *La question technocratique*, Strasbourg: Presses Universitaires de Strasbourg.

— (2008) 'La sociologie historique et politique de l'EU: un point d'ensemble et quelques contrepoints', *Politique européenne*, 25: 53–85.

— (2009) 'Bringing Elites Sociology Back in European Integration Theories: A Case Study Based on Commissioners and Directors General', EUSA Paper.

Georgakakis, D. and de Lassalle, M. (2007a) 'Les très hauts fonctionnaires de la Commission européenne: genèse et structure d'un capital institutionnel européen', *Actes de la recherche en sciences sociales*, 166–7: 39–53.

— (2007b) *La 'nouvelle gouvernance européenne': Genèses et usages politiques d'un Livre Blanc*, Strasbourg: Presses Universitaires de Strasbourg.

—   (2009) 'Where Have all the Lawyers Gone? Structure and Transformations of the Top European Commission Officials' Legal Training', EUI Working Paper.

Gerstlé, J. (1996) 'L'information et la sensibilité des électeurs à la conjoncture', *Revue française de science politique*, 45(5): 731–52.

—   (ed) (2001) *Les effets d'information en politique*, Paris: L'Harmattan.

Gerstlé, J. and Piar, C. (2005) 'Le cadrage du référendum sur la Constitution européenne: la dynamique d'une campagne à rebondissements', in *Le référendum de ratification du Traité constitutionnel européen du 29 mai 2005: comprendre le non français*, Paris: Cahiers du CEVIPOF.

Gillingham, J. (2003) *European Integration, 1950–2003: Superstate or New Market Economy,* Cambridge: Cambridge University Press.

Goffman, E. (1974) *Frame Analysis: An Essay on the Organization of Experience*, London: Harper and Row.

—   (1983) 'The interaction order', *American Sociological Review*, 48, 1–17.

—   (1990) *The Presentation of Self in Everyday Life*, London: Penguin Books.

Gombin, J. and Hubé, N. (2009) 'Le politologue, le journaliste et l'électeur: Les commentaires sur le référendum sur le Traité constitutionnel européen dans la presse quotidienne française', *Savoir/Agir,* 7: 65–76.

Góra, M. (2002) 'Wiedza o integracji europejskiej – rolnicy, przedsiębiorcy, kadra kierownicza i lokalni decydenci' (Knowledge on European integration – farmers, businessmen, managers and local decision-makers), in Z. Mach and D. Niedźwiedzki (eds) *Polska lokalna wobec integracji europejskiej*, Cracow: Universitas.

Grawitz, M. (2001), *Méthodes des sciences sociales*, Paris: Dalloz.

Greenwood, J. (1997) *Representing Interests in the European Union*, New York: St. Martin Press.

Grignon, J.-C. and Passeron, J.-C. (1989) *Le Savant et le populaire: Misérabilisme et populisme en sociologie et en littérature*, Paris: Gallimard-Seuil.

Grunberg, G. (2005) 'Le référendum français de ratification du Traité constitutionnel européen du 29 mai 2005', *French Politics, Culture and Society*, 23(3): 128–44.

Grunberg, G. and Schweisguth, É. (2003) 'La tripartition de l'espace politique', in P. Perrineau and C. Ysmal (eds) *Le vote de tous les refus. Les élections présidentielle et législatives de 2002*, Paris: Presses de Sciences Po.

Guiraudon, V. (2000) 'L'espace sociopolitique européen, un champ en friche?', *Cultures et Conflits, Sociologie de l'Europe*, 38–9: 7–37.

Harmsen, R. (2007) 'Is British Euroscepticism still unique? National exceptionalism in comparative perspective', in J. Lacroix and R. Coman (eds) *Les résistances à l'Europe: Cultures nationales, idéologies et stratégies d'acteurs*, Bruxelles: Editions de Université de Bruxelles.

Harmsen, R. and Spiering, M. (eds) (2004) *Euroscepticism: Party Politics, National Identity and European Integration,* Amsterdam: Rodopi.

Hassenteufel, P. (2000) 'Deux ou trois choses que je sais d'elle: Remarques à propos d'expériences de comparaisons européennes', in CURAPP, *Les méthodes au concret: Démarches, formes de l'expérience et terrains d'investigation en science politique*, Paris: PUF.

Hauray, B. (2006) *L'Europe du médicament: Politique, expertise, intérêts privés*, Paris: Presses de Science Po.

Hix, S. (1999) 'Dimensions and alignments in European Union politics: Cognitive constraints and partisan responses', *European Journal of Political Research*, 35: 69–106.

Hoggart, R. (1969) *The Uses of Literacy*, London: Penguin Books.

Hooghe, L. (2003) 'Europe Divided? Elite vs. Public Opinion on European Integration', *European Union Politics*, 4(3): 281–307.

Hooghe, L. and Marks, G. (1996) 'Europe with the Regions? Regional Representation in the European Union', *Publius: The Journal of Federalism,* 26(I): 73–91.

— (2004) 'Does identity or economic rationality drive public opinion on European Integration?', *Political Science and Politics*, 37: 415–20.

— (2005) 'Integration, calculation, community and cues: public opinion on European Union', *European Union Politics*, 6: 419–43.

— (2009) 'A postfunctionalist theory of European Integration: from permissive consensus to constraining dissensus', *British Journal of Political Science*, 39(1): 1–23.

Hooghe, L., Marks, G. and Wilson, C. J. (2002) 'Does left/right structure party positions on European Integration?', *Comparative Political Studies*, 35(8): 965–89.

Horolets, A. (2006) *Obrazy Europy w Polskim dyskursie publicznym* (The Images of Europe in Public Discourse), Cracow: Universitas.

Hubé, N. (2008) 'Le courrier des lecteurs: une parole journalistique profane? Le cas du traité constitutionnel européen', *Mots. Les langages du politique*, 87: 99–112.

Ina'stat, lettre trimestrielle no.9, juin 2008, www.ina.fr.

Inglehart, R. (1970) 'Cognitive mobilization and European identity', *Comparative Politics*, 3(1): 45–70.

— (1971) 'Changing values priority and European Integration', *Journal on Common Market Studies*, 10(1): 1–36.

— (1990) *Culture Shift in Advanced Industrial Society*, Princeton: Princeton University Press.

Inglehart, R. and Rabier, J.-R. (1979) 'Europe elects a parliament: cognitive mobilization, political mobilization and pro-European attitudes as influences on voter turnout', *Government and Opposition*, 14(4): 479–507.

Inglehart, R. and Reif, K. (eds) (1991) *The Dynamics of European Public Opinion: Essays in Honour of Jacques-René Rabier*, London: Macmillan.

Jarosz, M. (ed.) (2005) *Wygrani i przegrani polskiej transformacji* (The winners and losers of the Polish transformation), Warsaw: Oficyna Naukowa.

Jasiecki, K. (2005) 'Społeczności lokalne wobec członkowstwa w Unii europejskiej: Oczekiwania i przygotowania' (Local communities and the accession to the European Union: Expectations and preparations), in M. Jarosz (ed.) *Wygrani i przegrani polskiej transformacji*, Varsovie: Oficyna Naukowa.

Joana, J. and Smith, A. (2002) *Les commissaires européens* □ *Technocrates, diplomates ou politiques*, Paris: Presses de Sciences Po.

Jobert, B. (ed.) (1994) *Le tournant néo-libéral en Europe: Idées et recettes dans les pratiques gouvernementales*, Paris: L'Harmattan.

Joignant, A. (2007) 'Compétence politique et bricolage: Les formes profanes du rapport au politique', *Revue française de science politique*, 57(6): 799–817.

Juhem, P, (2001) 'Luttes partisanes et fluctuation des cadres cognitifs des journalistes', in J. Gerstlé (ed.) *Les effets d'information en politique*, Paris: L'Harmattan.

Juncos, A and Pomorka, K. (2006) 'Playing the Brussels game: strategic socialisation in the CFSP Council Working Groups', *EIOLP*, 10.

Kitschelt, H. (1995) *The Radical Right in Western Europe: A Comparative Analysis*, Ann Arbor: The University of Michigan Press.

Klapper, J. T. (1960) *Effects of Mass Communication*, New York: Free Press.

Kolarska-Bobinska, L. (1999) *Polska eurodebata*, Warsaw: ISP.

Kopecky, P. (2004) 'An awkward newcomer? EU Enlargement and Euroscepticism in the Czech Republic', in R. Harmsen and M. Spiering (eds) *Euroscepticism: Party Politics, National Identity and European Integration*, Amsterdam: Rodopi.

Labov, W. (1972) *Sociolinguistic Patterns*, Philadelphia: University of Pennsylvania Press.

Lacroix, J. and Coman, R. (eds) (2007) *Les résistances à l'Europe: Cultures nationales, idéologies et stratégies d'acteurs,* Bruxelles: Editions de l'Université de Bruxelles.

Lane, R. E. (1967) *Political Ideology: Why The American Common Man Believes What He Does*, New York: Free Press/ London: Collier-Macmillan Ltd.

Lau, R. R., Sears, D. O. and Jessor, T. (1990) 'Fact or artifact revisited: Survey Instrument Effects and Pocketbook Politics', *Political Behavior*, 12(3): 217–242.

Lazarsfeld, P., Berelson, B., and Gaudet, H. (1968) *The People's Choice: How the Voter Makes up his Mind in a Presidential Campaign*, New York: Columbia University Press.

Lefebvre, R. and Marrel, G. (2009) 'Logiques partisanes, territorialisation et capital politique européen: La constitution des listes socialistes françaises aux élections européennes', Communication au colloque, *Le lien électoral au Parlement européen.*

Lehingue, P. (2007a) 'Le Non français au traité constitutionnel européen (mai 2005). Sur deux lectures "polaires" du scrutin', *Actes de la recherche en sciences sociales*, 166–67: 123–39.

— (2007b) 'Les interprétations polyphoniques d'un scrutin' in A. Cohen and A. Vauchez (eds) *La Constitution européenne: Elites, mobilisations, votes*, Bruxelles: Editions de l'Université de Bruxelles.

— (2007c) *Subunda: Coups de sonde dans l'océan des sondages*, Bellecombe-en-Bauges: Editions du Croquant.

Leonardi, S. (2008) 'Classe laborieuse et orientation politique: Quelques thèses à partir du cas italien', *Les mondes du travail*, 6.

Lequesne, C. and Rivaud, P. (2001) 'Les comités d'experts indépendants: l'expertise au service d'une démocratie supranationale?', *Revue française de science politique*, 51(6): 867–80.

Lewis J. (2003) 'Institutional environments and everyday EU decision-making: rationalist or constructivist?', *Comparative Political Studies*, 36(1/2): 97-124.

Lindberg, L. N. and Scheingold, S. A. (eds) (1970) *Europe's World-Be Policy: Patterns of Change in the European Community*, Englewood Cliffs: Prentice-Hall.

Lodge, M. and McGraw, K. M. (eds) (1995) *Political Judgment Structure and Process*, Ann Arbor: The University of Michigan Press.

Lupia, A. and McCubbins, M. D. (2000) 'The Institutional Foundations of Political Competence: How Citizens Learn What They Need to Know', in A. Lupia, M. D. McCubbins and S. L Popkin (2000) *Elements of Reason: Cognition, Choice, and the Bounds of Rationality*, Cambridge: Cambridge University Press.

Lupia, A. and McCubbins, M. D. and Popkin, S. L. (2000) *Elements of Reason: Cognition, Choice, and the Bounds of Rationality*, Cambridge: Cambridge University Press.

Mach, Z. and Niedźwiedzki, D. (eds) (2002) *Polska lokalna wobec integracji europejskiej* (Local Poland and European integration), Cracow: Universitas.

Magnette, P. (2000) *L'Europe, l'Etat et la Démocratie: Le souverain apprivoisé*, Bruxelles, Complexe.

Mange J. and Marchand, P. (2007) 'Oui et non à la constitution européenne: L'éloquence du forum', *Mots. Les langages du politique*, 83: 121–37.

Marcussen, M., Risse, T., Engelmann-Martin, D., Knopf, H. J. and Roscher, K. (1999) 'Constructing Europe? The evolution of French, British and German nation state identities', *Journal of European Public Policy*, 6(4): 614–33.

Marquand, D. (1979) *Parliament for Europe*, London: Jonathan Cape.

Marrel, G. and Payre, R, (2006) 'Des carrières au parlement: longévité des eurodéputés et institutionnalisation de l'arène parlementaire', *Politique européenne*, 18: 69–104.

Mauger, G. (2001) 'Précarisation et nouvelles formes d'encadrement des classes populaires', *Actes de la recherche en sciences sociales*, 136(1): 3–4.

Mayer, N. (2002) 'Les hauts et les bas du vote le Pen 2002', *Revue francaise de science politique*, 52(5–6): 505–20.

McLaren, L. (2002) 'Public support for the European Union: cost/benefit analysis or perceived cultural threat?', *The Journal of Politics*, 64(2): 551–66.

Meinhoff, U. H. (2004) 'Europe Viewed from Below: Agents, Victims, and the Threat of the Other', in R. K. Herrmann, T. Risse and M. B. Brewer (eds) *Transnational Identities: Becoming European in the EU*, Lanham: Rowman and Littlefield Publishers inc.

Melich, A. (1998) 'Les enquêtes Eurobaromètres et la construction européenne', in P. Bréchon and B. Cautrès (eds) *Les enquêtes Eurobaromètres: Analyse comparée des données socio-politiques*, Paris: L'Harmattan.

Michel, H. (2007) 'La "société civile" dans la "gouvernance européenne": Eléments pour une sociologie d'une catégorie politique', *Actes de la recherche en sciences sociales*, 166–67: 30–7.

— (2007) 'Les groupes d'intérêts et la consultation sur le Livre Blanc: objectivation et institutionnalisation de la société civile', in D. Georgakakis and M. de Lassalle, *La ▢nouvelle gouvernance européenne▢: Genèses et usages politiques d'un Livre Blanc*, Strasbourg: Presses Universitaires de Strasbourg.

Moucharik, S. (2008) '"Classes populaires": peut-on enquêter sur les subjectivités politiques à partir d'un concept a priori?', *Les mondes du travail*, 6: 47–61.

Muller, P. (1995) *Politiques publiques en Europe,* Paris: l'Harmattan.

Neuman, W. R., Just, M. R. and Crigler, A. N. (1992) *Common Knowledge: News and the Construction of Political Meaning*, Chicago: University of Chicago Press.

Neumann, R. W. (1986) *The Paradox of Mass Politics: Knowledge and Opinion in the American Electorate*, Cambridge: Harvard University Press.

Nie, N. H., Verba S. and Petrocik, J. (1979 2nd edn) *The Changing American Voter,* Cambridge: Harvard University Press.

Osservatorio di Pavia, data (Sept.–Nov. 2008) presented at the seminar *L'unione Europea nei media italiani*, Milano, 09/02/2009, www.osservatorio.it.

Passeron, J.-C. (2006) *Le raisonnement sociologique: Un espace non-poppérien de l'argumentation*, Paris: Albin Michel.

Percheron, A. (1991) 'Les Français et l'Europe: acquiescement de *façade* ou *adhésion* véritable?', *Revue française de science politique*, 41(3): 382–406.

Pierru, E. (2004) '"Effets politiques des medias" et sociologie prophétique: Pour une sociologie des rapports ordinaires à l'information politique', in J.-B. Legavre (ed.) *La presse écrite: objets délaissés*, Paris: L'Harmattan.

Popkin, S. L. (1991) *The Reasoning Voter: Communication and Persuasion in Presidential Campaigns*, Chicago and London: The Chicago University Press.

Pounds, G. (2006) 'Democratic participation and letters to the editor in Britain and Italy', *Discourse and Society*, 17(1): 29–63.

Pudal, B. (1988) 'Les dirigeants communistes: Du "fils du people" à "l'instituteur des masses" ', *Actes de la recherche en sciences sociales*, 71–2: 46–70.

Rabier, J.-R. (1965) 'L'information des Européens et l'intégration de l'Europe',

Institut d'études européennes, Brussels (lecture).

Rabier, J.-R. (1993) 'La naissance d'une politique d'information sur la Communauté européenne (1952–1967)' in F. Dasseto and M. Dumoulin (eds) *Naissance et développement de l'information européenne*, Bern: Peter Lang.

Reif, K. and Schmitt, H. (1980) 'Nine Second-order National Elections. A Conceptual Framework for the Analysis of European Elections Results', European Journal of Political Research, 8(1): 3–44.

Reynié, D. (2008) 'L'avènement d'un stato-scepticisme européen', in D. Reynié (ed.) *L'opinion: européenne en 2008*, Paris: Lignes de Repères – Fondation Robert-Schuman.

Ricoeur, P. (1995) *Oneself as Another,* Chicago: University of Chicago Press.

Risse, T. (2004) 'European Institutions and Identity Change: What have we Learned?', in R. Herman, T. Risse and M. Brewer (eds) *Transnational Identities: Becoming European in the EU*, New York: Rowman and Littlefield.

Robert, C. (2004) 'Doing Politics and Pretending Not to: The Commission's Role in Distributing Aid to Eastern Europe' in A. Smith (ed.) *Politics and the European Commission: Actors, Interdependence, Legitimacy*, London: Routledge.

— (2007) 'L'impossible modèle social européen', *Actes de la recherche en sciences sociales*, 166–7: 94–109.

Rohrschneider, R. and Whitefield, S. (2006), 'Political parties, public opinion and European Integration in post-Communist countries: the state of the art', *European Union Politics*, 7 (1) 141–60.

Rowell, J. (2005) 'La domination en vertu du savoir? La construction et les usages des statistiques du logement en RDA', *Revue française de science politique*, 55(5–6): 865–87.

Rozenberg, O. (2009) 'L'influence du Parlement européen et l'indifférence de ses électeurs: une corrélation fallacieuse?', *Politique européenne,* 28: 7–36.

Sánchez-Cuenca, I. (2000) 'The political basis of support for European Integration', *European Union Politics*, 1(2): 147–71.

Sawicki, F. (1997) *Les réseaux du parti socialiste: Sociologie d'un milieu partisan*, Paris: Belin.

Scharpf, F. (1999) *Governing in Europe: Effective and Democratic?*, Oxford: Oxford University Press.

Scheuer, A. and Van der Brug, W. (2007) 'Locating support for European integration', in W. Van der Brug and C. Van der Eijk (eds) *European Elections and Domestic Politics: Lessons from the Past and Scenarios for the Future*, Notre Dame: University of Notre Dame Press.

Schild, J. (2001) 'National versus European identities? French and German in the European multi-level system', *Journal of Common Market Studies*, 39(2): 331–51.

Schmidt, V. (2006) *Democracy in Europe: The EU and National Polities*, Oxford: Oxford University Press.

—   (2007) 'Trapped by their ideas: French elites' discourses of European integration and globalization', *Journal of European Public Policy*, 14(7): 992–1009.

Schmitt, H. (2005) 'The European Parliament elections of June 2004: still second-order?', *West European Politics*, 28(3): 650–79.

Schmitt, H. and Binder, T. (2006) 'The Agendas of Voters and Parties in the European Parliament Election of 1999', in H. Schmitt (ed.) *Voters, Parties and European Unification*, London: Frank Cass.

Schoen, H. (2008) 'Identity, instrumental self-interest and institutional evaluations: explaining public opinion on common European policies in Foreign Affairs and Defence', *European Union Politics*, 9(5): 5–29.

Schwartz, O. (1990) *Le monde privé des ouvriers*, Paris: PUF.

Seidendorf, S. (2007) *Europäisierung nationaler Identitätsdiskurse? Ein Vergleich französischer und deutscher Printmedien*, Baden-Baden: Nomos.

Siblot, Y. (2005) 'Les rapports quotidiens des classes populaires aux administrations', *Sociétés contemporaines*, 58: 85–103.

Sievert, H. (1998) *Europäischer Journalismus. Theorie und Empirie aktueller Medienkommunikation in der Europäischen Union*, Opladen: Westdeutscher Verlag.

Slater, M. (1982) 'Political elites, popular indifference and community building', *Journal of Common Market Studies*, 21: 69–93.

Smith, A. (1998) 'La Commission et le peuple: L'exemple d'usages politiques des Eurobaromètres', in P. Bréchon and B. Cautrès (eds), *Les enquêtes Eurobaromètres. Analyse comparée des données socio-politiques*, Paris: L'Harmattan.

—   (2008) 'L'intégration européenne des politiques françaises', in O. Borrazn and V. Guiraudon (eds) *Politiques publiques 1, La France dans la gouvernance européenne*, Paris: Presses de Sciences Po.

Sniderman, P. (1998) 'Les nouvelles perspectives de la recherche sur l'opinion publique', *Politix*, 11(41): 123–75.

Sniderman, P. M., Brody, R. A. and Tetlock, P. E. (1991) *Reasoning and Choice Explorations in Political Psychology*, Cambridge: Cambridge University Press.

—   (1993) 'The New Look in Public Opinion Research', in A. Finifter (ed.) *The State of The Discipline II*, Washington, DC: The American Political Science Association.

—   (2000) 'Taking Sides: A Fixed Choice Theory of Political Reasoning', in A. Lupia, M. D. McCubbins and S. L. Popkin (eds) *Elements of Reason: Cognition, Choice, and the Bounds of Rationality*, Cambridge: Cambridge University Press.

Stewart, D. W., Shamdasani, P. N. and Rook, D. W. (2006) *Focus Groups: Theory and Practice*, London: Sage.

Strudel, S. (2008) 'Citoyenneté', in C. Bélot, P. Magnette, and S. Saurruger (eds) *Science politique de l'Union européenne*, Paris: Economica.

Szczerbiak, A. (2001) 'Polish public opinion: explaining declining support for EU membership', *Journal of Common Market Studies*, 39(1): 105–22.

Szczerbiak, A. and Taggart, P. (eds) (2008) *Opposing Europe? The Comparative Party Politics of Euroscepticism, Comparative and Theoretical Perspective*, Oxford and New York: Oxford University Press.

Taggart, P. (1998) 'A touchstone of dissent: Euroscepticism in contemporary Western European party systems', *European Journal of Political Research*, 33(3): 363–88.

Tanasoiu, C. and Colonescu, C. (2008) 'Determinants of support for European Integration: the case of Bulgaria', *European Union Politics*, 9(3): 363–77.

Topalov, C. (1999) '"Expériences sociologiques": les faits et les preuves dans les thèses de Maurice Halbwachs (1909–1913)', *Revue d'histoire des sciences humaines*, 1: 11–46.

Trondal, J. (2006) *An Institutional Perspective on Representation: Ambiguous Representation in the European Commission*, Working paper, EIOP, vol. 10.

Tucker, J. A., Pacek, A. C. and Berinsky, A. J. (2002) 'Transitional Winners and Losers: Attitudes toward EU Membership in Post-Communist Countries', *American Journal of Political Science*, 46(3): 557–71.

Vauchez, A. (2007) 'Une élite d'intermédiaires: Naissance d'un capital institutionnel européen (1950–1970)', *Actes de la recherche en sciences sociales*, 166–7: 54–65.

Verger, S. (2008) 'INTERREG versus configuration territoriale: quel modèle d'action pour la construction de "territoires transfrontalier"?' Paper presented at the workshop, *Des territoires ☐compétitifs': Genèse, usages, pratiques de catégories d'action publique et articulation des niveaux de gouvernement*, Strasbourg.

Wagner, A.-C. (1998) *Les nouvelles élites de la mondialisation: Une immigration dorée en France*, Paris: PUF.

— (2005) *Vers une Europe syndicale: une enquête sur la Confédération Européenne des Syndicats*, Bellecombe-en-Bauges: Editions du Croquant.

Weber, M. (1922) *Gesammelte Aufsätze zur Wissenschaftslehre*, Tübingen: JCB Mohr.

— (1978) *Economy and Society: An Outline of Interpretive Sociology,* Vol. 1, Berkeley: University of California Press.

Weiland, S. (2005) '95 Prozent Zustimmung, Null Begeisterung', *Spiegel*, 12 Mai.

Weisbein, J. (2006) 'Des mobilisations sous (inter)dépendance: Une approche configurationnelle du militantisme fédéraliste en Europe', in A. Cohen, B. Lacroix and P. Riutort (eds) *Les formes de l'activité politique: Eléments d'analyse sociologique (18è-20è siècles)*, Paris: PUF.

— (2007) 'Instituer la société civile européenne: la contribution des mouvements fédéralistes: L'expérience du forum permanent de la société civile', in D. Georgakakis and M. de Lassalle (eds) *La ☐nouvelle gouvernance européenne☐: Genèses et usages politiques d'un Livre Blanc*, Strasbourg: Presses Universitaires de Strasbourg.

Weisbein, J. and Mischi, J. (2004) 'L'Europe comme cause politique proche:

Contestation et promotion de l'intégration communautaire dans l'espace local', *Politique européenne*, 12: 84–104.

Zalc, C., and Lemercier, C. (2008) *Méthodes quantitatives pour l'historien*, Paris: La Découverte.

Zaller, J. (1992) *The Nature and Origins of Mass Opinion*, Cambridge: Cambridge University.

| subject index

| author index